Convergence of Deep Learning and Internet of Things:

Computing and Technology

T. Kavitha
*New Horizon College of Engineering (Autonomous), India & Visvesvaraya
Technological University, India*

G. Senbagavalli
AMC Engineering College, Visvesvaraya Technological University, India

Deepika Koundal
University of Petroleum and Energy Studies, Dehradun, India

Yanhui Guo
University of Illinois, USA

Deepak Jain
Chongqing University of Posts and Telecommunications, China

A volume in the Advances in Computational
Intelligence and Robotics (ACIR) Book Series

Published in the United States of America by
IGI Global
Engineering Science Reference (an imprint of IGI Global)
701 E. Chocolate Avenue
Hershey PA, USA 17033
Tel: 717-533-8845
Fax: 717-533-8661
E-mail: cust@igi-global.com
Web site: http://www.igi-global.com

Library of Congress Cataloging-in-Publication Data

Names: Kavitha, T., 1979- editor.
Title: Convergence of deep learning and internet of things : computing and
  technology / T. Kavitha, Senbagavalli Ganesan, Deepika Koundal, Yanhui
  Guo, Deepak Jain, editors.
Description: Hershey, PA : Engineering Science Reference, [2023] | Includes
  bibliographical references and index. | Summary: "For those interested
  in design and building intelligent Internet of Things, this research
  book offers solutions with the state-of-the-art and novel approaches for
  the IoT problems and challenges from a deep learning perspective"--
  Provided by publisher.
Identifiers: LCCN 2022034109 (print) | LCCN 2022034110 (ebook) | ISBN
  9781668462751 (h/c) | ISBN 9781668462768 (s/c) | ISBN 9781668462775
  (eISBN)
Subjects: LCSH: Internet of things. | Deep learning (Machine learning) |
  Convergence (Telecommunication)
Classification: LCC TK5105.8857 .C67 2023 (print) | LCC TK5105.8857
  (ebook) | DDC 004.67/8--dc23/eng/20220906
LC record available at https://lccn.loc.gov/2022034109
LC ebook record available at https://lccn.loc.gov/2022034110

This book is published in the IGI Global book series Advances in Computational Intelligence and Robotics (ACIR) (ISSN: 2327-0411; eISSN: 2327-042X)

British Cataloguing in Publication Data
A Cataloguing in Publication record for this book is available from the British Library.

For electronic access to this publication, please contact: eresources@igi-global.com.

Advances in Computational Intelligence and Robotics (ACIR) Book Series

Ivan Giannoccaro
University of Salento, Italy

ISSN:2327-0411
EISSN:2327-042X

MISSION

While intelligence is traditionally a term applied to humans and human cognition, technology has progressed in such a way to allow for the development of intelligent systems able to simulate many human traits. With this new era of simulated and artificial intelligence, much research is needed in order to continue to advance the field and also to evaluate the ethical and societal concerns of the existence of artificial life and machine learning.

The **Advances in Computational Intelligence and Robotics (ACIR) Book Series** encourages scholarly discourse on all topics pertaining to evolutionary computing, artificial life, computational intelligence, machine learning, and robotics. ACIR presents the latest research being conducted on diverse topics in intelligence technologies with the goal of advancing knowledge and applications in this rapidly evolving field.

COVERAGE

- Machine Learning
- Agent technologies
- Intelligent Control
- Adaptive and Complex Systems
- Algorithmic Learning
- Robotics
- Artificial Life
- Fuzzy Systems
- Cognitive Informatics
- Evolutionary Computing

IGI Global is currently accepting manuscripts for publication within this series. To submit a proposal for a volume in this series, please contact our Acquisition Editors at Acquisitions@igi-global.com or visit: http://www.igi-global.com/publish/.

Titles in this Series

For a list of additional titles in this series, please visit: http://www.igi-global.com/book-series/advances-computational-intelligence-robotics/73674

Controlling Epidemics With Mathematical and Machine Learning Models
Abraham Varghese (University of Technology and Applied Sciences, Muscat, Oman) Eduardo M. Lacap, Jr. (University of Technology and Applied Sciences, Muscat, Oman) Ibrahim Sajath (University of Technology and Applied Sciences, Muscat, Oman) M. Kamal Kumar (University of Technology and Applied Sciences, Muscat, Oman) and Shajidmon Kolamban (University of Technology and Applied Sciences, Muscat, Oman)
Engineering Science Reference • © 2023 • 269pp • H/C (ISBN: 9781799883432) • US $270.00

Handbook of Research on Computer Vision and Image Processing in the Deep Learning Era
A. Srinivasan (SASTRA University (Deemed), India)
Engineering Science Reference • © 2023 • 440pp • H/C (ISBN: 9781799888925) • US $325.00

Multidisciplinary Applications of Deep Learning-Based Artificial Emotional Intelligence
Chiranji Lal Chowdhary (Vellore Institute of Technology, India)
Engineering Science Reference • © 2023 • 296pp • H/C (ISBN: 9781668456736) • US $270.00

Principles and Applications of Socio-Cognitive and Affective Computing
S. Geetha (Vellore Institute of Technology, Chennai, India) Karthika Renuka (PSG College of Technology, India) Asnath Victy Phamila (Vellore Institute of Technology, Chennai, India) and Karthikeyan N. (Syed Ammal Engineering College, India)
Engineering Science Reference • © 2023 • 253pp • H/C (ISBN: 9781668438435) • US $270.00

Revolutionizing Industrial Automation Through the Convergence of Artificial Intelligence and the Internet of Things
Divya Upadhyay Mishra (ABES Engineering College, Ghaziabad, India) and Shanu Sharma (ABES Engineering College, Ghaziabad, India)
Engineering Science Reference • © 2023 • 279pp • H/C (ISBN: 9781668449912) • US $270.00

Convergence of Big Data Technologies and Computational Intelligent Techniques
Govind P. Gupta (National Institute of Technology, Raipur, India)
Engineering Science Reference • © 2023 • 233pp • H/C (ISBN: 9781668452646) • US $270.00

701 East Chocolate Avenue, Hershey, PA 17033, USA
Tel: 717-533-8845 x100 • Fax: 717-533-8661
E-Mail: cust@igi-global.com • www.igi-global.com

Table of Contents

Ekta Gandotra, Jaypee University of Information Technology, India
Deepak Gupta, Jaypee University of Information Technology, India

Jyoti R. Munavalli, BNM Institute of Technology, Visvesvaraya Technological University,
India
Bindu S., BNM Institute of Technology, Visvesvaraya Technological University, India
Yasha Jyothi M. Shirur, BNM Institute of Technology, Visvesvaraya Technological
University, India

Detailed Table of Contents

The phrase "intelligent device" refers to a package that contains either a full measurement system or a component inside a measurement system that includes a digital processor. The processing of measurement sensor output to adjust for flaws inherent in the measurement process results in significant gains in measurement accuracy. Intelligent device management is a technique used in corporate software applications to monitor and manage distant equipment, systems, and goods through the Internet. Device security in cloud platforms will be made using proactive attack surface management and improved protection against ransomware and other sophisticated threats safeguarding data and devices. Cloud security is a set of processes and technologies that are meant to handle both external and internal risks to enterprise security. This chapter explains about intelligent devices, the need for security and management of intelligent devices in cloud platforms, and finally ends with challenges associated with this.

Chapter 2

Data privacy is the common concern across different enterprises- applications deployed in multi-cloud environment will make it more challenging for the cyber security team to monitor the application traffic simultaneously to prevent any attacks or data leak or data privacy breaches. Handling different data privacy issues always demands for a complete visibility over data flow, which ensures to prevent vulnerability points, and best way to handle sensitive and personal data with right data retention policies and data protection schemes. Articulation of data privacy features from different cloud providers, particularly with their service and deployment model, help to plan cybersecurity teams and build the necessary security analytical models to predict and prevent the data privacy theft and attacks.

Chapter 3

V. A. Velvizhi, Sri Sairam Engineering College, Anna University, India
G. Senbagavalli, AMC Engineering College, Visvesvaraya Technological University, India
S. Malini, AMC Engineering College, Visvesvaraya Technological University, India

The heart of Industry 4.0 is established by a new technology called the internet of things (IoT). Through the internet, the IoT makes it possible for machines and gadgets to share signals. Using artificial intelligence (AI) approaches to manage and regulate the communications between various equipment based on intelligent decisions is made possible by the internet of things (IoT) technology. Data collection devices can be fundamentally altered to "lock in" to the best sensing data with regard to a user-defined cost function or design constraint by utilizing inverse design and machine learning techniques. By allowing low-cost and small sensor implementations developed through iterative analysis of data-driven sensing outcomes, a new generation of intelligence sensing systems reduces the data load while significantly enhancing sensing capabilities. Machine learning-enabled computational sensors can encourage the development of widely distributed applications that leverage the internet of things to build robust sensing networks that have an influence across a variety of industries.

Chapter 4

Amuthan Nallathambi, AMC Engineering College, Visvesvaraya Technological University,
India
Kannan Nova, Microsoft, USA

Deep learning is a new approach to artificial intelligence that enables edge-computing systems to learn from data and take decisions without human intervention. Edge computing is a technique for coping with the increasing demand for streaming data. This is especially important in the case of applications that involve computationally intensive tasks such as driverless cars, autonomous drones, and smart cities. Edge computing is the provision of computing, big data analytics, and storage in such a way that the data comes to the processing power and not vice versa. It relies on a decentralized approach where computational resources are provided at the edge of networks. Edge computing is an emerging field that's getting attention from many vendors and researchers. The data generated by IoT devices is usually too large and complex for cloud-based storage and processing. That's why edge computing can handle data at the source of generation in real time, which speeds up the process of decision making.

Chapter 5

Amuthan Nallathambi, AMC Engineering College, Bengaluru, India
Sivakumar N., Department of Mechanical Engineering, India
Velrajkumar P., CMR Institute of Technology, Visvesvaraya Technological University, India

Distributed deep learning is a type of machine learning that uses neural networks to learn and make predictions at scale. This is achieved by having many different computer systems that are connected via the internet. This allows for more parallel processing and faster results. In addition, when it comes to IoT, this type of technology can be used in conjunction with sensors and other devices to create more accurate predictions about the environment around us. Distributed deep learning can be used in many ways with the IoT because it can be applied to various aspects of IoT data processing, such as image recognition, speech recognition, natural language processing (NLP), or anomaly detection. The neural net is the most computationally intensive component of the system, and it requires a significant amount of energy. To make this system more cost-effective, there are two ways to lower the number of memory accesses: by reducing the size of images (so precision decreases), or by increasing network bandwidth so that there are fewer loop iterations required for each memory access.

The continued growth and widespread use of the internet benefit many network users in various ways. Meanwhile, network protection becomes increasingly essential as the internet becomes more widely used. Though, as the number of internet-connected systems in finance, e-commerce, and the military grows, they are becoming targets of network attacks, posing a noteworthy challenge and causing significant harm. Essentially, practical strategies for detecting and defending against attacks, as well as maintaining network protection, are needed. Furthermore, various types of attacks must typically be dealt with in different ways. This chapter summarizes some of the important deep learning techniques and reinforcement techniques for information security by providing various methods for attack detection and corrections.

The potential growth of internet of things (IoT) brings people and things together to handle daily tasks in a smart way. The major advancement the IoT offers is quality data sensing and faster data analytics through hurdle-free communication. The increasing number of devices and heterogeneous network natures unwrap more challenges in terms of quality of service. Currently, the deep learning algorithm explores different dimensions of service quality gradually in IoT scenarios. In order to effectively handle a dynamic IoT environment, it is essential that the design of IoT must be supplemented with an intelligent agent for providing effective QoS. The traditional methods are not capable of utilizing historical data to find insights into service quality improvement. In this chapter, a comprehensive analysis of deep learning techniques for improving QoS of the internet of things is carried out. Deep learning solutions for improving QoS and the challenges involved are compared. The deep reinforcement learning (DRL) for improving QoS in IoT and its evaluation technique are also explored.

Chapter 8

    Rajarajeswari S., Vellore Institute of Technology, Chennai, India
    Hema N., Vellore Institute of Technology, Chennai, India

We can perceive, analyse, control, and optimise the conventional physical systems thanks to pervasive IoT applications. Numerous IoT apps have recently had security breaches, which suggests that IoT applications could endanger physical systems. Numerous security issues in IoT applications are mostly caused by two factors: severe resource restrictions and inadequate security architecture. Edge-based security designs for IoT applications are still in their infancy, despite some research efforts in this direction. In addition to providing an in-depth analysis of current edge-based IoT security options, this study seeks to provide inspiration for new edge-based IoT security designs. A significant deal of progress in artificial intelligence (AI) opens up a number of potential avenues for addressing the security challenges in the setting that privacy preservation and security have become essential issues for EC. This chapter addresses issues with edge computing-based internet of things at the computation and security levels.

Chapter 9

    Hakki Soy, Necmettin Erbakan University, Turkey

Recently, the evolution of artificial intelligence has caused the emergence of smart systems exhibiting intelligent behavior like the human brain. Specifically, as a class of artificial intelligence methods, computer vision empowered with deep learning has tremendous promise for the accurate detection of crowds in real-time. In addition, the edge artificial intelligence approach allows for the development and deployment of artificial intelligence methods outside of the cloud. This study introduces the deep learning-based computer vision implementation to monitor public transport stops. The main aim is to determine the count of passengers through edge computing. The experimental study is realized with the popular YOLO object detector model on the Maixduino board developed for edge-based artificial intelligence (AI) applications with the internet of things (IoT). The experiments' results show that the obtained accuracy of crowd counting was found to be satisfactory.

Chapter 10

    Sanjay Rajendra Mate, Sangam University, India & Bhilwara and Government Polytechnic
        Daman (Gujarat Technological University), India
    Renuka Suryawanshi, MIT World Peace University, India
    Manjusha Taur, Canadian Imperial Bank of Commerce, Canada
    Kishor S. Wagh, All India Shri Shivaji Memorial Society's Institute of Information
        Technology, India

Consider a person with total mental capacity and an active lifestyle who can now not communicate or connect with the world around them due to a severe motor impairment to being locked into their body. Assume the person cannot notify their caregiver when uncomfortable or in distress. Caregivers dealing with locked-in patients must currently rely on their instincts, troubleshooting skills, and standard operating procedures to offer the best care possible. And with these safeguards in place, patients continue to suffer from needless rashes, illnesses, and deaths that should have been avoided. Modern technologies could significantly change this outcome and are being under-utilized in such healthcare environments. This chapter explores patient behavioral analysis with smart healthcare and IoT.

Chapter 11

Sujatha Kesavan, Dr. MGR Educational and Research Institute, India
Sivanand R., Dr. MGR Educational and Research Institute, India
Rengammal Sankari B., Dr. MGR Educational and Research Institute, India
Latha B., Dr. MGR Educational and Research Institute, India
Tamilselvi C., Dr. MGR Educational and Research Institute, India
Krishnaveni S., Dr. MGR Educational and Research Institute, India

The combustion quality determination in power station boilers is of great importance to avoid air pollution. Complete combustion minimizes the exit of NOx, SOx, CO, and CO2 emissions, also ensuring the consistency in load generation in thermal power plants. This chapter proposes a novel hybrid algorithm, called black widow optimization algorithm with mayfly optimization algorithm (BWO-MA), for solving global optimization problems. In this chapter, an effort is made to develop BWO-MA with artificial neural networks (ANN)-based diagnostic model for onset detection of incomplete combustion. Comparison has been done with existing machine learning methods with the proposed BWO-MA-based ANN architecture to accommodate the greater performance. The comprehensive analysis showed that the proposed achieved splendid state-of-the-art performance.

Chapter 12

Angela Diaz-Cadena, University of Guayaquil, Ecuador
Miguel Botto-Tobar, Eindhoven University of Technology, The Netherlands

As China's population grows, the country places a greater focus on the value of cultural education. A successful instructional approach includes ideological and political content within the context of cultural training. Students would do well to observe the facial expressions used by their lecturers in class to completely appreciate the themes being discussed and the strategies being used. A group of high school seniors from a Shanghai high school will take part in experimental research to determine the model's viability. The objective is to assess the effectiveness of education in the classroom is to conduct a poll with students and instructors to get a sense of their thoughts on the topic. More than half of the student body prefers competitions and lectures to other sorts of intellectual and political involvement in the classroom. This model's expression recognition accuracy is more than 2.9% greater than that of other models, and the model's improvement effect is incredible. The authors also investigated the influence of including experimentation in the quality evaluation process.

Chapter 13

    Meghna Dhalaria, Jaypee University of Information Technology, India
    Ekta Gandotra, Jaypee University of Information Technology, India
    Deepak Gupta, Jaypee University of Information Technology, India

Over the past few years, Android has been found to be the most prevalent operating system. The increase in the adoption of Android by users has led to many security issues. The amount of malware targeting Android has significantly increased. Due to the increase in the amount of malware, their detection and classification have become a major issues. Currently, the detection techniques comprise static and dynamic malware analysis. This chapter presents a comparative study of various feature selection methods through machine learning classifiers for Android malware classification. The study examines the features acquired through static malware analysis (such as command strings, permissions, intents, and API calls), and various feature selection techniques are employed to find suitable features for classifying malware to carry out the comparative analysis. The experimental results illustrate that the gain ratio feature selection approach selects relevant features for the classification of Android malware and provides an accuracy of 97.74%.

Chapter 14

    Jyoti R. Munavalli, BNM Institute of Technology, Visvesvaraya Technological University,
        India
    Bindu S., BNM Institute of Technology, Visvesvaraya Technological University, India
    Yasha Jyothi M. Shirur, BNM Institute of Technology, Visvesvaraya Technological
        University, India

In recent times, it is observed that many technologies converge to result into efficient systems. Among others, internet of things has wide applications. IoT is a collective network of devices that collect data, compute, communicate, and act accordingly. The data surge has resulted in various kinds of data analytics for which machine learning and deep learning are extensively used. IoT collects data in real time and processes this data. Deep learning mechanism has a potential to make IoT systems efficient. The deep learning in IoT is the disruptive innovation that leads to various smart things. This chapter highlights the prominent applications in which deep learning has blended with IoT and discusses the applications like smart cities, smart homes, smart farms, smart supply chain management, and smart healthcare. The chapter concludes with a discussion on the challenges and limitations of the IoT infrastructure.

Preface

ABOUT THE BOOK

The Internet of Things (IoT) is multidisciplinary, and it integrates a variety of domain technologies with electronics, communications, Mechanical, Civil, and computer technology. Evaluation of digital technology has enabled the number of Internet-enabled devices that generate a huge volume of data from different systems. This large amount of heterogeneous data requires efficient data collection, processing, and analytical methods. Deep Learning is one of the latest efficient and feasible solutions that enable smart devices to function independently with a decision-making support system. Technological advances and evaluation in the field of deep learning and the Internet of Things have attracted greater research on the use of Deep Learning in the Internet of Things. The amalgamation of deep learning and IoT gives the inherent opportunity for a wide range of emerging applications with diverse devices that are beyond our imagination, which has been discussed in recent literature surveys.

Each chapter of the book will contribute to technology and methodology perspectives in the incorporation of deep learning approaches in solving the wide range of issues in the Internet of Things domain to Identify, Optimize, Predict, Forecast, and Control the emerging IoT systems. Altogether, this book is expected to be the collection of academic and industrial researchers' contributions in DL algorithms for Edge Computing in the Internet of Things, Intelligent Internet of Things, and conceptual structures of Deep Learning concepts on IoT infrastructure. Deep Learning for the Internet of Things, there are a lot of scopes that need further investigation to embed the intelligence in the Internet of Things for accuracy and speed-up the decision. The audience who are interested in designing and building intelligent Internet of Things is in need of strong technical information; this book addresses the emerging technologies and applications of both deep learning and the Internet of Things that is the need of the audience. Moreover, this book is a collective effort of the contributors to highlight and promote the value of deep learning in the field of the Internet of Things.

ORGANIZATION OF THE BOOK

This edited book solicits contributions from the field of Convergence of Deep Learning and the Internet of Things. Each book chapter covers the solutions with state-of-the-art and novel approaches for the IoT problems and challenges in Deep learning perspectives. Topics discussed in this edited book include Intelligent devices, device management, device security for cloud platforms; Hardware Platforms for Deep Learning Framework for resource-constrained IoT devices, Deep Learning-based Intelligent sensing and assessing; DL enabled Edge Computing and IoT; Distributed DL for IoT; Deep Learning for Internet of Things Security – Device security, data security; Deep Learning for QoS in IoT; Edge Computing in Intelligent IoT; and at the end few applications of IoT that uses the deep learning and Survey of Application of Internet of Things with Deep Learning.

In Chapter 1, Nalini M. introduces the reader to intelligent devices with their importance. She describes in detail Intelligent device management in the IoT cloud platform. In the IoT cloud platform managing different intelligent devices is very important for effective utilization. Whenever intelligent devices are connected to the cloud it has many security issues like data privacy, backup, and storage, etc. The author also discusses the root causes of security challenges and also she gave possible solutions for the same. Therefore, this chapter gives a clear idea about the management of intelligent devices. The usage of Intelligent devices in IoT cloud platforms increases day by day, so proper handling of intelligent devices is achieved by reading this chapter. This chapter is useful for researchers, IoT developers, cloud security management, academicians, and students. Before handling an intelligent device one should have a clear understanding of its management and challenges so this chapter gives a clear idea about the same. This chapter covers the importance of intelligent devices in IoT with cloud Computing and also explains about its management, security issues, and possible solutions. This chapter gives an overview of Intelligent device management and security challenges. For developers' and researchers' understanding, this is important before developing an intelligent device-based IoT environment.

In Chapter 2, S. Balachandar and R. Chinnaiyan propose a novel Intelligent Broker Design for IoT using Multi-Cloud Environment. Data Privacy is a common concern across different enterprises, applications deployed in multi-cloud environments will make it more challenging for the cyber security team to monitor the application traffic simultaneously to prevent any attacks or data leaks or data privacy breaches. Handling different data privacy issues always demands for complete visibility over data flow, which ensures to prevent of vulnerability points and the best way to handle sensitive and personal data with the right data retention policies and data protection schemes. The authors have discussed the Articulation of data privacy features from different cloud providers, particularly with their service and deployment model, which help users to plan cybersecurity teams and build the necessary security analytical model to predict and prevent data privacy theft and attacks.

In Chapter 3, Velvizhi V. A. et al. provide readers with an intelligent sensor system in the Internet of Things. The main aspects of IoT are active sensing and efficient sharing of information. IoT is assisted by intelligent sensor devices which aid intelligent communication between connected devices. Billions of sensors and connected devices generate voluminous data. These sensors improve the intelligence of the IoT. Deep learning techniques have great potential to analyze the complex behavioral pattern of IoT devices. A Convolutional Neural network is one such platform where a very large amount of data can be assessed effectively to enhance the performance of Intelligent IoT. Computation and deep learning methods can fundamentally change the hardware designs of traditional sensors and can be used to holistically design intelligent sensor systems. Deep Learning works well for deciphering extremely complex data produced by IoT applications. The authors have described the architecture of IoT, the need for sensors in IoT, the framework of the intelligence sensor system, datasets for deep learning, and DL Algorithms for Sensor Data analysis and prediction. Applications, challenges, and case studies of intelligent sensing systems are also described in the chapter. The target audiences are researchers and engineers who need to apply state-of-the-art and reliable sensing and artificial intelligence technologies in manufacturing industries and engineers working closely with the industry using sensing and artificial intelligence (AI) technologies.

In Chapter 4, Amuthan Nallathambi and Kannan Nova explore the edge computing applications which are enabled by deep learning at scale by predicting user preferences. Edge computing can be used for various purposes, including but not limited to intelligent traffic management and automation, design and manufacturing, health care, the internet of robotic things, medical imaging and E-heath, autonomous vehicles, human facial recognition, smart garbage monitoring system and personal assistants. Deep learning and edge computing are two technologies that are developing fast and will be a challenge to business models. Edge computing is a term used to describe the distribution of computing tasks or workloads across multiple devices, data centers, or other computing resources. These two technologies are a challenge to business models because they can be used for good and bad purposes. The Internet of Things, some experts claim that the IoT is the world's fastest-growing technology, and it will soon become a billion-dollar industry.

In Chapter 5, Amuthan Nallathambi et al. provide the readers with distributed deep learning which extracts knowledge from many sources and processes them in an efficient way without human involvement. It has also been shown that this technique reduces the amount of data transfer from remote machines to central servers significantly. This chapter is for people who know the basics of artificial intelligence. Useful for the students and faculties in the universities who wants to know the fundamentals of Distributed Deep Learning for IoT. This chapter will also be helpful to professionals carrying out the real-time projects. The current research on remote DNN execution does not cover all networks and layers, nor does it take into account the possibility of layer fusion, which would cut down on the amount of communication that is required. To optimize memory, compute, and communication needs all at the same time in order to make it possible for neural networks to be executed in a totally decentralized manner. In order to accomplish this aim, methods are used that are able to permit cross-layer optimization.

In Chapter 6, Nayana Hegde and Sunilkumar propose a chapter on the deep learning algorithms that are utilized for improvement of network and cyber security. This chapter targets researchers who are working in the area of network and cyber security. This is also a suggested good reading for industry people who are currently working on the deep learning algorithms. This chapter can also be a suggested reading for the students of under graduates and post graduate in cyber security technology. Scholars both domestically and internationally have given the study of network attack prediction and detection methodologies considerable attention for a long time. In the context of deep hybrid learning, this research principally provides a multi-type low-rate assault revealing strategy for communication networks. This chapter summarizes some of the key helpful deep learning techniques for attack detection in order to improve the model's ability to adapt to the complicated network environment. This will increase the network's security. Reinforcement learning and its application for intrusion detection are explained. A comparative study report is provided for the review conducted. List of software tools for the implementation of deep learning algorithm are provided. Our review will offer direction and dictionaries for additional study in this area. The proposed chapter is a good reading for researcher and students.

In Chapter 7, K. UdayaKumar et al. presents the reader to explore the deep learning approach for improving Quality of Service in Internet of Things. They describe in detail about recent challenges in QoS. This chapter describes various applications of deep learning method in enhancing Quality of service. It motivates the reader to discourse real time problem in this direction. The exponential growth of IoT requires parallel advancement in terms of communication and computation infrastructure. Providing such infrastructure for IoT with essential resources requires investment and continuous effort. The effective allocation of resources turns an essential factor that directly influences the quality of service. Such allocation policy gains energy efficiency, delay minimization, maximum throughput, channel selection, and resource consumption. This chapter conducts a thorough review of deep learning methods for enhancing the QoS of the Internet of Things. Quantitative comparisons are made between deep learning approaches for enhancing QoS and the difficulties associated. Deep reinforcement learning, a technology that combines the strength of deep learning and reinforcement learning, is explored along with its QoS solutions for dynamic settings. Also investigated are the DRL and its evaluation method for the IoT. Deep learning technology has a lot of potential for handling several QoS concerns. Additionally, it can uncover the relationships between variables that would improve trading. Finally, it is concluded that deep learning is essential for improving IoT QoS and more research inquiries need to be done further.

In Chapter 8, S. Rajarajeswari et al. discuss about edge intelligence in the IoT. The discussion starts with an introduction to edge intelligence, the performance requirements of IoT, and the role of Edge computing in IoT. The authors discuss the challenges of Edge computing in IoT. Some of the Security designs of Edge computing in IoT have been analyzed in this chapter. Later privacy preservation for edge-enabled IoT services using AI is discussed. Further, blockchain for AI-based edge-enabled IOT services is analyzed in this chapter. It is concluded with the various areas of applying Edge computing in IoT

In Chapter 9, Hakki Soy targets to fill a gap in the crowd-monitoring literature by integrating the Internet of Things (IoT) and Artificial Intelligence (AI) technologies into public transportation systems. In this context, an edge computing-based crowd-monitoring application is presented for the realization of similar projects in other regions of the world. This chapter presents the crowd monitoring application that can be implemented on public transport stops in a typical smart city. The main aim is to monitor the crowd of people waiting at public stops and inform the public transport management center (PTMC) about the instantaneous crowding level.

This study introduces a deep-learning-based solution to estimate the density of passengers at bus/tram stops. Different from the conventional cloud computing-based solutions, the proposed method uses smart cameras, which are run on the edge node capable of dealing with AI algorithms. Thanks to the applied edge computing-based crowd-monitoring approach, the proposed application enables the analysis of captured images locally and quickly. In this way, the crowd-monitoring task can be realized independently from the storage of personal data on the cloud servers.

In Chapter 10, Sanjay Rajendra Mate et al. focus the patients with loss of control of the brain for a short period or in between periodic illnesses unable to recognize caretakers, and unable to perform daily activities with full control. IoT is an emerging sector and becoming very essential as many things get connected to the Internet. The Internet of Everything (IoE) makes IoT more popular. In the case of medical science smart devices are being preferred for precise input from patient health. This chapter discusses the human-brain interface. This chapter will help health science researchers, medical practitioners, and learning aspirants. This chapter introduces readers to different kinds of issues with patients especially elderly patient whose brain is not fully operative and whose other body organs are working in a good condition. The author(s) has added all views for various issues related to the brain-computer interface. It has ample opportunity for readers and learners to get self-explanatory information related to human-brain-computer interfacing.

In Chapter 11, Sujatha Kesavan et al. focus on the readers to monitor and control the combustion unit of the turbine using image processing with associating artificial intelligence techniques. The thermal power plant is selected for predicting the combustion quality and is also used to monitor the system. The turbine monitoring system is needed and must be mandatory in order to avoid damage caused by indecorous combustion in the power plant system. The power plant, which plays a major role in energy production, also causes global warming. This topic is of great importance because it will be helpful to control pollution thereby saving mother earth from destruction. This topic will provide knowledge to AI engineers, process control engineers, engineering students, researchers, faculty, scientists, and industrialists, and also in power-generating industries.

In Chapter 12, Angela Diaz Cadena and Miguel Botto-Tobar introduce the reader to China's population growth, the country places a greater focus on the value of cultural education. A successful instructional approach includes ideological and political content within the context of cultural training. Students would do well to observe the facial expressions used by their lecturers in class to completely appreciate the themes being discussed and the strategies being used. A group of high school seniors from a Shanghai high school will take part in experimental research to determine the model's viability. The objective is to assess the effectiveness of education in the classroom is to conduct a poll with students and instructors to get a sense of their thoughts on the topic. More than half of the student body prefers competitions and lectures to other sorts of intellectual and political involvement in the classroom. This model's expression recognition accuracy is more than 2.9 percent greater than that of other models, and the model's improvement effect is incredible also investigated the influence of including experimentation in the quality evaluation process.

In Chapter 13, Meghna Dhalaria et al. examine the features acquired through static malware analysis and employed various feature selection techniques to find suitable features for classifying malware to carry out the comparative analysis. In the current era, there is an increase in the usage of smartphones in our day-to-day lives. A lot of users use these smartphones due to the various functionalities they are providing like emailing, gaming, watching videos, banking, etc. There are various operating systems available in the market such as Windows, iOS, Android, BlackBerry, etc. Among these, Android is found to be the most prevalent one. Unfortunately, the renown of these devices has resulted in an increasing level of cybercrimes. The increasing use of Android applications lured attackers to build complex and sophisticated malware, which is difficult to analyze. The earlier signature-based approach is extensively used for identifying malware. The major constraint of this method is that it cannot detect unknown (i.e., zero-day) malware. Machine learning techniques are now being used by researchers to detect Android malware. These methods allow computers to think and make predictions. Static and dynamic malware analysis features can be used by machine learning approaches to classify apps. Therefore, various feature selection and ML methods are used to classify Android apps. A comparative analysis of feature selection and ML algorithms is carried out to finalize the method/technique that provides the best results for detecting Android malware. Experiments are performed on a dataset of real Android apps consisting of various features. The experimental results illustrate that the Gain Ratio feature selection approach selects relevant features for the classification of Android malware and provides an accuracy of 97.74%.

In Chapter 14, Munavalli J. R. et al. introduce the readers to various IoT applications that have applied deep learning mechanisms to become efficient as well as smart systems. The authors have discussed various applications that have applied deep learning mechanisms to IoT solutions. Smart cities and smart infrastructures applied deep learning methods for traffic monitoring, parking management, and road surveillance. Even during the pandemic, it is used for crowd management, mask detection, and social distancing. To make buildings smarter, environmental monitoring, visual management for security from intruders, waste management, energy management, and home automation are implemented. In agriculture, it is used in crop management, and livestock management is based on climate and soil, the crops are selected to get better yield. Plant diseases are identified at an early stage and necessary actions are taken. Autonomous planning and scheduling of tasks, market situation analysis, demand and supply logistics, and the behavior of customers are analyzed through deep learning methods. The wearables have changed the way health parameters are monitored. Now the necessary body vitals are monitored continuously through the sensors in wearables and the data analysis results in detecting diseases. Smart healthcare provides personalized healthcare.

Going forward, with the pace at which the world is moving ahead, there will be an increase in the number of connected devices, and this can pose various challenges. Issues like connectivity, handling of data, and its processing at edge devices could limit the implementations of IoT solutions. The industry, academicians, and researchers can explore various opportunities to tackle the limitations and implementation challenges of the IoT solution using deep learning techniques.

T. Kavitha
New Horizon Collee of Engineering (Autonomous), India & Visvesvaraya Technological University, India

G. Senbagavalli
AMC Engineering College, Visvesvaraya Technological University, India

Deepika Koundal
University of Petroleum & Energy Studies, Dehradun, India

Yanhi Guo
University of Illinois, USA

Deepak Jain
Chongqing University of Posts and Telecommunications, Chongqing, China

Acknowledgment

First and foremost, we would like to thank all of the contributors for their hard work and for spending their time and knowledge to bring their chapter to a greater extent of quality.

Second, we would like to express our gratitude to the reviewers for their significant contributions to the book's excellence and consistency by providing vital feedback. Their expertise and commitment are immensely valued.

Third, we would like to express our gratefulness toward the members of our affiliating organizations for their kind cooperation and encouragement for the successful completion of this book.

We would like to acknowledge the IGI publishers and their team for guiding us to meet the expectation of international-level readers. without their aid, this book would not have been possible. Their time and effort are greatly appreciated.

Finally, we would like to thank our family members, friends, and all who have directly or indirectly helped us in the successful completion of this book.

Chapter 1
Intelligent Devices, Device Management, and Device Security for Cloud Platforms

Nalini M.

Sri Sairam Engineering College, Anna University, India

ABSTRACT

The phrase "intelligent device" refers to a package that contains either a full measurement system or a component inside a measurement system that includes a digital processor. The processing of measurement sensor output to adjust for flaws inherent in the measurement process results in significant gains in measurement accuracy. Intelligent device management is a technique used in corporate software applications to monitor and manage distant equipment, systems, and goods through the Internet. Device security in cloud platforms will be made using proactive attack surface management and improved protection against ransomware and other sophisticated threats safeguarding data and devices. Cloud security is a set of processes and technologies that are meant to handle both external and internal risks to enterprise security. This chapter explains about intelligent devices, the need for security and management of intelligent devices in cloud platforms, and finally ends with challenges associated with this.

INTRODUCTION

The prefixes SMART and INTELLIGENT are frequently misunderstood in today's connected world and are used interchangeably by inexperienced users. Most people think it will be the same thing, but it's not. The functioning of the two is significantly dissimilar. The SMART gadget operates autonomously, doing tasks according to an internal algorithm that has been pre-programmed. On the other hand, intelligent gadgets carry out tasks based on algorithms that have evolved through time as a result of prior learning and human input. To put it another way, SMART devices adhere to the pre-established operational rules, but INTELLIGENT devices learn and develop together with the user which was discussed by Kumar et al. (2019), Kaur et al. (2018) and Parast et al. (2022).

DOI: 10.4018/978-1-6684-6275-1.ch001

Normal Device: To alter the temperature setting and turn the device on or off, the user must physically be present.

Smart Device: The user may enter a schedule for temperature and on/off switching. Without user input, the smart gadget will follow the timetable. The gadget may also be controlled remotely through the internet.

Intelligent Devices: A whole different degree of capacity is being discussed when we talk about intelligent devices, including artificial intelligence (AI).

- An intelligent air conditioner could be able to do things like turn on at a certain time and control the temperature depending on prior learning about user behavior.
- Alternatively, it may learn from the user's previous behaviors and automatically modify the temperature based on the temperature and humidity outside.

It can be accepted that intelligent devices may also be referred to as smart devices with understanding and adaptation capabilities based on the description and examples provided above. Therefore, it is clear that intelligent gadgets are "smarter" than smart ones and which was given by Walia et al., (2022). A machine, instrument, piece of equipment, or any other item having inbuilt processing capacity is referred to as an intelligent device. Currently, there are a wide variety of intelligent products on the market, including laptop and handheld computers, automobiles, household appliances, geological equipment, medical devices, airplanes, weapons, and cameras. As a result, managing IoT devices in such a complexed infrastructure will be a crucial task that addresses crucial FCAPS (fault, configuration, responsibility, performance, and security) concerns (Al-Ali et al., 2017)

An intelligent device's connectivity is its capacity to join a data network. Intelligent devices cannot be autonomous or context-aware if they are not connected. A key component of the internet of things is network connection, which allows a device to participate in the network. A network can have wired or wireless connection (Rimal, 2009). Users can finish computer activities utilizing services made available through the Internet thanks to cloud computing. The usage of intelligent devices in connection with cloud platforms has evolved into a sort of catalyst: cloud computing and intelligent devices are now interconnected. These are genuine future technologies that will have several advantages, Figure 1 depicts the overview of intelligent devices.

Figure 1. Intelligent device

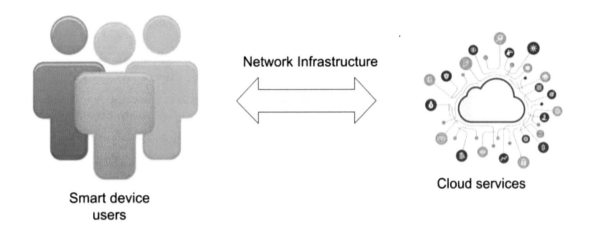

The challenge of storing, analyzing, and accessing massive volumes of data has emerged as a result of the quick development of technology. The collaborative use of cloud technology and intelligent devices is a major area of innovation. Combining advanced processing of visual data streams with new monitoring services will be feasible. For instance, sensor information may be transferred to the cloud and retained for use in intelligent monitoring and activation by other devices in the future. The objective is to turn data into insights, which will then motivate practical and profitable action (Ristenpart et al., 2009; Abdou et al., 2019).

THE ROLE OF CLOUD COMPUTING ON THE INTELLIGENT DEVICE

In combination with both the internet of things and cloud computing helps to improve the effectiveness of routine jobs. The aim of cloud computing is to provide data a way to go where it needs to go, yet the internet of things creates a tonne of data. Despite the clear advantages of cloud computing, security issues have been raised due to the model's complexity and shared technology (Takabi et al 2010 & Kaur, 2020). Four advantages of cloud computing:

- No need to estimate infrastructure capacity requirements
- Savings increase with the size of the scale since you only have to pay for the resources you really utilize.
- Platforms may be set up all over the world in a short amount of time.
- Flexibility and promptness in supplying developers with resources

Thus, cloud computing's function in the internet of things is to pool resources to save IoT data and make it accessible when needed. Companies will invest 47% more than on cloud computing in 2021 alone as a result of the COVID-19 effect, according to a 2020 poll of 750 worldwide cloud professionals (Alazab et al., 2022).

Provides features for remote computing: An intelligent device minimizes reliance on on-site infra-structure because of its vast storage capacity. Cloud computing has been more popular as a result of ongoing advancements in internet-based technology, including the internet and the devices that support sophisticated cloud solutions. Cloud solutions, which are jam-packed with intelligent devices, give busi-nesses the opportunity to quickly and easily use remote computing services.

Privacy & Security: With cloud technology and intelligent devices, tasks may be completed auto-matically, helping enterprises significantly lower security hazards. An intelligent device-enabled cloud technology is a system that offers control that is preventative, investigative, and remedial. It also offers consumers excellent security mechanisms with efficient authentication and encryption. intelligent device goods employ protocols like biometrics to manage and secure user identities as well as data.

Integration of data: In addition to seamlessly integrating intelligent devices and cloud, recent tech-nological advancements also offer real-time communication and connection. As a result, it is simple to extract real-time data on crucial business activities and carry out on-the-spot data integration thanks to constant connectivity. The volume of data created from various sources, along with its centralized storage, processing, and analysis, may be handled by cloud-based systems with strong data integration capabilities.

A minimal dependence on hardware: Currently, a number of intelligent device solutions provide plug-and-play hosting services, which are made possible by fusing the intelligent device with the cloud. To support the agility needed by intelligent device devices, cloud-enabled intelligent device hosting providers do not need to rely on any form of hardware or infrastructure. Organizations may now easily transition to omnichannel communication and deploy large-scale intelligent device initiatives across platforms.

Business Resilience: Cloud computing solutions, which are renowned for their adaptability and dependability, can guarantee company continuity in the event of almost any emergency, data loss, or disaster. Cloud services function through a variety of data servers spread over several different places that store numerous copies of backup data. Intelligent device-based activities continue to function in the event of an emergency, making data recovery simple.

Touchpoint and Multi-Device Communication: Response times and data processing rates are often shortened and increased when edge computing and intelligent device technologies are coupled. For best use, intelligent device implementation with cloud technology and edge computing technologies is necessary (Kaur, 2020).

Although cloud computing services help speed up intelligent device development, correctly using these services presents several difficulties. There are a few challenges which need to be resolved before combining intelligent devices with the cloud.

IoT CLOUD FUNCTIONS AND BENEFITS

The benefits of integrating these services are numerous. IoT cloud computing provides a wide range of connectivity options, demonstrating substantial network access. One of the various tools individuals use to access cloud computing resources is a mobile, tablet, or laptop device. Users will find this use-ful, but it raises the question of whether network access points are necessary. IoT cloud computing is readily accessible to developers. In other words, it's an internet service that doesn't require any help or special permission to access. The only requirement is Internet access. The service can expand based on user demands and requirements. Fast and versatile allow you to adjust the user count, expand storage capacity, and alter software settings. It is possible to provide both deep computing power and storage because of this property. Cloud computing implies resource sharing. It promotes greater collaboration and creates enduring ties among users. As the use of automation and IoT devices grows, security risks emerge. Thanks to cloud solutions, businesses may employ reliable authentication and encryption procedures (Abie, 2019, Chen et al., 2012).

Finally, since you get exactly what you paid for from the supplier, IoT cloud computing is practical. Since the supplier monitors your consumption habits, this suggests that rates vary based on use. There must be a growing network of IP-addressed objects for the network to be able to communicate with one another and connect to the Internet. It is crucial to remember that good cloud architecture is essential for ensuring dependability, security, economy, and performance optimization. A safe environment and agile development are produced by using well-designed CI/CD pipelines, organized services, and sandboxed environments (Perez et al., 2008)

IoT DEVICE MANAGEMENT

In order to supply, monitor, and maintain the expanding array of connected objects (also known as the internet of things endpoints or edge devices) in your residential or commercial network, you must use a variety of procedures, tools, and technologies. The need for IoT device management software is growing as more and more devices have network capabilities. By 2023, there would be 29.3 billion networked devices, or 3.6 gadgets for every person on the earth, predicts Cisco's Annual Internet Report (2018-2023). Architectures for IoT device planning typically carry out device provisioning to start machine-to-machine (M2M) communication, resource control that is required to set up functional parameters like bandwidth and availability time, and lastly device fault detection, Network infrastructure monitoring, and mitigation (Spring, J 2011). By abstracting the network enablers and protocols of the underlying infrastructure, the most well-known frameworks, such as Google IoT Core, Amazon Web Services (AWS) IoT, Azure IoT, or IBM Watson, link a large quantity of devices as a single domain and/or in a single place (Harnik et al., 2010)

IoT Device Management is Crucial due to Two Factors: Pull and Push

Intelligent IoT device management creates the foundation for advanced analytics, seamless automation, internal efficiency, and novel business models, therefore there is a definite pull factor. IoT device management is essential for business models like servitization, which replaces outright equipment sales with equipment leasing and services based on IoT data.

Additionally, there is a push aspect because more and more people are adopting linked gadgets. Without IoT device management, staff members would probably keep adding additional endpoints to the company network, adding significantly more shadow IT labour (Ramachandran et al., 2022). Due to these factors, according to a 2020 study analysis by Valuates Reports, the need for IoT device management will increase between 2021 and 2026 at a compound annual growth rate of 22.6 percent (CAGR). IoT device administration will be a $6.25 billion market globally by the conclusion of this projection period. IoT device management includes both the procedures and the tools you need to control your IoT environment, as was previously indicated, Figure 2 illustrates the required important key components. Throughout an IoT device's lifespan, several essential operations are:

Figure 2. Key components of Device Management

Device onboarding: An IoT device must be implemented into the network when it is turned on for the first time. However, they lack a fully featured, standalone interface to help users with the onboarding process, unlike conventional devices. Some of the tasks you could anticipate during device onboarding include verifying credentials, creating authentication methods, assigning a device identity, etc.

Device configuration: Each IoT device connected to your network must be set up to meet your company's requirements. For instance, if you have a fleet of connected vehicles, you would wish to group particular devices according to their normal operating location or destination.

Operational diagnostics: Diagnostics may provide you a wealth of information about how your IoT operations are doing. You need a centralised IoT device management capability since the majority of IoT devices lack the memory or computational power to interpret diagnostics on the device itself.

Device security: This is going to play a bigger role in IoT device management. Despite making up 30% of all endpoints, up to 98 percent of IoT device traffic in the U.S. was permitted to travel across unencrypted channels in 2020. IoT device administration provides the appropriate security procedures and brings unmapped endpoints under corporate control.

Device upkeep: In addition to updating device firmware to the most recent version, you should keep an eye out for any security flaws that could be introduced by recent releases. Similar to onboarding or configuration, IoT device management performs over the air (OTA) updates for device maintenance in bulk.

End of life: Intelligent Iot systems that are no longer in use but are still connected to the company network offer a serious security risk since an outside party might steal data from the device covertly. Furthermore, a dated or broken gadget might seriously harm operations. End-of-life policies and protocols outline the precise actions that must be taken to decommission an IoT device and how to recycle its parts (Abdou et al,. 2019, Almusaylim et al. 2020).

Key Requirements for IoT Device Management Features

Figure 3. Requirements for IoT Device Management Features

Important requirements for implementing IoT device management system shows in Figure 3 and which is explained below one by one.

Bulk device onboarding: The software has to make it possible to sign in using identifying credentials and a network key. To create a safe connection between the endpoint device and the IoT service, device onboarding must be done remotely.

Remote troubleshooting: To swiftly fix user difficulties and minimize manual work, assistance for remote troubleshooting should be provided. An integrated governance portal can aid in the centralized resolution of problems affecting several endpoints.

Analytics and reports: IoT devices often come with some edge analytics functionality. Through GUI dashboards, the IoT device management software will be able to show in-depth analytics findings in real-time. Reports based on this data can also be created for business users to comprehend.

Robust integrations: This software must be compatible with your hardware ecosystem and application codebase (i.e., the language in which they are developed). For integrated processes, it has to link to business apps and downstream data servers.

Strict security: The programme should provide you thorough device records that you may use to spot instances of unusual use and illegal access. The software's dashboard may send real-time notifications that can be used to swiftly conduct root-cause analysis and detect problems.

Even while these are the capabilities you must have, you should also give priority to value-added services that increase the functionality of your IoT devices. For instance, the solution can include application development tools that enable you to create your own IoT apps (complete with cloud hosting) and expand your company. Alternately, you might use machine learning (ML) and artificial intelligence (AI) to make IoT device management more contextual, for as by comparing diagnostics data to other infrastructure KPIs to determine the optimal operational configuration (Oke & Arowoiya, 2021) The top IoT device management software suppliers in the globe provide distinctive differentiators that make these solutions suitable for certain company requirements in recognition of these possibilities (Aboubakar et al., 2021). Let's evaluate a few of these suggestions.

Various data demands and devices functionality requirements need situational IoT device management, as shown by these high-level examples:

Agriculture: IoT devices used in agricultural applications must transmit a variety of data due to its shifting nature, including temperatures and moisture levels as well as the positions of vehicles and even mobile irrigation systems.

Solar systems: While these technologies don't go across space, many solar panels nowadays change their location in response to the sun's position and the surrounding weather.

Electric vehicle charging: It is possible to combine EV charging stations with applications that help drivers locate them. Additionally, they may report on their consumption, if they require maintenance, and more. To different users for various objectives, each of these sorts of data must be transmitted.

How May IoT Device Management Platforms be Chosen?

An IoT device management platform's precise purpose is to offer remote access, configuration management, and security to an IoT system. When choosing an IoT device management platform for your IoT devices, it's important to pay attention to features like sophisticated and robust APIs, a customizable dashboard, the platform's capability to send custom scripts to deployed devices, the platform's ability to organize and manage device groups, and access to edge devices. Even better, you can decide to hire a reputable IoT development company to help you create your own IoT Device management platform (Silva et al., 2022).

Problems with Remotely Managing IoT Devices

In the internet of things age, systems can use analytics and business intelligence more quickly and effectively than a person. Without any human intervention or acknowledgement, the responses are logged and modifications are performed.

Businesses rely increasingly on IoT devices nowadays to create better divisions, cut costs, and increase company efficiency. Even while IoT networks are quickly integrating into commercial processes, maintaining the networks still presents several difficulties. Let's examine some of the difficulties in managing distant IoT devices, from connection to scalability and security.

Security: Because it involves protecting technological information, cybersecurity is one of the main problems with IoT device management. Cybersecurity focuses on everything connected to the hardware, not only the data connection's susceptibility or brittleness.

Consider a smart manufacturing unit with IoT sensors. A management or maintenance worker in the equipped units can use a mobile device to read data, give commands, or check the equipment's status. What happens if an attacker tries to assault the computer and steal the data using the system's lax security measures? The chance exists that the technician may turn off all connected devices and systems, causing the system to overheat or become overloaded. The information would also be accessible.

System Reliability: The local ISP has outages, and the system as a whole goes dark when the power goes out. Similarly, disasters or climatic changes may have an influence on data centres, which are essential to the effective operation of most IoT solutions. These circumstances allow for a total shutdown of all systems or devices.

Privacy: The majority of internet connections are protected by encryption, which means that the data is securely locked behind the programme key and cannot be unlocked or translated without the appropriate authority. Even while many businesses are aware of this issue and continue to avoid using such encryptions, it is more dangerous when they store sensitive digital data, such as user accounts, passwords or pin numbers, and personal information, in a plaintext. Data which is not encrypted or encoded can be collected, transmitted, and used by IoT systems. It may increase the danger for companies that handle sensitive data.

Utilization of Power, Storage, and Resources: Energy is required to run any electronic equipment, including IoT. Even physical storage areas are required for the data. Remote services must also store digital data due to the abundance of cloud and edge computing services. These distant servers require a tremendous amount of power. Large-scale cooling systems are needed for the data centers.

Limitations and Features of Simple IoT Device Management

The ability to set up and manage a variety of fundamental IoT connection and functionality needs, which are important to almost all IoT applications, is provided by basic IoT device management (Walia & Garg, 2022).

Range: The device's internal power management system and its built-in or external antennas determine the device's communication range. Without any sophisticated IoT device management tools, communication range is therefore within the control of the business, but testing and reporting on range are considerably simpler with an IoT device management platform.

Bandwidth: A deployed IoT application's bandwidth depends on the device's internal features, including the modem type (e.g., 3G, 4G LTE, or 5G), and the existing network. Although they are not necessary to handle this feature, sophisticated (contextual) IoT device management technologies give the ability to evaluate bandwidth and acquire network awareness.

A battery's life: The battery life capacity is another issue for IoT technology. The design of the item and how it is used affect battery life. For instance, a deployed gadget in a far-off oil well will drain its battery every time it transmits data. Using cutting-edge IoT device management programmes like Digi Remote Manager, edge computing approaches can aid in the optimization of these procedures. One of the main issues that consumers who want to invest in IoT worry about is the battery life of an IoT device. The consumer will pay twice as much for networks that use more battery power and have shorter battery lives, and the firm's monitoring standards may even suffer. The control of battery life is essential for maintaining real-time updates. IoT investors must choose the appropriate network and device type for their business in order to maximize battery life. Therefore, the management of battery life depends on the network and device that customers choose. As an illustration, devices using wireless networks like 3G/4G or Wi-Fi consume more power and have shorter battery lives than those using LPWAN-based technologies like LoRaWAN, NB-IoT, LTE-M, and others.

Activation of a device: The operation of an enterprise with any of its customers' end IoT infrastructure depends critically on the activation of IoT devices. It is evident that an internet connection and reliable connectivity are necessary for the continuous flow of data, the coordination of commands and programmes, and the effective automation and monitoring of activities in the IoT device deployment environment. The over-the-air activation (OTAA) technique, on rare occasions, Activation by Personalization, are the two methods often used for device activation (ABP) activation by personalization. A unique extended unique identifier (EUI) address is allocated and safety keys are exchanged with the device during the join-procedure that OTAA devices conduct with the network. This easy step creates automated activation that doesn't require any form of manual interface. In rural places, this procedure is hampered by weak internet connectivity, frequent power outages without backup, and other issues (Grobauer et al 2010).

Location of an IoT device: The selection of an IoT device model and installation location for real-time data collecting is a problem that still faces IoT device adoption. The IoT market is expanding, as are the hardware device types (outdoor, indoor, waterproof, etc.) and their characteristics, which call for careful selection. The needs of a company are frequently not reviewed with the selection of hardware prior to deployment, resulting in a wasted investment in IoT technology, even when sensors and gateways are available in many networking facilities with new technologies like LoRa. Another issue is that the location or site of installation is not a desired factor that impairs IoT performance. Devices might be either indoor or outdoor; making a wise choice is what produces a successful outcome.

Update the firmware: Firmware, a piece of software that is integrated into hardware, is essential to the continued operation of IoT technology in a particular setting. In other words, firmware updates are required in IoT to enable automation and predictive maintenance as it works to correct bugs, unauthorized data, enhance encryption, upgrade features, and so on. Firmware is a code that runs on hardware and is important to the system's ability to function. Firmware upgrades for IoT devices become difficult when the over-the-air (OTA) technique is not available. Finding IoT equipment that offers OTA firmware upgrades is therefore crucial for continuous real-time data updates.

Maintaining Equipment Health: The device or sensor that provides real-time data, together with automation and predictive maintenance, is the key component of integrating IoT technology and ensures accuracy in management, monitoring, and business intelligence at all times. The deployed device's condition and health should be known in order to ensure the continued and guaranteed operation of the technology, since the device continues to be the core of IoT. The problem emerges when IoT technology is chosen without taking into account aspects that disclose device health. Make sure the IoT infrastructure you select reveals all information, no matter how insignificant, to reinforce openness in your business operations.

Difficulties with Accurate Data Capture: Even if we were to suppose that the IoT process had overcome all of its technological obstacles in the past and that a reliable system had been launched on the market, inaccurate data collecting would still be a problem. This is due to the fact that systems record everything, including any abnormalities, unintended occurrences, and IoT software failures. The inclusion of this data in analytical data may have a negative impact on decision-making, which will then have an impact on customers and the firm collecting the data.

Difficulties with IoT Data Analytics: The true benefit of an Iot infrastructure is in the generation of useful insights from the gathered IoT data. A high-performance analytical platform including tools capable of processing enormous volumes of data is necessary for this. Additionally, when IoT software is implemented, new challenges are created, such as the requirement for IoT analytics that deviate even more from traditional analytics due to the exponential growth of data quantities.

For businesses to profit from this form of data collecting, analytics must take place in real-time due to the nature of IoT data. Another problem is time series data, which is any data with a timestamp. Massive amounts of time series data must be able to be gathered, stored, and analyzed by an organization's IoT infrastructure. The difficulty in this situation is that the majority of standard databases are ill-suited to manage this kind of data (Tsai et al., 2012).

DEVICE SECURITY FOR CLOUD PLATFORM

In settings including smart infrastructures, smart cities, smart factories, and smart households, a variety of IoT devices are linked to clouds, edge servers, and edge devices like on-premises gateways. Moving client IP or other sensitive data from IoT devices to the cloud or edge might make that data more vulnerable to attack. Therefore, it is crucial to effectively safeguard connected IoT devices as well as cloud and edge server systems. This establishes a continuous chain of trust between cloud infrastructures. The demand for security is only increasing as more apps become compute-intensive and capable of making autonomous decisions (Moreno-Vozmediano et al., 2012).

With billions of devices connected to the internet of things, both manufacturers and customers need to be certain that each device's identification is safe and authentic. The problem for device makers is to safeguard the identity and integrity of every component of a cloud-connected system, regardless of whether it consists of cloud servers, edge servers with high computational demands, consumer electronics, or internet of things end nodes like sensors. This security is fundamental to enabling safe zero-touch provisioning and secure lifecycle management of internet of things devices. It also forms the foundation for secure cloud connectivity.

What Makes Cloud Security Crucial?

The adoption of cloud-based platforms and IaaS, PaaS, or SaaS computing paradigms has increased in contemporary organizations. When organizations effectively resource their departments, the variable nature of maintaining the infrastructure, particularly in growing applications and services, can present a variety of issues. Organizations may outsource the many time-consuming IT-related duties thanks to these as-a-service models.

Understanding the safety standards for keeping information secure has become important as businesses continue to shift to the cloud. Although the administration of this infrastructure might be transferred to third-party cloud computing service providers, there is no guarantee that the accountability and security of data assets will follow. With the continued development of the digital environment, security concerns have progressed. Because of an organization's lack of coverage in accessing data and movement, these risks specifically target suppliers of cloud computing. Organizations may experience serious governance and compliance issues when handling client information, independent of where it is housed, if they don't take proactive measures to increase their cloud security (Nawrocki & Osypanka, 2021).

Regardless of your duties, the complete breadth of cloud security is intended to safeguard the following:

- Physical networks, such as routers, cables, power sources, and temperature controls.
- Hard discs and other data storage devices
- Core network computing hardware and software are data servers.
- Frameworks for computer virtualization, include virtual machine software, host computers, and guest computers
- Operating systems (OS) are pieces of software
- Application programming interface (API) administration is a function of middleware.
- Runtime environments: where a programme is executed and maintained.
- Data is every piece of information that is saved, changed, or accessed.
- Traditional software services, applications (email, tax software, productivity suites, etc.)

- Hardware used by end users, such as laptops, smartphones, internet of things (IoT) devices, etc.

Cloud Security Working

Every step taken to secure the cloud aims to achieve the following:

- In the event of data loss, allow for data recovery.
- Defend networks and storage against nefarious data theft.
- Preventing carelessness or human mistake that results in data breaches
- Minimize the effects of any system or data breach

A component of cloud security which involves the technological side of threat prevention is data security. By leveraging tools and technology, providers and customers can put up barriers that stop sensitive data from being accessed or seen. Out of those, encryption is one of its most powerful techniques. Your data is encrypted, making it impossible for anybody other than the owner of the encryption key to decrypt it. If your data is lost or stolen, it will be nearly unreadable and worthless. (Umar et al., 2018) In cloud networks, emphasis is also placed on security measures for data transit, such as virtual private networks (VPNs).

The management of identity and access (IAM) relates to the accessibility rights provided to user accounts. Managing user account authorisation and authentication also applies here. IAM encompasses techniques like password management and multi-factor authentication, among others.

Policies concerning threat prevention, detection, and mitigation are the main concerns of governance. Threat intelligence, for SMBs and organizations, may assist with tracking and prioritizing threats to keep critical systems properly secured. However, emphasizing safe user behavior standards and training might be advantageous for even individual cloud customers. Although they are especially pertinent in professional settings, all users may gain from understanding safe usage rules and how to address threats (Viega, 2009).

Technical disaster recovery methods are included in data retention (DR) and business continuity (BC) planning in the event of data loss. Any DR and BC strategy must include techniques for data redundancy, such as backups. Having technical mechanisms in place to guarantee continuous operations might also be beneficial. For a complete BC strategy, frameworks for validating backups and adequate staff recovery instructions are just as important. Organizations must thus adhere to rules in order to uphold these principles. Data masking is one strategy that hides identity inside data using encryption techniques (Sabahi, 2011).

Cloud Security Solutions

Identity and access management (IAM): Enterprises may implement policy-driven enforcement methods for all users seeking to access both on-premises and cloud-based services using identity and access management (IAM) tools and services. IAM's primary role is to give all users digital identities so that they may be tracked and regulated actively throughout all data exchanges as needed (Parast et al., 2022).

Data loss prevention (DLP): The privacy of regulated cloud data is ensured by a collection of tools and services provided by data loss prevention (DLP) services. All stored data, whether at rest or in motion, is protected by DLP systems using a mix of remediation warnings, data encryption, and other preventative measures.

Security information and event management (SIEM): A complete security orchestration system, security information and event management (SIEM) automates threat monitoring, detection, and response in cloud-based settings. SIEM technology enables IT teams to properly implement their network security policies while being able to promptly respond to any possible threats. SIEM technology uses artificial intelligence (AI)-driven technologies to correlate log data across several platforms and digital assets (Fortino et al., 2022).

Business continuity and disaster recovery: Data breaches and disruptive disruptions can still happen despite the precautionary precautions enterprises put in place for their on-premise and cloud-based infrastructures. Enterprises need to be ready to respond as rapidly as possible to newly identified vulnerabilities or large system failures. Disaster recovery solutions are a cornerstone of cloud security and give businesses the tools, services, and standards required to quickly recover lost data and go back to business as usual.

Encryption: Data can be scrambled using encryption so that only people with the proper authorization can decipher it. Unencrypted data can be leaked, sold, used to launch more assaults, etc., if a hacker gains access to a firm's cloud and discovers the data there. The attacker, however, will only see scrambled data if the company's data is encrypted, which they cannot utilise until they somehow uncover the decryption key (which should be almost impossible). In this way, encryption aids in protecting data even though other security measures fall short.

Both at rest (while it is kept) and in transit, data can be encrypted (while it is sent from one place to another). In order to prevent hackers from intercepting and reading cloud data, it should have been encrypted both in transit and at rest. In a multi-cloud or hybrid cloud scenario, encrypting data in transit must cover both data moving between a cloud and a user and data moving from one cloud to another. Data which is kept in a database or through a cloud storage service should also be encrypted.

A VPN can encrypt communication across clouds in a multi-cloud or hybrid cloud system if the clouds are linked at the network layer. SSL/TLS encryption should be used if they are connected via the application layer.

Firewall: By preventing harmful online traffic, a cloud firewall adds an extra layer of security around cloud assets. Cloud firewalls are hosted in the cloud and provide a virtual security fence around cloud infrastructure, in contrast to traditional firewalls, which are housed on-premise and protect the network perimeter. This is the category in which most web application firewalls belong in.

DDoS assaults, malicious bot activity, and vulnerability exploitation are all blocked by cloud firewalls. As a result, there are fewer possibilities that a cyberattack will destroy the cloud infrastructure of a business.

CLOUD SECURITY CHALLENGES

For IT leaders, security has become one of the most difficult problems, especially when using clouds. Numerous security concerns exist and are keeping businesses from utilizing the cloud's benefits. In the realm of cloud computing, users have access to processing capacity that is greater than what is available in their physical surroundings. A user must transport data via the cloud in order to access this virtual environment. Implementing security solutions in the cloud environment presents a number of difficulties due to its size and flexibility. Figure 4 shows the important security challenges.

Figure 4. Cloud security challenges

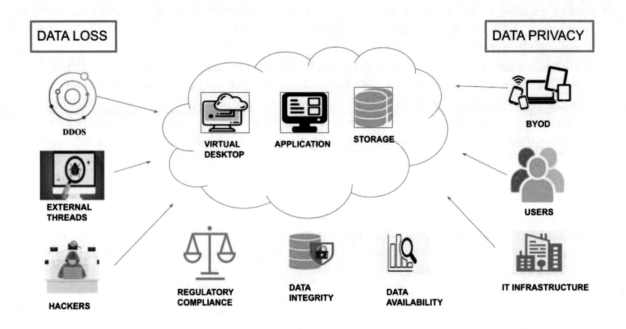

The categorisation shown above highlights a number of typical problems with cloud computing. Figure. 5 is a schematic diagram illustrating the cloud computing hierarchy along with security difficulties for both the deployment and service models as well as network-related problems. The deployment paradigm is further divided into Private, Public, and Hybrid Clouds, and the security concerns of each have been revealed.

The Service provider model is further divided into the SaaS, PaaS, and IaaS briefings, each of which highlights the security problems they share. The difficulties with network security are also demonstrated by the fact that networks are the foundation of all internet-based services, including cloud computing.

Figure 5. Classification of security challenges

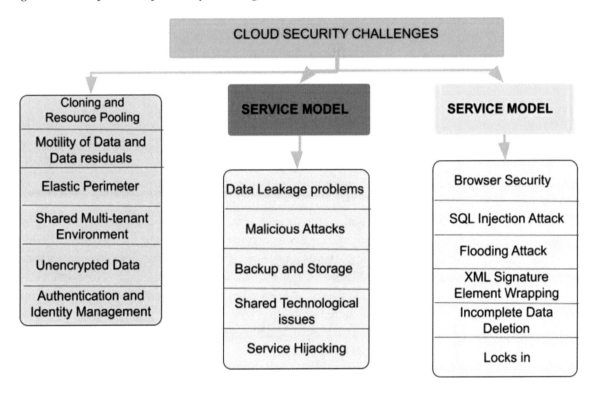

Security problems associated with deployment models: Three different deployment model options are available: private, public, and hybrid. Private type cloud models are often implemented within an enterprise and are only accessible internally by members of that organization. The company uses the public cloud model to access a variety of resources, online applications, and services via the internet, intranet, and extranet. A hybrid cloud is made up of two or more than two clouds, either private cloud or public. It is a setting with several internal and external service providers (Wang et al., 2022, Alazab et al., 2022).

Security Issues Relating to Certain Deployment Models

Resource pooling and Cloning: Cloning associated with data replication or duplication Cloning causes data leakage issues that expose the machine's legitimacy. Resource pooling is a service that allows users to share and use different resources in accordance with the demands of their applications. Resource pooling is concerned with unapproved access brought on by sharing across the same network. While a virtual machine can be provided simply, according to studies on virtual and cloud computing, they can also be reversed to earlier situations, halted, easily resumed, easily cloned, and easily transferred between two or more physical servers, posing non-auditable type security risks (Kaur et al., 2018) .

Data mobility and residuals: Data is frequently migrated to cloud infrastructure to make the greatest use of resources. As a result, the place where data is stored in the cloud would no longer exist for the company. With public clouds, this is valid. The leftover data that is left behind after this data transit might be accessed by unauthorized individuals. Although data leftover poses extremely few security risks in private clouds, public cloud contributions may experience serious security problems. Data security risks including data remains and leakage, and inconsistent data may result from this once again. The authors also noted that the ideal solution of cryptography may be successfully thought of in order to tackle the issues with data storage.

Elastic Perimeter: A private cloud-based cloud architecture, in particular, generates an elastic perimeter. The organization's many divisions and users permit resource sharing to boost accessibility, but this has the undesirable side effect of increasing the risk of data breaches. Resources are centralised and dispersed according to demand in private clouds. The resource management process distributes resources according to user needs, which causes data loss issues because any user may easily attempt to access sensitive data. Due to the flexibility of different cloud-based resources, duplicated data might end up being stored on unreliable hosts, posing serious privacy problems.

Shared Multi-tenant Environment: among the most crucial characteristics of the cloud computing is multitenancy, which will enables numerous users to execute individual apps simultaneously on the same physical infrastructure while keeping user data private. However, the shared multi-tenant nature of public clouds increases security vulnerabilities including unauthorised data access by other renters using the same infrastructure. When one tenant uses a disproportionate amount of resources, a multi-tenant setup may also show some resource contention problems. This might be the result of a cyber assault or legitimate recurring needs. The impact of a Virtual Machine Hopping attack may be greater than in a typical IT system due to multi-tenancy.

Unencrypted Data: Encryption of data is a method that aids in defending against numerous hostile external attacks. Data that is not encrypted is subject to attack because it lacks a security measure. Unauthorized individuals can simply access these unencrypted data. Unencrypted data puts user information at risk, making it possible for cloud servers to leak different sensitive information to unwanted users. For instance, well-known file-sharing site Dropbox was accused of storing all user data with a single encryption key. These are not encrypted, which encourages malevolent individuals to misuse the data in some way.

Authentication and Identity Management: The user is enabled to approach their private data and make it accessible to numerous services throughout the network with the aid of the cloud. By using their credentials, users may be authenticated with the use of identity management. The drawback of interoperability caused by various identity tokens, identity negotiation methods, and architectural patterns is known as identity management (IDM). IDM exacerbates the issue of unauthorized users intruding. They even highlighted the need to adopt multi-factor type authentication utilizing a smart card as well as fingerprint in addition to a password in order to provide authentication and achieve a greater level of security.

Service models and security issues they present:

The cloud is used to supply and utilize a variety of cloud services, which includes Software as a Service (SaaS), Platform as a Service (PaaS), and Infrastructure as a Service (IaaS). SaaS is a multi-tenant platform, also known as an application service provider, that facilitates the allocation of services across cloud customers. While PaaS gives programmers a platform to make work with all settings and systems for designing, testing, and deploying web applications using cloud services.

Without any guarantee of user data protection, SaaS customers must place a high reliance on the cloud provider for security needs. When using PaaS, cloud service providers give customers who are developing apps on their platform various controls but do not protect them against network or intrusion risks. IaaS, however, gives developers more control over the programme. Compliance and appropriate security are addressed here.

Below are some of the security issues with the service model challenges:

Data leakage and related issues: Without a backup, data loss or modification can cause serious issues with security, integrity, location, segregation, and breaches. As a result, unauthorized users could access private information. Cloud platforms should offer new services to gather context data, conduct analyses, and maintain data privacy in order to assist applications that use the data. Deduplication is one approach to addressing the issue of data leakage while enabling a cap on the number of times the user uploads per time window.

Malicious Attacks: Usage of diverse IT services that lack clarity between the method and process linked to service providers increases the possibility of malicious intruders for users of cloud services. Some personal data may be accessed by malicious people, resulting in data breaches. malicious assaults by unauthorized users on the physical server and IP address of the victim. To prevent unauthorized users from accessing secured data, one might consider an access control mechanism tool.

Backup and storage: Cloud providers must make sure that frequent data backups are done and that security is fully guaranteed. However, the fact that this backup data is typically available in an unencrypted format makes it vulnerable to abuse by unwanted parties. Data backups thus provide a number of security risks. However, when it comes to cloud storage, de-duplication is done improperly by using data backup.

Common technological problems: IaaS providers use shared infrastructure to scale the delivery of their services. However, this structure does not provide a multi-tenant design with good isolation qualities. Therefore, virtualization hypervisor intervenes in the access in between guest operating systems and the actual compute resources in order to close this gap. Despite having many benefits, some hypervisors have shown weaknesses that have allowed guest operating systems to gain excessive amounts of control or authority over the underlying platform. There are no doubts that this caused cloud security vulnerabilities. the use of IaaS by the client to make infrastructure or hardware more accessible.

Hijacking Service: Obtaining unlawful control over certain permitted services by several unauthorized users is referred to as service hijacking. It takes into account a number of methods, including fraud, software exploitation, and phishing. One of the greatest threats is thought to be this one. Account hijacking has been identified as one of the serious dangers. Due to the absence of native APIs for registering different cloud services, the likelihood of one's account being compromised significantly increases.

Virtual Machine Hopping: Virtual Machine (VM) hopping allows an attacker on one victim VM to obtain access to another target VM. The target VM's confidentiality, integrity, and availability are at risk since the attacker may examine its resource process, change its configurations, and even erase stored data. The two VMs should be running on the same host for this attack to succeed, and the attacker must be aware of the victim VM's IP address. An attacker may get or choose the IP address utilizing benchmark customer capabilities on the basis of different methods and combinational inputs, despite PaaS and IaaS customers having limited authority. So it follows that Virtual machine hopping is really a plausible hazard in cloud computing technology. Besides, compared to a traditional IT infrastructure, multi-tenancy increases the effect in this type of attack. There is a chance that all of the VMs running concurrently on the same host will end up becoming victim VMs. Therefore, this type of hopping is a serious weakness for IaaS and PaaS systems. In the infrastructure as a service (IaaS) concept, a provider makes resources and supporting hardware available as a service, and a user can create their own computing platform by importing a unique VM representation into the infrastructure service. The impact of VM mobility on integrity and confidentiality in the cloud may be greater than it would be in a traditional IT system due to the enormous scope of IaaS. While PaaS, SaaS, and DaaS (Database-as-a-Service) still are vulnerable to the elements in terms of confidentiality, integrity, and availability, the dangers from IaaS have increased (Kumar & Goyal, 2019).

Different deployment and service model security risks have been identified. This informs us of the fact that cloud computing frequently involves the internet, and one must assess numerous network security dangers as well. As a result, the following list of fundamental cloud network concerns has been provided.

Cloud Network Difficulties

In order to preserve data for a variety of applications, cloud computing mostly relies on the internet and distant computers or servers. All of the data is uploaded over the network. Network security concerns on the cloud are of particular importance. It gives customers on-demand access to virtual resources, high bandwidth, and software. But in practice, this cloud's network topology is vulnerable to several assaults and security problems, including XML signature wrapping, flooding attacks, locks-in, incomplete data erasure, and attacks from cloud malware injection.

Browser Security: To communicate information across a network, every client utilises a browser. The browser encrypts user credentials and identity using SSL technology. But using sniffer software placed on the intermediate computer, hackers from that host may obtain these credentials.

Attacks that Flood the Cloud: In this assault, the intruder quickly submits requests for resources, flooding the cloud with a large number of requests. The ability of the cloud to grow based on a high volume of requests. It will enlarge in order to satisfy the demands of the invader, rendering the resources unavailable to regular users.

Entire Data Erasure: In cloud computing, entire data deletion is seen as risky. When data is erased, the duplicated data stored on a dedicated backup server is not also lost. The server's operating system won't remove any data until the network service provider directly instructs it to. Because copies of the data are stored in replicas but are not accessible for use, precise data erasure is almost impossible.

Locks in: Locks in are small tenders in the way of tools, standard data formats or procedures, services edge that could embark on data, application, and service portability, not allowing the customer to transfer from one cloud provider to another cloud provider.

Possible Solutions for Cloud Security

The cloud security challenges and possible solutions are, the restriction mentioned by Ogiela (2020), Ogiela (2016) and Ogiela (2008) demonstrates the necessity for better secure data delivery techniques in intricate systems like the cloud. The second issue in Haykin et al. (2017) is brought on by the complicated nature of ransomware, which is challenging to handle since it generates dynamic patterns. The requirement for creating intricate authentication systems that are not just password secured but also impervious to attackers was outlined by Greenstadt & Beal, (2008) in their study. The fourth restriction in Table 1, as indicated in Andrade & Yoo (2019) and Krichene & Boudriga, (2008) demonstrates the security analyst's incapacity and findings that are prone to mistake when responding to a decision process because of the vast amount of data that has to be examined. The following restriction on False Data Injection (FDI) in Haykin et al. (2017) is a serious security issue that is not picked up by traditional methods. The last restriction in Table 1 by Abie (2019) results from the dynamic, complex, and unpredictable character of IoT healthcare services and cyber physical methods (CPS), which makes it impossible for current security systems to offer protection from potential attacks. Cognitive techniques can be used to overcome these constraints and create effective security systems.

Table 1. Issues and Possible solutions for cloud security

Reference Number	Issues	Possible solutions
22, 23, 24	For large secret data sets data sharing schemes	Linguistic Biometric threshold scheme
33	Ransomware and Malware pattern identification	Cognitive intelligent system for identification
10	Advanced security and authentication system	Cognitive and sensor based cryptography
7, 16	The incident response procedure is laborious.	Dynamic cognitive map modules
13	False data injection system for smart grid system	Cognitive dynamic system
2	CPS-IoT attack	Layered AI enabled cognitive model

FUTURE RESEARCH DIRECTIONS

Since cities have become more densely inhabited, which poses serious infrastructure challenges, the smart city idea is the IoT application field that is developing the fastest. IoT technologies' primary contribution to the smart city idea is their ability to solve major infrastructure problems in densely populated areas. The efficient development of different conventional services in urban areas is also anticipated to increase the quality of living there. The early identification of many and frequent everyday concerns in cities, such as transportation problems, energy and water shortages, security challenges, etc., might be effectively resolved with Intelligent devices with IoT. Therefore more research is needed in the area of data authentication, proper utilization of data and security of data in cloud computing.

CONCLUSION

The current need in digitization has opened up a lot of technical possibilities which have already started to progressively alter the major economic sectors and society at large. Different economic sectors have been able to progress and use scarce resources, systems, or processes more effectively thanks to digitalization. Information technology, or smart technologies enabled by the internet of things, is the primary force behind an effective digitalization across numerous industries. In the preceding sense, one of the important industries where "energy digitalization" has already been expanding quickly in a variety of energy-related fields is the energy industry. IoT technology application in the energy sector is now one of the fastest growing areas. Healthcare sectors also be significantly improved with the application of Intelligent IoT devices, i.e. via the E-health concept. Improved quality of services and patient safety could be enabled with an advanced IoT supported intelligent device monitoring system. Prediction of life threatening states could be detected efficiently with a better treatment of patients, such as timely therapy decisions and quali- tative rehabilitation. Major healthcare systems could also benefit from IoT, both in efficiency and from a cost aspect, which is very important for hospitals. The pandemic state with COVID-19 allowed for the consideration of different IoT applications or devices that could help in efficiently monitoring and controlling the pandemic, which proves the added value of IoT products. With safety as the primary concern, autonomous cars provide the most difficult IoT application sector. In this regard, major research improvements are anticipated in the near future.

End customers are now equally ecstatic and tense thanks to IoT cloud computing. They are eager about the security-related concerns it raises as well as the numerous options the cloud presents. Users would be concerned by the security holes built into the cloud environment when they migrated their data there. As a result, one of the highly conceivable problems has emerged: security threats with cloud computing. Nearly every security risk identified in the network and cloud models has been examined in this study, and it has also provided remedies for some of those risks. This study will be expanded upon in order to provide a systematic method for doing risk investigation in order to identify safety concerns associated with cloud deployment.

REFERENCES

Abdou, M., Mohammed, R., Hosny, Z., Essam, M., Zaki, M., Hassan, M., & Mostafa, H. (2019, December). End-to-end crash avoidance deep IoT-based solution. In *31st International Conference on Microelectronics (ICM)*, (pp. 103-107). IEEE. 10.1109/ICM48031.2019.9021613

Abie, H. (2019, May). Cognitive cybersecurity for CPS-IoT enabled healthcare ecosystems. In *13th International Symposium on Medical Information and Communication Technology (ISMICT)*, (pp. 1-6). IEEE.

Aboubakar, M., Kellil, M., & Roux, P. (2021). A review of IoT network management: Current status and perspectives. *Journal of King Saud University-Computer and Information Sciences*.

Al-Ali, A. R., Zualkernan, I. A., Rashid, M., Gupta, R., & Alikarar, M. (2017). A smart home energy management system using IoT and big data analytics approach. *IEEE Transactions on Consumer Electronics*, *63*(4), 426–434. doi:10.1109/TCE.2017.015014

Alazab, M., Manogaran, G., & Montenegro-Marin, C. E. (2022). Trust management for internet of things using cloud computing and security in smart cities. *Cluster Computing*, *25*(3), 1765–1777. doi:10.100710586-021-03427-9

Almusaylim, Z. A., Alhumam, A., & Jhanjhi, N. Z. (2020). Proposing a secure RPL based internet of things routing protocol: A review. *Ad Hoc Networks*, *101*, 102096. doi:10.1016/j.adhoc.2020.102096

Andrade, R. O., & Yoo, S. G. (2019). Cognitive security: A comprehensive study of cognitive science in cybersecurity. *Journal of Information Security and Applications*, *48*, 102352. doi:10.1016/j.jisa.2019.06.008

Chen, J., Wang, Y., & Wang, X. (2012). On-demand security architecture for cloud computing. *Computer*, *45*(7), 73–78. doi:10.1109/MC.2012.120

Fortino, G., Guerrieri, A., Savaglio, C., & Spezzano, G. (2022). A Review of internet of things Platforms through the IoT-A Reference Architecture. In *International Symposium on Intelligent and Distributed Computing*, (pp. 25-34). Springer, Cham. 10.1007/978-3-030-96627-0_3

Greenstadt, R., & Beal, J. (2008, October). Cognitive security for personal devices. In *Proceedings of the 1st ACM workshop on Workshop on AISec*, (pp. 27-30). 10.1145/1456377.1456383

Grobauer, B., Walloschek, T., & Stocker, E. (2010). Understanding cloud computing vulnerabilities. *IEEE Security and Privacy*, *9*(2), 50–57. doi:10.1109/MSP.2010.115

Harnik, D., Pinkas, B., & Shulman-Peleg, A. (2010). Side channels in cloud services: Deduplication in cloud storage. *IEEE Security and Privacy*, *8*(6), 40–47. doi:10.1109/MSP.2010.187

Haykin, S., Fuster, J. M., Findlay, D., & Feng, S. (2017). Cognitive risk control for physical systems. *IEEE Access : Practical Innovations, Open Solutions*, *5*, 14664–14679. doi:10.1109/ACCESS.2017.2726439

Kaur, A., Raj, G., Yadav, S., & Choudhury, T. (2018, December). Performance evaluation of AWS and IBM cloud platforms for security mechanism. In *international conference on computational techniques, electronics and mechanical systems (CTEMS),* (pp. 516-520). IEEE.

Kaur, C. (2020). The cloud computing and internet of things (IoT). *International Journal of Scientific Research in Science, Engineering and Technology*, *7*(1), 19–22. doi:10.32628/IJSRSET196657

Krichene, J., & Boudriga, N. (2008, December). Incident response probabilistic cognitive maps. In *international symposium on parallel and distributed processing with applications*, (pp. 689-694). IEEE.

Kumar, R., & Goyal, R. (2019). On cloud security requirements, threats, vulnerabilities and countermeasures: A survey. *Computer Science Review*, *33*, 1–48. doi:10.1016/j.cosrev.2019.05.002

Moreno-Vozmediano, R., Montero, R. S., & Llorente, I. M. (2012). Key challenges in cloud computing: Enabling the future internet of services. *IEEE Internet Computing*, *17*(4), 18–25. doi:10.1109/MIC.2012.69

Nawrocki, P., & Osypanka, P. (2021). Cloud resource demand prediction using machine learning in the context of qos parameters. *Journal of Grid Computing*, *19*(2), 1–20. doi:10.100710723-021-09561-3

Ogiela, L., & Ogiela, M. R. (2020). Cognitive security paradigm for cloud computing applications. *Concurrency and Computation*, *32*(8), e5316. doi:10.1002/cpe.5316

Ogiela, L., Ogiela, M. R., & Ogiela, U. (2016, July). Efficiency of strategic data sharing and management protocols. In *10th International conference on innovative mobile and internet services in ubiquitous computing (IMIS),* (pp. 198-201). IEEE. 10.1109/IMIS.2016.119

Ogiela, M. R., & Ogiela, U. (2008, December). Linguistic approach to cryptographic data sharing. In *Second International Conference on Future Generation Communication and Networking,* (Vol. 1, pp. 377-380). IEEE. 10.1109/FGCN.2008.89

Oke, A. E., & Arowoiya, V. A. (2021). *Evaluation of internet of things (IoT) application areas for sustainable construction.* Smart and Sustainable Built Environment. doi:10.1108/SASBE-11-2020-0167

Parast, F. K., Sindhav, C., Nikam, S., Yekta, H. I., Kent, K. B., & Hakak, S. (2022). Cloud computing security: A survey of service-based models. *Computers & Security*, *114*, 102580. doi:10.1016/j.cose.2021.102580

Perez, R., Van Doorn, L., & Sailer, R. (2008). Virtualization and hardware-based security. *IEEE Security and Privacy*, *6*(5), 24–31. doi:10.1109/MSP.2008.135

Ramachandran, V., Ramalakshmi, R., Kavin, B. P., Hussain, I., Almaliki, A. H., Almaliki, A. A., El-naggar, A., & Hussein, E. E. (2022). Exploiting IoT and its enabled technologies for irrigation needs in agriculture. *Water (Basel)*, *14*(5), 719. doi:10.3390/w14050719

Ramachandran, V., Ramalakshmi, R., Kavin, B. P., Hussain, I., Almaliki, A. H., Almaliki, A. A., El-naggar, A., & Hussein, E. E. (2022). Exploiting IoT and its enabled technologies for irrigation needs in agriculture. *Water (Basel)*, *14*(5), 719. doi:10.3390/w14050719

Rimal, B. P., Choi, E., & Lumb, I. (2009, August). A taxonomy and survey of cloud computing systems. In *Fifth International Joint Conference on INC, IMS and IDC*, (pp. 44-51). IEEE. 10.1109/NCM.2009.218

Ristenpart, T., Tromer, E., Shacham, H., & Savage, S. (2009, November). Hey, you, get off of my cloud: exploring information leakage in third-party compute clouds. In *Proceedings of the 16th ACM conference on Computer and communications security*, (pp. 199-212). 10.1145/1653662.1653687

Sabahi, F. (2011, May). Cloud computing security threats and responses. In *IEEE 3rd International Conference on Communication Software and Networks*, (pp. 245-249). IEEE. 10.1109/ICCSN.2011.6014715

Silva, J. A. H., & Hernández-Alvarez, M. (2017, October). Large scale ransomware detection by cognitive security. In *IEEE Second Ecuador Technical Chapters Meeting (ETCM)*, (pp. 1-4). IEEE.

Spring, J. (2011). Monitoring cloud computing by layer, part 1. *IEEE Security and Privacy*, *9*(2), 66–68. doi:10.1109/MSP.2011.33

Takabi, H., Joshi, J. B., & Ahn, G. J. (2010, July). Securecloud: Towards a comprehensive security framework for cloud computing environments. In *IEEE 34th Annual Computer Software and Applications Conference Workshops*, (pp. 393-398). IEEE.

Takabi, H., Joshi, J. B., & Ahn, G. J. (2010). Security and privacy challenges in cloud computing environments. *IEEE Security and Privacy*, *8*(6), 24–31. doi:10.1109/MSP.2010.186

Tsai, H. Y., Siebenhaar, M., & Miede, A. (2012). *Threat as a Service? Virtualization's impact on Cloud Security,* IEEE, 32-37.

Umar, B., Hejazi, H., Lengyel, L., & Farkas, K. (2018). Evaluation of IoT device management tools. In *Proc. 3rd Int. Conf. Adv. Comput., Commun. Services (ACCSE)*, (pp. 15-21).

Viega, J. (2009). Cloud computing and the common man. *Computer*, *42*(08), 106–108. doi:10.1109/MC.2009.206

Walia, R., & Garg, P. (2022). Performance and Security Issues of Integrating Cloud Computing with IoT. In *Emergent Converging Technologies and Biomedical Systems,* (pp. 1–12). Springer. doi:10.1007/978-981-16-8774-7_1

Wang, B., Liu, X., & Zhang, Y. (2022). *internet of things and BDS Application*. Springer. doi:10.1007/978-981-16-9194-2

Chapter 2
Intelligent Broker Design for IoT Using a Multi-Cloud Environment

Balachandar S.

CMR Institute of Technology, Visvesvaraya Technological University, India

Chinnaiyan R.

Presidency University, India

ABSTRACT

Data privacy is the common concern across different enterprises- applications deployed in multi-cloud environment will make it more challenging for the cyber security team to monitor the application traffic simultaneously to prevent any attacks or data leak or data privacy breaches. Handling different data privacy issues always demands for a complete visibility over data flow, which ensures to prevent vulnerability points, and best way to handle sensitive and personal data with right data retention policies and data protection schemes. Articulation of data privacy features from different cloud providers, particularly with their service and deployment model, help to plan cybersecurity teams and build the necessary security analytical models to predict and prevent the data privacy theft and attacks.

INTRODUCTION

The existing outbreak of Covid-19 (Novel Coronavirus) is one of the great examples for data privacy risks (Morgan & Smith, 2020) as per EY (Ernst & Young), it classified into four types and how best we need to handle the data privacy risks. As per Verizon Business 2020 Data Breach Investigations Report (2020 DBIR) published on May 2020, this study shares about 36 confirmed data breaches which were directly related to COVID-19 epidemic. The review also shows 474 data breach incidents from March to June 2020 based on contributor data and publicly disclosed incidents (Miles, 2020). Another major data privacy incident spotted during 2017 in the cloud environment particularly about "WWE" (World Wrestling Environment) database (Massive, 2017) contains information about more than three million

DOI: 10.4018/978-1-6684-6275-1.ch002

user's personal data (e.g., Email, Ages, Gender and) kept in the Amazon S3 Storage (Cloud Storage). The S3 Storage was accessible without user name and password, the database was misconfigured by WWE IT department which created this major incident. Post that WWE utilizes leading cybersecurity firms to proactively protect their customer data. It is utmost important to ensure the data movement across multi cloud servers and databases are safeguarded with right data protection techniques, enable proper data governance in place for the applications () which needs data from different cloud. This document explains different data analysis done for data privacy implementation of sweeping regulations like GDPR (Wikipedia, 2022a) (General Data Protection Regulation) promises well for data security in multi cloud platforms like Amazon Aws, Azure and Google Cloud Platform. We analyze the reviews from different authors and publishers mentioned about data privacy issues in cloud and what sort of regulations should be taken care, also the analysis done for different compliance mechanisms.

In Section III we cover the functional needs of data protection and handling privacy for cloud server and databases. In section IV we explain the basics of multi-cloud platform and section V we examine the what are different data classification method required for different security compliance. In section VI we will mention about different cloud security tools and its purpose. Section VII will mention about problem relevancy with high level approach and step by step component mapping with known issues. We will share the deployment considerations and issues in section VIII. In section IX we will present our significance and in section X we will share our recommendations and conclusion.

BACKGROUND

Multi Cloud environment is the key trend in the upcoming year as per Gartner 2020 Trends (Gartner, 2020). Gartner is estimating that by 2021, 75 percent of midsize and large organizations will have adopted multi-cloud or a hybrid strategy. This will significantly help integrating different applications for enterprise from their on-premise or private cloud to public cloud or multiple public clouds. The resiliency and service level agreement are thrown to different cloud providers who has to support with right balance of high availability, geo replication and fault tolerance and disaster recovery based on the down-time agreement. the data privacy and data hiding are important when data movement happens across cloud servers or database from on-premise application or cloud-based applications. We will be sharing the key literature reviews for different journals and notes which had been done by some of the researchers.

As mentioned by **Jiangshui Hong et.al (Hong et al., 2020)**, It details out the issues with cloud computing particularly about "Four Layer Cloud Computing Architecture" and how resources are managed in each layer. They also discussed about "Issues" with cloud computing and "Data Security & Privacy" is one of the biggest issues and its pressing matter for many researcher and business organizations. They also mentioned top 10 issues of multi-cloud environment. As referred in **Yunchuan Sun et.al (Sun et al., 2014)** explicitly mentioned about memory database encryption technique for privacy and security of sensitive data in untrusted cloud environment.

As mentioned **(Orekhova, 2022)" paper,** the role of blockchain for IOMT devices and not trusting members on the network (e.g., Healthcare providers, Care Takers). they covered on the data security & privacy of IOMT devices in the cloud platform. They described an algorithm of how a block is added to blockchain with an illustration of EMR (Electronic Medical Records)

Wencheng Sun e.al (Martin, 2018) focused on the security and privacy requirements related to the data flow for Internet of things. They mentioned the Lightweight Private algorithms (DES) which is considered as strong encryption for IOT devices. They referred "clustering method based-anonymity algorithm as the building block of privacy preserving for medical wearable devices."

"Preeti Barrow et.al (Barrow, 2016) discusses about cloud computing challenges and issues specifically about Confidentiality, integrity and authentication. They analyzed about "SaaS" cloud service model security challenges and how CSP (Cloud Service Providers) should propose a suit of SaaS which include various security measures. They also shared a table of security methods comparison for different cloud providers like Amazon, IBM, Rackspace, Windows Azure and Google Cloud Platform.

Zhao FeiFei,Dong et. al (Li et al., 2012) elaborated about "K-anonymity" model which forms at least K clusters by generalizing or inhibiting the original data, it enables each tuple can be distinguished with at least other K-1 records. They also compared Datafly algorithm, Samarati algorithm. Incognito algorithm uses k-anonymity node to prune searching and Optimal Lattice Algorithm (OLA) which makes an improvement on the bases of Incognito and Datafly algorithms. They also recommended to compare k-anonymity algorithm with enhanced OLA algorithms.

In the **MULTICLOUD DATA SECURITY (Data, n.d.)** research journal prepared by Arun Singh et.al articulates about movement of Single to multiple cloud. The data security towards 'multi-clouds' has emerged and they elaborated Customers do not want to lose their personal or sensitive information as an outcome of malevolent exists in the cloud, they also stressed about data intrusion and loss of service accessibility has caused many problems for a huge number of customers. They explained the SHAMIR SECRET SHARING algorithm in detail with concept of Lagrange interpolation and polynomial equations with different variables.

FUNCTIONAL NEEDS

Problem statement: How effectively analyze and compare the data privacy issues across different multi cloud and decide the need to additional controls and validations to mitigate the gaps from the cloud providers for accessing my applications.

Below diagram (Figure 1) shows an example of how application connects through multi cloud (Hong et al., 2020) platforms (both private and public) for fetching any data stored in either cloud.

Figure 1. Data Accessibility & Privacy checks for multi cloud environment

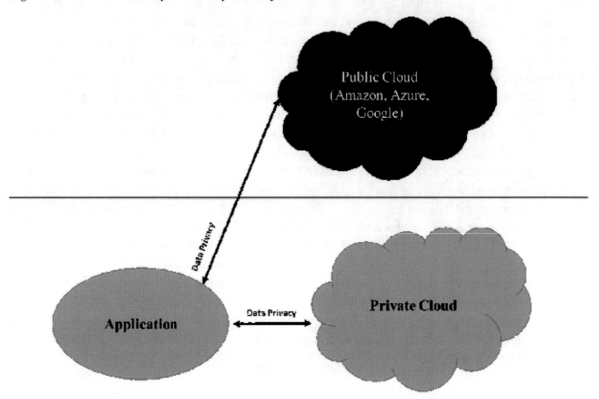

The data required for the application () should be protected and well handled with cloud provider's data masking, encryption and other standard operating procedures. The common issues we generally face while connecting the multi-cloud environments are from security stand point of view are.

I.   No Common API or API standards for authorizing and authenticating the application
II.   Data Masking techniques are not agnostic across multi-cloud platforms
III. Data Encryption and Decryption needs common algorithms (e.g., SHA 256)
IV.   Handling of Sensitive, Personal data with different data storage provided by cloud provider
V.   Data Retention policy across cloud platforms.

We will be analyzing the above issues in the subsequent sections

BASICS OF CLOUD & MULTI-CLOUD PLATFORM

This section explains the basics of cloud service and deployment model and the purpose of different multi-cloud platform and how it helps to build an application effectively.

What is Cloud Computing

In simple words availability of data centers over internet or on-demand provisioning of resources such as data storage, compute power (processors) without any direct intervention of users. Cloud computing comes in three service models and four ways of deployment.

Cloud Service Model

As mentioned in below figure 2 three service model (Wikipedia, 2022b) exists to support the enterprise application development or deployment. Many cloud providers are existing in the market to support these models. From the left "IaaS" (Infrastructure as A Service) model is helping to build an application from scratch through a hardware (e.g., provisioning of virtual machines, virtual servers, virtual database servers). Any organization who wishes to build their data center over internet or extend their data center with additional capacity over cloud can opt this model. It helps the organization to scale-out quickly when they have resource crunch during peak-time. It eliminates the man power & physical resource (e.g., building, cables, electricity, consumables like batteries) required to setup additional data center rather organization can build an on-demand data center on the fly and they can dismantle when they don't want it. It guarantees the extendibility of on-premise data center which are either having outdated server model or non-upgradable software which either might be out of warranty and user support period. Thus, on-premise data center can be scaled down with minimum or mandatory data requirements or which are not able to move to cloud can only reside, other applications or servers which needs storage, computing power can leverage "Cloud" model and provision it through "IaaS" option given by different cloud service providers in the market.

In the other model mentioned in figure 2 targets different user community of the organization, especially Developers who needs to provision the necessary application environment, middleware, cloud development platform which runs top of extendable hardware resource model. The developers do not require to worry about the hardware model, data base versions or dynamic scale-out feasibility of the hardware. The respective cloud service provider who enables the "PaaS" will take care of scale-up or scale-down the application instances along with hardware specific resources scale (e.g., When I would like to increase my Java Run Time Environment for an application from 1 instance to 10 instances, the underlying the Java Run Time Environment memory and disk will automatically managed by my cloud service provider who takes care of hardware resources in the backend)

Figure 2. Cloud Service Models – IaaS, PaaS and SaaS

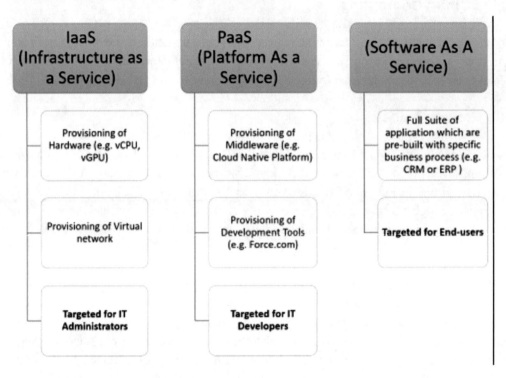

Third model of cloud service (SaaS) is where most of the organization are thriving their future application needs as well modernizing their current landscape with the help of market specific SaaS applications. (e.g., Purchase a CRM suite of application (i.e., Salesforce CRM) instead of building it from scratch by provisioning either IaaS or PaaS). The time to market for this model is really high and it will easy to adopt based on the current market trends as well enable additional analytics specific feature rather spending more time for building and integrating the same.

Cloud Deployment Models

Cloud providers facilitating with four ways to deploy the cloud model (Wikipedia, 2022b)[14] as mentioned in figure 3 below. Organization can leverage either one of the model or combination of different models to support their organization needs.

The choice of private or public or community or hybrid cloud is based on parameters of interest (e.g., time, cost, resource availability, organization's capability, business demand, economies of scale).

Public cloud is nothing but a data center available over internet with suite of services (e.g., Infrastructure specific services or application development specific service or market standard product with pre-built features), organization can leverage such services based on their demand.

Figure 3. Cloud Deployment Models – Public, Private, community and Hybrid

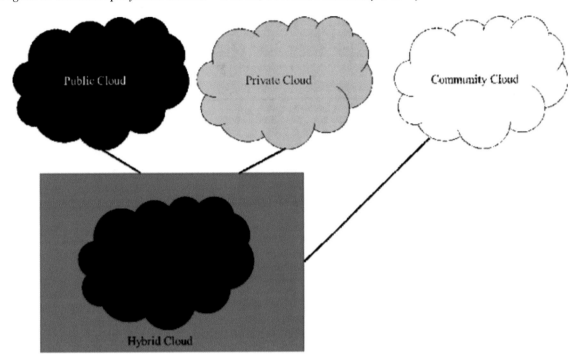

Private Cloud: it's another model (Microsoft, 2022) where organizations build it over the Internet or a private internal network and only to select users instead of the general public users. The access is restricted to specific user group.

Hybrid Cloud: It combines the private cloud with one or more public cloud services (Citrix, 2022). Organization use hybrid cloud when they want to expand their data center with public cloud and build a dedicated network tunnel for communication. Good example like an organization who are interested to offload their legacy data into different back-up servers, to setup the back-up server it will cost high at on-premise data center (considering the physical layout of the data center, rack mounting and cable foundation, etc..), instead of keeping on-premise option, they can offload the back-up to cloud based storage which is very less in cost.

What is Multi-Cloud: It is nothing but integrating more than one cloud service provider (Elkhatib, 2016) [15] (CSP) to connect an application which needs assorted services from different cloud. Simple Example here "An IOT Application() needs data from different sensors which needs to be stored, processed and build machine learning or deep learning model to predict the sensor health and communicate it with another sensor based on the recommendation value or score of the model" if we break the above example, we need to handle this problem statement into a multi-model cloud environment as single cloud provider will not able to address all the services that we need.

Figure 4. Multi cloud platform with an IOT Example

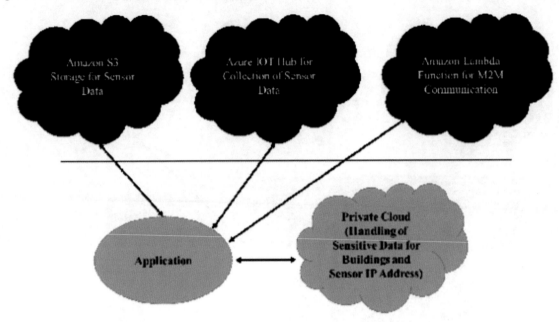

Figure 3 – Multi cloud platform with an IOT Example

As mentioned in above diagram, "Data Coming from Sensors or Devices" are going to collected by Amazon S3 Storage once the data collected by "Azure IOT Hub" where the devices are directly linked.

Amazon Lambada (Amazon, 2022) function used us to add custom logic to AWS resources (e.g., S3 Bucket where we kept the sensor data collected from Azure IOT Hub), making it easy to apply compute to data as it is entering or moves through the cloud. The function can be invoked through "Application" which needs to orchestrate and integrate data from diverse cloud platform as mentioned above. The below table Table 1 shows who does what for the above example.

Who Does What?

Table 1. Multi-Cloud Services and its functions example

Service	Provider	What it does
AWS S3 (Simple Storage Service)	Amazon	Collects the data from Azure IOT Hub and stores the data for subsequent actions/triggers performed by AWS Lambada function.
Azure IOT Hub	Microsoft	Here sensors or actuators or IOT Gateways are directly connected with Azure IOT Hub either directly or through IOT Edge module to orchestrate and monitor the data coming from different sensors
Amazon Lambada	Amazon	It's a serverless function which can robotically run code in reply to multiple events or triggers such as changes to objects in Amazon S3 buckets
Metadata/Master Data	Local Private Cloud from Enterprise	It is used to locate the data coming from Azure IOT Hub or processing in AWS S3 or Lambada function is valid from data authentication and authorization perspective.
AWS Sage maker	Amazon	It used to run the machined learning model required by the application to predict the health score and recommendation model for M2M (Machine to Machine) communication.

DATA CLASSIFICATION

The below Table 2 shows different data classification (Al-Fedaghi, n.d.) type required to handle the data security and privacy level. Some of the regulations (e.g., GDPR – Global Data Protection and Regulation) are mandating to keep these classifications irrespective of the application deployment model (either in cloud or on-premise).

Table 2. Data Classification and its support from different cloud providers

Data Classification type	What it means	Applicability and supportability
PCI – Payment Card Industry information (Primate Conservation, n.d.)	Any application that supports payment transactions through credit card or debit card and it shouldn't be stored without user's consent, even certain country regulation (e.g., GDPR) will not permit to store. Any breach of PCI compliance is also a breach of GDPR compliance therefore subject to the same scrutiny and potential fines.	Cloud Service Providers like Azure and AWS are supporting different levels of PCI DSS (Data Security Standards) to secure the application running on their cloud platform. https://docs.microsoft.com/en-us/compliance/regulatory/offering-pci-dss AWS Support for PCI: https://aws.amazon.com/compliance/pci-dss-level-1-faqs/
PII (Al-Fedaghi, n.d.) - Personally Identifiable Information (PII)	PII is information helps in distinctively detect, contact or trace a single person. Anonymized Personal information is not considered sensitive	Azure platform supports PII compliance and it ensure to protect personally identifiable information. As narrated in Microsoft site. Microsoft customers know what's happening with their PII. https://docs.microsoft.com/en-us/compliance/regulatory/offering-iso-27018 Similarly, Amazon Web Services (AWS) is PII complaint (Best practices for PII compliance in Amazon Connect, n.d.) and Amazon Connect contact center is PII compliant. https://aws.amazon.com/compliance/iso-27018-faqs/

Continued on following page

Table 2. Continued

Data Classification type	What it means	Applicability and supportability
PHI – Protected Health Information (AWS services in scope by compliance program, n.d.)	Protected Health Information (PHI) is controlled by the Health Insurance Portability and Accountability Act (HIPAA). PHI is individually identifiable health information that relates to the physical condition of an individual irrespective of Present, Past and Future.	This is very important compliance from healthcare domain perspective. None of the cloud services are fully complaint on Cloud HIPAA compliance is not so much about platforms and security controls, but how those services are used Is AWS HIPPA Certified. The Answer from AWS is There is no HIPAA certification for a cloud service provider (CSP) such as AWS. In order to meet the HIPAA requirements applicable to our operating model, AWS aligns our HIPAA risk management program with FedRAMP and NIST 800-53, which are higher security standards that map to the HIPAA Security Rule. https://aws.amazon.com/compliance/hipaa-compliance/
CSI – Customer Sensitive Information	Customer name, address or telephone number, Social Security number, account number, credit or debit card number, or a personal identification number or password are treated as Customer Sensitive Information. Event data containing racial, ethnic origin, trade union, genetic and bio metric data, health related data	AWS recommends different techniques to protect sensitive data with the help of "Encryption" and "Tokenization" and network isolation, etc. https://aws.amazon.com/blogs/database/applying-best-practices-for-securing-sensitive-data-in-amazon-dynamodb/

HARNESSING CLOUD SECURITY TOOLS FOR DATA SECURITY AND PRIVACY

Gartner (Gartner, n.d.) recommended three different categories of cloud security tools namely Cloud Access Security Brokers (CASBs), Cloud Workload Protection Platforms (CWPP) and Cloud Security Posture Management (CSPM). In today's multi cloud context, the cloud security tools (Cloud Security tools, n.d.) are becoming essential to support different cloud services and cloud deployment models mentioned in the above section. Out of these three tools, "CWPP" is important to protect the data and applications workloads on Infrastructure as A Service (IaaS) or Platform as A Service (PaaS).

The below Table 3 show the cloud security tools and its purpose from multi-cloud point of view.

Table 3. Different cloud security tools

Cloud Security Tools (Cloud Security tools, n.d.)	Purpose	Support from Multi-cloud point of view
CASB – Cloud Access Security Broker	It is used for Cloud-based security policy enforcement perspective and it is kept in between cloud consumers and CSPs like Amazon, Azure, Google Cloud, etc.. to consolidate and interpolate organization's security policies whenever the use accesses the cloud-based resources.	Microsoft's Cloud App Security is a Cloud Access Security Broker (CASB) that works across multiple clouds. How it will work: It secures the data traffic between application hosted on cloud and local applications (e.g., On-premise) with the same security policy. Similarly, if one cloud (e.g., Azure App Fabric service) application accesses another cloud's resources (e.g., AWS S3 Storage) from multi-cloud perspective, both the data flow from those two clouds should comply the same security policy while transferring the data for the application.
CSPM - Cloud Security Posture Management (Integrating azure security center with Azure Sentinel, n.d.)	Gartner states (Comparing the Use of CASB, n.d.) that "CSP concentrates on security assessment and compliance monitoring, primarily across the IaaS cloud stack". CSPM influencing API integrations with different providers in order to discover cloud resources and its related risks.	CSPM plays a critical role for identification of risks when any changes posted in the cloud application which are monitored through DevOps with logging mechanisms. It detects the log changes easily and identify whether that changes are done international or malicious or busines as usual based on the change pattern. Most of the multi-cloud architecture supports this and it is mandated for certain compliance monitoring perspective (e.g., PII or CSI)
CWPP- Cloud Workload Protection Platform	Cloud Workload Protection Platforms is agent based or agent driven solution that is required to handle the workload specific security protection solutions. It is even used for Hybrid cloud architecture and container-based architecture to handle the application security	As per Microsoft Azure Security Center (How to effectively perform an Azure security center PoC, n.d.) is categorized as a Cloud Security Posture Management (CSPM) and Cloud Workload Protection Platform (CWPP). Similarly, there are tools (Cloud workload security, n.d.) like Trend Micro, Symantec, cloudticity are available in AWS (Amazon Web Services Market place) to support the workload protection.

HIGH-LEVEL APPROACH

In this section, we will be elaborating a use case (What is context-aware security?, n.d.) on how the application security is centrally managed and controlled when the application requires resources across different cloud service providers and on-premise data center. The following diagram (Figure 4) shows that the steps are required to build a security control for multi-cloud.

Figure 5. Step by Step approach on data security control in Multi-Cloud

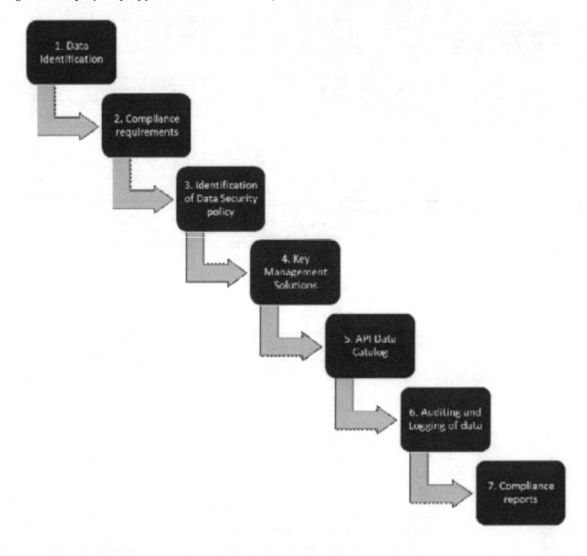

Step 1: Detailed data flow analysis from different sources and targets with in the multi-cloud points. It will help us to decide what sort of data encryption and data protection techniques are required and which of them are centrally going to be triggered and managed as per organization security framework or policies.

Example: API (Application Program Interface) is one of the common standards to communicate across different cloud providers however the secret key, authorization token shouldn't be localized so that the logic of creation might not comply with organization's IT security policy, thus API should be secured from on-premise data center or organization cloud which has full control on security policies and compliance requirements.

Step 2: Data Compliance requirement: based on the above section some of the country specific regulations for data privacy (e.g., GDPR) or personal data specific compliance (e.g., PII or CSI) needs to be assessed well before we recommend the right approach on implementing the security model (e.g., common keys or vault service)

Example: Applications which needs to protect personal and sensitive information has to agree on what sort of data masking required while transfer the data from one layer of cloud to other layer of cloud or with in the cloud environment. This demand us to either encrypt or anonymize the data before being sent to different cloud storage or application. Data retention is key to purge the personal and sensitive information or de-identify the personal information

Step 3: Identification of Data Security Policy or Data Privacy Policy:

Based on above steps, it definitely requests us to either propose a new policy to comply the data privacy and security or enrich the existing policy document to support additional controls to comply the data security

Step 4: Key Management Solution

Post Step3, the key management (e.g., encryption and decryption keys (i.e., Private and Public Key) location and communication through the API framework should be assessed. Also, the key management should constantly replicate whenever the central place goes for revision of their security policy or procedure. This is where "Security Key" agents which takes care of managing it across multi cloud environments (e.g., Trend Micro, Symantec, etc.)

Step 5: API Data Catalog

This is one of the important steps for multi-cloud deployments to build an API data catalog with a canonical model to help different cloud providers to ingest and follow the standard API naming conventions for that application which is going to communicate across different cloud service providers.

Step 6: Auditing and Logging:

It's a common process to take care of auditing the application at various transactions levels and ensure the necessary application and system logs are able to detect the changes.

Step 7: Compliance reports

At given point the application should able to disclose the compliance reports for specific compliance or data classification being used across the cloud service providers.

Example: if we are going to use the cloud to store CSI (Customer Sensitive Information) then we need to ensure what are the fields being accessed across the cloud providers should consistently anonymize, mask, encrypt and retain the data as per the central data security policy. The report should clearly show the data fields that are currently treated as sensitive and what are the retention period in respective cloud storage or cloud services perspective.

The above figure 5 shows the application hosted in AWS cloud (Amazon Web Services Cloud) and it uses AWS KMS (Key Management Services) to store the private keys being exchanged from On-premise data center which maintains the central keys for all applications and resources which needs to be consumed by the organization application. the application from AWS always communicate the common key being stored and replicated across other cloud service providers such as Azure and Google to ensure the data is being encrypted and decrypted with central key algorithm prescribed by the organization. The organization doesn't necessary to leverage any algorithm from cloud service providers and it can change any time and ensure the data and contents are protected well for the application hosted or consumed.

Figure 6. Sample application and its data flow

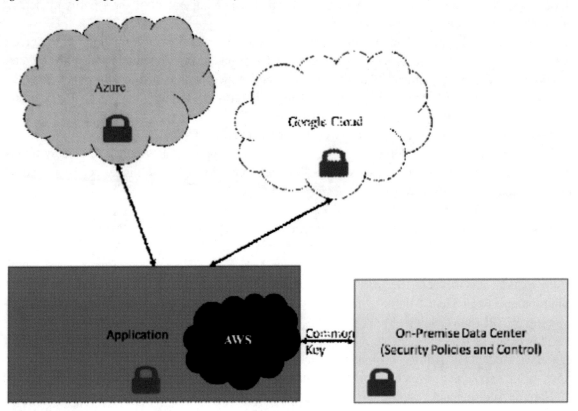

DEPLOYMENT CONSIDERATIONS

Following are multi-cloud deployment considerations (What is Cloud security?, n.d.) relating to data security and data privacy.

a) Deep data security and privacy analysis is required to understand the end-to-end flow of application's data across different cloud platform and its purpose
b) Assessment of legal, fiscal and regulatory requirement of the organization relating to the application which is going to be hosted in multi-cloud platform.
c) Capability analysis of multi-cloud environment or individual cloud service provider's capability
d) Cloud Security tool assessment to meet the data classification and data certification requirements mandated by global or local country regulators
e) API Integration is key challenge for multi-cloud environment, it might demand sophisticated integration pattern or integration platform (Untangling multicloud integration complexity, n.d.) as a service (iPaaS) to handle the API led approach.
f) Common key management service from either on-premise or cloud service provider should be considered in order to handle and manage the keys (e.g., encryption keys) required to protect the sensitive data held in the cloud. Even most of the multi-cloud service (Key, n.d.) provides are of-

fering "BYOK" Bring Your Own Key model (Key Management in a Multi-Cloud Environment, n.d.) and we need to ensure that it also supports "MYOK" Manage Your Own Key model as well.

g)   Establish the right "Orchestration" tool for multi-cloud to simplify application deployment and management.

h)   Enable right level load balancing either at "DNS" (Domain Name Services) or hardware or software level or application level, also we need to ensure the data synchronization and replication seamless across the cloud services.

i)   Conduct risk assessment for data storage, data integration and data availability and data obfuscation feature supported by each cloud provider in the multi-cloud environment.

j)   Data ingestion from different "Cloud Security" tools or agents going to deployed across multi-cloud environment.

k)   Analyze the ingested data and build a data usage pattern or data anomaly detection model using the above step J

l)   Correlate the data patterns being emitted by different applications, server, DEVOPS engine of cloud services and integrate that outcome with compliance report to identify the data leakage or data loss and how best the data loss prevention can be controlled across cloud.

m)   Keep an eye on latest compliance standards as per ISO (International Organization for Standardization) Example ISO/IEC 27017(Cloud security standards, n.d.) and ISO/IEC 27018, that provide more detailed guidance and recommendations for cloud services.

SIGNIFICANCE OF THE RESEARCH

This research signifies how well we need to prepare for building an application in a multi-cloud environment which should oblige data privacy and security challenges. The necessity of data classification, cloud security tools and key management with a step-by-step approach to handle the data privacy and data sensitivity related issues if we anticipate during deployment.

CONCLUSION

The aforementioned research topic is specific to the data privacy and security issues in multi-cloud environment and it needs to be customized for hybrid or private cloud or single cloud environments based on the need. It is not necessary to follow all the steps that we mentioned in the approach section. The solution that we recommended is able to accommodate different data privacy and security use cases. The cloud security tools and agents are absolutely not necessary if the existing cloud security tools and agents are satisfying the needs to data synchronization and replication of data across cloud service providers. There are lot of third-party tools are emerging at the time of writing this paper and even those tools might bring more value to solve this problem and it's an on-going research topic for most of the organization who wants to adopt multi-cloud solutions.

REFERENCES

Al-Fedaghi, S. (n.d.). Experimentation with personal identifiable information. Abdul Aziz Rashid Al-Azmi College of Engineering and Petroleum, Kuwait University.

Amazon. (2016). *AWS GovCloud (US) user guide.* Amazon.

Amazon. (2022). *Amazon AWS lambada function.* Amazon. https://aws.amazon.com/lambda/features/

AWS services in scope by compliance program. (n.d.). https://aws.amazon.com/compliance/services-in-scope/

Balachandar, S., & Chinnaiyan, R. (n.d.). A reliable agnostic data compression model between edge and cloud IOT platform. *International Journal of Computer Engineering and Applications, 12*(1), 139–143.

Balachandar, S., & Chinnaiyan, R. (2018a). A reliable troubleshooting Model for IoT devices with sensors and voice based chatbot application. *International Journal for Research in Applied Science & Engineering Technology.*

Balachander, S., & Chinnaiyan, R. (2018b). Internet of Things based Reliable Real–Time Disease Monitoring of Poultry Farming Imagery Analytics. ICCBI.

Balachander, S., & Chinnaiyan, R. (2019). Internet of Things based Agro based Monitoring using Drones with Block Chain. *ICICCS.*

Balachandar, S., & Chinnaiyan, R. (2020). *Reliable admin framework of drones and IOT sensors in agriculture farmstead using blockchain and Smart contracts BDET.* Academic Press.

Barrow, P. (2016). Security in Cloud Computing for Service Delivery Models: Challenges and Solutions. *Int. Journal of Engineering Research and Applications, 6*(4), 76-85. http://www.ijera.com

Best practices for PII compliance in Amazon Connect. (n.d.). https://docs.aws.amazon.com/connect/latest/adminguide/compliance-validation-best-practices-PII.html

Chinnaiyan, R. (2022a). Smart vehicle tracking system using Internet of things. *International Journal of Scientific Research in Science and Technology, 9*(2), 351–355.

Chinnaiyan, R. (2022b). Intelligent hospital monitoring system using Internet of things. *International Journal of All Research Education and Scientific Methods, 10*(4).

Chinnaiyan, R., & Balachandar, S. (2018a). Reliable digital twin for connected footballer. *Lecture Notes on Data Engineering and Communications Technologies, Springer International conference on Computer Networks and Inventive Communication Technologies (ICCNCT - 2018).*

Chinnaiyan, R., & Balachandar, S. (2018b). Centralized reliability and security management of data in Internet of things (IoT) with rule builder. *Lecture Notes on Data Engineering and Communications Technologies, Springer International conference on Computer Networks and Inventive Communication Technologies (ICCNCT - 2018).*

Citrix. (2022). Hybrid cloud. *Citrix*. https://www.citrix.com/en-in/glossary/what-is-hybrid-cloud.html#:~:text=Hybrid%20cloud%20is%20a%20solution,as%20needs%20and%20costs%20fluctuate

Cloud security standards: What to expect and what to negotiate version 2.0. (n.d.). https://www.omg.org/cloud/deliverables/CSCC-Cloud-Security-Standards-What-to-Expect-and-What-to-Negotiate.pdf

Cloud Security tools: CASB, CWPP and CSPM, Use Cases, for cloud security to success at scale, why do you need to use automation? Explained and Explored. (n.d.). https://www.linkedin.com/pulse/cloud-security-tools-casb-cwp-cspmuse-cases-success-praveen/

Cloud workload security. (n.d.). https://aws.amazon.com/marketplace/solutions/migration/cloud-workload-security

Comparing the Use of CASB. (n.d.). *CSPM and CWPP Solutions to Protect Public Cloud Services.* https://www.gartner.com/en/documents/3886773/comparing-the-use-of-casb-cspm-and-cwpp-solutions-to-pro

Dat Privacy Manager. (2022). *What is data privacy.* Data Privacy Manager. https://dataprivacymanager.net/5-things-you-need-to-know-about-data-privacy/

Data, M. (n.d.). Security. *International Research Journal of Engineering and Technology, 3*(3).

Divya, R., & Chinnaiyan, R. (2019). Reliable Constrained Application Protocol to Sense and Avoid attacks in WSN for IoT Devices, *International Conference on Communication and Electronics Systems (ICCES),* 1898–1901.

Elkhatib, Y. (2016). Mapping cross-cloud systems: Challenges and opportunities. *Proceedings of the 8th USENIX Conference on Hot Topics in Cloud Computing.*

Elkhatib, Y., Blair, G. S., & Surajbali, B. (2013). Experiences of using a hybrid cloud to construct an environmental Virtual Observatory. *Proceedings of the 3rd International Workshop on Cloud Data and Platforms.* 10.1145/2460756.2460759

Gartner. (2020). *Cloud trends coming up over the horizon: What to look out for in.* Gartner.

Gartner. (n.d.). *Cloud security tools: Understanding the differences between CASB, CSPM and CWPP.* Gartner.

Hari Pranav, A., Senthilmurugan, M., Pradyumna Rahul, K., & Chinnaiyan, R. (2021). IoT and Machine Learning based Peer to Peer Platform for Crop Growth and Disease Monitoring System using Blockchain. *International Conference on Computer Communication and Informatics (ICCCI),* 1–5. 10.1109/ICCCI50826.2021.9402435

Hong, J., Dreibholz, T., Schenkel, J. A., & Hu, J. A. (2020). An overview of multi-cloud computing, SimulaMet. *Pilestredet, 52.*

How to effectively perform an Azure security center PoC. (n.d.). https://techcommunity.microsoft.com/t5/azure-security-center /how-to-effectively-perform-an-azure-security-center-poc/ba-p/516874

Integrating azure security center with Azure Sentinel. (n.d.). https://techcommunity.microsoft.com/t5/azure-sentinel/integr ating-azure-security-center-with-azure-sentinel/ba-p/482847

Key, M.-C. M. (n.d.). *Service and deployment options.* https:// blog.entrust.com/2017/04/multi-cloud-key-management-service-and-deployment-options/

Key Management in a Multi-Cloud Environment – A blessing or a curse? (n.d.). https://www.crypto-mathic.com/news-events/blog/key-management-in-a-multi-cloud-environment-a-blessing-or-a-curse

Li, F., DKun, WYang, L. (2012). Study on privacy protection algorithm based on K-anonymity. *Physics Procedia International Conference on Medical Physics and Biomedical Engineering*, 33, 483–490.

Martin, R. (2018). *Internet of medical things (IoMT)—The future of healthcare. Ingite.*hnttps://ignite-outsourcing.com/healthcare/internet-of-medical-things-iomt-examples/

Massive, W. W. E. (2017). Leak exposes 3 million wrestling fans' addresses, ethnicities and more. *Forbes.* https://www.forbes.com/sites/thomasbrewster/2017/07/06/massive-wwe-leak-exposes-3-million-wrestling-fans-addresses-ethnicities-and-more/?sh=39c30eee75dd

Microsoft. (2022). What is private cloud? *Microsoft Website.* https://azure.microsoft.com/en-in/overview/what-is-a-private-cloud/

Miles, R. (2020). What impact has COVID-19 had on the data breach landscape? *Intelligent CISO.* https://www.intelligentciso.com/2020/09/10/what-impact-has-covd-19-had-on-the-data-breach-landscape/

Morgan, P., & Smith, P. (2020). EY's four data privacy risks for Covid-19. *Computer Weekly.* https://www.computerweekly.com/opinion/Four-risks-to-data-privacy-and-governance-amid-Covid-19

Nirmala, S., & Chinnaiyan, R. (2021). Blockchain based Secured Framework for Road Traffic Management using Fog Computing. *International Journal of Computational Intelligence in Control.*, *13*(2).

Orekhova, K. (2022). The Role of IoT in Healthcare Industry: Benefits and Use Cases. *Cleveroad.* https://www.cleveroad.com/blog/iot-in-healthcare

Primate Conservation. (n.d.). *Compliance – Amazon web services (AWS).* https://aws.amazon.com/compliance/pci-dss-level-1-faqs/

Sun, Y., Zhang, J., Xiong, Y., & Zhu, G. (2014). Data security and privacy in cloud computing. *International Journal of Distributed Sensor Networks, 10*(7), 190903. doi:10.1155/2014/190903

Swarnamugi, D. R. (2019). Context-Aware Smart Reliable Service Model for Intelligent Transport System. *ICRIC 2019.*

Swarnamugi, M., & Chinnaiyan, R. (2019). Smart and Reliable Transport System based on Message Queing Telemetry Transport Protocol. *ICICCS.*

Swarnamugi, M., & Chinnaiyan, R. (2021a). CNN based Vehicle Classification for Intelligent Transportation System in Unstructured Environments. *International Journal of Computational.*

Swarnamugi, M., & Chinnaiyan, R. (2021b). CNN based Single-level and Multi-level Vehicle Classification Framework in Intelligent Transportation System. *International Journal of Computational Intelligence in Control., 13*(2).

Tilak, R. (2019, December). IOT based Leaf Disease Detection and Fertilized Recommendation. *International Journal of Innovative Technology and Exploring Engineering, 9*(2).

Untangling multicloud integration complexity. (n.d.). https://blogs.mulesoft.com/api-integration/strategy/solving-multiclo ud-integration-conundrum/

Weak password = data breach? Common bad password habits, Password Best Practices: Explained. (n.d.). https://www.linkedin.com/pulse/weak-password-data-breachcommon-bad-habitspassword-praveen/

What is Cloud security? Critical Cloud Security Challenges: Its solution: Explained. (n.d.). https://www.linkedin.com/pulse/what-cloud-security-critical-challenges-its-solution-praveen/

What is context-aware security? What are use cases? (n.d.). https://www.linkedin.com/pulse/what-context-aware-security-use-cases-praveen/

Wikipedia. (2022a). GDPR: what it does. *Wikipedia.* https://en.wikipedia.org/wiki/General_Data_Protection_Regula tion

Wikipedia. (2022b). Basics of Cloud computing. *Wikipedia.* https://en.wikipedia.org/wiki/Cloud_computing

Yamini, R. (2020). Smart crop monitor using Internet of things, cloud, machine Learning and android app. *International Journal of Engineering and Advanced Technology, 9*(3).

Chapter 3
Deep Learning–Based Intelligent Sensing in IoT

V. A. Velvizhi

(iD) https://orcid.org/0000-0001-5139-7675

Sri Sairam Engineering College, Anna University, India

G. Senbagavalli

AMC Engineering College, Visvesvaraya Technological University, India

S. Malini

AMC Engineering College, Visvesvaraya Technological University, India

ABSTRACT

The heart of Industry 4.0 is established by a new technology called the internet of things (IoT). Through the internet, the IoT makes it possible for machines and gadgets to share signals. Using artificial intelligence (AI) approaches to manage and regulate the communications between various equipment based on intelligent decisions is made possible by the internet of things (IoT) technology. Data collection devices can be fundamentally altered to "lock in" to the best sensing data with regard to a user-defined cost function or design constraint by utilizing inverse design and machine learning techniques. By allowing low-cost and small sensor implementations developed through iterative analysis of data-driven sensing outcomes, a new generation of intelligence sensing systems reduces the data load while significantly enhancing sensing capabilities. Machine learning-enabled computational sensors can encourage the development of widely distributed applications that leverage the internet of things to build robust sensing networks that have an influence across a variety of industries.

INTRODUCTION

Internet of things (IoT) became inevitable as it enhances the lifestyle of humans in terms of intelligent living, healthcare, sustainable energy, and Industrial 4.0. IoT helps the globe to be connected together via smart devices and technologies. The domain covers various fields of automation and was predicted that billions and billions of devices would be connected and monitored 24/7. The term IoT helps to

DOI: 10.4018/978-1-6684-6275-1.ch003

connect devices that are readable, locatable and controllable (Intelligence, S. C. B. 2008). Researchers have predicted that the IoT market would be worth $2:7 to 6:2 trillion by 2025(Manyika et al., 2013).

Large volumes of data should be evaluated as the internet of things (IoT) expands, and the most recent algorithms should be adjusted to work with big data (Chen et al., 2015). IoT include sensors, software, and technologies of connecter network to exchange information. The main aspects of IoT are the active sensing and efficient sharing of information (Awin et al., 2019).

IoT is assisted by intelligent sensor devices which aids intelligent communication between connected devices. Billions of sensors and connected devices generate voluminous data. These sensors improve the intelligence of the IoT. Deep learning techniques have great potential to analyze the complex behavioral pattern of IoT ed devices. Convolutional Neural network is one such platform where a very large amount of data can be assessed effectively to enhance the performance of Intelligent IoT.

Many authors have contributed to intelligent sensing systems in IoT. Kavitha et al have proposed an intelligent system that can sense gas leakage in industries and vehicles over the globe. The authors integrated the data collected to google cloud through web servers that ease the monitoring of air pollution. Dinesh Kumar etal have proposed an intelligent sensing system that can collect data from scattered nodes to form a backbone node. This backbone node could balance and reschedule the incoming traffic (Sah et al., 2022).

The architecture of IoT for offline data analysis was done using traditional procedures such as classification, clustering and pattern recognition. Hung Li-Ling, 2022 Al proposed an action model that can advance the flexibility of sensors to enhance the intelligence of IoT. This model could sense and transmit parameters that could achieve reliable quality of service. Also, it adjusts the current status level of the sensors if it fails to satisfy the condition to achieve the required quality of service (QoS).

Architecture of IoT

There are many uses for Internet of Things (IoT) technology, and its use is accelerating quickly. The Internet of Things functions as it was intended or developed to in accordance with the various application areas for which it has been used. Architecture of IoT does not follow any standards internationally. Working principle and the domain where IoT is going to be implemented determine the architecture. The functioning and application of IoT in various domains determine its architecture. However, there is a fundamental process flow upon which IoT is founded. The four stages of IoT architecture are shown in figure 1.

Figure 1. Stages of IoT Architecture (Courtesy:www.geeksforgeeks.org)

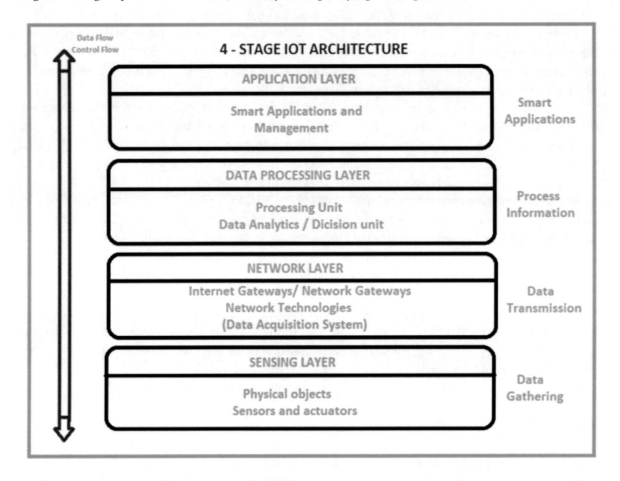

Sensing Layer, Network Layer, Data processing Layer, and Application Layer constitute the architecture of IoT.

Sensing Layer: Sensors, actuators, and devices present in this layer accept the data, process it and send it back across the network.

Network Layer: This layer contains Internet/Network gateways and data acquisition systems (DAS). DAS is responsible for data collection, gathering, and conversion duties (such as translating analogue sensor data from sensors to digital data). Advanced gateways provide a variety of core gateway tasks, such as malware protection, filtering, and occasionally making judgments based on data input and offering data management services, in addition to connecting Sensor networks to the Internet.

Data processing Layer: This is an IoT ecosystem processing unit. Prior to being sent to the data center, where it is accessed by software programmes commonly referred to as business applications, the data is examined, pre-processed, and ready for further action. Edge IT or edge analytics enter the picture at this point.

Application Layer: The fourth step of the IoT architecture is this layer. The management of data occurs in data centers or the cloud, where it is used by end-user applications for things like agriculture, healthcare, aerospace, farming, and defense.

Need for Sensors in IoT

Different types of sensors are needed for various applications in order to collect environmental data. This article examines a few typical Internet of Things sensors. The Internet and tangible objects like sensors and actuators play a crucial role in an Internet of Things (IoT) ecosystem. The IoT system's bottom layer, as depicted in figure 1, is made up of a network for information gathering and sensor connectivity. This layer is a crucial component of the Internet of Things (IoT) system and is network-connected to the gateway and network layer below it.

Sensors are placed in the front end of the IoT system. The signals were processed and then connected to the network. Connections between different devices were chosen as per the requirements of the applications. For example, digital sensors were connected to microcontrollers through serial peripheral interface (SPI). At the same time analog sensors require the signal to be digitized before using SPI.

Industrial Cyber-Physical Systems (CPSs), among other IoT systems, applications, and technologies, have recently advanced thanks to a variety of artificial intelligence-based sensors (AI). These intelligent AI-based sensors often include inbuilt intelligence and the capacity for group communication or Internet communication. Today's smart IoT applications demand a high level of automation, thus sensors built into nodes must be effective, intelligent, context-aware, dependable, accurate, and linked. Additionally, for users to engage with them safely and privately, such sensors need to be reliable. New capabilities recently developed by sensors utilizing cutting-edge AI technology have the potential to detect, identify, and prevent performance decline as well as uncover novel patterns. They can support product innovation, enhance operation level, and open up new business models in addition to knowledge from complicated sensor datasets. In this article, we'll go through the sensors, intelligent data processing, communication protocol, and artificial intelligence that will be necessary to deploy AI-based sensors for the next wave of Internet of Things (IoT) applications.

Types of sensors

Many sensors were available in the market. There are two key factors that must be taken into account in an IoT ecosystem: the internet and actual physical devices like actuators and sensors. In the IoT, the bottom layer is primarily where the sensors and network connectivity are located. The primary purpose of this is to gather data. This lowest layer in the Internet of Things is crucial because it includes network connectivity to higher layers like the gateway and network layer.

Figure 2. Sensors (Courtesy: thesecmaster.com)

These sensors' primary job is to collect data from the environment. Once the signal conversion and processing is complete, these devices can be connected to the IoT either directly or indirectly. Since different IoT applications require different kinds of sensors, not all sensors are created equal. For instance, using the SPI bus to connect digital sensors to a microcontroller (Serial Peripheral Interface). However, for analogue sensors, either an ADC or a Sigma-Delta modulator can be used to convert the data into an SPI open/closed circuit. The various IoT sensors are listed below.

Temperature Sensor: The heat energy produced by an object or other adjacent region is detected using a temperature sensor. These sensors can be used in a variety of Internet of Things (IoT) applications, from farming to manufacturing. These sensors' primary function in production is machine temperature monitoring. Similar to how they are used in other industries, these sensors are utilized in agriculture to measure the temperature of water, soil, and plants. Thermistors, thermocouples, integrated circuits, and RTDs are all types of temperature sensors (resistor temperature detectors). The major appliances that use temperature sensors are air conditioners and refrigerators

Figure 3. Temperature-sensor (www.elprocus.com)

Smoke Sensor: Smoke sensors have been used in a variety of settings, including residences, businesses, and more. Because of the advent of the Internet of Things, these sensors are incredibly practical and simple to use. Additionally, the additional functions can be made available to boost security & ease by adding a wireless link to smoke detectors.

Figure 4. Smoke-sensor (www.elprocus.com)

Motion Sensor: The movement of a physical object can be detected by motion sensors or detectors utilizing a variety of technologies, such as passive infrared (PIR), microwave detection, or ultrasonic, which detects objects using sound. These sensors can automate the control of doors, sinks, air conditioning and heating, and other systems in addition to being employed in security and intruder detection systems. These sensors can be used with the Internet of Things to check them using a computer or smartphone.

Figure 5. Motion-sensor (www.elprocus.com)

Humidity Sensors: Sensors that measure humidity keep track of how much water vapour is present in the air. If not, it will affect various industrialized processes as well as human comfort. RH (relative humidity), D/F PT (frost point), and PPM are the units used to measure humidity (parts per million).

Figure 6. Humidity-sensors (www.elprocus.com)

Pressure Sensor: IoT devices and systems that are controlled by force signals are monitored using pressure sensors. The gadget alerts the user to the problems that need to be repaired since the pressure range is outside the threshold stage. The BMP180 pressure sensor, employed in PDAs, mobile phones, peripheral devices, GPS navigation systems, etc., utilizes pressure sensors. These sensors can be used in aircraft and intelligent vehicles to determine altitude and force appropriately. The TMPS (tyre pressure monitoring system) in a car can also be utilized to warn the driver when the tyre pressure is dangerously low and could lead to dangerous driving scenarios.

Figure 7. Pressure-sensors (www.elprocus.com)

Gas Sensor: Toxic gas detection is the primary application for gas sensors. Electrochemical, semi-conductor, and photo-ionization technologies are the most often employed ones. Based on technical requirements and improvements to increase the connectivity of wired and wirelessly arranged inside IoT applications, several types of gas sensors are now available.

Figure 8. Gas-sensor (www.elprocus.com)

IR Sensors: The primary function of infrared sensors is to quantify the heat emitted by things. These sensors are utilized in a variety of IoT applications, including monitoring blood flow and other physiological indicators in the healthcare sector. It is used in smartphones to regulate, in wearable technology to measure light levels, in automobiles to identify blind spots, etc.

Figure 9. Infrared-sensors (www.elprocus.com)

Accelerometer Sensor: Smartphones, automobiles, and aircraft all use accelerometer sensors. Similar to how they are used to determine an object's direction, these are also used to determine an object's tilt, tap, shaking, placement, motion, vibration, or shock in many applications. Piezoelectric, Hall-effect, and capacitive accelerometers are a few examples.

Figure 10. Accelerometer-sensor (www.elprocus.com)

Image Sensor: Image sensors can be used in sonar, radar, biometric systems, thermal imaging equipment, digital cameras, night-vision equipment, media houses, and medical imaging systems. With the aid of a network like the Internet of Things, these sensors are utilized in the retail sector to track the number of people who visit the store. Image sensors are mostly used in offices and corporate buildings to monitor employees.

Figure 11. Image-sensor (www.elprocus.com)

Proximity Sensors: Without any physical contact, proximity sensors can determine if an object is present or absent. These sensors are divided into several categories, including magnetic, capacitive, inductive, ultrasonic, and photoelectric. These sensors are frequently employed for process control, object counts, and monitoring.

Figure 12. Proximity-sensors (www.elprocus.com)

These sensors are essential in our daily lives. They are widely used in the IIoT (Industrial Internet of Things) to monitor the industrial process as well health, home security, and air quality. The combination of detection, enhanced surveillance, and monitoring made possible by the Internet of Things can increase safety and improve health.

Sensors in general can also be categorized as follows.

Electromagnetism sensors: These include radioactivity sensors for safety and health applications, imaging and identification sensors for security purposes, and RFID sensors for use in retail and logistics.

Vibration and sound sensors: These include seismic sensors for regional safety, sound pressure for health monitoring and industrial process automation, specialized sound monitoring for civil management uses like gunshot noise detection, fitness and health wearables, or vibration sensors for reliability-based equipment maintenance in plants or for industrial organizations.

Matter and materials sensors: Specific fluid and gas sensors to detect a chemical presence or oxygen, carbon dioxide, humidity, or water levels, are needed for many applications in environmental, safety, health, agricultural, and environmental automation.

Time and space sensors: For instance, location sensors for personal applications, position, velocity, and acceleration sensors for vehicle and traffic management, or GPS location sensors for logistics management.

RFID: RFID tags are Internet of Things sensors that gather information about the particular object to which they are attached. RFID tagging includes conveying data utilizing certain radio wave emissions and is frequently used in supply chain management, ID badging, and access control. RFID comes in both active and passive forms. An inbuilt power source on an active RFID tag allows it to send data at any time and at greater distances. If a radio frequency emission does not activate a passive RFID tag, it will not be able to communicate. It then starts data collecting and powers the return communication link using the radio wave that was picked up by the antenna in the tag.

FRAMEWORK OF INTELLIGENT SENSOR SYSTEM

Nowadays the use of intelligent devices has increased abundantly. These intelligent devices produce information through different apps and sensors. This abundant data has to be stored on a daily basis. Many industries produce a large amount of data which has to be stored as the data is being produced consistently. With the evolution of IoT(Internet of Things),the era of sensors has also advanced. With this abundant data, which are organized and unorganized, these datas need to be analyzed for decisions to be taken.

A typical IoT architecture composed of edge, fog, and cloud layer. The edge layer is composed of IoT end devices. Edge computing means the processing of sensor data at the sources of data. Thereby reducing the amount of data that needs to be sent to a cloud location and hence money and bandwidth can be saved. The whole processing is done nearer to the data's source where it is being gathered. The edge devices can be switches, router, or iot sensors. Since processing and storage is done at places where data is collected, issues of latency can be reduced for real time data. The two different models used in edge computing are Edge Intelligence and Intelligent edge. The Edge intelligence deals with communicating with other devices and performs computations to provide a better result. Edge intelligence helps us to get a secure, accurate and a fast result without using a cloud location. Intelligent edge brings content delivery and machine learning closer to the user. The edge computing brings data sources and devices together saving the time and distance to process. Fog computing, a term created by Cisco, involves bringing computing to the network's edge. It provides a highly virtualized model of computation, storage and networking resources between end devices and classical cloud servers Fog computing includes edge processing as well as the necessary infrastructure and network connections for transporting the data.

In Cloud computing, the information being accessed is found remotely in the cloud or a virtual space. Cloud computing is developed to facilitate applications in storing and processing data. IoT sensors usually depend on cloud computing to store and process data

Edge computing takes place on IoT devices where IoT sensors are connected. Here computing takes place in IoT devices rather than data being taken to further places. Thereby data is stored in the entry point sensors only.

Fog Computing takes away data from IoT sensors which generate data and computation takes place further away from IoT sensors and actuators. The data are calculated inside fog nodes of IoT. The calculation of data in fog computing takes place with less interruption delay.

Figure 13. Intelligent farming framework(Ashay Rokade et.al (2022))

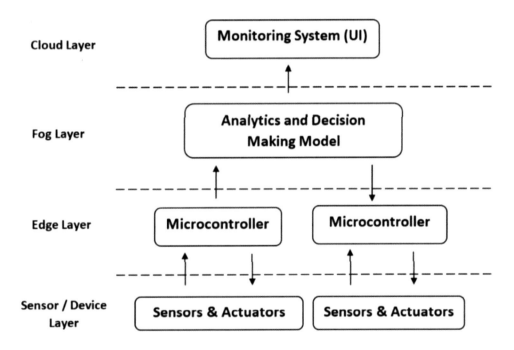

The architecture of an intelligent framework can be represented as sensor layer, edge layer, fog layer followed by cloud layer, as represented in figure 13. Different types of sensors and actuators are explained in the sensor layer. For data acquisition and further processing, we need to interface these sensor data. To control this data, the edge layer consists of a controller unit. The purpose of the fog layer is for developing the model which does the analysis and decision making. The other purpose being, providing control signals to the edge layer to control the actuators. The output of this fog layer, data will be displayed in the cloud layer.

DISTRIBUTED COMPUTING FRAMEWORK OF INTELLIGENT SENSOR NETWORK

Edge Computing Framework: This type of framework has 4 domains. They are application, data, network, and device domain. The device domain is where we make use of sensors, robots, etc. to get the data. The network domain provides connection services through which sensor data can be analyzed. The data domain helps us to get data extraction, analysis of data, services of data and the application domain provides the open interfaces provided by the device and network (D. Li et.al,2020).

   Distributed Computing Framework for Intelligent Sensor Networks: Deep learning and CNN have high advantages in sensor analysis. Therefore, the combination of deep learning and edge computing can improve the ability of computer application capabilities and smart grids. The edge-deployed convolutional neural network (ECNN) can systematically leverage the inherent advantages of neural networks and achieve similar advantages

Intelligent Sensor Design

Figure 14. Design flow of Intelligent Sensor (Zachary Ballard et al,2021)

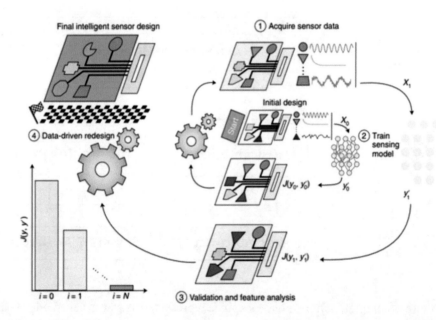

The collecting of sensing data is the first step in the deep learning-enabled intelligent sensor design process (2). These data, Xi, are then used to train a learning model that outputs sensing results as predictions, y′ I as shown below by a schematic of circular nodes and interconnections. (3) Using the ground-truth sensing data, yi, a cost function J(yi, y′ I is utilized to assess the learnt model with the additional goal of examining the group of transduction components or characteristics. (4) On the basis of the statistical analysis in (3), the sensing hardware is revised, represented here by the cog icons, deleting non-informative or less valuable characteristics and/or replacing such features with modifications to those features or other sensing components. This design cycle may be repeated to increase sensor performance in terms of a user-defined cost function (bottom left), and it concludes with a final deep learning-enabled intelligent sensor design, as shown by the subscript I = 0,.., N. (upper left).

DEEP LEARNING FOR INTELLIGENT SENSING

DL is a learning algorithm based on artificial neural networks. An artificial neural network works just like a biological neural network in human brain. It consists of neurons. Activation values are also associated with neurons like synapses. Artificial models do have different layers like input layer, output layer which will convert input to output with the help of hidden layer. A neural network containing multiple hidden layers is typically considered as a "deep" neural network—hence, the term "deep learning" (Litjens et al., 2017). Deep learning became a center of attraction in current years because of its high performance and this helped deep learning finds its application in almost all fields, mainly by outperforming all other meaning learning algorithm. Deep Learning has achieved great achievements in computer vision, robots, self driving car. For any of these applications, deep learning has to deal with tremendous data. Deep learning has advanced so much in recent years such that it can give an accurate model within less time period for complex problems.

DATASETS FOR DIFFERENT APPLICATIONS

A number of network datasets, including KDDCUP99, NSL-KDD (Tavallaee et al., 2009), UNSW-NB15 (Moustafa et al., 2015), and ISCX (Sharafaldin, et al., 2018), were created for the evaluation of IDSs; however, they do not include any specific characteristics of IoT/IIoT applications as they do not contain IoT network traffic.

The LWSNDR (Sharafaldin, et al., 2010) dataset does not include any attack scenarios and solely includes homogeneous data gathered from single-hop and multi-hop Wireless Sensor Networks (WSNs).

The AWID (Kolias et al., 2015) dataset is another well-known one; it exclusively comprises network features that were taken from the Media Access Control (MAC) layer frame of an 802.11 wireless network. Additionally, it lacks the telemetry data that IoT devices have.

Sivanathan et al. offered IoT-based datasets for IoT device classifications based on network traffic characteristics, but these datasets did not include attack scenarios.

Koroniotis et al. developed an IoT network that clearly shows both legitimate and hostile traffic (Sivanathan et al., 2018). The dataset includes attacks such as data exfiltration, DDoS, DoS, service scan, and keylogging. For the BoT-IoT dataset, network traffic logs from over 72 million simulated IoT devices were collected. A scaled-down dataset with roughly 3.6 million records was also provided by the author for review.

Hamza et al. (Hamza, et al., 2019) proposed an IoT-based dataset where they collected both regular and different types of DoS attack traffic (such as TCP SYN flooding, Ping of Death, and SNMP/TCMP flooding). This dataset may be used to detect DoS attacks in an IoT network. They created a fake smart home environment to collect their data. However, neither sensor data from IoT devices nor a variety of attack vectors, such as ransomware and XSS-Cross-site Scripting, are present in these databases.

DL ALGORITHMS FOR SENSOR DATA ANALYSIS AND PREDICTION

In today's IoT and fog networks, data analysis to identify meaningful trends and information is critical. The DL algorithms are good in this regard. Convolutional Neural Networks (CNN), Deep Neural Networks (DNN), Long Short-Term Memory Networks (LSTM), and Recurrent Neural Networks (RNN) are examples of traditional deep learning algorithms that we can use .For any application, data from several sensors is acquired and data from thousands of sensors is collected for analysis. Before an ML algorithm is applied to the sensor data, it is important to ensure that it is in the right format or structure. This is referred to as pre-processing. Preprocessing can be done for denoising and reduction in dimensionality. Data was gathered by IoT devices, particularly sensors, which can collect data in real time or in small batches. Deep Learning algorithms can be used for learning nonlinear models also the algorithms used for intelligent sensing are:

Convolutional Neural Network: CNN is a type of deep learning model for processing data. CNN is a mathematical construct that is typically composed of three types of layers (or building blocks): convolution, pooling, and fully connected layers. The first two, convolution and pooling layers, perform feature extraction, whereas the third, a fully connected layer, maps the extracted features into final output, such as classification. The architecture of CNN is made of convolutional layer, pooling layer and fully connected network for prediction or classification based on the model wanted. The gradient diffusion problem which exists in the traditional neural network is reduced in CNN. The other advantage of CNN being used is that it reduces the number of parameters in nets. The basic architecture of convolutional neural networks is as shown in figure 15 . Some CNNs used are Alexnet which has 9 layers, Resnet contains 152 layers, VGGNet contains 11-19 layers.

Figure 15. Architecture of a convolutional Neural Network

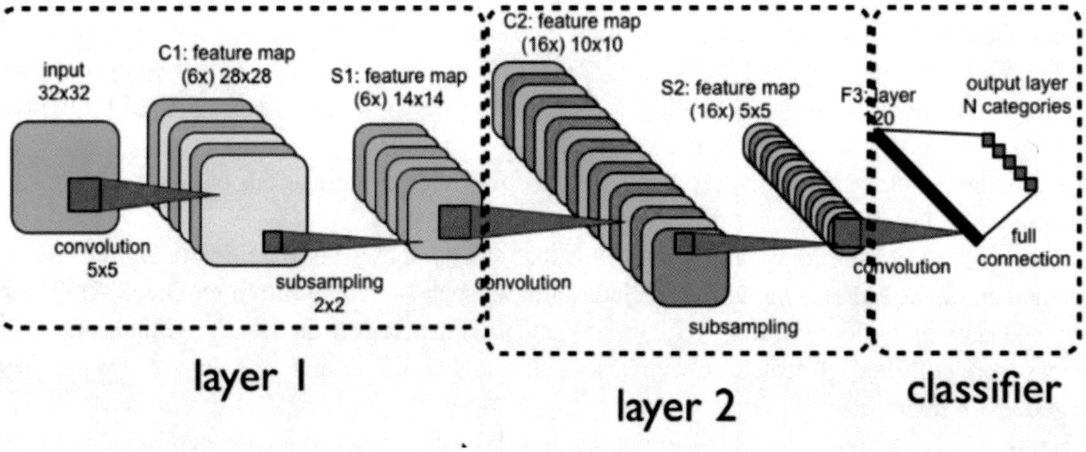

Smys et al., (2020), proposed a framework to manage the flood during emergency and normal conditions. The proposed work has been verified with a four tank system comprising IoT sensors and cloud computing algorithms. The CNN is used in this proposed method and is compared with SVM (Support Vector Machine)and ANN(Artificial Neural Networks).The result after comparing indicates that the

CNN algorithm based classification system performs efficiently with higher accuracy among the other two algorithms.

Omar Costilla-Reyes et.al (2018),used CNN for pattern classification and a raw sensor data transformation technique that allows the automatic extraction of features from the raw spatio-temporal tomography sensor data. Here the sensor data are processed by machine learning to enable classifications of the process conditions

Tawsif K et.al (2022),presented work on an emotion recognition system, which is built using physiological signals extracted from biosensors. From the data from biosensors, the extracted physiological signals are used to identify the user's emotional state using deep learning models. These deep learning models avoid human intervention.

Zhenyu Bao et.al (2021),proposed a method to find earthquakes in advance with the help of CNN model. An electromagnetic sensor was used to collect earthquake signals in order to assess. Then, a CNN model was proposed to classify the earthquake magnitude according to the data of the inductive electromagnetic sensor.

Recurrent Neural Networks (RNNs):RNN is a part of artificial neural networks. These RNN are used widely for processing the sequential data. They are following the feedforward networks which follow the human brain which can process longer sequences without any difficulties. The main advantage of RNN is the memory power which can remember the previous information that can be used for the next nodes. The two issues of RNN being used are exploding and vanishing gradient. To Solve these problems LSTM(Long Short-Term Memory) was modeled which will be effectively remove these problems by taking decision of keeping what to keep in current and previous memory discarding others

Jongho Shin et.al, proposed a method which focuses on deception attacks that modify sensing data in time. The procedure will be finding all possible attack categories on the sensors of it, and then choose the deep learning model and design its architecture.

Long-Short Term Memory (LSTM): It is a layer structure of deep learning used to analyze objects and phenomena so multi-level characteristics are extracted by learning objects. The layer structure enables computers to learn complex concepts by simple structures. Because of the powerful data fitting ability and great computing power of high dimensional data, deep learning achieves powerful representational ability of various kinds of data. So LSTM is used nowadays and preferred over RNN.LSTM with its more complex internal structure which includes memory cells that permits architecture to recollect the information that have been stored in the memory cells long back

F. D. Casagrande et.al, (2018), proposed a text sequence from the sensor data to predict the next event. Around 13 sensors were used to get sensor data. The sensors used are motion, power, magnetic sensors. The data from sensors are converted to letters using ALZ algorithm. LSTM algorithms are used as they have high storing and accessing capabilities. The result showed that LSTM algorithm has better accuracy and can be used for further applications related to finding patterns and relation between these patterns.

Awais, M et.al (2021),The deep learning-based physical activity classification (PAC) systems system was developed using the LSTM approach, by directly feeding in the raw data from the inertial sensors. (3 for linear acceleration, 3 for angular velocity),

Kanjo et.al (2019), proposed a methodology in which emotion detection often require modeling of various data inputs from multiple modalities, including physiological signals (e.g.EEG and GSR), environmental data (e.g. audio and weather), videos (e.g. for capturing facial expressions and gestures) and more recently motion and location data. Convolutional Neural Network and Long Short-term Memory

Recurrent Neural Network (CNN-LSTM) are used on the raw sensor data, thereby eliminating the needs for manual feature extraction and engineering.

Mekruksavanich et.al(2021), proposed a method in which a 4-layer CNN-LSTM is proposed. This proposal consists of a hybrid DL network which uses both LSTM and CNN layer . The advantage of using LSTM is that it could learn temporal and spatial features automatically. The result showed that this method has outperformed other DL network and has improved the recognition process, as shown in figure 16

Figure 16. Using CNN (Mekruksavanich et.al(2021))

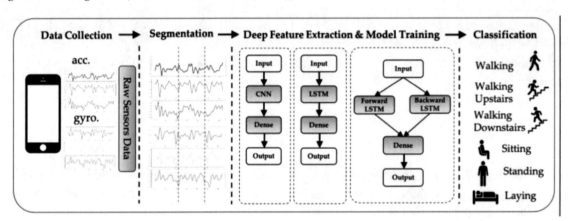

Younis et.al (2022) proposed a multi modal emotional predictor with the help of real and direct sensor data. In this, many sensors were used like the optical heart monitor which collected heart rate, galvanic skin sensors, skin temperature sensors, UV sensors . These were all collected with the help of wearable sensors used.

Generative adversarial Nets (GANs): GANs are basically made up of a system of two competing neural network models which compete with each other and are able to analyze, capture and copy the variations within a dataset.In GANs, there is a generator and a discriminator. The Generator generates fake samples of data(be it an image, audio, etc.) and tries to fool the Discriminator. The Discriminator, on the other hand, tries to distinguish between the real and fake samples. The Generator and the Discriminator are both Neural Networks and they both run in competition with each other in the training phase.

Vanilla GAN: One of the simplest GAN where discriminator and generator are used. Both of them are simple multi-layer perceptrons. We make use of stochastic gradient descent and thereby make the algorithm simple.

Conditional GAN (CGAN):When some conditional parameters are used, it becomes CGAN. To identify fake data from real data, we make use of labels.

Deep Convolutional GAN (DCGAN):ConvNets are used in DCGAN .The ConvNets are implemented without max pooling, which is in fact replaced by convolutional stride.

Laplacian Pyramid GAN (LAPGAN): As the name indicates, multiple numbers of generator and discriminator networks are used. Here, image is down sampled at lower layer and upscaled at each layer till it gets original size.

Super Resolution GAN (SRGAN): Here high resolution images are obtained with the help of deep neural networks. Thereby we can enhance minute details of images

Vaccari.et.al (2021),used the concept of generative adversarial networks (GANs) to perform a data augmentation from patient data obtained through IoMT sensors for Chronic Obstructive Pulmonary Disease (COPD) monitoring. The result was compared with the real data recorded by the sensors and found this method was an efficient one

Zhu.et.al, (2021), took up cases where only few samples are available as a result of physical restrictions and time costs, resulting in insufficient data and incomplete data representation. A new virtual sample generation approach based on conditional generative adversarial network (CGAN-VSG) was proposed

Deep convolutional Neural Network: The strength of DCNNs is in their layering. A DCNN has a three-dimensional neural network to process data at the same time. This considerably reduces the number of artificial neurons required to process data, compared to traditional feed forward neural networks.

Otebolaku et.al (2020), proposed a novel fast and robust deep convolutional neural network structure (FR-DCNN) for human activity recognition from the collected raw data from the inertial measurement unit (IMU) sensors.

Wei et.al (2019), proposed a method for human action recognition with the inertial signals and video images and inertial signals with the help of a video camera and a wearable inertial sensor. The data captured by these sensors are turned into 3D video images and 2D inertial images that are then fed as inputs into a 3D convolutional neural network and a 2D convolutional neural network, respectively, for recognizing actions

Yen et.al, (2021), make use of three parallel convolutional neural network after getting data from the wearable device which consists of a single-board computer (SBC) and six-axis sensors for human activity recognition

Ranieri et.al (2021), proposed the problem of recognising heterogeneous activities of daily living centered in home environments considering simultaneously data from videos, wearable IMUs and ambient sensors and data got is given to the Deep Learning (DL) framework, which provides multimodal activity recognition

Autoencoder: Autoencoders are a type of deep learning algorithm that are designed to receive an input and transform it into a different representation. An autoencoder is a fully connected neural network. It is a three layer architecture. Encoder consists of input and hidden layer and decoder consists of hidden and output layer. The encoder converts the input dimension into higher dimension. It also tries to make a nonlinear relationship between input data. Hidden layer will do the computation during the training period and the decoder converts the data back to input dimension

M. Şeker.et.al (2019), used an auto-encoder based unsupervised feature extraction method was used and a deep learning approach was investigated to classify focal-non-focal EEG records and with the result got can be used to diagnose epilepsy by using deep neural networks.

Hao et.al (2022), used sparse autoencoder in deep learning is integrated into the compressed sensing (CS) theory, and a reconstruction algorithm is designed based on the biological mechanism of human brain synaptic connections. LSTM network model was proposed for the reconstruction

Restricted Boltzmann Machine (RBM): The RBM is made of two layers: the visible layer and the hidden layer. The input is fed to the visible layer, and the hidden layer learns from the input layer. The neurons in the visible and hidden layers are connected in a way that they form a bipartite graph. Back-propagation and gradient descent techniques are utilized during training to determine the optimal parameters in the network.

Cao et.al (2018), proposed a classification system for activity recognition (AR) from the information gained from multi-sensors. These data received from different sensors are used for making features with high dimensionality. Restricted Boltzmann machines (RBM) and extended space forest (ESF) algorithms are used in this paper to create accurate classifiers.

Deep Belief Network: Deep Belief Networks (DBNs) is the adding up of individual unsupervised network that use each network's hidden layer as the input for the next layer. The structure of DBN is closely related to the number of hidden nodes and hidden layers; if the DBN structure is too simple, learning ability is so poor that it cannot effectively integrate the multi-information as mentioned in below figure 17.

Figure 17. Architecture of a deep belief network (DBN)

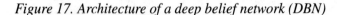
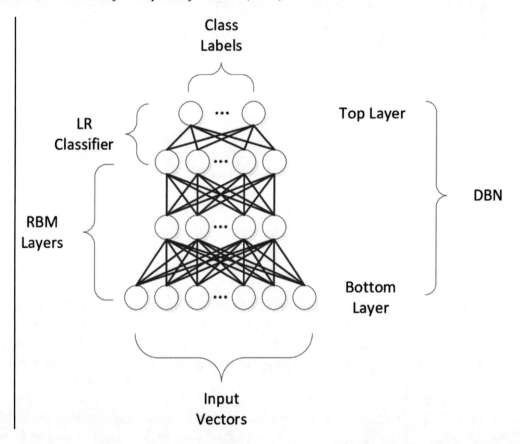

M.M Hassan.et.al (2019), used unsupervised deep belief network (DBN) for depth level feature extraction from sensors like Electro-Dermal Activity (EDA), Photoplethysmogram (PPG) and Zygomaticus Electromyography (zEMG). Once the sensor data are obtained, features of these sensor data are combined with DBN features to find the emotion recognition.

Li, C. et.al., (2019) proposed a novel deep belief network (DBN) hyperspectral image classification method based on multivariate optical sensors and stacked by restricted Boltzmann machines. This was done to get a new hyperspectral image classification model.

APPLICATIONS

Intelligent sensing systems are used in a variety of smart systems for the following applications (Tausifa Jan Saleem and Mohammad Ahsan Chishti 2021) .

Smart Home: used for energy demand prediction, behavior monitoring, human activity recognition and posture detection in smart homes.

Smart Health care: used for disease risk prediction, disease detection, health monitoring, mortality prediction and missing clinical data prediction.

Smart Grid: used for power demand forecasting, electricity price detection and electricity theft detection.

Smart Manufacturing: Machine condition monitoring, fault detection, remaining useful life prediction and worker activity recognition.

Smart Agriculture: used for plant classification, plant disease detection, crop yield prediction, fruit counting and weed detection.

Smart Transportation: used for traffic congestion management, traffic speed prediction, smart shift decision, obstacle detection, accident detection and car park occupancy prediction.

Reconfiguring a computational sensing system: For example, wearable devices (like the activity monitor or sensor arrays for monitoring blood pressure) could be reconfigured computationally by optimizing the relative weights of different signals within the sensor array to converge to a reliable and accurate readout for electrocardiogram or photoplethysmogram signals. Such computational sensing systems will have the primary benefit of learning "online" from evidence-based sensing results if linked in an IoT network in a broadly distributed manner, convergent to sensing solutions intractable with a single sensing unit. Distributed sensing networks for environmental monitoring, for instance, might select on their own where and how to collect samples. This flexibility might be controlled by an unsupervised framework for broad discovery or monitoring or a supervised learning framework with a specific sensing objective . Based on the variations from the ground-truth frequency and the source of a measured vibration, the vibration localization metamaterial sensor might be modified. Reconfigurable computational sensing solutions for wearable sensors might considerably improve data capture for various types of body, health conditions, misalignments and motion artifacts (Zachary Ballard et al,2021).

Remote Sensing: used for Land cover and land use classification, scene classification and object detection. (Lei Maa et al.,2019)

Predictive maintenance of sensors: provides a self re-calibrating system for correcting the sensor drift. (Srikanth Namuduri et al.,2020)

CHALLENGES

- Overfitting can also happen when training datasets are not sufficiently diverse in terms of dynamic range, test samples, performance variability frm sensor-to-sensor and resolution(Zachary Ballard et al., 2021).
- Once catastrophic sensing errors are recognised, a computational sensor that misses a significant event or merely misses outlier occurrences of 'small data' may be corrected by optimizing their respective weights and its measurement characteristics. (Zachary Ballard et al., 2021)

- Due to the relatively high acquisition costs of training samples, it is advantageous to use augmentation techniques to increase the quantity or effectiveness of training datasets, such as transfer learning or active learning. (Lei Maa et al.,2019)
- Identification of the pertinent parameters (such patch size), which have a significant impact on classification accuracy, is the key challenge with this technique. 2019 (Lei Maa et al.)
- To balance the global context and the local details in semantic segmentation, it is still difficult to enhance the network topology, particularly the decoder network. 2019 (Lei Maa et al.)
- To train the algorithms and forecast the hidden data, DL needs extensive labeled datasets. The difficulty of this task increases when the amount of the accessible datasets is constrained or when real-time processing is required. Therefore, it may be possible to work on ways to lessen this problem. (Mohammad Ahsan Chishti and Tausifa Jan Saleem, 2021)
- Frameworks that are unsupervised or semi-supervised are necessary for DL. The majority of algorithms used today are supervised, which need large amounts of difficult to get labeled training data. (Mohammad Ahsan Chishti and Tausifa Jan Saleem, 2021)
- Cost, latency, workload, feature extraction, recognition, etc.

CASE STUDIES

User recognition using smart triboelectric flooring system: A polyvinyl chloride (PVC) base layer, a silver electrode layer, and a polyethylene terephthalate (PET) film friction layer make up a smart flooring system. A randomized binary electrode design with various fill factors is included on each floor tile. The deep learning model can identify people by their gaits using two voltage readouts (V1 and V2). This model from ten independent users(U1–U10) with the confusion matrix giving an accuracy of 96%. The analysis of location sensing data is done concurrently using a microcontroller unit (MCU) as illustrated in figure 18.

Figure 18. Smart triboelectric flooring system (Shi, Q. et al.2020)

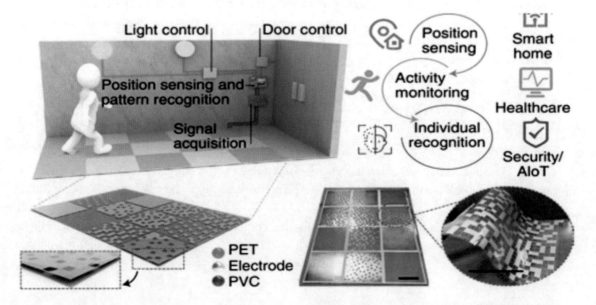

Figure 19. Signal acquisition and DL model for predicting the position of user (Shi, Q. et al.2020)

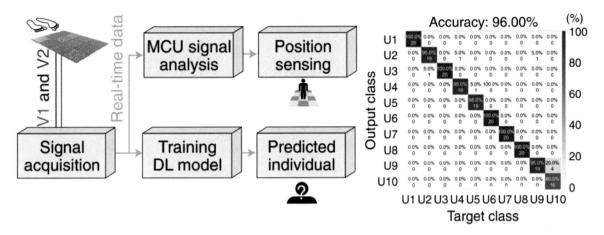

Magnetic induction-based wearable sensor network for activity recognition: The torso and limb segments are determined via magnetic induction-based wearable transceiver sensors (Txi, RX), designated by Mi, which are utilized to determine the location of the transceiver coils. Transceiver signals are used by a recurrent neural network (RNN) to categorize user behavior, with xt standing for the normalized input data at different time instants determined by a sliding window of 1 s. The RNN outputs the average prediction scores, represented by yˆt, before converting them into an average class probability, denoted by Oˆt.

Figure 20. magnetic induction-based wearable sensor network (Golestani, N. and Moghaddam, M. 2020)

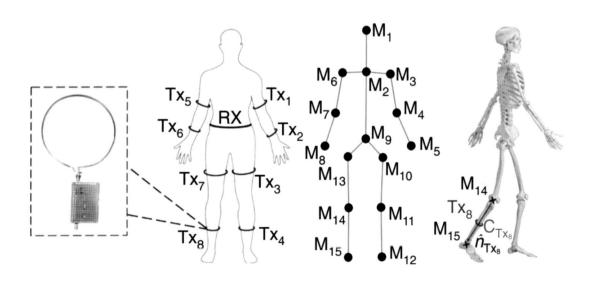

Figure 21. Deep RNN for Activity recognition (Golestani, N. and Moghaddam, M. 2020)

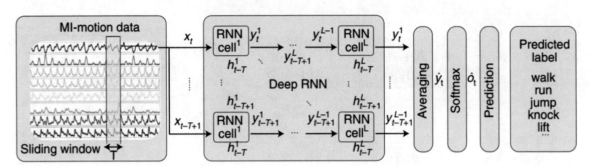

Deep learning-based diagnostic sensor for Lyme disease: The first step in this approach is to collect multiplexed sensory data using a mobile phone reader and a paper-based biosensor. When the colorimetric assay using gold nanoparticles is ended, the multiplexed sensing membrane captures various Lyme antibodies in patient serum and reports their relative concentrations. Two different assay cartridges are used to capture the IgM and IgG class of antibodies. The optimal antigen panel, a subset of the full antigen measurement features, is then determined through a feature analysis technique called sequential forward selection with the area under the receiver operating character.

Figure 22. Deep learning-based diagnostic sensor for Lyme disease (Joung, H.-A. et al 2020)

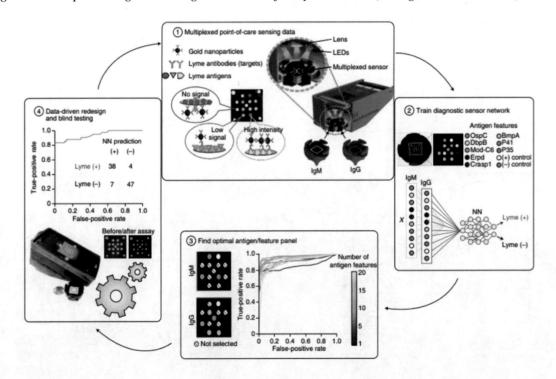

These sensing data are then used to train a neural network-based diagnostic algorithm that infers a Lyme positive or Lyme negative diagnosis from the multiplexed IgM and IgG antibody measurements. A final verified computational biosensor design is then produced utilizing the specified panel to measure blindfolded patient samples and infer a diagnostic outcome using a trained neural network model, along with the ROC curve and confusion matrix of the blind testing result.

Programmable RNA toehold switches: The first step in the process of choosing an RNA tool involves using a library of sequences for the synthesis of RNA toehold switches. The toehold switch architecture is shown in the bottom left and consists of an 18-nucleotide stem (b/b′) that has been unwound by trigger RNA and a 12-nucleotide toehold (a/a′). Following synthesis, the toehold switches are examined using a pooled sequential assay to describe them, and their functionality is predicted using a variety of learning models including convolutional neural network (CNN), long short-term memory (LSTM), and multilayer perceptron (MLP). In order to get biological insights regarding the essential RNA components that provide the desired function- Ribosome-binding site(RBS), the deep learning model is tested in turn.

Figure 23. Programmable RNA toehold switches (Angenent-Mari et al,.2020)

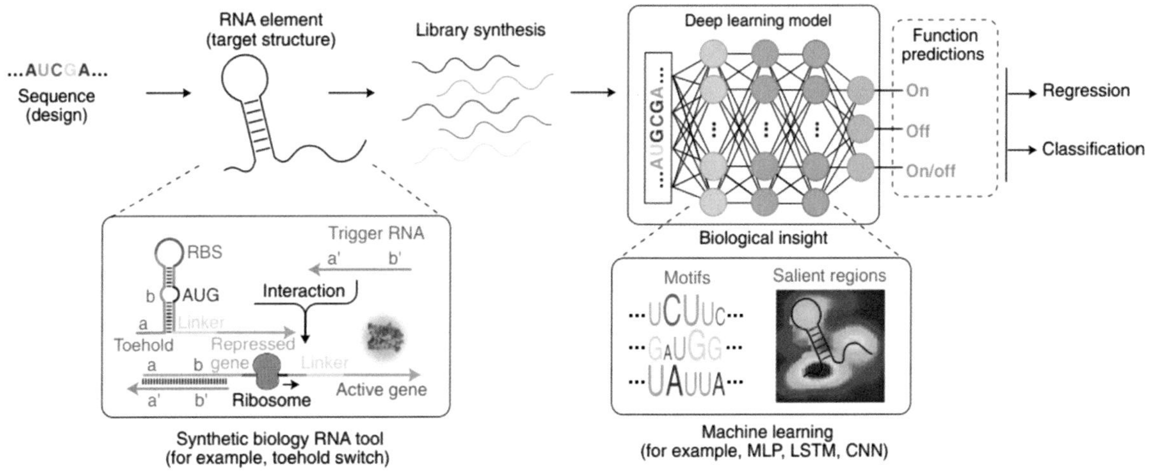

STORM is an optimization pipeline designed to use deep learning to redesign toehold switches that perform badly. Here, the model weights may be optimized via a conventional training approach starting from initialization (t = 0), in order to most accurately forecast the ON and OFF signals emerging from a given fixed sequence. The concepts of intelligent sensor design are demonstrated by the fact that this process may also be reversed by setting the model weights-Position Weight Matrix(PWM) and target ON and OFF signals in order to find a locally optimal sequence.

Intelligent hyperspectral image sensor: An assortment of various spectrum encoding components are built at the outset of the design process using approximations of electromagnetic transmission models. In order to train a reconstruction model, encoded spectral data from known incident spectra, Si (λ), is obtained and utilized to produce a predicted spectrum, S′.

Figure 24. DL based intelligent hyperspectral image sensor design

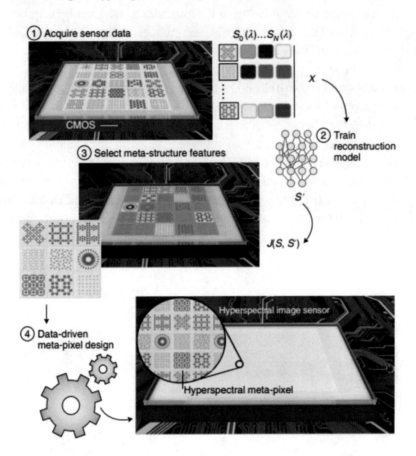

The subset of spectral encoders provide the best foundation for the encoding operation and reconstruction of the spectrum given a user-defined, application-specific cost function are then chosen using feature analysis. In a machine learning-inspired architecture, metapixels are created using the best subset of encoders for a hyperspectral image sensor.

CONCLUSION

Intelligent sensors are key to developing IoT applications, as they help modernize and streamline analytics and connectivity. The internet of things couldn't exist without intelligent sensors. Today, smart factories, smart cities, smart buildings and connected individuals are using an array of intelligent sensors to collect real-time data for real-time insights and decision-making. Intelligent sensing in the Internet of Things (IoT) can be used for almost any type of measurement and offers a method for connecting desired field observations to applications. With the introduction of 5G, edge computing became more prevalent, organizing the gathered data using machine learning and artificial intelligence algorithms. The intelligent sensors' connected IoT edge gateways will be able to make judgments more quickly and efficiently. The future sensor landscape will also alter as a result of continuing sensor shrinking since additional functions will be available on the same platform, supporting various sensing categories from the same devices.

Traditional sensors' hardware designs can be substantially altered by computational and deep learning techniques, which can also be utilized to create intelligent sensor systems holistically. Deep Learning works well for deciphering extremely complex data produced by IoT applications. Though deep learning is crucial for processing huge amounts of data, it can produce reliable prediction outcomes. Deep learning also aids in the analysis of complicated data sets that are challenging for the human brain to comprehend. To be completely reliable in deep learning, there are still a lot of obstacles to be solved. However, deep learning will soon play a significant role in IoT. There is a tremendous growth that is happening in intelligence sensing which in turn raises problems for the integrity, safety and secure communication of data produced from the sensors. The adaptation of deep learning algorithms makes this process easier and it gives a way for future applications. The different types of sensors, DL algorithms and the models were discussed.

REFERENCES

Angenent-Mari, N. M., Garruss, A. S., Soenksen, L. R., Church, G., & Collins, J. J. (2020). A deep learning approach to programmable RNA switches. *Nature Communications*, *11*(1), 5057. doi:10.103841467-020-18677-1 PMID:33028812

Awais, M., Chiari, L., Ihlen, E.A.F., Helbostad, J.L., Palmerini, L.(2021) Classical Machine Learning Versus Deep Learning for the Older Adults Free-Living Activity Classification. doi:10.3390/s21144669

Awin, F. A., Alginahi, Y. M., Abdel-Raheem, E., & Tepe, K. (2019). Technical issues on cognitive radio-based Internet of Things systems: A survey. *IEEE Access : Practical Innovations, Open Solutions*, *7*, 97887–97908. doi:10.1109/ACCESS.2019.2929915

Ballard, Z., Brown, C., Madni, A. M., & Ozcan, A. (2021). Machine learning and computation-enabled intelligent sensor design. *Nature Machine Intelligence*, *3*(7), 556–565. doi:10.103842256-021-00360-9

Bao, Z., Zhao, J., Huang, P., Yong, S., & Wang, X. (2021, June 28). A Deep Learning-Based Electromagnetic Signal for Earthquake Magnitude Prediction. *Sensors (Basel)*, *21*(13), 4434. doi:10.339021134434 PMID:34203508

Cao, J., Li, W., Wang, Q., & Yu, M. (2018). A Sensor-Based Human Activity Recognition System via Restricted Boltzmann Machine and Extended Space Forest. In G. Fortino, A. Ali, M. Pathan, A. Guerrieri, & G. Di Fatta (Eds.), Lecture Notes in Computer Science: Vol. 10794. *Internet and Distributed Computing Systems. IDCS 2017.* Springer., doi:10.1007/978-3-319-97795-9_8

Casagrande, F. D., Tørresen, J., & Zouganeli, E. (2018) Sensor Event Prediction using Recurrent Neural Network in Smart Homes for Older Adults. *International Conference on Intelligent Systems (IS)*, pp. 662-668, 10.1109/IS.2018.8710467

Chen, F., Deng, P., Wan, J., Zhang, D., Vasilakos, A. V., & Rong, X. (2015). Data mining for the internet of things: Literature review and challenges. *International Journal of Distributed Sensor Networks*, *11*(8), 431047. doi:10.1155/2015/431047

Golestani, N., & Moghaddam, M. (2020). Human activity recognition using magnetic induction-based motion signals and deep recurrent neural networks. *Nature Communications*, *11*(1), 1551. doi:10.103841467-020-15086-2 PMID:32214095

Hamza, A., Gharakheili, H. H., Benson, T. A., & Sivaraman, V. (2019, April). Detecting volumetric attacks on lot devices via sdn-based monitoring of mud activity. In *Proceedings of the 2019 ACM Symposium on SDN Research,* (pp. 36-48. 10.1145/3314148.3314352

Han, T., Hao, K., Tang, X. S., Wang, T., & Liu, X. (2022, June). A Compressed Sensing Network for Acquiring Human Pressure Information. *IEEE Transactions on Cognitive and Developmental Systems*, *14*(2), 388–402. doi:10.1109/TCDS.2020.3041422

Hassan, M., Alam, G. R., Uddin, Z., Huda, S., Almogren, A., & Fortino, G. (2019). Human emotion recognition using deep belief network architecture. *Information Fusion, 51*, 10-18. doi:10.1016/j.inffus.2018.10.00

Hung, L. L. (2022). Intelligent Sensing for Internet of Things Systems. *Journal of Internet Technology*, *23*(1), 185–191.

Intelligence, S. C. B. (2008). National Intelligence Council: Disruptive Technologies Global Trands 2025. *SRI Consulting Business Intelligence*, (Appendix), F-2.

Joung, H.-A., Ballard, Z. S., Wu, J., Tseng, D. K., Teshome, H., Zhang, L., Horn, E. J., Arnaboldi, P. M., Dattwyler, R. J., Garner, O. B., Di Carlo, D., & Ozcan, A. (2020). Point-of-care serodiagnostic test for early-stage Lyme disease using a multiplexed paper-based immunoassay and machine learning. *ACS Nano, 14*(1), 229–240. doi:10.1021/acsnano.9b08151 PMID:31849225

Kanjo, E., Younis, E., & Ang, C. S. (2019). Deep Learning Analysis of Mobile Physiological, Environmental and Location Sensor Data for Emotion Detection. *Information Fusion, 49*, 46–56. doi:10.1016/j.inffus.2018.09.001

Kolias, C., Kambourakis, G., Stavrou, A., & Gritzalis, S. (2015). Intrusion detection in 802.11 networks: Empirical evaluation of threats and a public dataset. *IEEE Communications Surveys and Tutorials*, *18*(1), 184–208. doi:10.1109/COMST.2015.2402161

Koroniotis, N., Moustafa, N., Sitnikova, E., & Turnbull, B. (2019). Towards the development of realistic botnet dataset in the internet of things for network forensic analytics: Bot-iot dataset. *Future Generation Computer Systems, 100*, 779–796. doi:10.1016/j.future.2019.05.041

Li, C., Wang, Y., Zhang, X., Gao, H., Yang, Y., & Wang, J. (2019). Deep Belief Network for Spectral–Spatial Classification of Hyperspectral Remote Sensor Data. *Sensors (Basel)*, *19*(1), 204. doi:10.339019010204 PMID:30626030

Li, D., Yu, R., Song, C., Jia, G., & Zhou, X. (2020) Distributed computing framework of intelligent sensor network for electric power internet of things. *9th Joint International Information Technology and Artificial Intelligence Conference (ITAIC),* pp. 68-71, 10.1109/ITAIC49862.2020.9338769

Litjens, G., Kooi, T., Bejnordi, B. E., Setio, A. A. A., Ciompi, F., Ghafoorian, M., & Sanchez, C. I. (2017). A survey on deep learning in medical image analysis. *Medical Image Analysis*, *42*, 60–88. doi:10.1016/j.media.2017.07.005 PMID:28778026

Ma, X., Yao, T., Hu, M., Dong, Y., Liu, W., Wang, F., & Liu, J. (2019). A Survey on Deep Learning Empowered IoT Applications. *IEEE Access : Practical Innovations, Open Solutions*, 7, 181721–181732. doi:10.1109/ACCESS.2019.2958962

Maa, L., Liuc, Y., Zhanga, X., Yed, Y., Yind, G., & Johnson, B. A. (2019). Deep learning in remote sensing applications: A meta-analysis and review. *ISPRS Journal of Photogrammetry and Remote Sensing*, *152*, 166–177. doi:10.1016/j.isprsjprs.2019.04.015

Manyika, J., Chui, M., Bughin, J., Dobbs, R., Bisson, P., & Marrs, A. (2013). *Disruptive technologies: Advances that will transform life, business, and the global economy*, (Vol. 180). McKinsey Global Institute.

Mekruksavanich, S. (2021). Jitpattanakul,(2019), A. LSTM Networks Using Smartphone Data for Sensor-Based Human Activity Recognition in Smart Homes. *Sensors (Basel)*, *21*, 1636. doi:10.339021051636 PMID.33652697

Moustafa, N., & Slay, J. (2015, November). UNSW-NB15: a comprehensive data set for network intrusion detection systems (UNSW-NB15 network data set). In *military communications and information systems conference (MilCIS)*, (pp. 1-6). IEEE.

Namuduri, S., Narayanan, B. N., Venkata, S. P. D., Burton, L., & Bhansali, S. (2020). Review—Deep Learning Methods for Sensor Based Predictive Maintenance and Future Perspectives for Electrochemical Sensors. *Journal of the Electrochemical Society*, *167*(3), 037552. doi:10.1149/1945-7111/ab67a8

Otebolaku A, Enamamu T, Alfoudi A, Ikpehai A, Marchang J, Lee GM,(2020). Deep Sensing: Inertial and Ambient Sensing for Activity Context Recognition Using Deep Convolutional Neural Networks. *Sensors (Basel)*, *20*(13), 3803. . doi:10.3390/s20133803

Qun-Xiong, Z., Kun-Rui, H., Zhong-Sheng, C., Zi-Shu, G., Yuan, X., & Yan-Lin, H.(2021),Novel virtual sample generation using conditional GAN for developing soft sensor with small data. *Engineering Applications of Artificial Intelligence, 106.* doi:10.1016/j.engappai.2021.104497

Ranieri,C,M., MacLeod S., Dragone M., Vargas PA., Romero RAF,.(2021) Activity Recognition for Ambient Assisted Living with Videos, Inertial Units and Ambient Sensors. *Sensors (Basel), 21*(3), 768. . doi:10.3390/s21030768

Sah, D. K., Nguyen, T. N., Cengiz, K., Dumba, B., & Kumar, V. (2022). Load-balance scheduling for intelligent sensors deployment in industrial internet of things. *Cluster Computing*, *25*(3), 1715–1727. doi:10.100710586-021-03316-1

Saleem, T. J., & Chishti, M. A. (2021). Deep learning for the internet of things: Potential benefits and use-cases. *Digital Communications and Networks*, *7*(4), 526–542. doi:10.1016/j.dcan.2020.12.002

Şeker. M., Özerdem, M.S. (2019). Autoencoders Based Deep Learning Approach for Focal-Nonfocal EEG Classification Problem. *Innovations in Intelligent Systems and Applications Conference (ASYU)*, pp. 1-4, 10.1109/ASYU48272.2019.8946412

Shaheen, A., Waheed, U. B., Fehler, M., Sokol, L., & Hanafy, S. (2021). GroningenNet(2021), Deep Learning for Low-Magnitude Earthquake Detection on a Multi-Level Sensor Network. *Sensors (Basel)*, *21*(23), 8080. doi:10.339021238080 PMID:34884084

Sharafaldin, I., Lashkari, A. H., & Ghorbani, A. A. (2018). Toward generating a new intrusion detection dataset and intrusion traffic characterization. *ICISSp*, *1*, 108–116. doi:10.5220/0006639801080116

Shi, Q., Zhang, Z., He, T., Sun, Z., Wang, B., Feng, Y., Shan, X., Salam, B., & Lee, C. (2020). Deep learning enabled smart mats as a scalable foor monitoring system. *Nature Communications*, *11*(1), 4609. doi:10.103841467-020-18471-z PMID:32929087

Sivanathan, A., Gharakheili, H. H., Loi, F., Radford, A., Wijenayake, C., Vishwanath, A., & Sivaraman, V. (2018). Classifying IoT devices in smart environments using network traffic characteristics. *IEEE Transactions on Mobile Computing*, *18*(8), 1745–1759. doi:10.1109/TMC.2018.2866249

Suthaharan, S., Alzahrani, M., Rajasegarar, S., Leckie, C., & Palaniswami, M. (2010, December). Labelled data collection for anomaly detection in wireless sensor networks. In *sixth international conference on intelligent sensors, sensor networks and information processing*, (pp. 269-274). IEEE 10.1109/ISSNIP.2010.5706782

Tavallaee, M., Bagheri, E., Lu, W., & Ghorbani, A. A. (2009, July). A detailed analysis of the KDD CUP 99 data set. In *symposium on computational intelligence for security and defense applications*, (pp. 1-6). IEEE.

Tawsif, K., Nor Azlina Ab. Aziz, J. Emerson Raja, J. Hossen, Jesmeen M. Z. H. (. (2022). A Systematic Thematic Review on Emotion Recognition System Using Physiological Signals. *Data Acquisition and Methodology*. doi:10.28991/ESJ-2022-06-05-017

Vaccari, I., Orani, V., Paglialonga, A., Cambiaso, E., & Mongelli, M. A. (2021). Generative Adversarial Network (GAN) Technique for Internet of Medical Things Data. *Sensors (Basel)*, *2021*(21), 3726. doi:10.339021113726 PMID:34071944

Wei, H., Jafari, R., & Kehtarnavaz, N. (2019, August 24). Fusion of Video and Inertial Sensing for Deep Learning-Based Human Action Recognition. *Sensors (Basel)*, *19*(17), 3680. doi:10.339019173680 PMID:31450609

Yen, C. T., Liao, J. X., & Huang, Y. K. (2021, December 11). Feature Fusion of a Deep-Learning Algorithm into Wearable Sensor Devices for Human Activity Recognition. *Sensors (Basel)*, *21*(24), 8294. doi:10.339021248294 PMID:34960388

Younis, E., Zaki, S. M., Kanjo, E., & Houssein, E. H. (2022). Evaluating Ensemble Learning Methods for Multi-Modal Emotion Recognition Using Sensor Data Fusion. *Sensors (Basel)*, *2022*(22), 5611. doi:10.339022155611 PMID:35957167

Chapter 4
Deep Learning–Enabled Edge Computing and IoT

Amuthan Nallathambi

https://orcid.org/0000-0001-8830-3353

AMC Engineering College, Visvesvaraya Technological University, India

Kannan Nova

Microsoft, USA

ABSTRACT

Deep learning is a new approach to artificial intelligence that enables edge-computing systems to learn from data and take decisions without human intervention. Edge computing is a technique for coping with the increasing demand for streaming data. This is especially important in the case of applications that involve computationally intensive tasks such as driverless cars, autonomous drones, and smart cities. Edge computing is the provision of computing, big data analytics, and storage in such a way that the data comes to the processing power and not vice versa. It relies on a decentralized approach where computational resources are provided at the edge of networks. Edge computing is an emerging field that's getting attention from many vendors and researchers. The data generated by IoT devices is usually too large and complex for cloud-based storage and processing. That's why edge computing can handle data at the source of generation in real time, which speeds up the process of decision making.

INTRODUCTION

In this chapter, we explore how deep learning enables edge computing applications at scale by predicting user preferences. Deep learning is an artificial intelligence algorithm which can learn from example data and improve its predictions. Deep learning enables edge computing applications at scale with real-time analytics. Deep learning is a subset of machine learning that use algorithms based on artificial neural networks to learn abstract concepts from data. Deep learning models have an architecture composed of many layers or modules, each designed to process and extract data from its inputs and pass it through multiple processing steps to generate outputs.

DOI: 10.4018/978-1-6684-6275-1.ch004

Deep learning models can be identified as following based on the number of layers in their architecture:

Single-layer networks: These models are composed of one layer with only one processing step. One layer includes a set of inputs and a single output. A single-layer network is an example of a perceptron model.

Multi-layer networks: These models have two or more layers in the architecture, each performing different tasks. The multiple hidden layers are introduced between input and output layers depends upon the optimization or hyper parameters. This can be achieved by means of a feed-forward architecture, whereby the output of one layer is input to the next layer, or a recurrent architecture with feedback. A multilayer network is an example of a deep neural network. The following diagrams illustrate three different types of multilayer networks: Feedforward multi-layer perceptron model: This is the simplest form of a multilayer network.

Recurrent neural network model: The recurrent neural network (RNN) model is an artificial intelligence technique used to process sequential data and produce a sequence of outputs where each successive value depends on the values of previous entries. This is an alternative to the backpropagation network This is a more sophisticated form of the feedforward architecture. They are trained using the standard batch training, but the time required for learning is reduced significantly compared to standard neural networks. This type of model is commonly used in machine learning to process time-based data. For instance, this kind of model can be used to predict the next word of a text or the next impulse (e.g., sound, gesture) that an actor makes in a video sequence.

Convolution Neural Network: A popular deep learning algorithm is called a Convolutional Neural Network. The Convolutional Neural Network works by using a lot of "neurons" and they work together to solve problems. It is used in image classification, image recognition, object detections, and autonomous self-driving cars.

Deep neural network model: This most complex and powerful type includes many layers, typically with multiple hidden or intermediate layers in each layer. As illustrated in the figure.1,

Figure 1. Deep neural network model

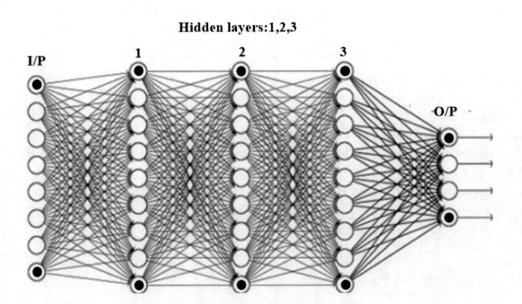

we have a network with two hidden layers. The input data is fed forward through the first hidden layer to output nodes for classification and prediction. The output from the input nodes is then fed to the second hidden layer and through it, to the output nodes. The output of these nodes is finally fed back to classification and prediction in a "backward pass" through the network after which an error function may be calculated.

The most important principle of neural networks is that a single neuron in one layer is connected to the output of neurons in the previous layer. The back propagation algorithm was largely developed by Geoffrey Hinton, who won the Turing Award in 2014. In its core, it consists of two steps: an error back propagation step and gradient descent optimization step. The error back propagation step iterates from the outputs of previously hidden nodes to calculate how much error is produced when the predicted output is compared to the actual active input.

The gradient descent optimization step iterates these calculations for each hidden node, updating the weights of nodes with a lower error back propagation and keeping those with a higher error. The least-squares minimization step calculates the error of each hidden node given the weight vectors of all weights in the network: The gradient descent optimization step iterates these calculations for each hidden node, updating the weights of nodes with a lower error back propagation and keeping those with a higher error. The final optimization step evaluates whether the update of the nodes has improved the overall error rate, and if not, it iterates the process again. In neural networks, this is achieved by applying an activation function to neurons and then multiplying all values in one neuron's inputs by that value.

The new Deep Learning enabled Edge Computing is changing the way we think of IoT. In this era, we can have more than one IoT device per person and they are interconnected to each other through the Internet. These IoT devices are also connected to the Cloud. Edge Computing provides a perfect infrastructure for handling these smart IoT devices that can be anywhere in the world and can connect to each other. This is the next phase of evolution for IoT. A good example of this is an autonomous car with Deep Learning enabled computer vision. Let's say, we are driving a taxi. We are the driver and there is an autonomous car coming up behind us. It could be at high speed, and it could take any action when it gets close to our taxi. The car will have Deep Learning enabled computer vision, so it can make decisions in real time without much input from the driver or passengers. With Deep Learning enabled Edge Computing, it becomes possible for these devices to communicate with each other directly through their microphones and cameras without going through an external server. This saves time and reduces latency in communication with these devices. The Edge Computing in this case is a distributed system that consists of a set of nodes spread across different geographical area and the task is to process the data locally.

The Edge Element is responsible for the processing of data, and it takes care of the following:

1. Routing the incoming messages to one or more processing elements which can be local on that node or remote.
2. Receiving messages from one or more processing elements and sending them out to another node in the cluster if required.
3. Receiving a message from the outside and if required, it will be stored in the data queue.
4. Converting messages to an appropriate format for the destination node
5. Processing messages
6. Sending messages to another processing element on that node or remote.
7. Sending a message to the outside if required.

Edge Computing has been applied to IoT devices such as wireless sensors. and smart meters, as well as distributed computing on mobile devices. Edge computing is a component of IoT. Edge computing refers to the practice of processing data at its source rather than in a central location and can be applied to all sorts of hardware including sensors or even smartphones. The edge would be the device itself, or could be an intermediary system - for example, sending data to a centralized system. Edge computing has been around in the industry for a decade, but industries have only recently started to adopt it because of the cost savings over centralized cloud computing. The technology is still relatively new, and many organizations are still researching how it can be implemented into their businesses. The technology has the potential to improve data-analyzing and machine learning.

The new Deep Learning enabled Edge Computing is changing the way we think of IOT. In this era, we can have more than one IOT device per person and they are interconnected to each other through the Internet. These IOT devices are also connected to the Cloud. The engineer is using an edge device to execute the deep learning model and process the data, with all processing taking place at that location. The engineer then uses a web service for display purposes, for example, to generate reports or show graphical models of potential causes. of failure, or to visualize the state of a machine.

There are two phases of each processing element that can communicate with other nodes in cluster: the local and remote phases, one phase contains three separate sub-phases: The local phase, which is either one or more messages sent to the node's in-bound queue for processing by the node's local state engine. The remote phase, which is the processing of a message from the in-bound queue by one or more nodes in the remote state engine, followed by messages that are sent to the node's out-bound queue for further processing. One can think of logical communication between nodes as an alternating pattern of local and remote phases: A first messaging event with an in-bound queue, followed by a local phase of processing the message, followed by an out-bound queue event. A messaging event can be thought of as an "interaction between the internal state of a node and the external world outside that node".

DEEP LEARNING IN EDGE COMPUTING

Deep Learning is a new approach to artificial intelligence that enables edge-computing systems to learn from data and take decisions without human intervention. Edge computing is a technology that stores and processes data at the source location to reduce latency and network congestion. Edge computing has received a lot of attention in the recent years due to its advantages over conventional cloud computing. The edge platforms are designed to execute deep learning algorithms efficiently. However, such platforms are costly and limited to specific use-cases. Edge computing can be used for various purposes, including but not limited to intelligent traffic management and automation, design and manufacturing, health care, and personal assistants. The most important advantage of edge computing is that data can be analyzed at the relevant place and time without the latency imposed by a centralized system. With the rapid development of new technologies, edge computing has also found its way into people's lives. Edge computing and edge devices provide a more personalized and interactive experience for people in their daily life. A recent study found that consumers are becoming increasingly satisfied with the value of a device that is 'small enough to fit in your pocket' but powerful enough to interact through voice, touch, vision, and movement.

Edge computing is a technology that stores and processes data at the source location to reduce latency and network congestion. Edge computing has received a lot of attention in the recent years due to its advantages over conventional cloud computing. The edge platforms are designed to execute deep learning algorithms efficiently. However, such platforms are costly and limited to specific use-cases.

In this section, we will discuss three key aspects of edge computing that are worth exploring:

1. Edge computing can be implemented in almost all the software and hardware systems. Every data-intensive application or service can benefit from it in some way. The most popular examples of edge computing today include mobile voice, internet of things (IoT), and augmented reality.
2. Edge computing helps in managing the vast amount of data that data-intensive applications generate. It can reduce the number of backend servers required for running these applications, as well as their associated costs.
3. Edge computing makes it easy to manage changes in a dynamic environment by reducing service outages. Edge computing also helps in understanding the data that is being generated, while it may not be possible to collect the same level of information from the backend.
4. Edge computing can be applied to a wide range of domains and data-intensive applications, with IoT being one of them.
5. Edge computing is a cost-effective mechanism for handling tens of petabytes (10^{15} bytes) of data on a daily basis.
6. Edge computing is more resilient, secure, and cost-effective than centralized cloud computing.
7. New applications can be created that leverage the combination of edge computing and blockchain technology to create decentralized solutions.
8. The software development community needs to be aware of edge computing in order to ensure that their applications are designed for mobile devices and will be able to scale and perform optimally on edge devices.

Edge computing can be used in many different fields such as communication and transportation systems, industrial control systems, embedded systems, medical devices, etc. Edge computing has been changing the way information is processed and managed. Edge computing is a significant shift in how data is handled. The three major types of edge computing are CDN edge, IOT edge, and MEC (multi-access edge).

a) **CDN edge**

Figure 2 shows the CDN Edge diagram. CDN edge is a form of edge computing that uses content distribution networks. This type of edge computing uses computer networking to bypass traditional data centers. CDN edge can span multiple locations and includes the use of machine learning for improved network performance. This type of technology achieves near-perfect connectivity using diverse routes and redundancies across a wide area network. CDN Edge is used to improve latency from users to content providers.

Figure 2. CDN Edge

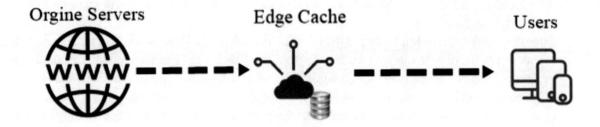

The cost of using CDN Edge versus using servers is comparable because you are only paying for what you need at that given moment. With this model, you can dodge traffic spikes and reduce latency which is critical when you are streaming video. CDN Edge also has the security advantage of not relying on a server, which can be hacked or shut down to be the middleman. The downside of CDN Edge is that it can affect performance for a short time, meaning users might see slowdowns during times of peak traffic. Reliability and Security CDN Edge can reduce latency and improve performance, but it also has increased security risks compared to a traditional CDN. It presents less vulnerabilities to attack because it is not connected directly to the internet, but its remote status means that if someone manages to compromise the server, they will have access to an enormous amount of data. The company has a security policy that covers customer data, and the company is monitored by multiple third parties that regularly investigate breaches.

b) **IoT edge**

Figure 3 shows the general IoT edge. IoT edge is a form of edge computing that refers to the growing number of data-driven, sensor-laden devices connected to the Internet. The applications and processing power on these devices can be deployed in or near their point of use to create intelligent networks. Figure 3 shows the IoT edge flow diagram. The IoT Edge is used when devices are too far away from centralized servers and power sources or when there are too many devices to connect them all at once. This can be implemented in different ways depending on the manufacturer, but typically involves independent processing of tasks. An example of this is when you turn your computer on it can be difficult for the computer to communicate with the CPU. The CPU is a centralized computing device that is usually not within reach. IoT edge devices are closer to the task and can communicate more quickly while taking on some of these responsibilities themselves.

Figure 3. IoT edge

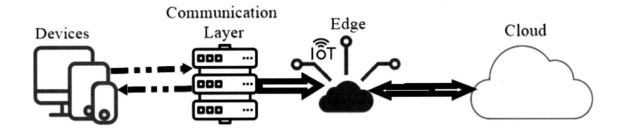

c)   **MEC (Multi-access Edge Computing)**

Figure 4 shows the Multi-Access Edge Computing. MEC reduces network congestion and improves application performance. MEC is designed to be placed in cellular base stations or other edge nodes, allowing customers to deploy new applications and services quickly and easily. By merging components of information technology and telecommunications networking, MEC allows cellular carriers to provide their radio access network (RAN) to licensed third parties, such as application developers and content providers. 'Multi-access edge' will allow for seamless collaboration across geographic distance which creates an important shift in how businesses operate today. Figure 4 shows the MEC flow diagram. The multi-access edge is an infrastructure component that will power the internet of things (IoT). IoT enables machines and devices to share data across vast distances. This technology is needed as it provides greater opportunities for people who live far away from each other to create value (Wikimedia Foundation, 2021).

Edge computing is a way to organize and connect devices, data, apps, and services to create a cohesive ecosystem. Edge computing can be achieved by leveraging two or more cloud providers. This results in the creation of an edge network that connects the cloud provider with various devices. Data centers store data on one central location and provide fast access to users. However, this centralized architecture makes data centers less secure since they can be hacked and exfiltrated. The Edge Network combines the reliability of the Cloud Network with the security of the Data Center network. This design allows users to maintain a single secure connection to their cloud provider regardless of where they are located. The Edge Network offers significant benefits for users who access their information in different geographic locations. and time zones. Users who access their information in different geographic locations and time zones may benefit from the Edge Network. The Edge Network offers a more robust connection for users who connect to their nearest edge location, which provides greater bandwidth and reliability than the core network. Users therefore experience a more high-speed data connection, as well as reduced latency. The Edge Network also offers some measure of redundancy, which is important for the integrity of the network Access Points. The Edge Network offers a more robust connection for users who connect to their nearest edge location, which provides greater bandwidth and reliability than the core network. Users therefore experience a more high-speed data connection, as well as reduced latency. The Edge Network also offers impressive download speeds.

Figure 4. Multi-Access Edge Computing (Juniper Networks, 2022)

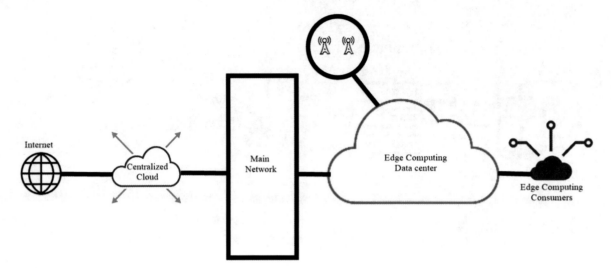

DEEP LEARNING IN IOT

The internet of things (IoT) is a network of physical objects that have been embedded with electronics, software, sensors, and connections in order to interact with one another. This section will cover what Deep Learning is and how it might be used as a technology in IoT devices.

Deep learning networks are composed of multiple layers of increasingly more abstract artificial neurons that process information in a hierarchical manner. This learning model is based on the premise that neural networks can automatically find formations in any data according to their own rules. Deep learning is a type of machine learning that is based on a set of algorithms that focus on mapping inputs from one layer to outputs in another layer. It can lead to the automation of tasks like image classification or speech recognition by systems that are self-learning. It is likely that deep learning will be used on IoT devices. To improve their ability to function autonomously without human intervention or supervision. The infrastructure component of the internet of things is just one aspect of a much broader topic of how IoT will affect society. Our society has many implications from the technology. It is expected that due to advances in technology and accessibility in the upcoming years that there will be a sharp increase in IoT-related jobs. These new jobs are needed due to the increasing use of IoT and its adoption as a technology. The internet of things (IoT) is a network of physical objects, vehicles, home appliances, and other devices with electronics, software, or sensors that connect with one another through the internet. It is expected that due to advances in technology and accessibility in the upcoming years that there will be a sharp increase in IoT-related jobs. One of the main reasons for this increase in jobs is the increasing use of IoT. More and more companies are turning to IoT as a technology due to its ability to make business more efficient, increase security, and provide customers with a better experience.

Deep Learning will be instrumental in developing more intelligent machines, which would make IoT more productive and meet our increasing needs in a better way.

1. AI can be used to help reduce military casualties, with increased accuracy and efficiency and fewer civilian casualties.

2. The use of AI for healthcare and robotics is a future that is not too far off, as the technology will provide more insight and greater understanding to medical professionals.
3. AI will make people better able to understand and predict human behavior, as it is being harnessed for such tasks.
4. The use of AI can help us avoid the risks that come with terrorism and crime.
5. It will be beneficial to those in underdeveloped countries, as children in these areas have the least access to education and technology in general.
6. Data will not be misused by malicious entities such as hackers.
7. It will allow people to monitor the effectiveness of police forces and governments in different countries and learn from their successes and mistakes.
8. There will be more transparency in the justice system, as evidence can be collected and presented on a large scale through AI.
9. The use of AI can increase public safety by catching criminals faster than traditional methods for the same cost.
10. AI could lead to a faster and more efficient court system which is beneficial for the people.-Jury members will be able to review evidence through video, audio, and transcripts.-Juries can be comprised of many jurors who don't have to travel across the country.-More accurate eyewitness testimony-Court proceedings will take less time due to automated calculations of sentence length Reduced crime rate-Court proceedings will take less time due to automated calculations of sentence length and decrease in crime rate The overall cost of criminal proceedings will be decreased due to automated calculations of sentence length and decrease in crime rate. the time spent on processing a case will decrease.
11. With over half of the US population working remotely or in a flexible work environment, AI is an important factor in worker productivity. and the future of work.
12. AI is helping to reduce global military casualties, with increased accuracy and efficiency and fewer civilian casualties.
13. AI has already been used in industries such as finance, manufacturing, and logistics to help cut costs, save time and improve productivity.

Deep learning has already proven to be successful in a number of medical and life sciences applications, such as providing an effective treatment for diabetic retinopathy by improving diagnostic accuracy. It has also been successfully used in cancer research, specifically targeting the detection of specific molecules associated with tumor growth. Deep learning is currently being used in the research and development of new drugs as well. Applications for Deep Learning include autonomous driving and self-driving cars, visualizing big data with interactive 3D visualizations, facial recognition software for law enforcement, and automated translation of text. Edge computing is a technique of deploying the computing power required for executing an application, algorithm, or data processing task at the edge of a network. Edge Computing has enabled industries to collect and analyze data in real time to create predictive insights and offer better customer service.

The following are deployment modes for edge computing: -

Cloud-based Edge Computing: where the computation is performed at one or more cloud servers and then transmitted to (or polled from) an edge device. -

Distributed Edge Architecture: which splits a workload between a cloud component and multiple edge components, all connected over the Internet. -

Centralized Edge Architecture: which offloads compute tasks exclusively to one central location, with all communication handled by a dedicated high-capacity network link. -

Hybrid Deployment Modes: where high compute tasks are offloaded to the cloud, and lower compute tasks are processed by the edge device. -

Mobile Edge Computing: where computation is spread between a mobile device, a local network infrastructure and a cloud server.

Hosted Edge: for the Hosted Edge in the cloudOne or more backend nodes are used to process data and applications. A typical configuration would have one or more public cloud servers that provide a cloud-based backend service, such as Amazon Web Services.

Publicly hosted application: This model exists at the intersection of self-hosting and hosted edge. The user is in full control of the front end and back end but uses a public cloud provider to handle managing scaling, load balancing, and so on. This model may be the most common for public cloud providers to offer as part of their service offerings.

Edge computing requires new efficiencies at three different levels; in data reception, data storage and data analysis: -

Data Receipt: The devices at the edge can be used to capture sensor data, sending information back to the cloud. This is important for applications such as smart cities. -

Data Storage: Edge storage reduces storage costs by offloading computation from the cloud and instead storing data on the device. It is also increasing available capacity. -

Data Analysis: At any point in time, edge devices can analyze voluminous data in real time, producing insights with a granularity that the cloud cannot provide. –

There are number of ways of applying edge computing. It can be done as a point solution, distributed, in the cloud and in the enterprise edge computing is a capability that many enterprises look for to help accelerate their business and build new products. One strategy for applying edge computing is to build a point solution. It can be done in the cloud, on-premises or as an in-house solution. One benefit of a point solution is that it can be easily extended to multiple locations. The downside is that you have to manage the entire infrastructure. With a distributed system, you get more flexibility because the infrastructure is managed for you by your cloud provider. However, with this approach, configuring and managing edge computing may be more difficult than with a point solution. There are various technologies that can be used to deploy edge computing such as Hadoop, Apache Spark, Kafka, Apache NiFi and more.

In-house solution: To deploy an in-house edge computing solution such as a Hadoop cluster that can be managed by an IT team.

Cloud solution: The most common way of deploying an edge computing point solution is to use a cloud-based service such as Azure. This can be done in order to have a self-managed edge computing solution.

Some simple Edge applications examples are:

1. At the edge, users can have extremely personalized experiences, because they are operating on their own devices. For example, if someone was cycling in a city and saw an interesting landmark on their way to work, they could take a picture of it or post it onto social media without ever having to leave their cycle. This Increasing the value of physical objects and services.
2. At the edge, users are able to have increasingly customizable experiences. For example, they can pick out a set of colors that they like and have physical objects printed with those colors. The value of physical things increases as the options for customization increase.

CLOUD BASED DEEP LEARNING

Cloud computing is usually defined as "computing services delivered over the Internet from a diverse set of providers". The next step in this field is Deep learning, what is Deep learning? Deep learning is a subset of machine learning and is characterized by "the use of many layers of nonlinear transformations to analyze data with hierarchical abstractions and gain high-level insight about the data". An example of this would be an artificial neural network. The essential idea behind deep learning is that these levels can be analyzed with nonlinear transformations.

The different categories of cloud computing are now being used by enterprises to gain advantages in particular markets or application domains. For example, a cloud computing service might be used for a public cloud infrastructure that supports multiple websites, an enterprise private cloud infrastructure, and a mobile phone application. A scalable computing platform that can be billed on a pay-as-you-go model or offered as a service by the provider. Fees are determined by the type of work requested and how long it takes to complete the task. A transactional store of information in which users can create, read, update, and delete documents, and share them with other users. A software-as-a-service product that is composed of a set of web services that run as part of an application in the cloud. A software as a service product can be used to build, host, and run applications such as CRM, ERP, ecommerce, or content management systems. A collection of hardware components, including servers, networking, and storage, which are used to run a software-as-a-service application. Software as a service (SaaS) is the delivery of computer software over the Internet using an online service provider's infrastructure such as cloud computing. The provider licenses use of some or all major functionalities for a fixed period of time, after which the customer is required to buy additional paid subscription service.

With new advancements in Deep Learning, Cloud Computing is not just limited to storing data or processing information like before. It is now being used by neural networks that learn on their own without any human supervision. In the short run, this can-do wonders for organizations that need many Machine Learning models to quickly create new features and strategies. Deep Learning with Cloud Computing has been used by banks, credit card companies, and insurance companies to detect fraud patterns in real time, and by using these deep learning models, the people responsible for identifying patterns in the data can spend their time on more important tasks. Deep learning models are able to process visual information at a much higher level than humans and detect objects in real time. The future of deep learning will contain new and more powerful methods for processing data and providing better outcomes for AI projects.

Cloud-based deep learning systems consume a vast amount of computing power and data. They are typically developed for specific applications or devices. such as self-driving cars or drones. For example, TensorFlow is a popular deep learning framework that is widely used to develop image recognition systems. Some of the more interesting applications of deep learning include image and speech recognition, natural language processing, cybersecurity, and control systems. Deep learning is a branch of machine learning employing techniques of data mining to achieve artificial intelligence by using neural networks with multiple layers. Over time, deep learning has been applied to many tasks where it has helped develop technologies such as computer vision, speech recognition, natural language processing and bioinformatics.

Storage Management (Cloudian, 2020):

a) **Scalability**: Because highly effective algorithms can only be developed with the assistance of large data sets, it is essential for artificial intelligence systems to be able to process massive amounts of data in a relatively short amount of time. This is because highly efficient algorithms can only be developed with the help of big data sets. Because of the sheer amount of data, there is a high level of competition for the storage space that is currently available. For instance, for Microsoft's voice recognition algorithms to be trained, the company needs continuous speech data over a period of five years. Tesla has logged data from over 1.3 billion miles of driving and is already using this information to train its autonomous vehicles. A storage system that has the potential to scale indefinitely is necessary for the administration of massive data collections.

b) **Cost Efficiency**: Scalability and cost-effectiveness are two elements that aren't always compatible with corporate storage, but they are essential for any practical storage solution. Scalability refers to the capacity to add more storage space as required. Scalability is the ability to expand the quantity of data saved without simultaneously increasing the amount of space that is necessary. The history of cost-effectiveness measurements has consistently shown that highly scalable systems tend to have overall higher costs. If there is not enough storage capacity to hold all the data that is necessary for an artificial intelligence system, then the project is doomed to fail.

c) **Software-Defined Storage Options**: Massive data sets may at times make it necessary to use hyperscale data center's, which often consist of already developed server architectures that are tailored specifically to the needs of the organisation. It is probable that the usefulness of pre-configured appliances will also be beneficial for other types of deployments.

d) **Hybrid Architecture**: The hardware must take into account the differing performance requirements that are presented by the various forms of data. In order to achieve the competing priorities of scalability and performance, computer systems need to make use of a variety of storage options rather than a single, all-encompassing strategy that is destined to fail. This is because scalability and performance are antithetical goals. Implementing an approach that is tried and true will almost always result in failure.

e) **Parallel Architecture**: A strategy based on parallel access is essential for data sets that have the potential to grow without limit. In the case that this does not take place, bottlenecks will form, and progress will be slowed down as a result.

f) **Data Durability**: Because doing so would need an excessive amount of time and would be prohibitively expensive, backing up a training data set that is several petabytes in size is not always feasible. This is because doing so would demand an excessive amount of time. You, on the other hand, cannot afford to overlook the fact that it is secure, nor can you afford to do so even if you wanted to. Another possible answer would be for the storage system to come equipped with its own security features from the factory.

g) **Data Locality**: The vast majority of the data that is used for artificial intelligence and deep learning will continue to be stored in the data centre for a variety of reasons, including compliance with regulations, performance, and cost. While some of the data that is used for artificial intelligence and deep learning will be kept in the cloud, the vast majority of it will continue to be kept in the data centre. If on-premises storage options are to maintain their viability, they will need to be able to adapt to changing needs and provide prices that are comparable to those offered by cloud-based services.

h) **Cloud Integration**: Interacting with a public cloud is necessary for a variety of reasons, the most significant of which are described in the following paragraphs. This is true regardless of the physical location at where the data is stored. To begin, the great majority of new work in the domains of AI and DL is currently being done on the cloud. These fields include artificial intelligence (AI) and deep learning (DL). When it comes to making advantage of cloud-native technologies, on-premises solutions that also embrace cloud computing will give the most degree of flexibility possible. In addition, as new data is produced and analyzed, we may anticipate seeing an ongoing flow of information both into and out of the cloud. Something like this is definitely something that we should anticipate seeing. This process needs to be simplified by an on-premises solution rather than made more challenging in order to better serve the demands of the organisation.

DEEP LEARNING ENABLED EDGE COMPUTING AND IOT

Edge computing and IoT are two of the most talked about topics in the tech industry these days. They are closely tied together and there is a lot of potential for businesses that invest in them. Edge computing is an emerging field that's getting attention from many vendors and researchers. The data generated by IoT devices is usually too large and complex for cloud-based storage and processing. That's why edge computing can handle data at the source of generation in real time, which speeds up the process of decision making.

Edge computing enables real-time interactions between IoT devices and other computing systems to provide faster responses to queries than possible from analysis in a central cloud-based data center. IoT (Internet of Things) technology connects machines to the internet around us, enabling them to collect and share data. These two trends are making the IoT spectrum the most dynamic growth area in next-generation internet technology.

The edge device might have access to more specific contextual details than can be inferred from a global view of the IoT network. Edge intelligence is also expected to lower total energy consumption for the IoT by enabling more power efficient operations at the device level without requiring extensive processing in centralized locations. IoT networks are set to become increasingly important as the world comes to rely on them for resource allocation and decision-making. As such, it is important to know that these networks are subject to new risks and vulnerabilities not traditionally associated with traditional computing environments. Networked devices in IoT environments represent a unique type of target for cybercriminals because of their complexity, scale, and the fact that they are often poorly secured.

Edge computing is a technique for coping with the increasing demand for streaming data. This is especially important in case of applications that involve computationally intensive tasks such as driverless cars, autonomous drones, and smart cities. Edge computing is the provision of computing, big data analytics, and storage in such a way that the data comes to the processing power and not vice versa. It relies on a decentralized approach where computational resources are provided at the edge of networks. Edge computing, which is enabled by deep learning enabled devices, will bring us the next wave of innovation with IoT applications. A possible use for deep learning is for self-driving cars. With new frameworks and techniques, it will be possible to build step-by-step policies where different components of the car learn from each other. Today's self-driving cars are limited by what they can see with their cameras, but with advances in algorithms and hardware, it is likely that tomorrow's cars will be able to see 360 degrees around themselves and react more quickly. There is a lot to love about self-driving cars, but one of these things is that they will likely reduce the number of accidents caused by human error. Computers are not only better at spotting potential hazards than humans, but they can also handle situations without causing unnecessary harm. Computers can do a lot of things that are outside of human capability, such as scanning for potential hazards and keeping the environment safe.

The rise of these decentralized devices has led to a new approach in data processing at the edge of the network. The edge is where much of the data processing takes place, and this greatly reduces latency by making users make decisions based on real-time information. Increasingly, companies are employing artificial intelligence (AI) powered solutions for edge computing including deep neural networks (DNNs) which are trained locally at the edge device itself with only occasional connection back to a central server or storage location for updates. The rise of DNNs has been aided by the success of this approach in industries such as computer vision and machine learning. The convergence of these fields with the development of edge computing devices creates a new opportunity for AI to be deployed at the edge device level. This is particularly true when considering that data which needs to be processed needs to be very small-scale. The processor's job is to take sensor data and convert it into usable data. Data analysis software then takes the processed data and produces actionable insights. This is an important distinction because it means that these two software programs work in tandem. One will be responsible for the conversion and the other will be responsible for the analysis, with each playing its role in providing insight. Along with a company's data analysis software, they may also choose to implement tools like predictive analytics or data science machine learning models to generate insights. Predictive analytics can be used to help companies predict which customers are likely to churn, or the likelihood that a customer will purchase another product in the future. The model would provide an estimate of those probabilities and allow for adjustments, should new information come to light. Figure 5 shows the Deep Learning Enabled Edge Computing and IoT.

Figure 5. Deep Learning Enabled Edge Computing and IoT

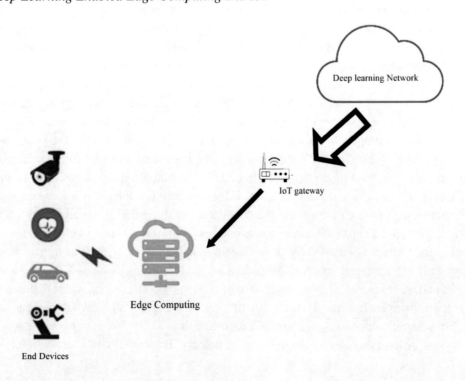

Data science machine learning models, on the other hand, leverage advanced methods in order to generate predictions with a high degree of accuracy. Data science machine learning models are computationally intensive and typically require large amounts of data to be properly represented in the model. Data scientists use machine learning models to extract insights into the behavior of a population based on information collected from a sample. The data science community is standardizing and setting guidelines for the creation, design, and use of machine learning models.

APPLICATION STUDY

Internet of Robotic Things

The Internet of Robotic Things (IoRT) mixes IoT with robotics. It's a novel concept in which autonomous robots communicate with one another by combining data from numerous sensors to do complex jobs. The integration of IoT/IIoT, AI, and robotics accelerates IoRT application development by increasing contextually aware decision-making help for resolving complex tasks and enabling machine intelligence. This trend allows for more efficient programming methods, tools, and controls, as well as the use of basic semantic web technologies and robotic object interfaces (Vermesan, et.al, 2020).

The essential characteristics and functional blocks of IoRT systems

a. **Perception and sense—** The IoRT system's capacity to perceive its surroundings through a range of equipment like as microphones, ultrasonic, radar, LiDAR, cameras, and antennas. The data collected by perception devices at the robotic object and application levels must be in a format that can be utilized by different and distinctive cognitive processes.

b. **Processing—** More efficient data processing methodologies (energy, speed, code size, etc.) applied into robotic objects and across dispersed settings are employed for optimal information processing at the local, edge, and cloud levels.

c. **Cognition and intelligence—** the function that generates data and combines it with sensor and contextual inputs to provide intelligence in the form of judgments or knowledge in order to regulate the system's activities.

d. **Planning—** the capacity to plan actions based on the mission, fleet operations, data from other robotic entities, people, animals, the environment, fleet management, and other aspects.

e. **Decision and control—** The IoRT system can create a trajectory, choose a direction, act by sensing/actuating/moving/manipulating, manage energy depending on the task and context, diagnose and handle difficulties, and participate in reactive control.

f. **Propulsion—** the ability of an IoRT system to perform tasks, move in coordinated space in response to its environment (static or dynamic), and control that movement based on the surrounding conditions—as defined by safe collective system and fleet operations—by following a planned trajectory with steering, body movements, braking, and body stabilization.

g. **Connectivity—** The ability of the IoRT system to connect with anything and anyone at any time via various paths/networks and services, enabling the required level of autonomy and capacity to build and make decisions based on the collective exchange of information among robotic things, humans, infrastructure, and other IoT/IIoT applications.

h.   **Storage of data/information/knowledge and energy**— the capacity to store data, knowledge, and expertise locally as well as remotely (memory, cloud, other robotic devices, infrastructure), as well as the energy required for propulsion (e.g., batteries for self-charging or as a source of pre-charged energy).

Medical Imaging and E-Heath

Deep learning is applied particularly to medical imaging analysis: using MRI scans and other digital images, deep neural networks have been trained to identify pictures of certain types of cancerous lesions on mammograms with an accuracy rate higher than that of a human expert. To learn to detect cancerous lesions on mammograms, machines analyze thousands of digital images labeled as either healthy or with cancerous lesions to predict which images are which. The model learns by analyzing the data and observing patterns, such as specific shapes of cells or shadows. DLPRS may be able to help diagnose skin diseases from photos or video clips (U.S. National Library of Medicine, 2022). The majority of e-health efforts are concentrated on the development of systems for remote health monitoring that are underpinned by the Internet of Things (IoT). The term "e-Health" refers to the new "consumer-centered paradigm" of health systems, which integrates health science and technology with information and communication technologies to produce positive effects on people's health both on an individual and societal scale. This paradigm shift was brought about as a result of the rise of the internet and the widespread use of mobile devices. This paradigm change came about as a direct consequence of the proliferation of mobile device usage in conjunction with the emergence of the internet (Dr. M. Sathya et al, 2022).

Autonomous Vehicles

Self-driving automobiles are vehicles that are capable of sensing their environment and navigating without the assistance of humans. They use inputs from sensors such as cameras, sonar, and GPS to detect obstacles on the road, track lane lines and maintain a safe distance from other traffic. They can also steer and brake automatically to avoid collisions. Autonomous vehicles are self-driving cars that can sense, decide, and act with little or no human input. They do not require a steering wheel, brake pedal or gas pedal to operate. Autonomous cars have been around for decades (Dr. Amuthan Nallathambi et al., 2022). Smart materials are more important to improve the autonomous vehicle performance with IoT systems (Sivakumar, N., & Kanagasabapathy, H., 2018).

Human Facial Recognition

The recent innovation of Deep Learning enables AI to perform tasks without the need for human input or explicit instructions. It can be used in applications that require image recognition, such as video surveillance and facial recognition. Human Facial Recognition is used in surveillance videos to automatically identify people by comparing faces in database with faces seen in camera feed. "The main benefits of facial recognition are convenience, ease of use, and the elimination of manual data entry." In a CCTV camera, facial recognition is the use of software to compare all the faces captured over time with stored or live face images in order to automatically identify specific people. The comparison is based on features of faces including color, expression, shape, and texture (Dr. N. Amuthan et al., 2022).

Smart Garbage Monitoring System

Due to the detrimental effects that junk trash has on the ecology in its immediate environment, the monitoring, collection, and management of garbage trash have emerged as one of the most pressing issues of our day. The manual monitoring and collecting of waste are a time-consuming and labor-intensive procedure that requires a large number of personnel and a significant investment of resources. This procedure likewise needs a significant amount of time to complete. An overview of Thingspeak, an open platform for the Internet of Things that will form the foundation of a waste monitoring system, is presented in this article. This arrangement has a load cell, an ultrasonic sensor, and a Wi-Fi module. The microcontroller in this configuration is an Arduino. The information that is gathered from the ultrasonic sensor as well as the load cell is sent to the Arduino microcontroller to be processed. A load cell is used to detect how much weight the full bin is holding, and an ultrasonic sensor is used to determine how deep the rubbish is. Both of these measurements are carried out by the same device. A liquid crystal display (LCD) screen shows the information. The aforementioned information will be uploaded to the worldwide web thanks to the Wi-Fi module's efforts. Thingspeak, which is a platform for the internet of things (IoT) that is open to the general public and free to use, is what is used to monitor the rubbish collection system. If this method is implemented, it will be much easier for the administrator to keep track of the timetable for trash collection as well as the routes (Bhuvaneswari, T. et al, 2020).

Simple Deep Learning Algorithm to Predict Weather Forecast

The Deep Learning Algorithm is used to predict the weather forecast. These algorithms have been improving their predictions over time to help with the accuracy. of weather forecasts. It can be used for short-term and long-term forecasts. Figure 5 shows the High-Level Architecture Flow of weather forecast prediction. The system predicts the weather forecast for current or future using deep learning from IoT sensor data. It captures the data from IoT device Raspberry Pi online simulator which will act as IoT device, and it is a compatible with real Pi devices. It collects temperature and humidity from the geolocation or region and sends them into deep learning to predict whether it will be rainfall or not. This simulator has BME280 sensor and a LED. It sends the sensor data in real time into Azure IoT Hub.

Figure 6. High Level Architecture Flow

Once IoT hub receives the data, it will be sent to Azure deep learning / machine learning platform to predict the outcome. In Deep learning, we do the following steps such as collect the training data, Prepare the data (clean and EDA), Train or model, deployment, run and production support or maintain.

The end-to-end practical example or solution can be implemented with real raspberry Pi IoT device. Here the simulator is used instead of real hardware device but output from hardware or simulator is the same. The entire solution is developed by python programming language and azure cloud platform. The sample working code will be downloaded from the following github repository (https://github.com/kan-nannova/DeepLearningEnabledIoTDevices) (Kannannova, 2022).

For making the end-to-solution working, we need to do the following steps and configurations

Step 1: Create IoT Hub in Azure as below, Figure 6 shows the IoT Hub Creation

Login into azure using subscription id and go to IoT hub

Figure 7. IoT Hub Creation

Once click then the deployment will take place and once done, we get the following, Figure 7 shows the IoT Creation and Deployment Completion

Figure 8. IoT Creation and Deployment Completion

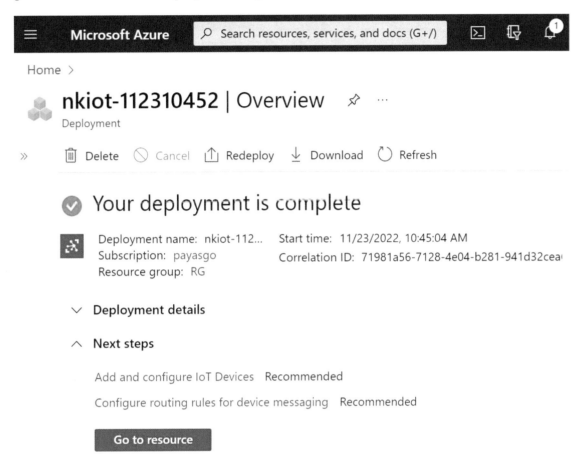

Now we need to configure the IoT device or Edge in IoT Hub and their details are given below, Figure 8 shows the register IoT Device to IoT hub.

Figure 9. Register IoT Device to IoT Hub

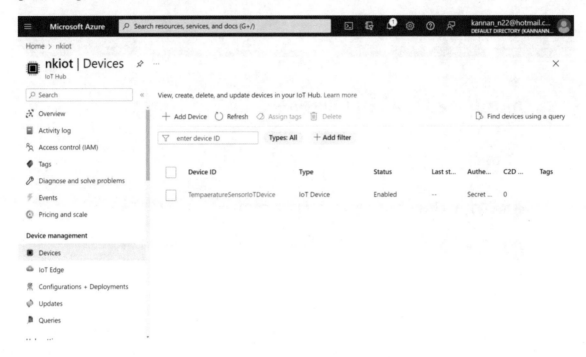

Once done, copy the connection string from device registration as below, Figure 9 shows the Connection String Details

Figure 10. Connection String Details

Step 2: Figure 10 shows the Raspberry IoT device simulator. Azure provides a few IoT simulators and here the raspberry pi temperature sensor used. We can access the simulator through https://sanajitghosh. medium.com/azure-iot-with-raspberry-pi-emulator-and-temperature-sensor-663490262c2d. We need to

update the connection string which we copied from step 1 as below into simulator HostName=<u>nkiot.</u> <u>azure-devices.net</u>; DeviceId=TemperatureSensorIoTDevice;SharedAccessKey=

Figure 11. Raspberry IoT Device Simulator

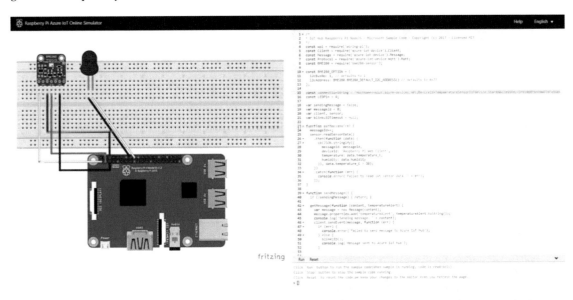

Step 3: Figure 11shows the Azure stream analytics for reading data from IoT device. Create Stream Analytics and configure the input, output, and query. The raspberry pi is input here, and storage contained is output here. the query will be used to fetch the data from input device and insert them into output container.

Figure 12. Azure Stream Analytics for reading data from IoT Device

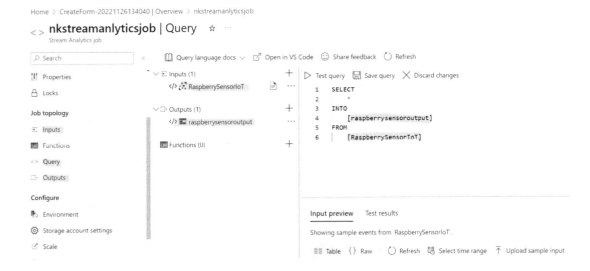

Store the data into Azure Storage-Container, Figure 12 shows the Azure Storage Container

Figure 13. Azure Storage Container

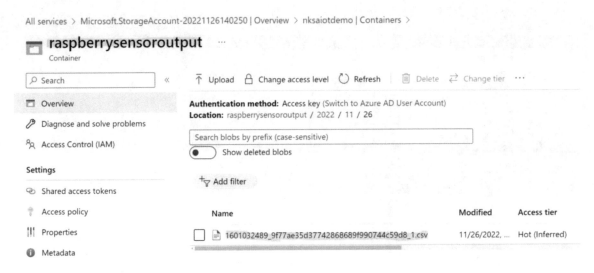

The sample IoT sensor data is shown below, Figure 13 shows the sample IoT sensor data

Figure 14. Sample IoT sensor data

	messageId	deviceId	temperature	humidity	EventProcessedUtcTime	PartitionId	EventEnqueuedUtcTime	IoTHub
2	1	Raspberry Pi Web Client	20.4511996	76.25564181	2022-11-26T19:36:15.7614124Z	1	2022-11-26T19:35:30.7740000Z	Record
3	2	Raspberry Pi Web Client	23.1241905	76.55011282	2022-11-26T19:36:15.8005056Z	1	2022-11-26T19:35:32.6450000Z	Record
4	3	Raspberry Pi Web Client	30.16069948	66.26066503	2022-11-26T19:36:15.8015771Z	1	2022-11-26T19:35:34.6300000Z	Record
5	4	Raspberry Pi Web Client	20.64225066	76.70888478	2022-11-26T19:36:15.8016692Z	1	2022-11-26T19:35:36.6460000Z	Record
6	5	Raspberry Pi Web Client	26.13621852	63.41034972	2022-11-26T19:36:15.8017067Z	1	2022-11-26T19:35:38.6460000Z	Record
7	6	Raspberry Pi Web Client	29.32954129	77.03891752	2022-11-26T19:36:15.8017385Z	1	2022-11-26T19:35:40.6310000Z	Record
8	7	Raspberry Pi Web Client	28.66311161	72.19681907	2022-11-26T19:36:15.8017740Z	1	2022-11-26T19:35:42.6370000Z	Record
9	8	Raspberry Pi Web Client	21.56008738	78.17124227	2022-11-26T19:36:15.8018051Z	1	2022-11-26T19:35:44.6370000Z	Record
10	9	Raspberry Pi Web Client	26.74489717	74.22206285	2022-11-26T19:36:15.8018359Z	1	2022-11-26T19:35:46.6380000Z	Record
11	10	Raspberry Pi Web Client	21.65035805	69.95768113	2022-11-26T19:36:15.8018656Z	1	2022-11-26T19:35:48.6380000Z	Record
12	11	Raspberry Pi Web Client	26.02831767	62.11737185	2022-11-26T19:36:15.8018959Z	1	2022-11-26T19:35:50.6390000Z	Record
13	12	Raspberry Pi Web Client	20.71668239	64.61817127	2022-11-26T19:36:15.8019268Z	1	2022-11-26T19:35:52.6390000Z	Record
14	13	Raspberry Pi Web Client	21.92080218	68.91547488	2022-11-26T19:36:15.8019570Z	1	2022-11-26T19:35:54.6390000Z	Record
15	14	Raspberry Pi Web Client	30.53477454	68.90825072	2022-11-26T19:36:15.8019876Z	1	2022-11-26T19:35:56.6550000Z	Record
16	15	Raspberry Pi Web Client	21.43260309	73.16477535	2022-11-26T19:36:15.8020236Z	1	2022-11-26T19:35:58.6390000Z	Record
17	16	Raspberry Pi Web Client	28.63375393	73.73454205	2022-11-26T19:36:15.8020566Z	1	2022-11-26T19:36:00.9220000Z	Record
18	17	Raspberry Pi Web Client	25.07531388	69.28787788	2022-11-26T19:36:15.8020872Z	1	2022-11-26T19:36:02.8910000Z	Record
19	18	Raspberry Pi Web Client	29.83077208	67.25578529	2022-11-26T19:36:15.8021200Z	1	2022-11-26T19:36:04.8750000Z	Record

Step 4: Figure 14 shows the deep learning algorithm, Apply Deep Learning Algorithm to predict weather forecast. We are using the linear regression algorithms with deep learning for prediction. It accepts the temperature, humidity, fast history rainfall status and predicts the current or future weather conditions.

Figure 15. Deep Learning Algorithm

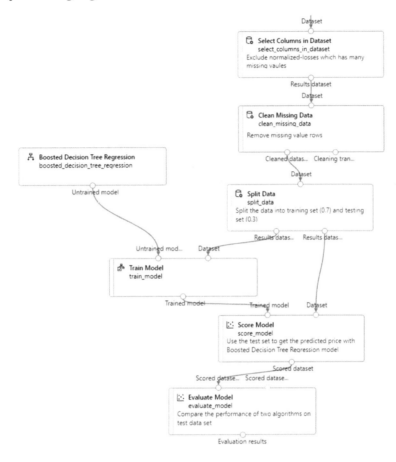

CONCLUSION

To conclude, deep learning and edge computing are two technologies that are developing fast and will be a challenge to business models. Edge computing is a term used to describe the distribution of computing tasks or workloads across multiple devices, data centers, or other computing resources. These two technologies are a challenge to business models because they can be used for good and bad purposes. The Internet of Things, some experts claim that the IoT is the world's fastest growing technology, and it will soon become a billion-dollar industry. The IoT has been a reality for years, but people are just starting to realize how significant it is. More and more devices are being connected to the Internet each day as they become more technologically advanced. The IoT is extremely varied, with devices ranging from appliances like coffee machines to cars. The IoT can help companies and individuals save time, money, and energy. While the IoT is an exciting new technology that has many benefits, it also presents a significant amount of risks due to its complexity.

The internet of things some experts claim that the IoT is the world's fastest growing technology, and it will soon become a billion-dollar industry. The IoT has an estimated $3.9 trillion value mainly due to its efficiency, ease of use, and convenience. The IoT is a system that allows appliances like washing machines, fridges, and heating systems to connect to the internet through sensors and software applications. These aspects allow the IoT to monitor itself remotely for changes in performance as well as implement automatic actions so that users need not take additional steps. The IoT is a system that allows appliances like washing machines, fridges, and heating systems to connect to the internet through sensors and software applications. These aspects allow the IoT to monitor itself remotely for changes in performance as well as implement automatic actions so that users need not take additional steps.

The IoT is extremely varied, with devices ranging from appliances like coffee machines to cars. And because the Internet can now connect these devices, many people are concerned that this technology could be used to turn them into "smart" appliances. There are many advantages of these two technologies, but they also bring challenges to the businesses. There are possible solutions to these challenges. How do you see deep learning impacting business models? Deep learning will impact business models in many ways. One way is in the recommendation engines. With deep learning, you can now recommend products to consumers that are more specific according to their needs. For example, if a consumer wants to buy a new espresso machine, there is a possibility that they will be recommended for buying an espresso maker or an espresso machine with milk frothier.

Another way deep learning impacts business models is that they could be applied to product recommendations. For example, if a consumer is looking for a new mattress, the deep learning algorithm might be able to recommend a better-quality mattress that was designed by the manufacturer of specific types of mattresses. It could also recommend other types of furniture such as beds and sofas. Deep learning enables AI applications that are often hard for humans to learn, such as recognizing faces in photographs. The algorithm is fed millions of images and learns how to identify the important features of a face, like eyebrows and lips. Keep your apps up to date with new AI technologies that could improve user experience.

A common use for deep learning is image recognition. Deep learning algorithms allow applications like the app to recognize a photo of a person and automatically suggest that user's name. In order for deep learning applications to work, developers must include the latest AI technologies in their code. Otherwise, users may experience unexpected results due to outdated features. For example, it can be used to predict consumers' spending and the most suitable product for them before they even know what they want or need. It is also helping create a new class of "smart businesses" that are more responsive to their customers' needs. "On the other hand, companies who leverage this disruptive technology will not only benefit from cost-saving but also gain insights into how other users interact with their products. In the future, deep learning might be used in more complicated fields like medicine, where it will be able to identify diseases and predict when they will come up.

REFERENCES

Amuthan, N. (2022). *Smart Surveillance System with Facial Recognition and Image-Processing Approach using AI*. 202241013636.

Bhuvaneswari, T., Hossen, J., Amir Hamzah, N. A., Velrajkumar, P., & Hong Jack, O. (2020). Internet of things (IOT) based Smart Garbage Monitoring System. *Indonesian Journal of Electrical Engineering and Computer Science*, 20(2), 736. doi:10.11591/ijeecs.v20.i2.pp736-743

Cloudian (2020, August 11). *Eight Storage Requirements for AI and Deep Learning.* https://cloudian.com/resource/data-sheets/eight-storage-requirements-artificial-intelligence-deep-learning/

Juniper Networks. (2022). What is multi-access edge computing? *Juniper.* https://www.juniper.net/us/en/research-topics/what-is-multi-access-edge-computing.html

Kannannova. (2022). *Kannannova/deeplearningenablediotdevices.* https://github.com/kannannova/DeepLearningEnabledIoTDevices

Nallathambi, A. (2022). *Autonomous Electric Vehicles Auto Monitor and Control.* 202241015720.

Sathya, M., Nirmala, S., Shivananda, S., Jeyaseelan. V. D., & Amutha, R. (2022). Smart E-Health Records using IoT. *International Journal of All Research Education and Scientific Methods, 10*(3), 2488–2493. http://www.ijaresm.com/uploaded_files/document_file/Dr.M_.Sathya_march_2022_l4jL.pdf

Sivakumar, N., & Kanagasabapathy, H. (2018). Optimization of Parameters of Cantilever Beam Using Novel Bio-Inspired Algorithms: A Comparative Approach. *Journal of Computational and Theoretical Nanoscience, 15*(1), 66–77. doi:10.1166/jctn.2018.7057

U.S. National Library of Medicine. (2022). *National Center for Biotechnology Information.* NCBI. https://www.ncbi.nlm.nih.gov/

Vermesan, O., Bahr, R., Ottella, M., Serrano, M., Karlsen, T., Wahlstrøm, T., Sand, H. E., Ashwathnarayan, M., & Gamba, M. T. (2020). Internet of robotic things intelligent connectivity and platforms. *Frontiers.* https://www.frontiersin.org/articles/10.3389/frobt.2020.00104/full

Wikimedia Foundation. (2021, July 27). Multi-access Edge Computing. *Wikipedia.* https://en.wikipedia.org/wiki/Multi-access_edge_computing

Chapter 5
Distributed Deep Learning for IoT

Amuthan Nallathambi

https://orcid.org/0000-0001-8830-3353

AMC Engineering College, Bengaluru, India

Sivakumar N.

Department of Mechanical Engineering, India

Velrajkumar P.

CMR Institute of Technology, Visvesvaraya Technological University, India

ABSTRACT

Distributed deep learning is a type of machine learning that uses neural networks to learn and make predictions at scale. This is achieved by having many different computer systems that are connected via the internet. This allows for more parallel processing and faster results. In addition, when it comes to IoT, this type of technology can be used in conjunction with sensors and other devices to create more accurate predictions about the environment around us. Distributed deep learning can be used in many ways with the IoT because it can be applied to various aspects of IoT data processing, such as image recognition, speech recognition, natural language processing (NLP), or anomaly detection. The neural net is the most computationally intensive component of the system, and it requires a significant amount of energy. To make this system more cost-effective, there are two ways to lower the number of memory accesses: by reducing the size of images (so precision decreases), or by increasing network bandwidth so that there are fewer loop iterations required for each memory access.

INTRODUCTION

Deep neural networks are able to recognize objects in an image through pattern recognition and learn from these patterns to recognize text in a piece of text. Because of the way deep neural networks operate, they are able to train themselves with minimal supervision. This makes them a popular choice for machine learning and artificial intelligence applications because they can learn on their own rather than

DOI: 10.4018/978-1-6684-6275-1.ch005

be programmed explicitly (Wikimedia Foundation, 2022, July 9). A few notable examples of deep neural networks in action are Google Translate, AlphaGo, and the Microsoft Tay Twitter bot.

In the typical method of training for deep learning, users first upload a local dataset to a cloud centre, where it is then trained using the huge computer capabilities of the cloud centre. The uploading of a local dataset to a centralized cloud centre that is controlled by a third party puts the user's data privacy at risk. Additionally, the uploading of multimedia data will use up a lot of mobile users' bandwidth as well as the storage space of the cloud centre, making it difficult to add more edge devices. We present an edge-enabled distributed deep learning platform that tackles these two difficulties by dividing a conventional deep learning training network into a front subnetwork and a rear subnetwork. This allows the platform to make use of distributed computing resources. In particular, the front subnetwork, which is comprised of multiple layers, is established in close proximity to the data source and trained independently at each edge device using the information that is local to that device. In order for the back subnetwork to be trained at a later time, the outputs of all of the front subnetworks are transferred to the back subnetwork, which is installed in a cloud data centre (Sun, Q., 2021).

Because edge devices do not send their original data to the cloud centre, the platform safeguards the data's confidentiality while still allowing for rapid expansion. On top of that, there are two more steps taken to protect data privacy: asymmetric encryption technology is used to make sure that parameters sent between edge servers and the cloud centre are safe and complete, and blockchain technology is used to track what people do on this platform and build trust among them. Both of these technologies are used to ensure that parameters sent between edge servers and the cloud centre are safe and complete.

In neural networks, there are a million parameters that make up the model, and learning these parameters requires a massive amount of data. This approach is time-consuming and computationally costly. A new approach to artificial neural networks is tackling one of the main problems in AI: training and deployment. Distributed Deep Learning (DDL) uses a simple technique that can potentially reduce the typical AI development time by half., Distributed deep learning allows for parallel experiments over many devices in order to reduce training time. This is accomplished with the use of remote GPUs, software containers, and cloud computing services. Using this, the company is able to train deep learning models with a single CPU in just a few hours. As well as this, it's possible to train models with many CPU cores as the power of two is still being used.

The future of artificial intelligence will likely be powered by DDL, which will help improve the usability, performance, and accuracy of the systems. DDL is a data-driven decision-making tool that helps in the execution of business strategies by providing algorithms and insights that can be used as models. These models are capable of predicting outcomes, identifying high risks, and optimizing performance.

The following are the features of Decision Lens:

- Provides insights and actionable information to help companies make better decisions.
- Challenges and opportunities based on unique business challenges -Predicts outcomes (both positive and negative) in a variety of industries.
- Helps identify high-risk areas that can improve performance by highlighting promising

Artificial intelligence (AI) has been the topic of a lot of speculation and debate in recent years. The future of AI is bright as scientists continue to tinker with the technology. With advancements in machine learning, machine learning algorithms will be used to power the future of AI and improve its usability, performance, and accuracy as well. As AI becomes more widespread, the need for a standardized framework for machine learning algorithms will become apparent. In order to establish a standard framework, the following are key factors that need to be addressed:

1. The development of machine learning (ML) frameworks in multiple languages and technologies is a must.
2. The creation of a global ML ecosystem with open standards governing interoperability.
3. The promotion of ML for enabling and empowering the most vulnerable sectors in society, including children and people living with disabilities.
4. The application of AI to solve social issues such as: societal challenges; inequality; access to education/healthcare; poverty; environmental sustainability Research in AI varies in scope and approach. AI can be applied to diverse fields such as astronomy, mathematics, medicine, finance, and robotics.

Distributed Deep Learning (DDL) is a new way of using computers to supercharge machine learning algorithms. DDL can be applied to any type of learning problem. DDL puts artificial intelligence more into the hands of regular people than ever before. This technology enables people without extensive technical knowledge to learn and master new skills with less effort and at a much faster rate than traditional methods would let you do. Distributed deep learning offers benefits such as not having to buy and maintain a large amount of hardware, which can be costly. More importantly, this approach allows for scalability in performance for a larger range of tasks and more customers. Scaling neural networks is a challenging task. In theory, distributed deep learning is scalable, yet in practice it often has to be modified or even rebuilt from scratch. Algorithms that make use of deep learning have become popular across multiple industries, from finance to manufacturing (Sait, S. 2021). Distributed deep learning is a type of machine learning that applies techniques to allow the processing of many individual computations over large datasets. It was previously used in the field of computer vision but has since been applied to many other fields. Distributed deep learning has been made possible by recent advances in multi-core, multi-threading, and graphics processing units (GPU).

Figure 1. Basic Distributed Deep Learning

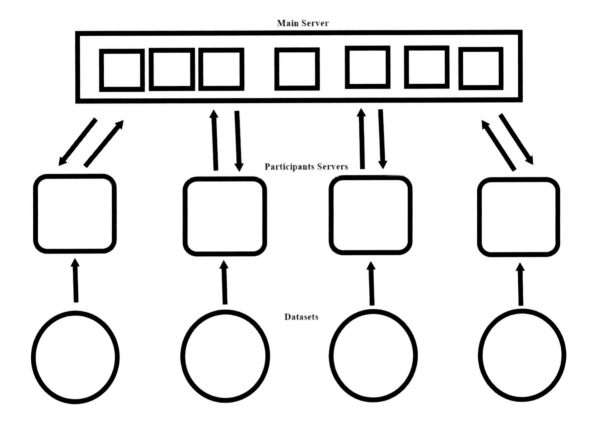

Figure 1. shows the Basic Distributed deep learning. The two powerful ways in deep learning is (i) data parallelization or (ii) model parallelization (Poulopoulos, D. 2021). Distributed deep learning for wavelength analysis is a new technology that can help save energy and improve quality of life in the future. The idea of distributed deep learning for wavelength analysis is to send images from different cameras in the same area to a centralized server, which then sends them back to the different cameras. The server uses deep learning algorithms to identify objects and compare them with each other. The algorithms can then determine whether a person is walking, running, or standing still. The server will also be able to compare whatever object it is with the images of other objects in the same area and find out how similar they are. While this helps in determining who's doing what, we're not there yet when it comes to determining what the object is. For example, if the server is using facial recognition to find out who the person in an image is, it needs to know what those people look like in order to compare them. wavelength Distributed deep learning for wavelength analysis has many potential applications across industries such as security, medicine, and manufacturing. It is also applicable for use in home appliances such as smart TVs or even drones (Dmaa, 2022).

DISTRIBUTED DEEP LEARNING AND HOW DOES IT WORK IN THE IOT?

Distributed Deep Learning is a new approach to AI that is based on the idea of using many small computers instead of just one. This allows for more parallel processing and faster results. In addition, when it comes to IoT, this type of technology can be used in conjunction with sensors and other devices in order to create more accurate predictions about the environment around us. For example, with the help of their AI solution, it is possible for them to connect sensors in manufacturing facilities and have them process information without having any humans involved. This allows companies to create more accurate data, which enables them to make better decisions.

The Internet of Things is an emerging technology that will have a huge impact on the automation industry. The automation industry is one of the most important sectors in the manufacturing and service sector. The IoT helps automate processes while also making it possible for machines to communicate with each other and make decisions without human intervention. Distributed deep learning is also applicable to the IoT because it is basically just a set of algorithms that can process data from all sensors. These algorithms can be implemented to automatically detect certain events, such as an intrusion or fire in an industrial facility.

Distributed deep learning is a type of machine learning that uses neural networks to learn and make predictions at scale. This is achieved by having many different computer systems that are connected via the internet. The IoT is a term for the network of devices and sensors that are connected to the internet. These devices are used in homes, offices, hospitals, and other places for everyday tasks like home automation, remote monitoring, and smart factories. The IoT is growing exponentially with many applications across many industries.

Distributed deep learning can be used in many different ways with the IoT because it can be applied to various aspects of IoT data processing such as image recognition, speech recognition, natural language processing (NLP), or anomaly detection.

THE FUTURE OF THE INTERNET OF THINGS

The Internet of Things (IoT) is a network of physical objects that are able to connect and exchange data. It provides automation, convenience, security, and efficiency in the workplace. IoT technology has become a well-known topic of discussion in recent years due to the implications it has on our lives. The internet of things has given rise to billions of interconnected devices that are able to collect data from sensors. With these sensors come problems such as security issues like password cracking, etc. Deep learning tools can help solve these problems with ease by creating a better platform for the IoT future. Deep Learning is the application of neural network models that receive signals from connected devices. These models are powerful at inferences and predictions and have been used in various applications, such as speech recognition, spam filtering, image recognition, and text summarization. Deep learning is an umbrella term, which includes many models, such as neural networks, Bayesian networks and support vector machines. These models can be characterized as "training deep" because they are trained to learn rather than programmed to solve problems.

In the future, we will be seeing more and more internet-connected devices. We need to prepare for this shift by preparing for the future of IoT technology. Here are some tips on how to prepare for the future of IoT technology:

1. Understand what IoT is and what it can do:
2. To understand how it works,
3. Understand your company's needs:
4. Learn about security issues with IoT technology:
5. Make sure you have adequate insurance coverage:
6. Conduct a risk assessment:
7. Understand how your company can benefit from IoT technology:

Manufacturing industry: In the manufacturing industry, IoT can be used to collect data on equipment such as production lines. This helps in making decisions about the production process, such as how many products are being made per hour or what machines need to be replaced in order for efficiency to increase.

Healthcare industry: IoT can help healthcare organizations track patients' health and reduce medical errors by providing real-time information about the status of machines and patients. Healthcare organizations are developing methods to track patients' health remotely. The IoT can help these organizations reduce medical errors by providing real-time information about the status of machines and patients, such as their heart rates or blood oxygen levels. Artificial intelligence medical applications are continuously being tested in order to increase the efficiency of healthcare providers. AI is utilized as part of a diagnostic application, which assists doctors with interpreting MRI scans, diagnosing patients, and predicting different outcomes based on their symptoms. The AI system can also identify abnormalities within specific organs that help doctors determine the severity of a potential disease. Some examples of AI in healthcare are: - Automatic diagnosis of diseases based on biotechnological information. AI is used to detect patterns and make predictions based on symptoms that doctors have never seen before. Nurses can use this system to predict patient outcomes in order to optimize treatments. This system can be used to identify a patient's symptoms and determine the right medicine to give them. These are some examples of how AI is impacting healthcare.

Retail industry: The retail industry can use IoT to monitor supply chains, which helps retailers reduce their inventory costs and improve customer service. In the retail industry, the IoT can help companies monitor supply chains to reduce inventory costs, improve customer service, and provide real-time information about items in stock. IoT is used by businesses for many purposes: Smart factories track production levels and adjust manufacturing methods; accordingly, utilities detect leaks remotely; retailers break down sales by region and collect customer data; and more. Also, Retailers use IoT for better customer service. They can reduce associated costs, increase store revenue, and improve the customers' shopping experience. Companies like Home Depot are using IoT in retail to offer better customer service and reduce associated costs.

Transportation: The transportation industry can use IoT to monitor the behavior of cars, trucks, trains, and other vehicles, as well as the behavior of travelers. IoT is used in transportation to monitor cars, trucks, trains, and other vehicles, as well as the behavior of travelers. Transportation companies can use IoT for many purposes: Smart cities use sensors to track traffic patterns; smart buses optimize routes and reduce stops; self-driving cars adjust their speed according to the surrounding traffic.

Utilities: Utilities can use the IoT to monitor energy usage and detect leaks remotely, especially in crumbling infrastructure. Utilities use IoT for a variety of purposes, like monitoring energy usage and detecting leaks remotely (especially in crumbling infrastructure).

Manufacturers: Manufacturers are using the Internet of Things to automate production by tracking factory conditions and adjusting manufacturing methods accordingly. Companies like Siemens and

Amazon are using IoT in manufacturing to automate production, explore new markets, and make supply chains more efficient.

IoT devices generate a large amount of data, especially now with cars and other IoT-enabled appliances. We can use this information to train AI models with better accuracy and precision than traditional methods. Predictive Maintenance Unmanned aerial vehicles (UAVs) can detect deterioration on the road before cars get there. This system would save millions in repairs. Drones are being tested for use in other applications, such as crop management, traffic management, and disaster relief.

Deep belief networks (DBNs) are a type of deep neural network designed for machine learning problems that involve patterns, sequences, and time. DBNs consist of multiple layers where each layer is composed of numerous units that can represent a number of variables. A DBN can have any number of layers, with the top layer containing one unit to represent the entire input space. DBNs are particularly suited for datasets with large numbers of outputs and that might not be well represented by a one-layer neural network. DBNs work best for problems where data is continuous, and time is either treated as a continuous variable or not present in the dataset at all.

DISTRIBUTED LEARNING FOR FOG COMPUTING

Machine learning is a field of computer science that gives computers the ability to learn without being explicitly programmed. The more data is obtained, the better the performance of a machine learning algorithm becomes. Deep learning is one subfield of machine learning in which many layers of processing are stacked together to interpret data and make predictions at a high level, with each hidden layer representing an abstraction of the data. Fog computing is a paradigm in which the computing is done at the edge of the network, closer to the data. It is a way of distributing the data-processing power so that it can be treated as needed. from any place and from any device. Fog computing is also a way of thinking of the cloud, with a difference: in contrast to the cloud, where data is stored at remote locations and accessed by users via the internet, fog computing datacenters are located closer to the data. Processing will be distributed among several linked devices in fog computing, which will make it possible for machine learning jobs to operate with massive volumes of data. This objective is difficult to accomplish because (i) devices have varying levels of computational capability and (ii) the topology places restrictions on how devices may communicate with one another.

Figure 2. Fog Architecture

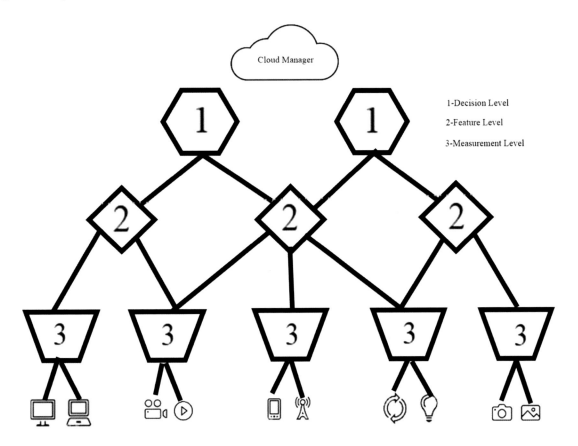

Figure 2. Shows the Fog Architecture. Distributed deep learning is a way to process information without needing to centralize it in one location, like that required by traditional distributed computing. The computations are done using distributed edge devices and embedded systems with only minimal communication with a centralized computer somewhere on a network, like the cloud computing. Distributed deep Learning is a powerful technique that is currently being used in Fog Computing. It has been shown to be more energy efficient and accurate than centralized deep learning architectures. The main motivation behind the adoption of deep learning for Fog computing is its scalability, which enables more diverse use cases including systems that are not as data intensive. However, the way that organizations have adopted distributed deep learning architectures has been somewhat limited. This is because it is difficult to build and maintain these networks on a large scale due to the high workload on the data centers.

The main challenge with building a distributed system is scaling it to support more analysis and processing power. First, the architecture of the software has to be able to support parallelization in order to scale across multiple servers. Second, all servers must cooperate with each other through a communication layer that is like a bus so that the data can be shared across multiple nodes. Third, all nodes need to know where and what data is located on them for it to be able to be used. And lastly, there must be a robust way of managing how the data is divided amongst the nodes. As with most complex distributed systems, these challenges can often result in architectures that are difficult to scale and manage. For example, some of the most common software solutions that are implemented for this purpose are Apache

Spark and Apache HDFS. Apache Spark is a cluster computing framework that runs on top of HDFS and provides support for iterative data processing. Apache Spark provides fast, resilient data analysis on large datasets. As the name suggests, it is a "spark" in the sense that it is designed to process huge volumes of data that are both fast and resilient with minimal hardware cost.

Fog computing is a type of cloud computing that has been optimized for edge devices. Fog is the system that sits between the data center and the end user device and processes data on site. Fog clouds are composed of edge devices that can be anything from sensors and connected devices to data centers and the internet. There is a fog cloud in every room of your house, and you can access it with your personal smartphone. Fog computing has many applications, but one that is especially relevant to IoT is smart cities. Connected sensors in fog clouds provide significant advantages over sensors in houses or even individual buildings. For example, sensors inside of a building can use Wi-Fi signals to detect when an accident has happened and relay the event to multiple people on the scene. But if it is raining outside and the sensor cannot see, it could miss important information about what happened at the scene. Fog computing systems dynamically adjust their priorities based on the data they collect. If they identify a lot of data that is related to rain, such as rainfall or dew points, then the system would prioritize reporting these findings first and less important information would be reported second. For example, it could send an alert about an accident instead of reporting that it's raining on the way to work in the morning. The future of distributed deep learning when it comes to fog computing can help us process data faster and make things simpler for developers. If we're able to create an API with fog, then we can focus on other fields like data privacy and security. The biggest challenge for the industry is how to avoid data privacy and security concerns. With fog computing, it is possible to provide solutions that are more secure than traditional computing (Rocha Neto et al, 2020).

Fog Computing is a novel paradigm that provides scalable, sustainable, and fault-tolerant network of computing elements. A fog computing platform is a type of software that allows for data to be processed more quickly in real-time by moving data closer to the edge of the network. It provides decentralized services to the endpoints of IoT networks where the infrastructure is not available or affordable. Fog Computing is a relatively new concept that is being implemented around the world because it gives better results than traditional cloud computing. It uses less power, requires less storage space, and has better tolerance for poor network conditions. The goal of Fog Computing is to bring together computation and data processing at the place where data are generated. It reduces latency in computation and enhances security as well. This paradigm changes the way data flows from sensors/cameras to mobile devices/desktops. Fog computing: Simplified architecture for a distributed computing paradigm in which the compute devices are dispersed and the network is used for data transfer, computation, and storage. The goal of Fog Computing is to bring together computation and data processing at the place where data are generated. It reduces latency in computation and enhances security as well. This paradigm changes the way applications are developed. A major characteristic of fog computing is that applications are deployed in the cloud with their own compute, storage, and network resources. Applications interact with cloud services in order to access or process data while achieving application-level portability, even when communicating across public or private networks. As cloud computing matures, the demand for data processing capabilities will grow exponentially. In the process of cloud computing, data is stored and processed on remote servers in computer centers or data centers. Cloud computing hardware is typically housed in a computer center (or cloud provider). The advantages of using cloud services are that they offer significant cost savings, scalability, guaranteed availability, and ongoing support. Data stored in the cloud may be accessed from any location where Internet is available. The disadvantages of using cloud services are that they may have a large footprint and require extensive operational management, capacity planning and ongoing support. Fog computing can be applied to any business sector, such as manufacturing or logistics. It is important for the company to be able to determine what their data is, in order to be able to use it for the best possible purpose. The more storage space a company has, the more data they can store. It uses less power, requires less storage space, and has better tolerance for poor network conditions (Wang, S. et al, 2021).

APPLICATIONS OF DISTRIBUTED DEEP LEARNING

Distributed deep learning technologies are used in a large number of commercial and consumer applications. With these applications, distributed deep learning is able to perform tasks that were not possible using traditional deep learning models. One of the main application areas for DDL is video recognition, which is being used to identify objects and scenes in videos. This technology enables these tasks by understanding natural language and general category terms.

According to Cisco, one of the primary companies that pioneered fog computing, the cloud is brought closer to the things that create Internet of Things data via the fog infrastructure, which consists of smart switches, routers, and specialized processing nodes. This is accomplished by bringing the cloud closer to the things that create the data. This method is predicated on the age-old principle of locating processing resources as near as possible to the data source, which in this instance refers to the Internet of Things devices. This will result in a decrease in the application's total latency as a consequence of less network traffic being required for these resources and a greater degree of cloud independence being achieved.

The ability for computers to automatically learn the concepts in a dataset has created many new opportunities for businesses, especially small businesses. Deep learning is applied in a variety of commercial and consumer applications. Some of them are:

Navigation: In order to provide assistance in navigating from one location to another, smartphones use deep learning to understand natural language terms such as "find a restaurant nearby," or "help me find the fastest route."

Self-service Kiosks: This technology allows self-service kiosks to serve as a more accessible and convenient way to do business. Several different deep learning frameworks may be implemented in Spark workflows in an end-to-end pipeline using Apache Spark, making it a crucial enabling platform for distributed deep learning. Distributed deep learning now has Apache Spark as a key enabler. Distributed deep learning may benefit greatly from Apache Spark's ability to handle large amounts of data in real time.

Voice search: This technology is still in the process of being developed, but it will allow users to speak their queries into smart speakers, which will be processed by deep learning. This technology is still in the process of being developed, but it will allow users to speak their queries into smart speakers, which will be processed by deep learning.

The blockchain is the best example of a distributed deep learning technology. It has already established itself as one of the leading technologies in machine learning, and it is predicted that in the next few decades, this decentralized model will become mainstream and lead to most AI models being distributed across multiple machines. Basically, on a blockchain, the data is encrypted and then duplicated across the network to secure it. This creates what is called a "distributed ledger." Blockchains make it possible for everyone with access to the internet to contribute pieces of information to a decentralized mass database that is open and transparent.

The main benefits of distributed deep learning are cost-effectiveness and scalability. Companies can use them to create IoT devices without the need for huge server farms from Amazon or Google. In addition, this type of AI is more easily distributable across multiple devices. Some examples of distributed deep learning are: - Autonomous cars can be trained using deep learning components such as Honda's autonomous car. - Using several GPUs, companies such as Nvidia have created algorithms to process data faster and more effectively in a distributed environment. For instance, a deep learning algorithm is able to recognize patterns in data from a network so that it can identify a security threat, like a hacker gaining access to data.

Deep neural networks are creating a new wave of traffic analysis. Traffic analysis is the process of mapping the relationship between the popularity and the flow of web traffic. This data is then used for strategic decision making on how to optimize websites for a better user experience. The demand for traffic analysis has risen significantly because of the advancements in deep learning software. The competition to analyze traffic is becoming more intense than ever before. For example, Google is using deep neural networks for the purpose of analyzing web traffic to improve user experience and monetize their business. Traffic analysis companies can use deep neural networks as a substitute for human traffic analysts. Deep neural networks are superior to humans in analyzing traffic because they are computer programs that do not experience boredom, fatigue, or the need for breaks. Additionally, deep neural networks never forget what they have learned and require less data to achieve the same results. The most important resource in the deep neural network is memory. Deep neural networks can also learn to recognize patterns and make decisions based on them. For example, a deep neural network could use time of day, location density, or behavior to decide when traffic will reach a certain level and where it is best to funnel that traffic.

Mobile Locking System: The internet of things (IoT) refers to the method by which individuals are linked together through a global network that comprises, among other things, the internet, processors, sensors, and software. This method is also known as the "Internet of People." With the use of this technology, inanimate objects, the data they gather, the actions they carry out, and even a user on the outside may all communicate with one another. It is a hybridized electronic infrastructure that is capable of analyzing and using data in real time, which has the potential to increase both production and efficiency. The rapid advancement of technology in recent years has resulted in cellphones playing an increasingly significant role in our day-to-day lives. These are portable personal computers that are tiny enough to fit in your back pocket. They use a mobile operating system such as Android or Windows Mobile, or a platform that is functionally equivalent to any of them. An integrated broadband mobile network links smartphones to both traditional landlines and the internet. This network also connects smartphones to one another. You may utilize a wireless or wired interface, such as WiFi, Bluetooth, or USB, as well as other technologies that are functionally equivalent, in order to link them to other devices in the area.

By combining a mobile device, a front-end embedded controller, and a variety of sensors and actuators, the goal of this project is to make effective use of the internet of things (IoT). Building an application for Android that simplifies the process of locking and unlocking a vehicle door is the objective of this project. The process of registering vehicles and generating permission codes is made possible with the assistance of a server-based technology. On a regular basis, the server will document the present condition of the system in a written format. This gives the authorized owner the ability to access these details through a smartphone from any location in the globe. With the help of this invention, the objective is to build and test a suitable combination of components that can be used to make a smart door lock that is not only reliable but also simple to use. The privacy and safety of IoT devices are also significant concerns that will need to be addressed by this initiative. Therefore, the innovation will provide a comprehensive look into the safety and privacy of the technologies that make up the Internet of Things. Because of this, the lock mechanism will be improved by being connected to the Internet, which will result in it being more resilient, productive, and creative (Amuthan Nallathambi et al, 2022).

It is a kind of high-frequency short-range wireless communication technology that enables electric rooms to transmit and receive data without the need for a connected connection between any two sites that are within 10 centimeters of one another. Radiofrequency discrimination the transmission range of NFC technology is much less than that of RFID, which is one of the reasons why RFID is focused on developing NFC technology. The transmission range of an RFID reader might be anything from several meters to tens of meters. NFC, on the other hand, restricts the range of its transmissions to a distance of no more than ten centimeters by using a method known as "signal attenuation." Radiofrequency discrimination (RFID), which is trying to enhance RFID technology, has a transmission range that is less than that of RFID technology. However, RFID is striving to improve RFID technology. The transfer of data via RFID makes it feasible for automobiles to have a system that automatically opens and shuts the doors. On the other hand, radio frequency identification (RFID) has a wide effective transmission range, which means that wireless communications may be readily intercepted and read. This poses a threat to the safety of vehicles. The mobile phone has evolved into an essential technological gadget throughout the course of time and has become an essential component of people's day-to-day life. The Near Field Communication (NFC) function will be one of the following mobile phone capabilities; nevertheless, the phone will be referred to as an NFC phone due to the fact that it has an NFC chip. Additionally, near-field communication (NFC) is a kind of communication that is risk-free and consumes very little energy. This is made possible by the one-of-a-kind and completely smooth wireless network that NFC and identification provide. You can get access to content and services in the neighborhood by touching an NFC smart device or by using an NFC smart device to gain access to content and services in the neighborhood directly. After the data interchange and connection with other NFC equipment rooms have been completed, an NFC mobile phone may then be utilized for a variety of purposes, including acting as a passive label.

The read-write line of the NFC analogue card, the connection between the mobile phone and the NFC equipment room for sending and receiving data, and the capability of the NFC-capable mobile phone to be the same as or similar to the contactless smart card are all things that should be the same or similar. The current invention provides a solution to the flaw that was discussed earlier. Its purpose is to create a type of vehicle door-opening and-closing lock system that is based on the NFC mobile phone. This system will have the ability to solve the problem that was caused by RFID energy bedding in the prior art by intercepting and capturing wireless messages, closely sending the shutter door signal by the NFC mobile phone and using a safe identification signal to catch a car thief. This system will also have the ability to solve the problem that was caused by RFID energy bedding in the solution. The prior art has been located and confiscated. An NFC mobile phone transmits the signal for the shutter door in close proximity, and a safe identification signal successfully completes the task of auto theft; in addition, the NFC mobile phone is connected to the body control system of the vehicle. The aforementioned objective may be accomplished via the use of the following technical programs thanks to the current invention: A system that allows an NFC phone to open and shut a vehicle door includes an NFC identification module, a car body controller, and a door-lock motor. Each of these components is a part of the larger system. An NFC communication unit, a data processor, a storer, and an input/output interface are the four components that come together to form the NFC identification module that is discussed in this article. The storer, the input/output interface, the vehicle body controller, and the door-lock motor are all linked to the data processor. The NFC communication unit is connected to the data processor, and the data processor is connected to the storer. Additionally, the NFC connection device is linked to the controller for the body of the car. The data processor does a comparison with the automobile body controller using the signal and identification tag information. This determines whether or not the rear output recognition was successful. The signal received from the NFC communication unit as well as the information contained on the identification tag are both used by the vehicle body controller in order to regulate the operation of the door lock machine. When it comes to automobiles, the input/output interface and the body controller are both connected to the CAN bus. This is the most effective technique to link the two together. A sort of car door opening and shutting lock system that makes use of an NFC phone incorporates a double jump light as one component of the system. The double jump light is connected to the automobile body controller in the most desirable implementation of this concept. However, the sequence number of the mobile phone is the single most crucial piece of identifying tag information that has to be stored in the aforementioned device.

The information that is shown on the identification tag may be altered by the vehicle body controller to reflect the preferences of the driver. The data processor receives the instructions to alter the functioning of the automobile body controller via the input/output interface. This allows the data processor more flexibility. Despite this, the data processor modifies the information about the ID tags that is stored in the keeper.

A vehicle performance monitoring system for an electric vehicle: A display for this performance monitoring system needs to be located on the dashboard, and it ought to be connected to the display that is located where the driver sits. Another is to integrate the instrument cluster and dashboard display of an electric vehicle to function as a single unit. Additionally, the monitoring system needs to use the minimum amount of power from the battery that is humanly feasible. The various sensors that are mounted on an electric vehicle should capture data in a consistent and reliable manner.

This innovation is a tracking device that may be installed in electric vehicles (EVs) to monitor how efficiently they are operating. The vehicle is equipped with a variety of sensors, each of which measures something relevant to the vehicle's performance. Displays on the dashboard provide the driver with the most useful representation of the information gleaned from the sensors. When you look at the operating parameters, you are able to view the speed, the distance travelled, the temperature of the motor, and the amount of gas that is currently in the tank. The current voltage of the battery is shown on an indicator for the fuel level.

In addition to this, the voltage of the main battery, the temperature of the primary battery, and the instantaneous current draw are all indicators of how well the electric car is operating and how it functions in general. A data collection system is responsible for transmitting sensor information to a processing unit. The processing units might then utilize this information to make decisions on what to do depending on the data that was gathered from the sensors. A portable computer, which comes equipped with its own power source, is the most effective processing unit for preventing the auxiliary battery from running down to an unsafe level. When the ignition switch is switched off, the processing unit enters what is known as "sleep mode," which helps conserve even more power from the battery. A battery temperature management system that is able to maintain a battery's temperature within a predetermined range regardless of the temperature of the air that is around the battery.

When an electric car is driven in a region that experiences extremes of temperature, the passenger compartment will often be equipped with both a heating unit and a cooling unit to maintain a comfortable temperature inside the vehicle. This is accomplished by using a mechanism that either cools or warms the air in order to manage the temperature of the battery, which is said to be the purpose of the innovation.

Let's imagine you're behind the wheel of an electric vehicle equipped with an air-cooling system and you manage to exceed a certain temperature. In this scenario, the battery temperature control system described in the present invention serves as the power source for the air-cooling device. The air-cooling device is equipped with both a temperature sensor and a control unit.

The inventor of an air-heating device for electric cars includes one in this battery temperature management system that was invented by him. It contains a control unit that will switch on the air-heating device if the battery temperature sensor detects a decrease below a specific temperature, an air intake port in the battery that is set to a given temperature, and a battery temperature sensor that measures the temperature of the battery.

If the battery temperature is above or below a certain limit, the control unit of an electric vehicle equipped with an air conditioner that is capable of both cooling and heating the interior of the vehicle is programmed to activate the air conditioner in either the cooling mode or the heating mode, respectively, as appropriate. Additionally, it instructs the charger to handle the procedure of charging the battery on its own. When the phone is being charged with an air conditioner running, the charger puts out a greater amount of power than it would otherwise.

For instance, if the temperature of the battery gets beyond a specific level while it is being charged in the summer, a device that cools the air or the air conditioner in the car will switch on to cool down the inside of the vehicle. The result of this is that the chamber of the battery is completely filled with chilly air. When the internal temperature of the battery, which is what drives the automobile, rises to an unsafe level, the air-cooling mechanism or air conditioner in the vehicle is activated. This allows cold air to enter the battery chamber, either from the device itself or through the air conditioner. Therefore, the temperature outdoors does not impact the cooling of the battery in any way. This prevents the battery from overheating, which would be detrimental to its performance and would lower its overall lifespan. Because of this, the battery does not get very warm while it is being charged, allowing for a rapid charging process even when the temperature is high outside the vehicle. When the temperature of the battery goes below a specific threshold, such as in the winter, warm air from the air-heating equipment or the air conditioner is used to heat the battery. This is done to prevent the battery from being permanently damaged. Therefore, the temperature of the battery is maintained at a level that is safe. If the battery chamber is cold when the vehicle is initially charged or switched on in the winter, warm air from the heating or cooling system may be delivered there to warm it up. As a result of this, it is feasible to prevent the low temperature from making the battery less strong and the process of charging less effective than it would have been otherwise (Shashishankar et al, 2022).

If the air conditioner is configured to charge the battery, the charger's electric power will be raised when the air conditioner is operating in this manner since the air conditioner consumes more electricity. Therefore, the electricity that is required to operate the air conditioner comes from the charger. While the battery is being charged, this power is not being used to maintain a constant temperature inside the battery. The Internet of Things is able to maintain complete awareness of its surroundings with the use of a portable design. Piezo electric transducers have made significant advances in the technology of electric vehicles (N, Sivakumar, 2018, January 1). Analyses the use of cutting-edge machine learning technology in energy grids, offers some novel ideas that haven't been discussed before, and provides forecasts based on those investigations. In the field of power generation, machine learning applications on the leading edge of technology have already been proposed and put into use, and more are on the way (M, Nirmala et al., 2021).

Natural language processing: Since neural networks excel in tasks where the knowledge is deeply embedded and data-filled, they are well suited for tasks such as image recognition, voice recognition, and natural language processing. The continuous improvements in deep learning algorithms have led to a big surge in the popularity of deep learning techniques in recent years. The Current Problems in Natural Language Processing Natural language processing, a subfield of artificial intelligence and machine learning, is concerned with the computational modeling and simulation of human language. Some researchers are interested in developing systems that can understand and generate natural language sentences, while others are focused on developing systems that can deconstruct text from different sources in order to gain insight into underlying structures.

Figure 3. Natural Language Processing Architecture

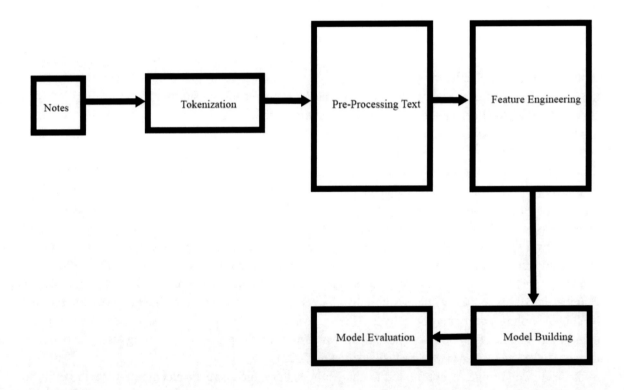

Figure 3. Natural Language Processing Architecture. One of the primary problems in natural language processing is how to generate appropriate, grammatically correct sentences that are free of syntactic ambiguity. The Current Problems in Natural Language Processing Natural language processing, a subfield of artificial intelligence and machine learning, is concerned with the computational modeling and simulation of human language. Some researchers are interested in emulating human language capabilities, while others are interested in applications that build on natural language processing. Natural Language Processing Natural language processing, a subfield of artificial intelligence and machine learning, is

concerned with the computational modeling and simulation of human language. Some researchers are interested in emulating human language capabilities, while others are interested in applications that build on natural language processing. Natural language processing, a subfield of artificial intelligence and machine learning, is concerned with the computational modeling and simulation of human language. Some researchers are interested in emulating human language capabilities, while others are interested in applications that build on natural language processing. Natural language processing (NLP) can be used in an app for text automation, natural language understanding, and retrieval of information. It is very useful for companies that want to automate customer service tasks, such as troubleshooting. It can identify certain patterns in customer data. It is valuable for companies that want to provide customer service robots or AI. It can be useful in identifying customer intent through analysis of website data to identify client needs, such as website conversions. It is useful for eCommerce sites that want to know what products their users are interested in. It also provides various insights from a wide range of data.

CONCLUSION

Distributed deep learning is a promising technology because it is able to extract knowledge from many sources and process them in an efficient way without human involvement. It has also been shown that this technique reduces the amount of data transfer from remote machines to central servers significantly. The three main methods of deep learning are convolutional neural networks (CNN), recurrent neural networks (RNN), and long short-term memory networks (LSTM). The first two are used to achieve supervised classification tasks, such as image recognition and natural language processing, while the last one is used for unsupervised tasks, such as video classification. CNNs are used for the following tasks: image recognition, natural language processing, time series prediction, and reinforcement learning. RNNs are used for the following tasks: speech recognition and sequence modeling. LSTMs with more than one input layer are used when two or three inputs are needed to be processed at once. LSTM's high-order states help with time series prediction and reinforcement learning.

Distributed deep learning is changing the way businesses and industries are tackling tasks and will continue to change the future of technology. The following are some of the key takeaways from this paper on distributed deep learning: Distributed deep learning is a new way of approaching data processing in machine learning models. -Distributed deep learning is being applied to many areas, including industrial automation, security, and healthcare. -The increased efficiency and breadth of AI applications due to distributed deep learning will have significant impacts on the future.

In order to make these algorithms widely available, companies must first embrace the idea of data-sharing by developing and deploying software that can process large amounts of data in parallel, which will help them scale their deep learning models. In the near future, we may see a significant shift in how we learn. With the increased use of AI and machine learning, it is possible to make technologies that are more personal without the need for humans. Distributed deep learning research is a faster and more cost-effective way of solving problems that can't be solved by traditional systems. By using the power of AI and machine learning, it can help solve some of the most difficult problems in machine learning and AI.

REFERENCES

Dmaa (2022). Distributed-deep-learning-algorithm-for-wavelength-analysis. *Business Insider.* https://www.businessinsider.com/dmaa-distributed-deep-learning-algorithm-for-wavelength-analysis

Nallathambi,A. B., Kanammai, D. Sandip, S., Gummadi, J. M., Dhanasekaran, S., & Balkeshwar, S. (2022). *Mobile Locking System for Vehicle Using Machine Learning*, Registration Number-1192615. Canadian Copyright.

Nirmala., M., Sathya, M., Shukla, A. K. C. S., Ravichandran, P. N. M. H., & Lakshminarayana, M. (2021). An Intellectual Monitoring of Power Sector by Machine Learning Applications, *NVEO – Natural Volatiles & Essential Oils, 8*(5), 6609–6619.

Poulopoulos, D. (2021, January 26). Distributed Deep Learning 101: Introduction. *Medium.* https://towardsdatascience.com/distributed-deep-learning-101-introduction-ebfc1bcd59d9

Rocha-Neto, A. F., Delicato, F. C., Batista, T. V., & Pires, P. F. (2020). Distributed machine learning for IOT applications in the fog. *Fog Computing*, 309–345. . doi:10.1002/9781119551713.ch12

Sait, S. (2021, August 19). Distributed deep learning-illustrated. *Medium.* https://towardsdatascience.com/distributed-deep-learning-illustrated-6256e07a0468

Shashishankar, A., Dule, C. S., Ananthapadmanabha, K., Rajasekharaiah, K. M., Sathya, M., & Nallathambi, A. (2022). *Cloud based Electric Vehicles Temperature Monitoring system using IoT*, Registration Number- 1191845. Canadian Copyright.

Sivakumar, N. (2018, January 1). *Shodhganga@INFLIBNET: Performance analysis and optimization of microcantilever beam smart structures.* http://hdl.handle.net/10603/257919

Sun, Q., Xu, J., Ma, X., Zhou, A., Hsu, C.-H., & Wang, S. (2021). Edge-enabled distributed deep learning for 5G privacy protection. *IEEE Network, 35*(4), 213–219. doi:10.1109/MNET.021.2000292

Wang, S., Ruan, Y., Tu, Y., Wagle, S., Brinton, C. G., & Joe-Wong, C. (2021). Network-aware optimization of Distributed Learning for Fog Computing. *IEEE/ACM Transactions on Networking, 29*(5), 2019–2032. doi:10.1109/TNET.2021.3075432

Wikimedia Foundation. (2022, July 9). Artificial Intelligence. *Wikipedia.* https://en.wikipedia.org/wiki/Artificial_intelligence

Chapter 6
Approaches for Detecting and Predicting Attacks Based on Deep and Reinforcement Learning to Improve Information Security

Nayana Hegde

 https://orcid.org/0000-0001-7467-2553

REVA University, India

Sunilkumar S. Manvi

REVA University, India

ABSTRACT

The continued growth and widespread use of the internet benefit many network users in various ways. Meanwhile, network protection becomes increasingly essential as the internet becomes more widely used. Though, as the number of internet-connected systems in finance, e-commerce, and the military grows, they are becoming targets of network attacks, posing a noteworthy challenge and causing significant harm. Essentially, practical strategies for detecting and defending against attacks, as well as maintaining network protection, are needed. Furthermore, various types of attacks must typically be dealt with in different ways. This chapter summarizes some of the important deep learning techniques and reinforcement techniques for information security by providing various methods for attack detection and corrections.

INTRODUCTION

The ongoing growth and worldwide usage of the Internet satisfies numerous network users in a variety of methods. Meanwhile, as the Internet becomes more widely used, network protection becomes very important and challenging task. Network protection is concerned with computers, networks, applications

DOI: 10.4018/978-1-6684-6275-1.ch006

and different data, among other things, with the aim of preventing unauthorized access and alteration as given in Mohamed Amine (2020). Originally, essential approaches for identifying and securing attacks, additionally sustaining network protection, are entailed. Additionally, different categories of attacks typically should be taken care with specific methods. The key problem in the area of information security need to be resolved is how to identify different types of network risks, especially those attacks that were not experienced earlier.

Due to diverse possessions regarding the technological breakthrough, threats to computer networks, IoT systems, and devices gets translated as increasing privacy issues. IoT systems were practical and efficient due to their characteristics such as: collecting a lot of data, connecting the physical and virtual worlds, complicated environments, architecture that is more centralized. Malicious hackers, though, might exploit vulnerabilities. An overview of the IoT attack surface areas can be found below:

- Device: Device might be the primary means of starting a cyber-attack. Memory, computing micro-programs, the hardware interfacing, the Internet application, and communications networks are illustrations of modules where vulnerability might well be found inside a device.
- Channels: Attacks may come through the media that connects different IoT devices together.
- Software applications: System may be harmed as a result of bugs in internet apps and Internet of things applications. Web apps can be used to steal user credentials or fraudulent system software updates, for example.

Numerous computer and network security research areas fall under the umbrella of cyber situational awareness or have some connection to it. However, an enterprise's capacity for cyber situational awareness is currently severely constrained for a number of reasons, including but not limited to:

- Incomplete and inaccurate forensics, intrusion detection, and vulnerability analysis.
- Unable to track certain microscopic systems or assault patterns.
- Restricted capacity for navigating ambiguity.

Challenges of Predicting Cyber-Attacks

Given the number of potential entry points, the attackers' goals, and the increasing reliance on connection and cloud storage, it is difficult to forecast cyber-attacks with current technology. Some of the challenges in predicting cyber-attacks are discussed as follows.

- Rising number of cyber-attacks: The frequency and severity of attacks are only going to increase as cyber threat actors hone their methods and make use of automation and machine learning.
- Active cyber pandemic: In order to enable the remote workforce and achieve the aims of the digital transformation, the development of remote work made users, computers, and personal devices the first line of defense, and the spike in cloud use generated new avenues of attack for cyber threat players.
- Mobile devices create more security threats: Cybercriminals changed their strategies to benefit on the rising use of mobile devices. There are several new mobile virus Trojan.

Types of Attacks

Numerous attacks have the potential to compromise the network's security and the nodes' privacy. A few of the security services in the system are impacted by each sort of assault. The most frequent and harmful types of attacks that a network can encounter are listed below.

- Sybil attack: In this kind of attack, the perpetrator simultaneously assumes multiple identities. The system can be subjected to any kind of assault using these identities. Additionally, these bogus identities give the impression that there are more nodes. By delivering fake signals, it creates an illusion for the other nodes.
- Denial of Service (DOS) attack: The attacker's goal in this case is to take down the network by flooding the communication channel with pointless messages. A DOS attack can jam the channel system, preventing any genuine node from accessing it.
- Black Hole attack: This kind of attack involves a node refusing to join the network or a node that is already in the network leaving to create a black hole. This results in data loss because the entire network's traffic is diverted to a single node that actually doesn't exist.
- Message suppression attack: Attackers can use this to deliberately remove packets from the network that might contain information that the recipient needs.
- Tunneling attack: The attacker creates a tunnel between two remote network nodes utilizing an additional communication channel. As a result, two remote nodes mistakenly believe they are neighbors and use the tunnel to send data.
- Spoofing user identity: Attackers pose as authorised users in order to obtain data for their own illicit gain. The man-in-the-middle attack is an example of a typical attack.
- Tampering: This attack occurs when an attacker modifies already-existing data. It may involve postponing the information's transmission, replaying an earlier transmission, or changing the entry of the delivered data itself.
- Repudiation: The attackers alter or fabricate new data, actions, and operations' identity.
- Information disclosure: Attackers find personally identifying information, including names, dates of birth, ethnicity, financial status, legal standing, and medical information.

There are several approaches employed by various researchers for the detection of network attacks. Using data mining algorithms, such as white list or black list models, is one of the crucial techniques. Signature-based detection is one of the most popular detection strategies. This approach can enhance signature-based detection by lessening the burden of detection, accelerating the signature matching procedure, and minimizing the false alarm rate. It is employed to create models of typical behavior. Both use statistical and analytical techniques to create signatures for their systems. However, the comprehensive and in-depth data gathered over secured networks is used to develop the signature-based models.

Situation Awareness

Situation perception, situation comprehension, and situation projection are the three phases of the cyber situation awareness process. Among these phases perception is considered as level 1. The state, characteristics, and dynamics of important environmental factors are revealed via perception. Level 2 is situation comprehension which corresponds to: understanding a situation that involves combining, interpreting, storing, and remembering information. Level 3 is situation projection which includes: making predictions based on information learned through perception and comprehension. The projecting of the aspects of the environment (situation) results into the near future attack detection. In a system, typically the one that is in charge of acquiring situation awareness cyber-attacks that are either random or planned poses a threat to the system.

Researchers have accustomed a various machine learning approaches to characterize network attacks without having earlier knowledge of their specific characteristics in the past. Machine learning has now made a huge advance by modeling the human brain using the architecture of neural network, which is known as deep learning architecture because of its design layout of deep layer and its ability to handle complicated issues as mentioned in Ayei (2020).

Attacks Detection and Prediction

It is necessary to provide context information in addition to giving a broad summary of successful attack detection using deep learning methods. As a result, the chapter begins with a brief overview of attack detection principles, which can serve as a foundation for researchers in this domain. Following that, a brief representation of effective cyber security applications is described.

A.   Developing an Attack Detection Process

Attacks may be defined as endeavour to circumvent the system's security policies, by making it easy for the attacker easier entry to acquire or modify information or maybe kill the system. Since the wireless channels are characterized by sharing with many users, it has significant threat to computer networks. Safety of wireless networks of communication in particular, has challenging issues and many methods have been proposed to secure the same (Rezvy, 2019). Given that we are now living in machine learning and big data, users must protect their data, computers and networks with cyber systems in wireless communication systems. To deal with such cyber security attack streams, researchers have proposed a lot of remedial solutions. Attack detection that includes a complete and complicated security model for tracking, avoiding, and preventing attacks, were the most significant approaches. In latest years, machine learning had also progressed at a rapid speed. Deep learning frameworks, one of the many machine learning approaches, generate artificial neural networks that replicate the linking neurons in human brains, providing them a particular benefit in tackling complicated issues (Shone, 2018). As a response, researchers are employing a range of deep learning algorithms to detect assaults, which has resulted in significant improvements.

In general, the two primary classifications of threats detection techniques are anomaly detection systems (profile-based detection systems) and abuse detection systems (signature-based detection systems). While misuse finding system target activity by which it resembles the known attack scenario, anomaly detection systems target behaviour that deviates from the typical profile of the system (Mohamed Amine, 2020). Over the previous few years, several predictive techniques in the field of cyber security have been put out. While they are useful proofs of concept that it is feasible to foresee future assaults, their current capabilities make them of extremely limited practical value. In this chapter, we suggest a novel deep-learning algorithm-based strategy for predicting network's attacks from known malicious sources. This approach is able to predict not only the likelihood of an attack observation, but also specific attack parameters, allowing for the application of more effective defence measures.

B.   Intrusion Identification System

By gathering and analysing data about internet activity, security logs, and also other options data on the network one can build the intrusion identification system for the malicious tasks. In that concern, an intrusion identification system collates suspicious activity to system security strategies and measures of attack in the system, and it is competent to defending the legitimate set of components. In typical device configurations, an intrusion identification system will be an active, logical and effective add-on to a firewall, which is a passive security mechanism (Vinayakumar, 2019).

C.   Malware Identification

A malware can be defined as the software that will degrade the performance of the wireless network, network server or any device present in the network. Malware can destroy the entire system under some serious circumstances. Initially, malware will be implanted into the device that is targeted. Later, it will execute the program and other software routines on its as per the inputs given by the attacker (Zhang, 2019). Malware identification approaches are separated into two groups: signature-based detection and anomaly-based detection. Traditional antivirus software, which detects malicious files based on file signatures, falls into the first group. However, malicious codes that are subtly deformed can be bypassed, resulting in several hundred false-positive rate (Thanh, 2021).

Deep Learning Approaches for Intrusion Detection

Deep learning is a subbranch of artificial intelligence and machine learning. It makes use of neural networks to learn unsupervised, unstructured, or unlabeled data. Deep learning is now associated with artificial neural networks, that are algorithms based on the structure and function of the brain. The deep neural network not only follows the algorithm, but it can also predict a artificial neural networks, which are algorithms based on the structure and operation of the brain, are now linked to deep learning. The deep neural network may forecast a task's outcome and make inferences based on prior experience in addition to just following the algorithm. Intrusion detection (ID) functionality in network security may be improved by the implementation of such learning algorithms. For information security malware detection, ten deep learning techniques are used, like, (A) deep neural network, (B) feed forward deep neural network, (C) recurrent neural network, (D) convolutional neural network, (E) restricted Boltzmann machine, (F) deep belief network, (G) deep auto-encoder, (H) deep migration learning, (I) self-taught learning, and (J) replicator neural network (Mohamed Amine, 2020). Various network security intrusion detecting strategies, employing deep learning methods are shown in figure1.

Figure 1. Network Security Intrusion Detection Techniques Using Deep Learning Approaches

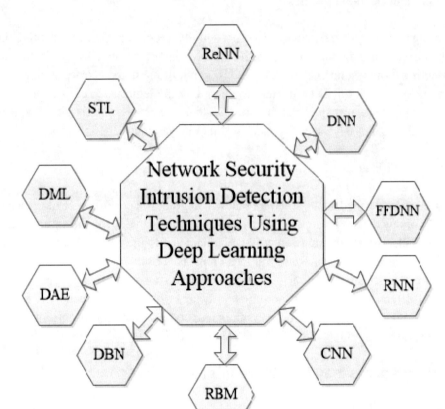

Applying various deep learning algorithms to detect attacks will provide numerous advantages. Here, two types of approaches we come across. The first is a method based on supervised learning, whereas the second is a method based on unsupervised learning. In supervised learning based approach, the data generated are manually labeled samples and thus the approach produces high accurate outcome. Whereas, unsupervised learning-based approaches performance is considered poor as there are insufficient labeled data available. Manual labeling, on the other hand, is a work that needs more time, particularly for challenging attacks. Because actual network attacks are inherently complicated, there are also cases that cannot be identified by a single label.

A.   Deep Neural Network (DNN)

A deep neural network (DNN) is an artificial neural network (ANN) having numerous layers in-between both the layers of input and output. A deep neural network is a machine learning system that uses numerous layers of nodes to construct high-level functions from incoming data. The training is becoming more challenging as the tasks you resolve are becoming deeper. It means repurposing facts into something more conceptual and inventive. DNN is a multilayer perceptron (MLP) with more than three layers. MLPs are a kind of artificial neural network with feed-forward determined by the number of layers that make up the network and follow one another, as seen in the figure 2. The input layer is the initial layer, followed by the hidden layer and the output layer.

Figure 2. Deep Neural Network

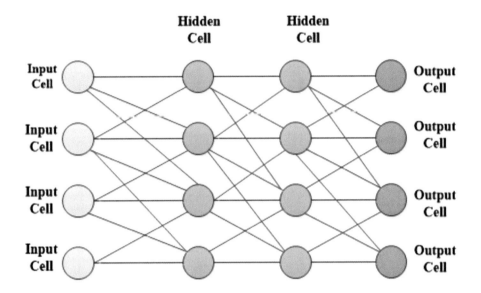

The layer of DNN is described with help of parameters such as: [a_m, b_m and n], that is DNNm={ a_m, b_m and n }.The parameter a_m gives the number of neurons in the layer. The parameter b_m specifies the value of the bias vector and W_m gives the weight of the matrix (Mohamed Amine (2020)). Algorithm 1 explains the calculation of weight matrix for DNN network.

Figure 3. Algorithm for calculating weight matrix

Algorithm 1 DNN network weight matrix

Input: $nlayers, learning pair(x_1, c_1)$

1: Select a learning pair(x_1, c_1)
2: $h \leftarrow 0$
3: $n \leftarrow total\ number\ of\ layers$
4: **for** $k \leftarrow 1$ to n **do**
5: $\quad W_k \leftarrow h_k + b_k$
6: $\quad h_k \leftarrow a_k(W_k)$
7: **end for**
8: **return** h_k

The work (Tang, 2016), suggested a software-defined intrusion prevention system for wireless network that uses a deep learning approach. The proposed scheme was developed in the SDN controller that has capability of monitoring every OpenFlow switch. The work (Kang, 2016), suggested a novel intrusion detection and prevention approach that is based on neural networks to solve issues of the VANETS (Vehicular Networks). Attacks scenarios were implemented by injecting the malicious data packet to the in-vehicle controller area. The developed scheme sends the inputs node with the feature space in accordance to categorize packets into one of two categories: normal or attack. There are four important types of attacks which can be predicted using datasets like: 1) Daniel of Service 2) Probe attack 3) User to Local attack and 4) root to local attacks.

B.   Feed Forward Deep Neural Network

A feed forward neural network (FFDNN) is a part of artificial neural network in which the relation between the nodes does not form a cycle. So, it varies from recurrent neural networks, its progeny. The feed forward neural network is perhaps fundamental form of artificial neural network. Multi-layered network (MLN) of neurons is a synonym for feed forward neural networks. The knowledge only flows forwards in the neural network, via the input nodes, next using the hidden layers (one or many layers), and at last through the output nodes, thus the name feed forward. In work (Kasongo, 2019), FFDNN was utilized to detect intrusions. In order to create appropriate feature subsets with minimal duplication for wireless networks, they employ an FFDNN with a filter-based features selecting technique. The main training dataset for the proposed intrusion detection system was separated into two sets (i.e., the trained dataset as well as testing dataset). After that, a two-way normalization process and feature transformation takes place. Finally, the FFDNN is used by the proposed system to develop and validate the models.

C.   Recurrent Neural Network (RNN)

A Recurrent neural network (RNN) is a category in artificial neural network within which nodes are associated in a pointed graph that preserves a time-related succession. This helps in making working procedure temporally more complex. Utilizing their internal model, RNNs which are derived from feed-forward neural networks can interpret input variables of varying length. They can therefore be applied to tasks like voice or handwritten text recognition or segmentation. Finite impulse as well as infinite impulse networks are duo large categories of networks with a roughly comparable structure that are both referred to as RNNs. These two types of networks exhibit complex temporal patterns. To detect cyber-attacks in connected vehicles, a novel approach is proposed in work (Loukas, 2017). This helps in protecting a cyber-physical intrusion. The system employs deep multilayer perceptron and recurrent neural network architecture to achieve excellent quality and validity compared to traditional machine learning methods (e.g., k-means clustering and SVM). Malware attack, command injection attack and denial of service attack are the three categories against which the system is tested for a robotic vehicle system. In figure 4 RNN is shown. These layers are connected in multiple layers (Buczak, 2016)(Mohammed Harun Babu, 2018).

Figure 4. Recurrent Neural Network

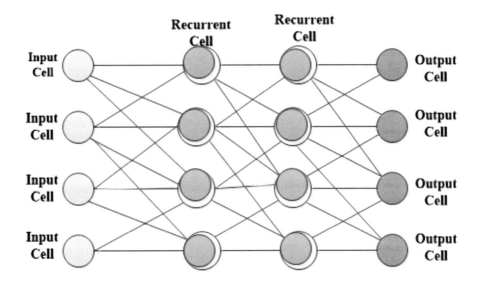

D.   Convolutional Neural Network (CNN)

The visual imaginary procedures can be frequently analysed using a type of deep neural network called Convolutional neural networks (CNNs). These networks are also named as shift invariant or space invariant artificial neural networks (SIANN) due to the common load model in the convolutional filters or kernels which slew across input characteristics and provide answer equal in translation (Qasem, 2020) (Daniel, 2019). But many CNN are same as translational in nature compared to invariant type. Some of the major applications where these are used can be listed as follows: recognising videos and images, commend system, image detection, image decomposition, interpreting medical images, natural language process and interfacing brain computer. Convolutional neural networks were employed in (Basumallik, 2019) for the packet-data intrusion identification system in the phasor measurement units-based simulation model. Data filters which are based on CNN were utilized for extracting feature from event signatures with the help of phasor measurement units. The units' buses in phasor measurement are dependent on IEEE 30 bus and IEEE 118 bus systems (Yirui, 2020). Figure 5 shows the convolutional neural network.

Figure 5. Convolutional Neural Network

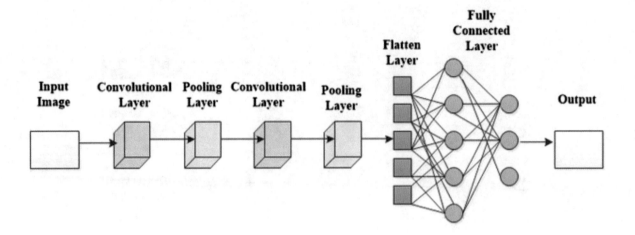

E.   Restricted Boltzmann Machine (RBM)

The probability distribution over given inputs can be trained and learnt using a type of artificial neural network by name restricted Boltzmann machine (RBM). A Restricted Boltzmann computer, developed by Geoffrey Hinton, is an algorithm for topic modelling, collaborative filtering, categorization, regress, and proportionality reduction. Figure 6 illustrates restricted Boltzmann network. The RBM has a regular symmetrical bipartite graph with no connections between units in the very same group. Many RBMs can be stockpiled and customized using the gradient descent and back-propagation algorithms. The deep belief networks (DBN) are some important type which belongs to this category of RBM. The DBN are developed using fundamentals of RBMs that are simplistic neural networks consisting of two-layers. The first layer of RBM is referred to as the visible layer or input layer, while the second layer is referred to as the secrete layer (Gupta, 2022).

Figure 6. Restricted Boltzmann Machine

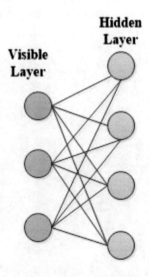

In work (Fiore, 2013), the intrusion detection was implemented using RBM algorithms. For combining and expressing power of generative model with correct categorization, discriminative RBM was employed (Ying-Feng Hsu, 2019).

F.   Deep Belief Network (DBN)

There are multiple layers with several latent variables which are also known as hidden units in deep belief network (DBN) which is an important subset of DBN. There will be interrelation within various layers of DBN but the individual units of the layers are not connected. Figure 7 shows the structure of DBN.

Figure 7. Deep Belief Network

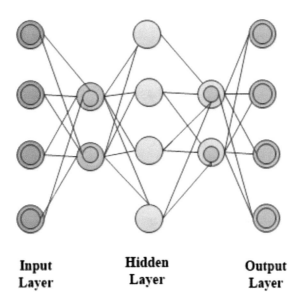

**Input
Layer**   **Hidden
Layer**   **Output
Layer**

Figure 6 shows deep belief network. The deep belief networks were utilized for detecting intrusions in work as explained in (Thamilarasu, 2019). The researchers aware of the needs a binary cross-entropy loss function to reduce the overall cost in the simulation environment. In another study, (Zhao, 2017) authors suggested a framework utilising probabilistic neural networks and deep belief networks.

G.   Auto encoder

An auto encoder is a neural network which could utilized for learning representation of raw data that is in compressed format. An auto encoder consists of two different sub models: one encoder and other is decoder. Figure 8 shows deep auto encoder. The data compression is carried out by the encoder and the reconstruction of the input of the encoder is done by the decoder (Rodriguez, 2021)(Rahim,2018). Thus, an encoder, input code and a decoder together make up the auto encoder. The deep auto-encoder is employed in work [25] for detecting intrusions in the area of cyber security. Authors have utilized the non-symmetrical multiple hidden layers for facilitating and improving results in comparison with DBN.

This work utilizes two different data sets by name KDD CUP 99 and NSL-KDD which has five different performance parameters like: F-score, accuracy, false alarm, recall and precision. In (Shone, 2016), the authors have explained an intrusion detection framework that uses the basics of the two-stage deep learning system (TSDL). The TSDL system makes utilization of a stacked auto-encoder. It is associated by a soft-max classifying model that consists of three layers (Maimo, 2018) (Wang, Q, 2019). Those layers names such as: (1) the input layer, (2) the hidden layers, and (3) the output layer. The auto encoder methods were employed by the authors in work (Papamartzivanos, 2019) for designing a self-adaptive and autonomous intrusion detection model. The system proposed by the authors consists of four stages that are: 1) Monitoring 2) Analysing 3) Planning and Executing and 5) Knowledge. Monitoring stage will determine the requirement of changes for adaptation of an intrusion detection system (Wang Y, 2016).

Figure 8. Deep Auto Encoder

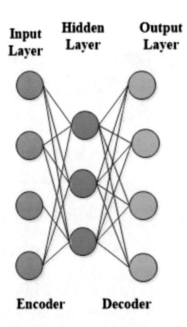

H.   Deep Migration Learning (DML)

Detecting intrusions in the field of cyber security, deep migration learning (DML) is used. The research incorporates a DML and an intrusion detection framework. There are four important classifications of DML namely; parameters migration, samples migration, related information migration and features representation migration which will help the research work. The DML is used in work, (Li D, 2019) for intrusion detection of network security.

I.   Replicator Neural Network (RNN)

Replicator neural networks (RNN) are used for cyber system's intrusion detection. To track down anomaly, the work needs employ the eccentric strategy. Figure 9 shows replicator neural network. Three steps make up the entropy extraction required for detection method Ullah, F, 2019) (Alavizadeh, 2022)(P. Deepa,2021). There are total three stages involved in the work like: 1) Data packet aggregation 2) Flow segmentation into time windows 3) The collection of features of interest from the flows. The replicator neural networks are used in work (Cordero CG, 2016), for cyber security intrusion detection utilizing above mentioned three stages.

Figure 9. Replicator Neural Network

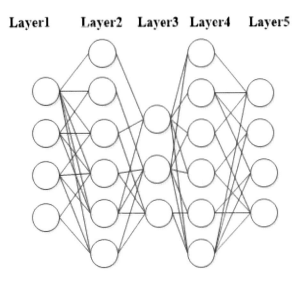

Performance Evaluation and Comparison

In this part, we provide comprehensive statistics on the results of attack detection accomplished by the various approaches indicated above. The majority of the deep learning techniques included here are intended to detect malware and network intrusions.

Table 1. Comparison of various DL algorithms

Deep Learning Algorithm	Reference	Data set used	Accuracy (%)
DBN	Zhao et al. (2017)	KDDCup 99	99.14
DNN	Wang et al. (2019)	KDDCup 99	95.45
CNN	Wang et al. [2016]	ISCX	95.5
RNN	Yin et al. (2020)	NSL-KDD	83.3

Reinforcement learning

Deep reinforcement algorithms can be used for intrusion detection by utilizing the labelled datasets. There are many advantages of using DRL algorithms for intrusion detection in network security (Mohammad Samar, 2022)(Koustav Kumar, 2021). Some of the important advantages are listed as follows. 1) DRL algorithm that are used for implementing classifiers are very easy and are having high speed of computation which makes it very much suitable for IoT applications. 2) The DRL algorithms are very appropriate for the design of distributed high performance computational systems. 3) There is flexibility of design and reduced differentiation task in drive detection in reward function. 4) Updating parameters in the system are very easy and simple. This is shown in figure 10.

The process of DRL is described by three terms namely state, action and reward. It uses experimenting and finding mistakes method by that the agent performs a task and gets a reward or penalty in return to that performed action. The environment will transition to a new state from its current condition (Cheng Ru Wang, 2018). In every state, the reward received by the agent conveys whether action performed was good or bad. Depending on the received rewards by the agent it learns to perform more good actions and slowly eliminates the bad actions (Lu Lv, 2020).

Figure 10. Agent and environment interactions in Reinforcement learning

Action taken (A$_t$)

Agent

Environment

(S$_{t+1}$)

(R$_{t+1}$)

Status (S$_t$)

Rewards (R$_t$)

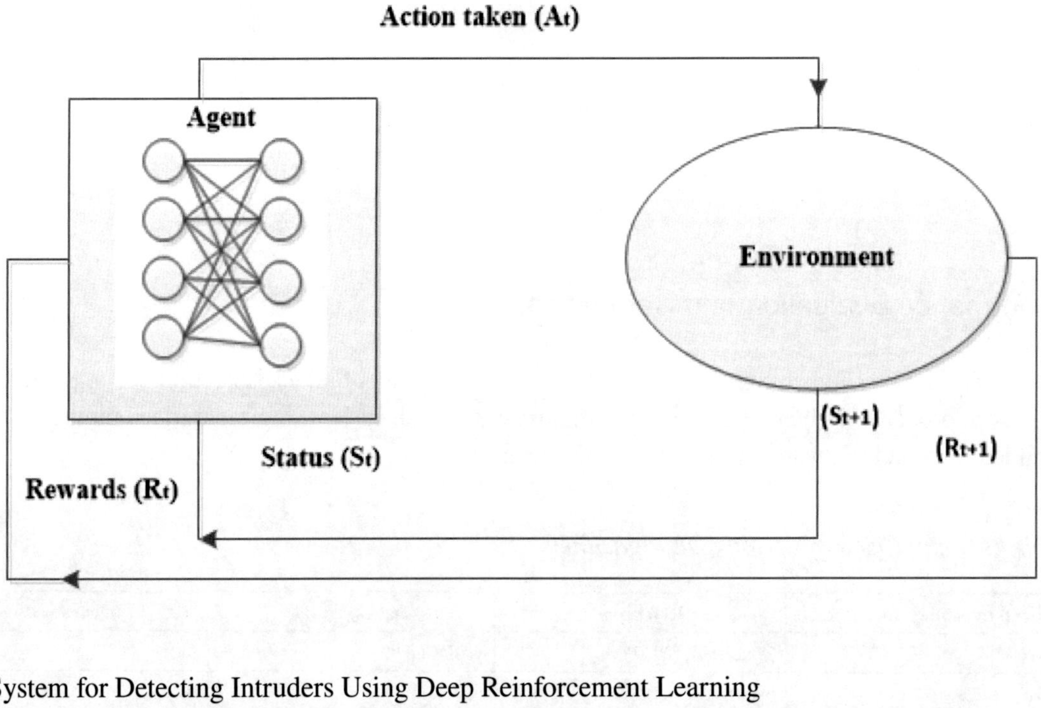

A. System for Detecting Intruders Using Deep Reinforcement Learning

The intrusion detection system mainly consists of three important entities namely: 1) data handling model 2) agent for intrusion detection and 3) training model for agents. The data handling model basically works on feature selection and pre-processing of the data. It mainly emphasise on reducing the noise redundancy of the input data (Manuel lopez-Matrin, 2020). Agent explains the components involved:

state model of the environment, training strategies and values function. The agent performs the actions randomly on the environment and it receives the rewards for the actions performed. In addition to the rewards, it also receives new status details at time t+1 for the action performed at time t. Depending on the reward received, the agents learns to select the proper actions. Thus randomness of the actions will gradually decrease and good actions are increased. Considering the network flow for the intrusion detection is discrete as well as independent, whenever an attack is identified it gives a positive feedback on the action conducted at time t+1. This helps to train for the next action.

Important Tools for Implementation of Deep Learning Mechanisms

This section contains a list of some of the key tools that can be used to execute deep learning techniques and their characteristics.

Table 2. List of Software Tools for Machine Learning algorithms implementation

Software Tool Name	OS Details	Type	Program used in developing tool	Features
TensorFlow	Linux, Mac OS, Windows	Open Source	Python, C++, CUDA	offers a collection for programming workflow.
KNIME	Linux, Mac OS, Windows	Open Source	Java	Can handle a big volume of data. via plugins, supports text mining and image mining
Apache Mahout	multiplatform	Open Source	Java Scala	Regression, clustering, recommenders, and distributed linear algebra, pre-processors.
Keras.io	multiplatform	Open Source	Python	a neural network API
Weka	Linux, Mac OS, Windows	Open Source	Java	Classification of data preparation Regression mining using association rules and clustering
Colab	Cloud Platform	Open Source		PyTorch, Keras, TensorFlow, and OpenCV libraries are supported

CONCLUSION

This chapter first briefs about requirement of network security and types of attacks. Next, detection and prevention of the attacks are briefly discussed. Deep learning approaches for intrusion detection are discussed for each type of neural network. Reinforcement learning and its application for intrusion detection are explained. A comparative study report is provided for the review conducted. List of software tools for the implementation of deep learning algorithm are provided. We firmly believe that this chapter is helpful for individuals who have suggestions for enhancing the accuracy of attack detection; our review will offer direction and dictionaries for additional study in this area.

REFERENCES

Alavizadeh, H., Jang-Jaccard, J. (2022), Deep Q-Learning Based inforcement Learning Approach for Network Intrusion Detection. *Computers*, pp.11-41 doi:10.3390/computers11030041

Ayei, E., Ibor, F. A., Olusoji, B., & Okunoye, O. E. (2020). Conceptualisation of Cyberattack prediction with deep learning. *Cybersecurity*, *3*, 14. doi:10.118642400-020-00053-7

Basumallik, S., Ma, R., & Eftekharnejad, S. (2019). *Packet-data anomaly detection in PMU-based state estimator using convolutional neural network. Int. J. Elec- tric*. Power Energy System.

Buczak, A. L., & Guven, E. (2016). A survey of data mining and machine learning methods for cyber security intrusion detection. *IEEE Communications Surveys and Tutorials*, *18*(2), 1153–1176. doi:10.1109/COMST.2015.2494502

Cheng, R. W., Rong, F. X., Lee, S. J., & Chie, H. L. (2018). Network intrusion detection using equality constrained-optimization-based extreme learning machines. *Knowledge-Based Systems*, *147*, 68–80. doi:10.1016/j.knosys.2018.02.015

Cordero, C. G., Hauke, S., Mühlhäuser, M., & Fischer, M. (2016), Analysing flow-based anomaly intrusion detection using replicator neural networks. In: *14th Annual Conference on Privacy, Security and Trust (PST)*. IEEE, pp. 317–24

Daniel, S. (2019). A Survey of Deep Learning Methods for Cyber Security. *Information*, *10*(4), 122. doi:10.3390/info10040122

Fiore, U., Palmieri, F., Castiglione, A., & De Santis, A. (2013). Network anomaly detection with the restricted Boltzmann machine. *Neurocomputing*, *122*, 13–23. doi:10.1016/j.neucom.2012.11.050

Gupta, C., Johri, I., Srinivasan, K., Hu, Y. C., Qaisar, S. M., & Huang, K. Y. (2022). A Systematic Review on Machine Learning and Deep Learning Models for Electronic Information Security in Mobile Networks. *Sensors (Basel)*, *22*(5), 2017. doi:10.339022052017 PMID:35271163

Kang, M.-J., & Kang, J.-W. (2016, June 7). Intrusion detection system using deep neural network for in-vehicle network security. *PLoS One*, *11*(6), e0155781. doi:10.1371/journal.pone.0155781 PMID:27271802

Kasongo, S. M., & Sun, Y. (2019). A deep learning method with filter based fea- ture engineering for wireless intrusion detection system. *IEEE Access : Practical Innovations, Open Solutions*, *7*, 38597–38607. doi:10.1109/ACCESS.2019.2905633

Khan, F. A., Gumaei, A., Derhab, A., & Hussain, A. (2019). A Tsdl: A two stage deep learning model for efficient network intrusion detection. *IEEE Access : Practical Innovations, Open Solutions*, *7*, 30373–30385. doi:10.1109/ACCESS.2019.2899721

Mondal, K. K., & Guha Roy, D. (2021). *IoT Data Security with Machine Learning Blckchain: Risks and Countermeasures*. Springer Science and Business Media LLC.

Li, D., Deng, L., Lee, M., & Wang, H. (2019). IoT data feature extraction and intrusion detection system for smart cities based on deep migration learning. *International Journal of Information Management*, *49*, 533–545. doi:10.1016/j.ijinfomgt.2019.04.006

Lu, Lv., Wang, W., Zhang, Z., & Liu, X. (2020). A novel intrusion detection system based on an optimal hybrid kernel extreme learning machine,Knowledge Based Systems, 195, Loukas G, Vuong T, Heartfield R, Sakellari G, Yoon Y, Gan D (2017), Cloud-based cyber-physical intrusion detection for vehicles using deep learning. *IEEE Access : Practical Innovations, Open Solutions*, 6(3), 491–508.

Lopez-Matrin, M., Carro, B., & Sanchez-Esguevillas, A. (2020). Application of deep reinforcement learning to intrusion detection for supervised problems. *Expert Systems with Applications, 141*.

Maimo, L. F. (2018). A Self-Adaptive Deep Learning-Based System for Anomaly Detection in 5G Networks. *IEEE Access : Practical Innovations, Open Solutions*, 6, 7700–7712. doi:10.1109/ACCESS.2018.2803446

Ferrag, M. A., Maglaras, L., Moschoyiannis, S., & Janicke, H. (2020). Deep learning for cyber security intrusion detection: Approaches, datasets, and comparative study. *Journal of Information Security and Applications, 50*.

Babu, M. H., Vinayakumar, R., & Soman, K. P. (2018), A short review on applications of deep learning for cyber security.

Ansari, M. S., Bartos, V., & Lee, B. (2022). GRU-based deep learning approach for network alert prediction. *FGCS, 128*, 235–247.

Papamartzivanos, D., Mármol, F. G., & Kambourakis, G. (2019). Introducing deep learn- ing self-adaptive misuse network intrusion detection systems. *IEEE Access : Practical Innovations, Open Solutions*, 7(135), 46–60.

Deepa, P., Rashmita Khilar. (2021). A Report on Voice Recognition System: Techniques,Methodologies and Challenges using Deep Neural Network, 2021 Innovations in Power and Advanced Computing Technologies (i-PACT), Qasem Abu-Hajira, Saleh Zein-Sabatto(2020), An Efficient Deep-Learning-Based Detection and Classification System for Cyber-Attacks in IoT Communication Networks. *Electronics (Basel)*, 9, 2152. doi:10.3390/electronics9122152

Rahim, N., Ahmad, J., Muhammad, K., Sangaiah, A. K., & Baik, S. W. (2018). Privacy-preserving image retrieval for mobile devices with deep features on the cloud. *Computer Communications*, 127, 75–85. doi:10.1016/j.comcom.2018.06.001

Rezvy, S., Luo, Y., Petridis, M., Lasebae, A., & Zebin, T. (2019), An efficient deep learning model for intrusion classification and prediction in 5G and IoT networks, In *53rd Annual Conference on Information Sciences and Systems (CISS)*, IEEE, pp 1–6.

Rodriguez, E., Otero, B., Gutierrez, N., & Canal, R. (2021). A Survey of Deep Learning Techniques for Cyber security in Mobile Networks IEEE Communication. Survey. *Tutor, 23*, 1920–1955.

Shone, N., Ngoc, T. N., Phai, V. D., & Shi, Q. (2018). A deep learning approach to network intrusion detection, IEEE Transactions on Emerging Top Computer. *Intelligence, 2*(1), 41–50.

Tang, T. A., Mhamdi, L., McLernon, D., Zaidi, S. A. R., & Ghogho, M. (2016). Deep learning ap- proach for network intrusion detection in software defined networking. *International Conference on Wireless Networks and Mobile Communi- cations (WINCOM)*, IEEE, p. 258–63.

Thamilarasu, G., & Chawla, S. (2019). Towards deep-learning-driven intrusion detection for the internet of things. *Sensors (Basel)*, *19*(9), 1977. doi:10.339019091977 PMID:31035611

Nguyen, T. T., & Reddi, V. J. (2021). Deep Reinforcement Learning for Cyber Security, IEEE Transactions on Neural Networks and Learning Systems, Ullah, F., Naeem, H., Jabbar, S., Khalid, S., Latif, M.A., Al-Turjman, F., Mostarda, L(2019), Cyber Security Threats Detection in Internet of Things Using Deep Learning Approach. *IEEE Access : Practical Innovations, Open Solutions*, *7*, 124379–124389.

Vinayakumar, R., Alazab, M., Soman, K. P., Poornachandran, P., Al-Nemrat, A., & Venkatraman, S. (2019). Deep learning approach for intelligent intrusion detection system. *IEEE Access : Practical Innovations, Open Solutions*, *7*, 41525–41550. doi:10.1109/ACCESS.2019.2895334

Wang, Q., Yang, H., Wang, Q., Huang, W., & Deng, B. (2019). A deep learning based data forwarding algorithm in mobile social networks Peer-to-Peer Network. *Application*, *12*, 1638–1650.

Wang, Y., Cai, W., & Wei, P. (2016). A deep learning approach for detecting malicious JavaScript code. *Security and Communication Networks*, *9*(11), 1520–1534. doi:10.1002ec.1441

Wu, Y., Wei, D., & Feng, J. (2020). *Network Attacks Detection Methods Based on Deep Learning Techniques: A Survey*. Security and Communication Networks Volume., doi:10.1155/2020/8872923

Hsu, Y.-F., & Matsuoka, M. (2019). A Deep Reinforcement Learning Approach for Anomaly Network Intrusion Detection System Communications and Networking: A Survey. *IEEE Communications Surveys and Tutorials*, *21*, 3133–3174. doi:10.1109/COMST.2019.2916583

Zhang, Y., Li, P., & Wang, X. (2019). Intrusion detection for IoT based on improved genetic algorithm and deep belief network. *IEEE Access : Practical Innovations, Open Solutions*, *7*, 31711–31722. doi:10.1109/ACCESS.2019.2903723

Zhao, G., Zhang, C., & Zheng, L. (2017), Intrusion detection using deep belief network and probabilistic neural network. In: *IEEE International Conference on Computational Science and Engineering (CSE) and IEEE International Conference on Embedded and Ubiquitous Computing (EUC)*, IEEE, p. 639–642 10.1109/CSE-EUC.2017.119

Chapter 7
Enhancing Quality of Service in Internet of Things:
Deep Learning Approach and Its Challenges

Udayakumar K.
SRM Institute of Science and Technology, India

Ramamoorthy S.
SRM Institute of Science and Technology, India

Poorvadevi R.
Sri Chandrasekharendra Saraswathi ViswaMahavidyalaya, India

ABSTRACT

The potential growth of internet of things (IoT) brings people and things together to handle daily tasks in a smart way. The major advancement the IoT offers is quality data sensing and faster data analytics through hurdle-free communication. The increasing number of devices and heterogeneous network natures unwrap more challenges in terms of quality of service. Currently, the deep learning algorithm explores different dimensions of service quality gradually in IoT scenarios. In order to effectively handle a dynamic IoT environment, it is essential that the design of IoT must be supplemented with an intelligent agent for providing effective QoS. The traditional methods are not capable of utilizing historical data to find insights into service quality improvement. In this chapter, a comprehensive analysis of deep learning techniques for improving QoS of the internet of things is carried out. Deep learning solutions for improving QoS and the challenges involved are compared. The deep reinforcement learning (DRL) for improving QoS in IoT and its evaluation technique are also explored.

DOI: 10.4018/978-1-6684-6275-1.ch007

INTRODUCTION

The growth of computation and communication technology empowers people to manage daily task digitally on the fly. Evolutionary areas such as machine learning, Cloud computing, Internet of things, big data analytics, virtual reality, digital twin and augmented reality changed the traditional approach of solving problem. Internet of things perceived as one of the hot area for more than one decade. Today, IoT is the most widely using technology in smart home, smart city, smart industry and so forth. It brings physical and digital worlds together to make the environment smarter and responsive. The IoT was first most intriguing to business and manufacturing. But, the focus is now on populating our homes and offices with smart gadgets, making it relevant to practically all.

According to international data corporation (IDC) USA, it is expected that by 2025 41.6 billion IoT devices will be deployed across the world. Industries have largest possibility of adapting IoT technology than the smart home and wearable gadgets in the near future.

The amount of data generated by IoT devices exponentially increasing and all of these IoT data must be gathered, saved, and analysed either locally or at cloud. due to limited resources in local system data transmission between IoT device and cloud become unavoidable. It subsequently increases latency and decrease the overall performance. As the number of IoT devices grows possibly millions, managing QoS for all of those devices will be difficult.

Due to complex service requirements and heterogeneous network, IoT applications face computational and communication delay. Edge technology as distributed paradigm allows execution near to the user end. Even though edge computing technology allows local execution, a resource allocation scheme is required to meet complex and customised service requirements. The branches of Artificial intelligence (AI) offers more flexibility to collect and process data in IoT through improved service quality even under dynamic environment.

An advancement in IoT data sensing and faster data analytics by removing connection barriers. However, as the number of devices grows and the network becomes more heterogeneous, new issues in terms of quality of service emerge. In the IoT, several parameters of service quality have been continuously growing with the help of machine learning algorithms. Energy efficiency, delay minimization, throughput, bandwidth, and resource usage are major concerns in this. To efficiently handle a dynamic IoT environment, IoT architecture must be augmented by intelligent agents for optimal QoS provisioning. Traditional methods are incapable of exploiting historical data to uncover insights about how to improve service quality. Quality of service can be increased by forecasting optimal or near optimal service that fits in dynamic IoT by introducing intelligent models built using historical data.

BACKGROUND

Response time, throughput, latency, computing cost, training cost, offloading, load balancing, path selection, channel allocate, security, and energy cost are the terminology that are most frequently used in QoS enhancement. The research studies used one or more parameters to improve overall system performance.

In (Vimal, S., *et al.*, 2020) have proposed resource allocation in MEC using the swam intelligence and reinforcement learning algorithm. In Mobile Edge Computing (MEC) environment, execution delay-causing factors are anticipated to improve Quality of Services. IoT resource allocation strategies must ensure at least two qualities: good performance and a reasonable turnaround time for resource allocation strategy development. Energy cost, response time, transmission rate, delay minimization, and security are notable aspects of system performance.

DL is a subset of ML approaches. The functionality of the human brain in analysis and learning is mimicked by trained DL models. Models in DL create neural networks that are inspired by the structure of the human brain. Large datasets can be handled by DL using GPUs, making it a popular choice for feature extraction and model fitting. DRL refers to RL architecture coupled with artificial neural networks that allow an agent to achieve high rewards by selecting the environment's most advantageous actions. DRL, then, is suitable for the complex, high-dimensional environment of the IoT.

In (Irshad, *et al.,* 2020) have proposed an approach to predict the upcoming behaviour and optimization needs of distributed biological systems. To provide interactive and responsive system to the end users, multi-agent based performance optimization approach used in cache, persistence and computing levels. IoT and deep learning paradigm plays significant part in collecting big biological data and big biological analytics which also provides fused information to its end users.

In (Amanullah, M. A., *et al.,* 2020) have suggested deep learning and big data technologies for IoT security. Since IoT allows communication with other devices, it has more chances to be vulnerable to security breaches. Research directions of IoT security are given by incorporating big data and deep learning. The number of IoT systems will increase as part of an advancement in cloud/edge based computing and new generation 5G communication. Intelligent techniques must be explored for improving QoS. In the direction, to handle large scale IoT system a novel scheduling approach has been proposed. The performance of heterogeneous IoT applications tuned based on packet priorities and network characteristics (Al-Turjman, *et al.,* 2019).

In (Saniya zafar, *et al.,* 2019) have explored QoS enhancement in mobile IoT using deep learning based interference prediction. Authors developed Threshold Percentage Dependent Interference Graph (TPDIG) using Deep Learning-based resource allocation algorithm for city buses mounted with moving small cells (mSCs). The cellular coverage impact due to dynamic interference present between small cells have been predicted through large short term memory based neural network.

In (Xuancheng Guo, et al., 2019) have proposed QoS-aware secure routing protocol for software defined network(SDN)-IoT. SDN as an emerging technique meets scale and flexibility requirements of IoT. Effective routing protocols with low latency and strong security are needed as the size of SDN-IoT expands, while the default routing protocols of SDN are still susceptible to dynamic flow control changes. To solve the fore-mentioned problem, deep reinforcement learning-based secure routing protocol proposed. This method can interact with network environment to extract required knowledge for creating dynamic secure routing protocol.

In (Liang, S.D., 2018) have explored smart and fast data processing for real time applications where computational expensive deep learning is deployed. Simulation conducted on automated handwritten digit recognition shows better performance in processing IoT data for deep learning.

INTERNET OF THINGS IN TECHNICAL PERSPECTIVE

Technically IoT can be viewed as integration of things/device, connectivity, application software, edge/cloud for sensing or collecting data about environment. The collected data utilized to make decision and control end system after processing (Wortmann, F & Flüchter, K., 2015) User end things embedded with sensor captures data when changes occur in the environment. for example, industrial machine slow down its operation when vibration sensor data crosses the threshold value. Since, seamless data flow occurs among IoT devices, IoT-edge and IoT-cloud network, QoS plays key role in IoT system performance.

Sensors, microcontroller devices for control, servers, and an edge or gateway are examples of IoT hardware. IoT software consists of mobile and web applications that collect data, integrate devices, do real-time analysis, and extend applications and processes. Sensing devices (thermostats, microphones) that interact with the environment, as well as an actuator (electric motor) that converts energy into motion. The communication channel over which devices can communicate and share information is known as connectivity or gateway.

Data from devices and sensors are translated into an easy-to-read and process format for analytics. The Internet of Things generates a lot of data, and the cloud platform allows us to store and handle those data. Automation and artificial intelligence help us attain the true potential of technology by giving more control over the system (Sethi, P & Sarangi, S. R., 2017). The Internet of Things provides a visual interface that the user can simply access and operate.

IoT Stack Architecture

The architecture of IoT stacked as three layers namely physical, network and application. Various component and its functionalities are illustrated in Figure 1.

Figure 1. IoT stack architecture

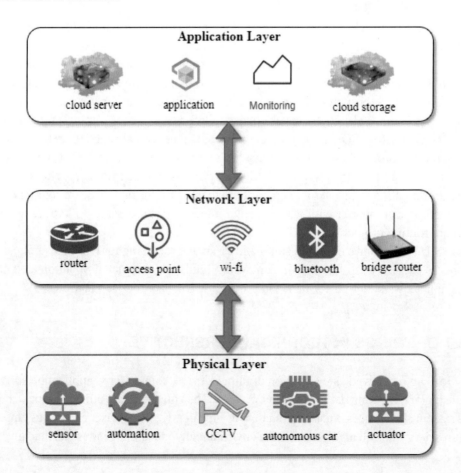

Physical layer

It detects certain physical factors or locates other intelligent devices in the surrounding region. Based on the requirement different sensors can be integrated with the real world object/thing. Those sensors perceive and transmit data about environment for further processing to edge or cloud. Processed data used to control the system through actuator. For example, Heat energy changes in a source is measured by temperature sensors.

Network layer

This layer responsible for establishing connectivity and transmit sensor data to other smart objects, network devices, and servers through different network. The Internet protocol(IP) stack is commonly used by IoT devices to connect to the Internet. This stack requires a lot of memory and processing power from the connected devices due to its complexity.

Application layer

The IoT users are facilitated with an application based services. It is the primary goal of an application layer. It outlines a variety of uses for the IoT, including smart homes, smart cities, and smart health.

QUALITY OF SERVICE IN IOT

Quality of service is a technique to enhance service quality with corresponding performance metrics. Service quality must be ensured and managed in different levels of IoT ecosystem. For an instance, network capabilities and resources must be managed from QoS perspective to deliver consistent connectivity among IoT devices. The efficient and effective utilization of available resources can be achieved by implementing QoS techniques.

Many research work explored technique to attain the optimal quality of network service but service quality requirement of things, computing, and caching are need to be investigated under dynamic environment. Due to heterogeneous IoT devices and complex network traditional techniques encounters various challenges in maintaining optimal service quality (Singh, M & Baranwal, G., 2018)

The IoT devices like wearables, autonomous vehicle needs seamless connectivity regardless of time and place. It creates dynamic environment in IoT ecosystem. Providing quality service in such environment become complex task.

In order to provide IoT services, QoS aids in managing the system's resources and capabilities. It helps the service providers to clearly communicate to the customers about performance and usability of their services. service level agreements (SLAs) between IoT service provider and IoT customer can be enforced on QoS based. Customers may find the finest IoT service for their application with the use of QoS measurements, which also deal with service quality improvement.

With IoT, the field of information and communication technology might take on a new dimension by adding a business enablement component. It is composed syntactically of the phrases Things and Internet, which work to focus attention on items so they can be included into a common framework.

Internet works to advance a network-driven IoT vision. However, it is clear that the Internet of Things, consists of things, communication, and computing.

Things

Things embedded with sensor and has the ability to connect to the internet. It includes intelligent objects, sensors, people, and any other items that are aware of the context and are able to communicate with other entities at any time and place.

Communication

The networking element are used in establishing communication between IoT devices and with the outside world. Internet gateway and non-IP networks are deployed to offer connectivity. Privacy and security are the major concern when data transmit over communication network (Sheikh, *et al.,* 2019).

Computing

The data collected from heterogeneous sources via communication networks are organized at edge or cloud infrastructure. Those infrastructures provide essential computational and storage service for data processing and storage.

QOS ISSUES

1.   Classification and Data Sorting

Traditional QoS tools has the ability to categorize the applications passing through a network. It follows standard well-defined policy to assign priority and manage network traffic. Initially, packets passing over a network is classified according to its type based on data type. Then, priority is marked. whenever traffic congestion occurs, Packets with a high-priority mark considered for transmitting over low-priority. But, today scenario have changed. Prioritizing real-time applications become more crucial due to its latency sensitiveness. An environment based dynamic priority need to be assigned for time sensitive IoT applications. An absolute necessity of dynamic QoS directs way to conduct further research.

2.   Congestion management

   Congestion control is the process of analysing a packet's marks and queuing it up using intricate algorithms. However, monitoring network traffic to identify high risk zones congestion avoidance is helpful. When such high risk situations are found, the congestion avoidance mechanism will discard low-priority packets in order to preserve high-priority packets at that specific moment. Avoiding and managing congestion helps keep a network from not being overloaded. Using a packet revealing policy high-priority services are processed and transmitted first in order to manage congestion. This is an important concern in network congestion management by priority mechanism.

3. Maximize bandwidth use

The current generation highly rely on internet-based applications that requires effective bandwidth management. Those applications including AR/VR and real time video processing must be properly handled. A variety of differentiated services are included in QoS bandwidth management, such as specifying a minimum throughput, guaranteeing a minimum throughput, and preventing packets from going above a certain size on the communication link. But, recent research showing that DL model can ensure effective bandwidth management with its prediction ability. Still more solution expected to come in future in this track.

4. Resource-intensive applications

Another QoS issue is managing resource-intensive applications like augmented reality, virtual reality and video processing applications. Traditional priority based QoS methods need to be replaced with prediction based methods for handling dynamic scenario. a seamless user experience must be ensured with effective approach for managing resource-intensive applications.

5. Minimizing latency

The deployment of latency sensitive application demands negligible latency across different communication networks. even though more solution proposed with machine learning, big data, and deep learning due to network heterogeneity optimal QoS and zero latency become more challenge for research community.

6. Packet loss prevention

There must be a traffic warden to guide the flow of data by priority and manage data traffic in order to make sure that all information reaches the cloud or other required destination given the large number of devices linked over a network. In the IoT, a lack of QoS could lead to instability, information overload, and the loss of crucial data.

QOS PARAMETERS AND METRICS

The service quality of IoT specifically measured through different parameters. Those parameters are classified based on layers of IoT architecture. Namely, sensing layer, communication layer and computation layer. The Quality of service parameters in IoT are illustrated in Table 1.

Table 1. QoS Parameters/Metrics of IoT

Layers	QoS metric/parameter	Description
Sensing layer	Weight	Weight and cost
	Interoperability	Compatibility and performance Measure
	Availability	Availability of resources and its range.
	Reliability	Recoverability and self-configurable
	Accuracy	Error calculation
	Stability	Device life time, high deviation in input
	Precision	Correlation measures
	Security	Authorization and authentication
	Energy	Power Consumption
Communication layer	Jitter	Delay between each packet varies
	Throughput	Successful transmission of data packets
	Bandwidth	The volume of data that can be transferred through a network.
	Packet Loss/delivery ratio	The number of undeliverable and deliverable packets.
	Security and Privacy	Safeguard the availability, reliability, and accuracy of the communication channel and the data passing over it.
	Delay	Variation in packet transfer time.
	Reliability	Ability to connect without any loss or security breach.
Computing layer	Scalability	Achieving maximum throughput with quick response
	Dynamic Availability	whether the system is usable when needed and in typical operation conditions
	Reliability	Mean time between failure
	Capacity	metrics like CPU, RAM, and storage capacity
	Response Time	Depends on application and infrastructure.

CHALLENGES IN QOS

1. Dynamic QoS

The unresolved problem might be addressed in future research on dynamic QoS providing methods. QoS-aware approaches must be adapted to dynamic network conditions. For instance, if the deadline, delay, or energy requirements of the service applicant or server change, the QoS-aware approach may adapt to the new situation and be able to maintain the QoS optimal condition during service delivery.

2. Mobility

Since IoT devices may be mobile, predicting where nodes and devices will be in the future helps with data forwarding and decreases overall delay in network, which can improve QoS by analysing behavioural and mobility tendencies. Semantic support and any available contextual data help in providing QoS solutions

3.   Real time evaluation

The current proposed methods achieve prominent improvement in QoS through machine learning and deep learning. But, the majority of the proposed works evaluated by a simulation environment to analyse the practicality of suggested strategies. Only few QoS-based techniques performed evaluation in the real world. A task scheduling strategy, for instance, ought to be able to mimic real-world patterns, even though these algorithms might operate strangely in practise. Therefore, it is quite challenging to put offered solutions into practise.

4.   Scalability

Some of the techniques proposed ought to be effective on a large scale. The viability of these technologies in confined contexts cannot be guaranteed for specific devices or nodes. Despite the importance of this criterion, most of the suggested techniques were only tested in a few specific situations. As a result, it provides a different direction for upcoming works.

5.   Energy

Energy is one of the essential elements of QoS requirement. There are many dispersed nodes in the environment, and it could have a significant energy and carbon footprint. As a result, we must develop new energy-saving techniques and novel architectural designs for the green system. Thus, the intriguing energy management strategy of green computing.

TRADITIONAL METHODS OF QOS

Diverse services lead to a significant rise in network traffic, which could lead to packet loss, network congestion, or an increase in forwarding time. Any of these circumstances will result in decline service quality or perhaps disruption in service. Therefore, a method to avoid network congestion is needed for real-time services. Increasing network bandwidth is the greatest answer, but doing so is expensive. The most economical strategy to handle traffic congestion is to implement a "guarantee" policy.

Depending on the needs of various services, QoS ensures the quality of the service from beginning to end. By allowing different forms of traffic to pre-empt network resources according to their priorities, it helps the network better utilise its resources. For instance, audio, video, and key data applications can be processed preferentially on network devices. Businesses can employ a number of strategies to ensure the excellent performance of their most important applications.

Prioritization of Time-Sensitive

Many business networks get too congested due to high packets flow, which causes unnecessary rejection of packets at routers and switches. Time critical application like VR, Autonomous vehicle and Streaming applications suffer as a result (Habeeb, F, *et al.,* 2022). Prioritisation technique assign high priority for such time critical application to handle traffic and avoid packets rejection. Due to the ability to send packets with a higher priority before other traffic, this is very helpful in situations of extreme congestion.

Reserved Resources

The resource reservation protocol (RSVP), reserves network resources through certain factors that causes traffic. In this method, traffic nature, frequency of occurrence, and origin are taken into account for classifying the network. Those classified network resource is reserved to provide particular degrees of QoS for application data streams. But this method not suitable for ever changing network environment.

Queuing

In addition to prioritization, queuing method is introduced to hold high priority application data over others. the specific rules need to be defined prior by the companies for time critical applications. Each router and switch maintain memory buffer called queue to hold passing packets for high priority applications (Mijuskovic, A, *et al.,* 2021).

Traffic Marking

Once it has been determined which applications on a network deserve priority over other bandwidth, the traffic has to be tagged. There are two techniques used in this process. One is differentiated services code point (DSCP) and second, class of service (CoS).

AN OVERVIEW OF DEEP LEARNING

DL is a subset of machine learning, which mimic the human brain structure. Deep learning gains more popularity later 2006. A neural network with some layers attempts to match and learn from large volume of data. The learning stage of DL can handle unstructured data like text and images and vanish preprocessing phase of traditional machine learning. the data input, weight, and bias together helps DL to recognise, categorise, and characterise the data objects with accuracy.

Deep neural networks are made up of many layers of interconnected nodes, each of which improves upon the prediction or categorization made by the previous layer. Basically, input and output layers are called visible layers and additional layers which help to optimize and refine accuracy called hidden layers. Traditional neural networks typically have two or three but it turns deep neural network with more hidden layers. Deep neural network has an ability to extract features by its own.

Deep Learning Algorithms

With the help of deep learning techniques, terrific development has been stretched in manufacturing industries, health care, agriculture, and many. Enormous amount of data and advanced data analytic techniques made decision making process more rapid and accurate.

Those data extracted from IoT based services in various formats. DL draws more attention due to effective feature extraction, prediction accuracy, high volume of data handling, structured/unstructured data support, and scalability. This increase the implementation of DL in different scenario rather than traditional machine learning.

IoT services mainly classified as finance critical or lives critical. It directly means that service quality of such system is an important factor. Due to increasing IoT services and limited resources, it is hard to offer stable QoS in dynamic environment. DL as a promising technique, that makes computational automation and intelligence more efficient (Kimbugwe, N, *et al.*, 2021). In this direction, methods for improving QoS have been proposed with DL algorithms. Such algorithm used in predicting class label and learn useful pattern with available data. Some of such DL algorithm and its functional procedures are discussed below.

Convolutional Neural Networks (CNN)

It (CNN/ConvNet) belongs to deep neural networks category and widely used technique to interpret visual data in deep learning. Normally, neural network deals with matrix multiplications, but in ConvNet deals with mathematical procedure that takes two functions and creates a third function. this unique method is called convolution.

Convolution neural network basically consist of three layers namely input, hidden, and output. Hidden layer further branched as normalizing, pooling, and convolution layer. The Convolved Feature's spatial size is condensed by the Pooling layer. By lowering the dimensions, the lower amount of CPU power needed to process the data. Average pooling and maximum pooling are the two types of pooling. The essential CNN module is the convolution layer, and different CNN structures are needed for various problems. The network's normalising layer enables each layer to learn more independently. The output of the earlier layers is normalised using it. In normalisation, the activations scale the input layer.

Recurrent Neural Networks (RNN)

It is the most advanced algorithm for sequential data. Due to its internal memory, it is the first algorithm to recall its input, making it ideal for machine learning issues while processing sequential data. RNN operates on the tenet that each layer's output is saved and fed back into the system's input in order to forecast that layer's output.

The information in RNN loops back on itself. It takes into account both the current input and the lessons it has learnt from prior inputs when making a decision. Information in a feed-forward neural network only passes from the input layer through the hidden layers and onto the output layer in one way. it never visiting a node more than once, the information travels in a straight line through the network. The processing flow of RNN and a feed-forward neural network is compared in Figure 2 and Figure 3.

Figure 2. Feed-Forward Neural Network

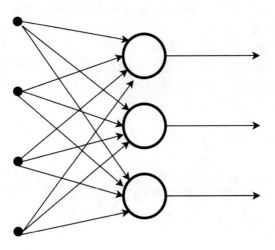

Figure 3. RNN

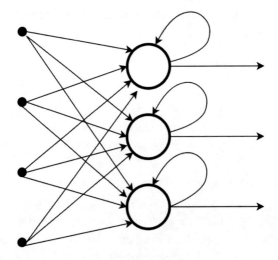

Deep Reinforcement Learning

The power of deep learning technique combined with reinforcement learning called deep reinforcement learning. It gains more popular because of its sequential decision making capability. DNN is coupled with RL since RL alone cannot manage situations when there are many system states, and data and the environment is not stationary. Functional procedure of DRL and its application scenario are elaborately discussed on separate section.

CHALLENGES IN DEEP LEARNING

1. Generalization

The generalization of DL model completely relies on the amount of data taken for training. If a user takes large amount data from different source, DL model can be trained with more parameters which leads powerful and accurate model with large functional area. High volume of data assures generalized deep learning model.

2. Bias

Biases are another significant concern with deep learning algorithms. When a model is trained on biased data, it will project those biases into its predictions.

3. Learning rate

Deep learning models encounters significant difficulties in defining learning rate. Model trained with high learning rate may failed to give optimal outcome. It stuck in the process and be even more difficult to find a solution if the rate is too low.

4. Inflexible

Deep learning models are rigid and incapable of multitasking after they have been trained. Only one unique problem can they effectively and precisely solve. Even resolving a similar issue would necessitate model retraining.

5. Hardware requirements

To ensure increased effectiveness and lower time consumption, high-performance graphics processing units (GPUs) are needed for DL. However, these devices are pricey and consume a lot of energy.

CONVERGENCE OF DEEP LEARNING AND IOT

The exponential increase in real time data, connections, and services has resulted in considerable problems, especially when it comes to meeting the demanding requirements of the IoT. Artificial Intelligence and IoT convergence perceived as an emerging platform to provide better real time solutions through efficient information retrieval. It technically aids a lot to data analysis and decision making. Each layer of an IoT architecture powered with AI that prompting digital and intelligent services (Shi, F, *et al.*, 2020). Adopting AI in sensing layer enables selective sensing that handles trade between limited sensing resources and data explosion. Various AI algorithms are defined in the sensing layer to increase the accuracy and effectiveness of sensing. AI in communication layer improves QoS by adapting DL and neural networks (Saleem, T. J., & Chishti, M. A., 2021). DL algorithms adopted to accomplish best path selection, network scheduling optimization, reliable connection, and low latency communication. AI in computation layer makes a significant contribution to better understanding customised services and increasing consumer satisfaction. The challenges of deep learning and IoT convergence are discussed in Table 2.

Table 2. Challenges of Deep learning and IoT convergence

Layers	Challenges	Solutions	Application Scenario
Sensing layer	· uncertainty and complexity due to sudden data flow. · Limited sensing resources.	Selective sensing	Deep learning-based classifiers used in selective sensing algorithm
Link layer	There is a significant difficulty for the limited communication capacity with extraordinarily vast connections.	adopting deep learning and neural networks	DL based prediction for best routing path and network scheduling
Application Layer	Adaptive services for different user requirement	Ontology modelling and Machine learning	DL based information mining and recommendation systems for providing the most appropriate service.

APPLICATION OF DL IN QOS

The deep learning algorithm have been adopted in internet for things to enhance QoS and provisioning of intelligent services.it mainly focuses on improving overall IoT ecosystem performance at all the level like sensing data, data transmission and data processing. Some of improvement observed in IoT by applying DL are discussed below.

1. Network traffic forecasting

Network traffic forecasting is an important aspect in IoT network where high number of connected objects including delay sensitive are involved. A novel DL architecture called generic additive Network (gaNet) proposed as supervised regression problem for IoT network traffic prediction (Lopez-Martin, M., *et al.*, 2019).

2. Signal Authentication and Security

The potential goal of IoT ecosystem is protecting IoT device and related resource from cyber-attacks. In this line-up, many researches have been focused on addressing security and privacy threats. For the purpose of dynamic authentication of IoT signals and the detection of cyberattacks, a unique watermarking method is proposed using deep reinforcement learning. By using this technique, the IoT gateway, which gathers signals from IoT devices and authenticate IoT signals (Ferdowsi, A., & Saad, W., 2018).

3. Channel assignment

In wireless SDN-IoT, promising communication quality of service achieved through partially overlapping channel assignment technique. In order to effectively handle dynamically changing data traffic,

DL based solution was proposed to predict IoT traffic load and assign channel through prediction result (Tang, F, *et al.,* 2018).

4.   Intrusion detection

Recently, the security vulnerabilities to IoT networks are being detected and mitigated using deep learning techniques. For identifying intrusion threats in IoT networks, feedforward neural networks (FNN) have been employed extensively. In this direction, a novel technique presented for the identifying intrusion threats in an IoT network called self-normalizing neural network (SNN) which is based on FNN (Ibitoye, O, *et al.,* 2019).

5.   Resource allocation

The dynamic resource allocation policy is required to handle computation and communication delay in IoT system. To make functional judgments at the source end, complicated services provided by edge nodes are also needed. As a distributed paradigm, edge technology enables execution closer to the data source. The resource allocation (RA) strategy is necessary to provide dynamic optimal allocation and usage of resources even while it permits local execution (Gai, K., & Qiu, M., 2018).

6.   Offloading decision

Due to limited computing resources at user end task offloading technique widely used in edge and cloud. But, it increases transmission latency and energy consumption. In order to enhance service quality, the cost of resources needed for task offloading and increase server resource utilization, optimized DRL algorithm used the task offloading problem presented as a joint decision-making problem for cost minimization that integrates processing latency, processing energy consumption, and the task throw rate of latency-sensitive tasks (Lin, L, *et al.,* 2019)

DEEP LEARNING ALGORITHM FOR QOS

Based on the number of layers, deep learning algorithms are classified as deep neural networks (E.g. convolutional neural network) and shallow neural networks (E.g. Feedforward neural network). In IoT network, DL algorithms and DL based reinforcement learning algorithms are adopted to improve quality of service as given in Table 3. this section attempting to present comprehensive analysis of deep learning for improving service quality in IoT environment.

Table 3. Deep learning for QoS

Methodology	QoS measurement factor	Application Scenario	Performance Result
DL based resource allocation (Saniya zafar et al., 2019)	Resource allocation	Interference prediction	22.5% improved data rate achieved
DRL based QoS aware Secure routing protocol (Xuancheng Guo et.al., 2019)	End to end delay, packet delivery ratio	Traffic prediction	10% relative performance gains
Proposed algorithm speed up data processing (Liang,S,D, et al., 2018)	Data processing	Automated handwritten digit recognition	99.7% accuracy
Hybrid CNN+LSTM model for DDoS attack prediction (Roopak, M et al., 2019)	security	Intrusion detection	97.16% accuracy
LSTM based missing data prediction (Kok, I, *et al.*, 2019)	Data analytics	Sensor data missing in IoT	average total delays reduced
DNN models for inference tasks (Zhang, W, *et al.*, 2021)	Resource allocation	Task scheduling and resource management	inference accuracy by 31.4%
Dynamic power management policy using DRL (Liu, N, et al., 2017)	Resource management	Power allocation	energy saving upto 16.20%
TOW-dynamic-based channel assignment algorithm (Ma, J., et al., 2019)	Resource allocation	Channel assignment	Quick decision made on channel selection
Online Predictive Offloading (OPO) algorithm (Tu, Y, et al.,2022)	Resource optimization	Off loading	Reduced offloading cost by 25.6%

DEEP REINFORCEMENT LEARNING

DRL is the most popular kind of machine learning since it can tackle a variety of difficult decision-making problems (Hussain, F, *et al.*, 2022). Due to efficacy in addressing difficult sequential decision-making problems, reinforcement learning(RL) has gained a lot of popularity. An intelligent agent in deep reinforcement learning learns from its actions much like people learn from experience. An agent is rewarded or punished according to its taken action. DR Learning strategies rely on interacting with the environment rather than large training data sets. IoT devices can employ RL based agent to make decisions based on inference in the face of dynamic and unpredictable network conditions. An agent interacts with environment to learn best policy function(model) which is achieved through maximizing reward.

Key Elements

The power of deep learning technique combined with reinforcement learning called deep reinforcement learning. It gains more popular because of its sequential decision making capability. Deep neural network(DNN) is coupled with RL since RL alone cannot manage situations when there are many system states and data and the environment is not stationary. Some of the key elements of DRL are illustrated in Figure 4.

Figure 4. Key elements of deep reinforcement learning

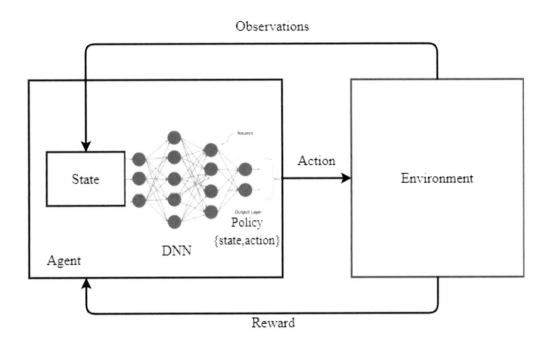

Agent - a software code which makes decision on choosing action with reward maximization as an objective under uncertainty.

Environment - An environment, which is everything that happens after an agent makes a choice, is a depiction of an issue.

State- finite set of variable and its possible values

Action- finite set of action that an agent can choose

Reward- it's an evaluation metric through which an agent action is measured. The goal of an agent is defined in a way to maximize the reward.

Policy- it's a function that represents state and action mapping.

DNN- By stacking layers of neural networks along the depth and width of smaller structures.

DRL algorithms

The IoT devices adopts deep reinforcement learning to make decisions based on inference in the face of dynamic and unpredictable network conditions. Most of the discrete action-state reinforcement Learning problem can be resolved using the MDP framework. An agent can reach the best policy using the Markov Decision for maximising rewards over time.

MDP= {A, S, R, N, V}

S-finite Set of states

A-Finite set of action

R-Rewards assigned for each action

N-Policy that maps action and state

V-Value function for rewards

Markov Decision Process:

States : S

Model : T (current state S, action, next state S')

Actions : A(S), A

Reward : R(S), R(S, a), R(S, a, S')

Policy : Π(S) -> a

Π*

The traditional Q-learning method not suitable for handling high dimensional state space. It requires more memory to store each state and action pair and equivalently it increases complexity in computation and Q-table update. On other side, DRL capable of taking more continuous state variable that represents Quality of service. DRL agent makes an action decision in discrete action space. Whereas a value vector is used to represent action in continuous action space. A set of all the state S that the agent can transition is called state space. In values based RL algorithm Q-function is used to determine the Q-Values to define the optimal Action-selection policy. Some of deep reinforcement learning algorithm given in Table 4.

Table 4. Deep reinforcement learning algorithms

Algorithm	Action Space(A)	State Space(S)	Function
Deep Quality Network (DQN)	Discrete	Continuous	Q-value
Double DQN	Continuous	Continuous	Q-value
Deep deterministic policy gradient(DDPG)	Continuous	Continuous	Q-value

1.   Deep Quality Network (DQN)

When dealing with a complicated environment with numerous potential outcomes, the Q-learning algorithm becomes ineffective. Deep RL resolves this problem by merging the Q-Learning approach with Deep Learning model. The basic task is to construct and train a neural network that can estimate the various Q-values for each action given a state as depicted in Figure 5. The memory replay and separate target network introduced by Deep Q-Learning make it possible to perform better.

Figure 5. Deep quality network

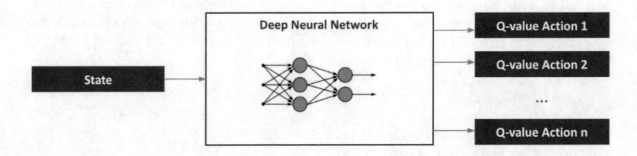

2.   Double DQN

By breaking down the target's maximum operation into its action selection and action evaluation, double Q-learning aims to reduce overestimations. Because Deep Q-learning involves a maximising step over estimated action values, which favours overestimated over underestimated values, it is known to occasionally learn action values that are unreasonably high.

3.   Deep Deterministic Policy Gradient (DDPG)

An algorithm called Deep Deterministic Policy Gradient (DDPG) simultaneously learns a Q-function (critic) and a policy (actor) as illustrated in Figure 6. The Q-function is learned using off-policy data and the Bellman equation, and the policy is then learned using the Q-function. it is an actor-critic, model-free technique that may operate over continuous action spaces. It is based on the deterministic policy gradient.

Figure 6. Deep deterministic policy gradient

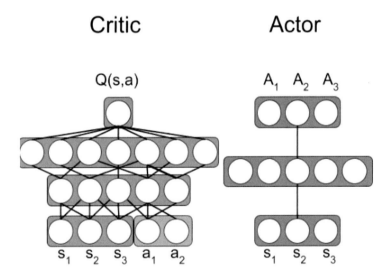

QOS AWARE RESOURCE ALLOCATION USING DRL

Resource management has been considered as one of major concern in Quality of service. The optimal resource management leads high QoS through related extents like task scheduling, task offloading, and resource allocation. Many literatures given noteworthy contribution in handling resource allocation and offloading problem. Specifically, In IoT communication and computation resources must be managed effectively and dynamically for consistent QoS (Filali, A., *et al.*, 2022). The communication resource like routers, switches need to be designed towards high service quality through energy consumption, latency, bandwidth utilization and security. In same way, high service quality can be achieved through computing resource management. It involves task scheduling, task offloading, resource allocation and resource provisioning.

The resource allocation and offloading decision problem in mobile edge computing considered as sample subject issue here. Task initiated from IoT devices queued in edge node or mobile edge server for processing (Udayakumar K. & Ramamoorthy S., 2022). The reinforcement learning agent at edge node and mobile edge server observes an environment. Based on observation input information given to deep neural networks as state description. Input layer is initiated to take state information as input. Neurons on hidden layers will be activated by activation function (E.g. ReLu) with QoS parameters. The output layer predicts optimal action for the given state. Suggested action given to mobile edge host to perform resource allocation or offloading. Evaluated reward (feedback) as a performance metric of an action given to deep neural network as depicted in Figure 7. State and action pair stored in memory for exploitation(repeat) in near future. The updated environment information given as next input to DNN and process continuous till an agent reach optimal policy for resource allocation. The derived policy can be utilized for optimal resource allocation.

Figure 7. Resource Allocation using DRL

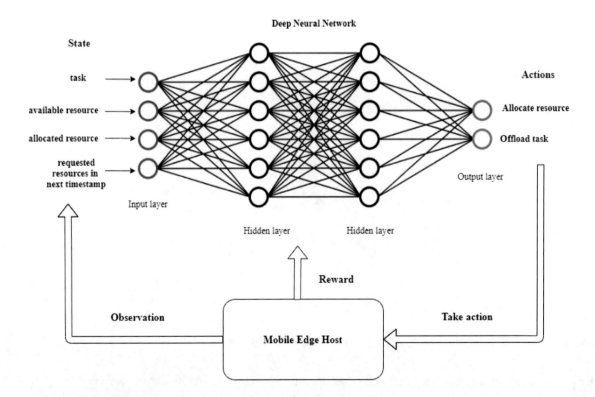

COMPARATIVE ANALYSIS

The recent researches proving that service quality in IoT is improved through machine learning specifically deep reinforcement learning. Traditional QoS improvement technique enhanced through machine learning approach with the help of enormous data about the environment. Most of the current research works focus on QoS from 5G,6G, IoT device, edge, fog and cloud computing perspectives (Haghi Kashani, M, *et al.,* 2020). The important concerns of QoS are energy consumption, response time, execution time, throughput, reliability, resource utilization, security, and mobility. Each QoS parameter has its own potential contribution in overall performance. In this section, various QoS factors of IoT from different DL based literature are considered.

In general, QoS can be approached in the three levels namely application level, communication level, resource level. In most of the literature, highest priority (50-60%) is given to QoS at resource level as shown in Figure 8. Followed by resource level QoS, communication and application level has 30-40% and 20-30% contributions respectively.

Figure 8. Quality of service level

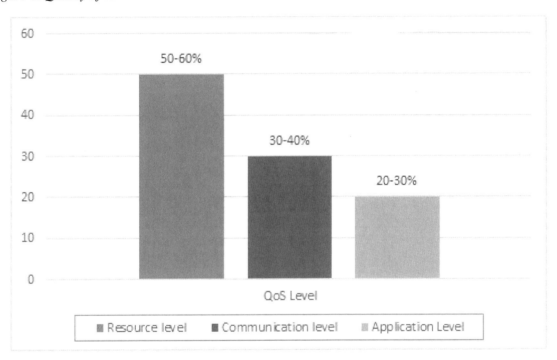

the resource management has significant part in improving QoS. The optimal resource management policy brings cost effective, improved performance and functionality of the system.The computing resource at edge,fog, and cloud offers various services required for IoT.IoT demands seemly infrastucture for processing task. provision of such infrastrcture must include cost,functional requirements, and QoS. The methods for improving QoS at different level is depicted in Table 5.

Table 5. QoS improvment methods

QoS approached level	QoS improvement methods
Resource management	Task Scheduling
	Energy efficient resource management
	Resource allocation
	Task offloading
	Reducing service delay
	Resource provisioning
	Service composition
Communication management	Traffic management
	Load balancing
	Network slicing
	Resource optimization
	Bandwidth prediction
	Latency and energy aware resource scheduling
Application management	Security models
	Real time stream monitoring
	Data analytics
	Routing protolcols
	Interoperatable services

Under three levels, different QoS factors are considered and those factors are improved using DL based solutions in Internet of Things.the statistical analysis of service quality factors are depicted in Figure 9. Response time is an important concern with high priority in most of the literature.followed by that, resource utilization and energy consumption cosidered as significant QoS factor. Implementation part in most literature uses simulator like Matlab, iFogSim, CPLEX and CloudSim and python as preferable language.

Figure 9. Service quality factors

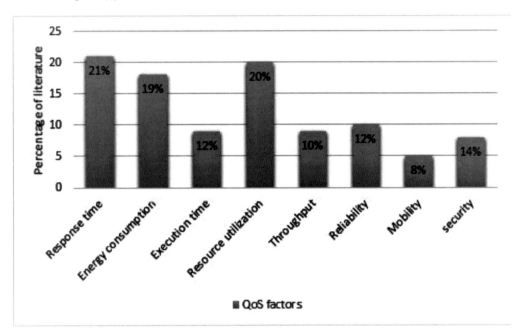

CONCLUSION

Due to increasing IoT applications and high load pressure communication network suffers to provide optimal quality of service. Also, Heterogeneous network involved in connecting IoT dynamic QoS policy become mandate for effective handling of services. Even though traditional (heuristic and metaheuristic) technique improves QoS dynamic network condition and uncertainty cannot be handled effectively. machine learning gears up QoS with its prediction and pattern discovery techniques. In specific, deep learning algorithms are adopted in internet for things to enhance QoS and provisioning of intelligent services.it mainly focuses on improving overall IoT ecosystem performance at all the level like sensing data, data transmission and data processing. In IoT scenario, QoS can be approached in the three levels namely application level, communication level, resource level The important concerns of QoS are energy consumption, response time, execution time, throughput, reliability, resource utilization, security, and mobility. Each QoS parameter has its own potential contribution in overall performance. The deep learning algorithm has significant potential to handle QoS factors together. And, it can find the correlation among factors for achieving better trade. Finally, it is concluded that deep learning plays key role in enhancing QoS in IoT.

REFERENCES

Al-Turjman, F., Ever, E., Zikria, Y. B., Kim, S. W., & Elmahgoubi, A. (2019). SAHCI: Scheduling approach for heterogeneous content-centric IoT applications. *IEEE Access : Practical Innovations, Open Solutions*, 7, 80342–80349. doi:10.1109/ACCESS.2019.2923203

Amanullah, M. A., Habeeb, R. A. A., Nasaruddin, F. H., Gani, A., Ahmed, E., Nainar, A. S. M., & Imran, M. (2020). Deep learning and big data technologies for IoT security. *Computer Communications*, *151*, 495–517. doi:10.1016/j.comcom.2020.01.016

Ferdowsi, A., & Saad, W. (2018). Deep learning for signal authentication and security in massive internet-of-things systems. *IEEE Transactions on Communications*, *67*(2), 1371–1387. doi:10.1109/TCOMM.2018.2878025

Filali, A., Nour, B., Cherkaoui, S., & Kobbane, A. (2022). *Communication and Computation O-RAN Resource Slicing for URLLC Services Using Deep Reinforcement Learning*. arXiv preprint arXiv:2202.06439.

Gai, K., & Qiu, M. (2018). Optimal resource allocation using reinforcement learning for IoT content-centric services. *Applied Soft Computing*, *70*, 12–21. doi:10.1016/j.asoc.2018.03.056

Guo, X., Lin, H., Li, Z., & Peng, M. (2019). Deep-reinforcement-learning-based QoS-aware secure routing for SDN-IoT. *IEEE Internet of Things Journal*, *7*(7), 6242-6251.

Habeeb, F., Szydlo, T., Kowalski, L., Noor, A., Thakker, D., Morgan, G., & Ranjan, R. (2022). Dynamic Data Streams for Time-Critical IoT Systems in Energy-Aware IoT Devices Using Reinforcement Learning. *Sensors (Basel)*, *22*(6), 2375. doi:10.339022062375 PMID:35336544

Haghi Kashani, M., Rahmani, A. M., & Jafari Navimipour, N. (2020). Quality of service-aware approaches in fog computing. *International Journal of Communication Systems*, *33*(8), e4340. doi:10.1002/dac.4340

Hussain, F., Hassan, S. A., Hussain, R., & Hossain, E. (2020). Machine learning for resource management in cellular and IoT networks: Potentials, current solutions, and open challenges. *IEEE Communications Surveys and Tutorials*, *22*(2), 1251–1275. doi:10.1109/COMST.2020.2964534

Ibitoye, O., Shafiq, O., & Matrawy, A. (2019, December). Analyzing adversarial attacks against deep learning for intrusion detection in IoT networks. In *2019 IEEE global communications conference (GLOBECOM)* (pp. 1-6). IEEE.

Irshad, O., Khan, M. U. G., Iqbal, R., Basheer, S., & Bashir, A. K. (2020). Performance optimization of IoT based biological systems using deep learning. *Computer Communications*, *155*, 24–31. doi:10.1016/j.comcom.2020.02.059

Kimbugwe, N., Pei, T., & Kyebambe, M. N. (2021). Application of Deep Learning for Quality of Service Enhancement in Internet of Things: A Review. *Energies*, *14*(19), 6384. doi:10.3390/en14196384

Kok, İ., Çorak, B. H., Yavanoğlu, U., & Özdemir, S. (2019, December). Deep learning based delay and bandwidth efficient data transmission in IoT. In *2019 IEEE International Conference on Big Data (Big Data)* (pp. 2327-2333). IEEE.

Liang, S. D. (2018). Smart and fast data processing for deep learning in Internet of Things: Less is more. *IEEE Internet of Things Journal*, *6*(4), 5981–5989. doi:10.1109/JIOT.2018.2864579

Lin, L., Liao, X., Jin, H., & Li, P. (2019). Computation offloading toward edge computing. *Proceedings of the IEEE*, *107*(8), 1584–1607. doi:10.1109/JPROC.2019.2922285

Liu, N., Li, Z., Xu, J., Xu, Z., Lin, S., Qiu, Q., . . . Wang, Y. (2017). A hierarchical framework of cloud resource allocation and power management using deep reinforcement learning. In *2017 IEEE 37th international conference on distributed computing systems (ICDCS)* (pp. 372-382). IEEE.

Lopez-Martin, M., Carro, B., & Sanchez-Esguevillas, A. (2019). Neural network architecture based on gradient boosting for IoT traffic prediction. *Future Generation Computer Systems, 100*, 656–673. doi:10.1016/j.future.2019.05.060

Ma, J., Nagatsuma, T., Kim, S. J., & Hasegawa, M. (2019, February). A machine-learning-based channel assignment algorithm for IoT. In *2019 International Conference on Artificial Intelligence in Information and Communication (ICAIIC)* (pp. 1-6). IEEE. 10.1109/ICAIIC.2019.8669028

Mijuskovic, A., Chiumento, A., Bemthuis, R., Aldea, A., & Havinga, P. (2021). Resource management techniques for cloud/fog and edge computing: An evaluation framework and classification. *Sensors (Basel), 21*(5), 1832. doi:10.339021051832 PMID:33808037

Roopak, M., Tian, G. Y., & Chambers, J. (2019, January). Deep learning models for cyber security in IoT networks. In *2019 IEEE 9th annual computing and communication workshop and conference (CCWC),* (pp. 452-457). IEEE.

Saleem, T. J., & Chishti, M. A. (2021). Deep learning for the internet of things: Potential benefits and use-cases. *Digital Communications and Networks, 7*(4), 526–542. doi:10.1016/j.dcan.2020.12.002

Sethi, P., & Sarangi, S. R. (2017). Internet of things: Architectures, protocols, and applications. *Journal of Electrical and Computer Engineering, 2017*, 2017. doi:10.1155/2017/9324035

Sheikh, A., Ambhaikar, A., & Kumar, S. (2019). Quality of services improvement for secure iot networks. *International Journal of Engineering and Advanced Technology.*

Shi, F., Ning, H., Huangfu, W., Zhang, F., Wei, D., Hong, T., & Daneshmand, M. (2020). Recent progress on the convergence of the Internet of Things and artificial intelligence. *IEEE Network, 34*(5), 8–15. doi:10.1109/MNET.011.2000009

Singh, M., & Baranwal, G. (2018). Quality of service (qos) in internet of things. In *2018 3rd International Conference on Internet of Things: Smart Innovation and Usages (IoT-SIU),* (pp. 1-6). IEEE.

Tang, F., Mao, B., Fadlullah, Z. M., & Kato, N. (2018). On a novel deep-learning-based intelligent partially overlapping channel assignment in SDN-IoT. *IEEE Communications Magazine, 56*(9), 80–86. doi:10.1109/MCOM.2018.1701227

Tu, Y., Chen, H., Yan, L., & Zhou, X. (2022). Task offloading based on LSTM prediction and deep reinforcement learning for efficient edge computing in IoT. *Future Internet, 14*(2), 30. doi:10.3390/fi14020030

Udayakumar, K., & Ramamoorthy, S. (2022). Intelligent Resource Allocation in Industrial IoT using Reinforcement Learning with Hybrid Meta-Heuristic Algorithm. *Cybernetics and Systems.* Advance online publication. doi:10.1080/01969722.2022.2080341

Vimal, S., Khari, M., Dey, N., Crespo, R. G., & Robinson, Y. H. (2020). Enhanced resource allocation in mobile edge computing using reinforcement learning based MOACO algorithm for IIOT. *Computer Communications, 151*, 355–364. doi:10.1016/j.comcom.2020.01.018

Wortmann, F., & Flüchter, K. (2015). Internet of things. *Business & Information Systems Engineering,* *57*(3), 221–224. doi:10.100712599-015-0383-3

Zafar, S., Jangsher, S., Bouachir, O., Aloqaily, M., & Ben Othman, J. (2019). QoS enhancement with deep learning-based interference prediction in mobile IoT. *Computer Communications, 148,* 86–97. doi:10.1016/j.comcom.2019.09.010

Zhang, W., Yang, D., Peng, H., Wu, W., Quan, W., Zhang, H., & Shen, X. (2021). Deep reinforcement learning based resource management for DNN inference in industrial IoT. *IEEE Transactions on Vehicular Technology, 70*(8), 7605–7618. doi:10.1109/TVT.2021.3068255

Chapter 8
Edge Computing in Intelligent IoT

Rajarajeswari S.
Vellore Institute of Technology, Chennai, India

Hema N.
Vellore Institute of Technology, Chennai, India

ABSTRACT

We can perceive, analyse, control, and optimise the conventional physical systems thanks to pervasive IoT applications. Numerous IoT apps have recently had security breaches, which suggests that IoT applications could endanger physical systems. Numerous security issues in IoT applications are mostly caused by two factors: severe resource restrictions and inadequate security architecture. Edge-based security designs for IoT applications are still in their infancy, despite some research efforts in this direction. In addition to providing an in-depth analysis of current edge-based IoT security options, this study seeks to provide inspiration for new edge-based IoT security designs. A significant deal of progress in artificial intelligence (AI) opens up a number of potential avenues for addressing the security challenges in the setting that privacy preservation and security have become essential issues for EC. This chapter addresses issues with edge computing-based internet of things at the computation and security levels.

EDGE INTELLIGENCE

Even though the term edge AI or EI is relatively research, new, and methodology in this area have existed for some time. As indicated before, Microsoft developed an edge-based prototype to support mobile voice command recognition, an AI application, in 2009 to show the advantages of edge computing. Despite the early stages of research, EI still lacks a defined definition. EI is currently referred to as the concept of demonstrating AI algorithms on an device with sensor data / signals) which are formed on the device by the majority of businesses and presses. It is important to highlight that, while this description reflects the current most popular tactic to EI in the real world Ike usage of high end AI chips), it significantly reduces the range of possible solutions. (O.salman et al.,2015) Running computation intensive methods

DOI: 10.4018/978-1-6684-6275-1.ch008

locally, as demonstrated by DNN models, is particularly resource-intensive and necessitates the inclusion of high end processors into the device. Such a mandatory requirement in addition to increase the price of EI but is also unsuited and unfavourable to legacy devices that currently exist and have constrained processing power.

This work states that EI is not limited to only using edge servers or devices to execute AI models. In fact, running DNN models with edge cloud collaboration can decrease end-to-end energy usage and latency when compared to the remote execution method, as shown by a numerous recent research. Because of these useful benefits, it is concluded that such a collaborative hierarchy ought to be incorporated into the creation of effective EI solutions. Additionally, current ideas about EI mostly concentrate on the inference phase (i.e., execution the AI model), assuming that the training of the AI model is carried out in the power cloud data centres because the training phase consumes substantially more number of resources than the inference phase. The vast volume of training data must, however, be transported either from end devices or from the cloud, results in excessive communication costs and worries about data protection (O.salman et al.,2015). As a result, it can be seen that EI does not essentially imply that the DNN model is completely trained or inferred at the edge but instead that it can function in a cloud-edge device synchronization manner via data offloading. EI can be categorized into six stages in accordance with the quantity and path length of data offloading, as displayed in Figure. 1. The following list includes a definition for each degree of emotional intelligence.

Figure 1. Six-level rating for EI

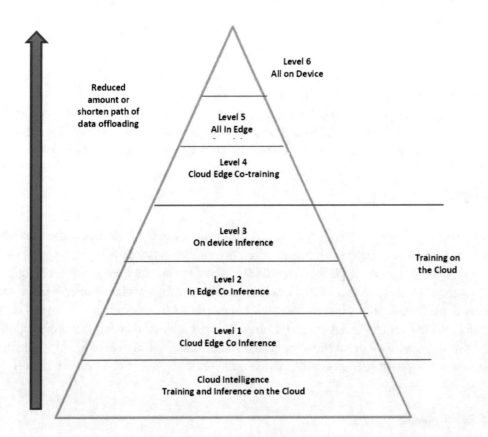

1) Cloud intelligence: The DNN model is entirely trained and inferred in the cloud.

2) Level 1—Cloud-Edge Coinference and Cloud Training: Inferring the DNN model using edge-cloud cooperation while training the DNN model in the cloud. In this case, edge-cloud cooperation entails a partial data offload to the cloud.

3) Level 2—In-Edge Coinference and Cloud Training: This level involves DNN model training in the cloud while inferencing it using in-edge technology. The term "in-edge" here refers to the model inference that is being performed within the network edge (using D2D communication).

4) Level 3—On-Device Inference and Cloud Training: The DNN model is trained in the cloud, but it is inferred entirely locally on the device.

5) Level 4—Cloud-Edge Cotraining and Inference: The DNN model is inferred and trained through edge-cloud cooperation.

6) Level 5—All In-Edge: The DNN model is inferred and trained both in-edge.

7) Level 6—All On-Device: On-device inference and training of the DNN model.

The quantity and path length of data unloading decrease as EI increases. As a result, data offloading transmission latency is decreased, data privacy is increased, and WAN bandwidth costs are decreased. This is accomplished, nevertheless, at the expense of higher processing latency and energy use. (P.Du et.al,2016) This disagreement shows that there isn't really a "best-level" in general; rather, the "bestlevel" EI depends on the application and should be chosen by taking into account a variety of factors, including energy efficiency, latency, WAN bandwidth cost and privacy.

INTEGRATION OF EDGE COMPUTING AND IOT

General

In keeping with what we previously discussed, edge computing and IoT are each experiencing significant growth. Even if they are independent, the edge computing environment can assist IoT in resolving some pressing problems and enhancing performance. Thus, it has become obvious in recent years that they should be incorporated.

Table 1. Features of edge computing, cloud computing and IoT

	IoT	**Edge**	**Cloud**
Deployment	Distributed	Distributed	Centralized
Components	Physical Devices	Edge Nodes	Virtual resources
Computational	Limited	Limited	Unlimited
Storage	Small	Limited	Unlimited
Response Time	NA	Fast	Slow
Big Data	Source	Process	Process

Figure 2. Layered architecture of IoT with Edge computing

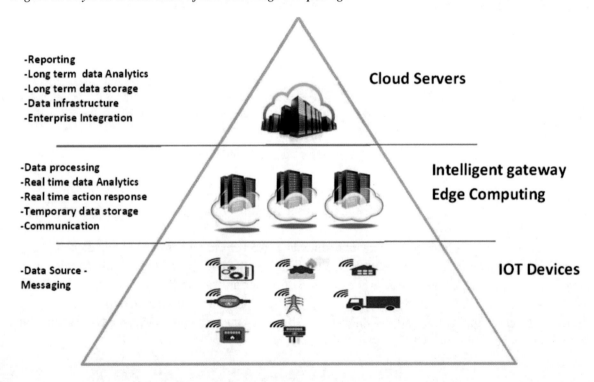

The three-layer architecture of edge computing-based IoT is shown in Figure. 2. In general, because of the traits of the two structures, IoT can profit from both edge computing and cloud computing. Even though edge computing has less computational power and storage than cloud computing for IoT, it nevertheless has additional benefits. IoT specifically needs quick response times rather than vast storage and high computational capacities. To meet the needs of IoT applications, edge computing provides an acceptable compute capability, adequate storage, and quick reaction times. On the other side, edge computing get profit from IoT by using the edge computing framework to handle the distributed and dynamic nature of the edge computing nodes. Edge nodes can be employed as service providers and can be either IoT devices or devices with leftover computational capability.

IoT Performance Demands

Transmission

The sum of the transmission and processing times can be used to calculate the overall reaction time. IoT devices typically produce a large volume of data continuously, yet have few computational needs. In fact, high network latency is inappropriate and incompatible with QoS standards. Vehicle-to-infrastructure and Vehicle-to-vehicle communications are two specific examples.

Response times must be incredibly quick as well, in relation to issues with public safety and the requirements of first respondents. Edge computing, in contrast to the typical cloud, can offer a large number of distributed compute nodes that are proximate to the users to support real-time data gathering and analysis.

Storage

IoT produced enormous amounts of data, as was already mentioned, and if it isn't already the most significant aspect of big data generation. IoT must therefore upload the vast amounts of data to edge / cloud storage. The quick upload time is one advantage of using edge-based storage. However, approach has the disadvantage that edge-based storage security is a worry. It is challenging to guarantee the information safety, integrity, calculation of anonymity, non repudiation, and data originality because the edge nodes are operating in many companies. Additionally, edge nodes' storage capacity is constrained, and they lack the kind of large-scale, long-lasting storage seen in cloud computing data centres (A.Ahmed et al.,2016). Finally, multiple edge nodes are used and synchronized for storing the data when it is important to upload the data, adding to the difficulty of data management.

Computation

Because the majority of IoT devices have constrained processing and energy capabilities, it is impossible to perform sophisticated computational operations locally. IoT devices typically just collect data and send it to more potent processing nodes, where all of the data will be processed further and analysed. However, most IoT devices don't need a lot of processing power, and edge nodes can adequately meet IoT demands, particularly for real-time applications. More discussion about Edge Computing-based IoT role in achieving the needs for transmission, computing ad, storage in the paragraphs that follow. Additionally, we will offer several instances so that you may evaluate each quality.

Figure 3. The problem space of IoT with Edge Computing

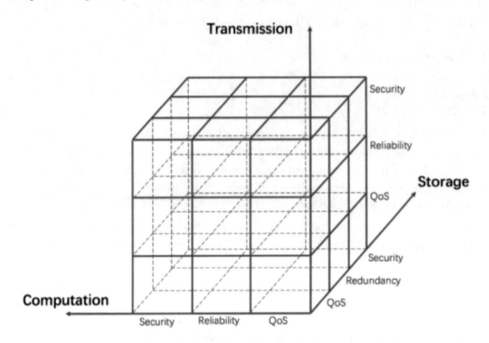

BENEFITS OF INTEGRATING EDGE COMPUTING AND IoT

Transmission

The transmission time is influenced by network performance, which is measured, among other things, by bandwidth, latency, and packet loss. As discussed earlier, main advantage of edge computing is its ability to meet the quality of service requirements of time sensitive applications, such as Microsoft's "Live Video Analytics" project. The goal of this work is to create a low-cost, real-time system for analysing live videos that are acquired from all the cameras that are present in a nearby open space. This project's ability to forecast the flow of moving traffic, which is apparently time sensitive, is one of its goals. Edge computing's hierarchical architecture ensures faster transmission times than any other network. In the meantime, edge computing has also been created to address the IoT network resource bottleneck issue. Traffic flow and response time will be greatly improved by delegating storage and data computation to end users.

Bandwidth

The IoT deploys a many sensors, which results in enormous amounts of data being produced. It is unacceptable for these data to be sent uncompressed or unprocessed directly to cloud servers. Massive amounts of data will use up a lot of network bandwidth, which can cause packet loss and transmission delays, among other problems. Therefore, before sending data to distant cloud servers, IoT gateways must pre-process it and even aggregate it. Therefore, the challenge is to efficiently migrate data processing and aggregation processes to lower end users' bandwidth needs while retaining the integrity of the data.

Numerous research projects have been focused on this problem. For instance, Abdelwahab et al. presented the REPLISOM memory replication protocol and an LTE which is an aware edge cloud architecture.

The planned protocol can plan memory duplication tasks successfully. In this method, it is possible to address radio resource contention caused by devices using the resources at the same time.

Energy

The IoT endpoints may differ in terms of power and battery capacity in addition to network resources. Therefore, it is important to carefully evaluate these elements when an end device needs to perform data processing or data forwarding. It's critical to extend the lifespan of end devices, particularly those with finite batteries. Edge computing can feature a variable job offloading strategy that takes into account the power capabilities of each device to accomplish this purpose.

Numerous studies have been conducted on the subject of energy. For instance, Gu et al. introduced the idea of medical cyber-physical systems backed by fog computing to host virtual medical device applications. A thorough approach for IoT-cloud service optimization was put forth by Barcelo et al. This approach formalises the service distribution problem as a min-cost mixed-cast _ow problem in the network under investigation. After the suggested problem is fixed, it is shown that the smart IoT services can cut power usage by more than 80%.

In order to solve the optimization challenge, Zhang et al. additionally presented an energy-efficient computation offloading scheme. The energy consumption of the MEC offloading mechanism in 5G heterogeneous networks can be reduced in this way.

Overhead

Each data packet sent across a network has a payload as well as header overhead. Even though the majority of IoT data packets are tiny, many IoT devices result in important network overhead due to the features of IoT data patterns. Another unresolved issue for edge computing is how to lower network overhead. The superfluous overhead can be reduced by aggregating and pre-processing insignificant packets with the help of cloudlet/ edge servers. Plachy et al. developed a cross-layer strategy in relation to this problem, intending to reduce overhead and boost transmission effectiveness for 5G networks.

Storage

Storage powered by cloud computing is typically centrally located and executed as complicated, multi-layered systems made up of collections of common servers and disc drives. It is the moment where the network topology converges and is constructed on top of the network. Edge computing based storage use failure recovery and load balancing strategies to achieve the availability and necessary performance in order to meet QoS requirements. By shifting storage demands to various edge nodes, these load balancing techniques can reduce traffic on the network connection lines. The failure recovery strategies are crucial for edge computing storage in order to differentiate between data failures (such as power difficulties software, packet loss, hardware, and noise) in the huge dataflow from several data sources.

Storage balancing

Devices often have extremely little storage space in IoT networks. The devices must communicate and store all data that is generated or gathered in a storage server. Additionally, many IoT devices are simultaneously producing a lot of data. There will be severe network obstruction if all devices are storing data in cloud storage at the same time. For Example, the Microsoft "Live Video Analytics" project creates enormous amounts of data that must be transferred to storage in a hurry and promptly incorporated into the analysis process. The cameras or sensors providing data into cloud computing based storage will certainly not meet these requirements. Instead data can be transmitted to storage nodes.

Recovery policy

Reliability is crucial for storing and retrieving accurate data representations, as was said above, and the recovery policy is a crucial requirement for edge computing based storage systems. The system will monitor the readiness of the storage nodes, data duplication, or employ more nodes for redundancy in order to boost reliability.

Availability

There are several reasons why a storage service can stop working. Monitoring systems often use frequent pinging or heartbeats to determine the availability of edge nodes and to confirm the health of storage systems. Storage services will inevitably go offline at some point.The edundant storage servers are set up in cloud computing-based applications. However, the other available edge nodes in edge computing storage systems will function as redundant storage. Massive numbers of devices always need data storage in IoT contexts. So it's crucial to choose the best storage service provider. To address this issue, a number of measurement systems are available and proposed. They can all choose from a list of storage service providers.

Data replication

The enormous number of connected devices in IoT contexts creates a constant need for data storage. Sensitive data, such as information about a person's health, energy usage patterns, speed or traffic conditions for smart vehicles, etc., must obviously be accurate. For the distributed storage systems to manage this enormous demand and guarantee data accuracy, IoT environments are therefore a must.

By employing replication, distributed storage systems can improve dependability and lengthen the MTTF. Data is split up into numerous parts in distributed storage systems, and each one has a set size and set of code blocks. Additionally, there are predetermined overlaps between the data segments. As a result, using information from linked pieces, it is possible to reassemble the data kept on each piece.

Computation

Each edge node in edge computing has less processing power than what is offered by cloud servers. As a result, several edge nodes must be given the same calculation duties in order to satisfy the requirements. Remember that edge computing offloads computation and storage to the edge of the networks to serve end user needs, making the task scheduling system a crucial part of edge computing. Generally speaking, several objectives can be used to construct task scheduling strategies.

Computation offloading

Edge computing requires shifting the sites of various calculation jobs in order to achieve higher computational efficiency.

Local

Embedded chips have become increasingly affordable and popular in contemporary IoT systems. As a result, end devices now have much more computer power. As a result, it's feasible that some computational jobs will be carried out by end users in the Machine-to-Machine network, which is made up of a variety of IoT end devices. The shortest response time can be obtained by end users with huge number of nearby devices.

Cloudlet / edge

Even though the M2M network of devices offers some computational resources, M2M is insufficient to meet all the end users' needs for resources. Thus, the most of network resources in the Internet of Things must be provided by edge/cloudlet servers. The task scheduling of the cloudlet/edge servers is the most important issue to properly accomplish this.

The goal of task scheduling for cloudlet/ edge servers is to determine the best subgroup of servers to allocate given the limitations. The ideal solution to this issue will produce the least amount of computation latency and transmission latency, the least amount of energy used for communication and computing, and the least amount of bandwidth needed for IoT applications.

Cloud

It is evident that few data processing or data storage jobs call for more resources than Machine to Machine or Edge/Cloudlet can feasibly supply without using up all available resources. The storage and computation in this scenario must be carried out using conventional cloud servers. The least computational latency will be experienced by tasks run on cloud servers because they have the biggest processing capacity in the network. Due to the great distance between end devices and cloud servers, the cloud servers have the highest transmission delay. Thus, finding a balance between compute slowness and transmission latency is a significant challenge.

Pricing policy

A suitable pricing strategy for the resources in the networks can therefore be used to develop resource allocation methods.

Single service provider

Traditionally, a single service provider has been in charge of overseeing the computing and communication resources in the edge/cloudlet servers. In other words, the service provider will determine the various costs for the computing and communication capabilities of the edge/cloudlet servers installed at various ranges from the end devices. By choosing the best edge/cloudlet servers that are available and moving the appropriate workload, end users can thus reduce their financial costs.

Multiple service providers

The computational or storage resources might not fit to a single service provider because IoT connects a wide range of devices from several parties. As a result, consumers who demand data processing activities must pay various edge computing service providers for the necessary resources. With the right pricing structure, third parties will be encouraged to contribute their computing/storage capabilities to IoT in order to ultimately receive service and money from end users. Furthermore, edge computing service providers will engage in both rivalry and collaboration. The future edge computing networks must therefore make some attempt to balance pricing amongst various service providers. To manage resources in this direction, economics-driven methods like auction could be used.

Priority

Another crucial component of the computation task schedule in edge computing is priority. Priority allows for the maximisation of the overall advantages of various IoT applications. So that the overall network performance may be enhanced, real-time IoT apps, such as monitoring applications, will be given a greater priority. Rest of the applications, however, that use more resources, like multimedia, can be given a lower priority.

CHALLENGES OF IoT BASED ON EDGE COMPUTING

As discussed earlier, incorporating edge computing to support the IoT has many advantages.

System Integration

Supporting multiple IoT device types and service requirements in an edge computing environment is a difficult task. In edge computing, a variety of platforms, servers and network topologies are combined. As a result, programming and managing resources and data for many applications that run on various and heterogeneous platforms, in various places, will be challenging. All user programmes and applications in cloud computing are deployed to and operating on cloud servers, from a programming standpoint. It is the duty of the cloud service providers, like Google and Amazon, to distribute these apps and programmes over the appropriate hardware and make sure they are functioning properly. The majority of users are unaware of how these programmes operate or distribute their data and resources. Being centralised and simple to maintain, the cloud service is one of the advantages of cloud computing.

Edge computing, in contrast, differs significantly from cloud computing. Although the dispersed topology has its advantages, edge nodes are typically heterogeneous platforms. In this scenario, creating an application which can be installed and run on an edge computing platform will be extremely challenging for developers. Some strategies have been developed to deal with the programmability issues associated with edge computing, but none take particular IoT uses into account. Since the identification of edge nodes is the initial stage in the Internet of Things (IoT), IoT devices are unaware of the types of surrounding platforms prior to the discovery process. Additionally, a sizable number of server-side applications must be installed on the edge nodes. (Kewei sha et al.,2020) Therefore, another difficult issue is distribution of edge node providers and management that server side programmes.

For instance, edge node owners can easily administer the NDN naming scheme, which offers a hierarchically structured name for the distributed network. However, in order to incorporate several communication protocols, a proxy server must be added to the network. Additionally, the NDN naming method requires knowledge of the source hardware, which increases the risk of information leaking. To better facilitate mobility, the name in the MobilityFirst naming scheme is separated from the IP and MAC addresses. The Globally Unique Identification (GUID) required by the MobilityFirst plan is a concern because it is not user-friendly.

Resource Management

Resource management must be fully understood and optimised in order for IoT and edge computing to work together. IoT devices, which frequently lack resources and processing capacity, will be significantly impacted by network delay and congestion, requiring more power to retransmit data in crowded environments. Device latency can be reduced by using edge computing, which is the closest computing and storage resource. Decentralized resources will be crucial in encouraging and sharing these resources.

As long as it is computationally affordable, the management of resources can be done in a variety of ways. Nevertheless, it is important to remember that the enormous variability of service providers, gadgets, and apps significantly increases complexity.

Auction-based

It is possible to manage network resources using a variety of economically motivated strategies. Auction techniques are widely used in a variety of computer science study fields, including smart systems, mobile and cloud computing, and diverse research spheres. Auction schemes must offer privacy preserving and secure bidding on services by need and bid value in order to satisfy user needs for edge resource management. Auction systems must be considered in the context of edge computing and the Internet of Things in order to conceal users from service providers and distribute services in a fair and impartial manner. There is an incentive for service providers to utilise their capacity to the fullest extent possible in order to maximise profit. This idea assumes that several organisations serve as data centre for edge computing providers, and that various edge nodes are hosted by diverse organisations as well.

Optimization

Resource allocation and division in edge computing could be handled by the use of optimization. Similar to auction systems, optimization can offer useful characteristics to system users, maximising welfare or profit. Although enterprises may plan for local edge systems to depend on on subscription/patron services, this idea may not be practical given that edge infrastructures act as an intermediate layer between cloud services and users. Optimization has shown increasing potential when used in conjunction with auction systems and other resource management applications, including cloud and edge computing.

Security and Privacy

Security and privacy are crucial issues that necessitate careful study since they are moving targets that cut across all sectors. These are actually the most crucial difficulties in the adoption of Edge Computing-based IoT. Wireless networks, Peer-to-peer systems, virtualization, and other diverse technologies are at the heart of edge computing, which necessitates the adoption of a thorough integrated system to protect and manage each technology platform as well as the system as a whole. Despite this ambitious ambition, edge computing will ultimately lead to some unexpected and novel security concerns. The interaction of diverse edge nodes and the transfer of services between the global and local scales are two uncommon and unexplored scenarios that have the potential to introduce new channels of harmful activity. Additionally, the fundamental characteristics of edge computing may very well determine which security and privacy solutions can be implemented and which cannot. There are various unique security concerns and issues in edge computing systems, just like there are with cloud computing. There are many advantages of the distributed structure for IoT. However, distributed structures have a substantial security and privacy difficulty. Edge computing might offer a secure computing platform for the IoT in the future. The sensitive data related to end users' privacy may be used while edge computing processes data at the edge. Observe that IoT systems' sensing data is kept on edge nodes, which can be more prone to attack than cloud servers. As a result, edge computing must take privacy protection into account, and efficient privacy preserving solutions such differential privacy with high utility and local differential privacy must be developed to safeguard users' privacy in the IoT ecosystem based on edge computing. The need to authenticate gateways at various levels is one of the common security issues with edge computing. Smart metres in residential buildings are one example, with each having its own IP address.

Transmission

One of the main issues facing Edge Computing-based IoT is certifying security during the data transmission procedure. Some assaults could be thrown during message communication between servers and end users to disable the links by clogging the network, or could monitor network data flow. The con-Figureurations entered by a network administrator often need to be reliable and verified in a traditional network. However, because Edge Computing based IoT is placed at the edge of the network structure, it will be difficult to operate networks like Wi-Fi, Mobile Wireless Networks, and Ultra Dense Networks. As a result, controlling edge networks would inevitably generate a lot of management traffic, making it harder to distinguish it from normal data traffic. In this scenario, enemies would have simple access to network control. SDN- Software Defined Networking must be implemented to reduce this issue. From the aforementioned views, SDN will reduce the security hazards:

I.   Detection: The ability to monitor data to detect malicious code is provided by the deployment of a Network Monitoring and Intrusion Detection System. Using SDN, it is simple to set up an IDS system and enhance the traffic flow management for Edge Computing based IoT.

II.   Security: Traffic prioritisation and isolation is the most effective way to secure data during transmission. Here, SDN may quickly aggregate various traffic types into VLANs using VLAN ID, and it can be utilised to further isolate harmful traffic. As a result, traffic isolation and prioritisation are frequently employed to stop certain sorts of attacks, such as those that try to overwhelm the network or take control of shared resources and hardware.

III. Responses: some researches are going on to measure and mitigate cyber attacks in edge computing platforms building on a long history of traditional remedy against network risks in cyber physical systems.

Storage

Massive amounts of data are produced by the countless sensors and devices used in Edge Computing-based IoT, and all of the storage is provided by various outside vendors. The storage providers who deploy their storage equipment at the network's edge and place it at numerous different physical addresses are hired to handle user data. This definitely increases the likelihood of attacks for a variety of reasons. First, because the data is divided into numerous pieces and spread across numerous storage sites, it is challenging to ensure data integrity because it is simple to lose data packets or store inaccurate data. Second, the stored data that has been uploaded may have been altered or misused by hostile parties or unauthorised users, resulting in data leaks and other privacy concerns.

Numerous methods, including homomorphic encryption, can be applied to solve these issues and ensure the integrity, secrecy, and verifiability of edge storage systems. Additionally, the technologies improve user security so that they can keep their data on any unreliable servers. For instance, the authors suggested using a third-party auditor to do public auditing while securing data stored in the cloud (TPA). Edge storage can also employ the same method

Computation

In general, Verifiable Computing allows the computing chores to be offloaded to an untrusted compute node. As a check that the computation was correctly finished, this computational node keeps track of the verifiable results and utilises them to compare them with those computed by a few other trusted computation nodes. All IoT device could be able to confirm the accuracy of the outcomes calculated by edge nodes in the case of edge computing based IoT. A technique called Pinocchio was created in that enables clients to validate computation results using nothing but cryptographic presumptions (Shi et al., 2016). Using Pinocchio, clients produce a public evaluation key that specifies the calculation task, and servers compare the key's value against the computation result to verify accuracy.

It is a tough and challenging task to maintain and protect networks with such a vast number of linked devices due to the decentralised organization of edge networks, which don't support suitable security and managing capabilities. For instance, Hafeez et al. suggested Securebox, a service based approach to protect the network edge. The developed system can permit security services by sensing and responding to hostile activity in the system by making use of the security and network management capabilities offered by the proposed system.

There are various preliminary works intended to solve other security challenges, such as software verification / intrusion detection. For instance, Tan et al. introduced the BUFS method, which stands for bottom up and fundamental approach, for evaluating the security of the software stack in an IoT system.

This method enables bottom-up verification of the end devices' software. A defence method against malicious D2D -device-to-device communication named HoneyBot was put forth by Mtibaa et al. The HoneyBot nodes can recognise and detach D2D insider attacks using this technique (R.Hsu et al., 2018). Additionally, it has been demonstrated that assessments of speed and accuracy can be considerably impacted by the amount and positioning of HoneyBot nodes in the network.

Three general defence strategies like proactive defence, reactive defence, and predictive defence—should be included in the design of an integrated defence system contrary to cyber attacks on edge servers. It is very important to create ways for proactive defence at both the system level and data level. The detection should take into account the allocation and usage of edge resources

Up to Date Communication

Edge computing is dismantling the obstacles to low-latency, quick, high-computation applications as a change in the established paradigm of remote computation and storage. Similarly, the technologies of upcoming 5G cellular networks, such as massive Multiple Input and Multiple Output-MIMO, Ultra-Dense Networks (UDNs), and millimeter-wave, are advancing everyday, increasing throughput, reducing latency and supporting massively interrelated groups in dense networks. Edge computing will evolve more as a result of these developments in communication technology because integration of various technologies is now a given.

Communication over 5G: The newest communication technology is called as 5G. Its objective is to give people access to information they need and ubiquity of network connectivity. In order to create flexible and effective communication, the ideas of 5G, IoT, and edge computing can be combined. Additionally, 5G technology can aid in increasing the effectiveness of numerous IoT applications.

For instance, under 5G scenarios, Cau et al. offered plans for efficient subscriber state management. In their thorough analysis of fog network and cloud radio access network architectures, Hung et al. emphasise the need to combine both for 5G. A VoWiFi solution incorporating edge computing technology was developed by Chagh et al., which can assist overcome its primary flaw (i.e., the lack of user location). The suggested approach makes it possible to retrieve location data for VoWiFi users.

EDGE BASED SECURITY DESIGNS FOR IOT

Since edge computing has becoming more prevalent, many scholars have looked into edge computing-based designs to address IoT security issues. These designs include intrusion detection systems, distributed firewalls, authorization and authentication, and privacy preserving methods, as well as more specialised designs to fulfil specific security objectives.

Complete Security Architectures at the Edge Layer

The edge offers a fresh setting for developing and implementing innovative, all-encompassing security solutions for IoT applications. These approaches aim to satisfy the majority of end device security requirements by outsourcing end device security protection as much as possible to the edge layer. The security issues brought on by resource limitations at the IoT device layer can be resolved by placing security measures at a trusted edge layer. User-centric, device-centric, and end to end security are three of the main categories of edge-based comprehensive security architectures shown in Figure 3. User centric IoT security architecture with an edge focus. The most alluring aspects of IoT applications are their accessibility. However, there are two important issues to consider when it comes to security. On the one hand, the user may not sign in using a consistently reliable and secure device. On the other side, it's possible that most everyday users lack the knowledge necessary to manage security successfully. Consequently, it is dangerous to rely on users for security. It becomes appealing to have the edge layer control the security for each individual user, which leads to security architecture solutions like offloading personal security to the network edge and virtualizing security at the network edge. Figure 3 illustrates the key concepts of user-centric security architecture design. Both of the designs in the Figure aim to create a trustworthy domain at the edge layer. Users must first connect to these trusted virtual domains (TVD), which are set up at the edge, in order to access resources in IoT applications from a variety of devices. (K.Sha et al.,2016) The secure access to IoT resources is managed by the TVD. There are numerous formats for the edge. consists of a number of secure gateways in the edge layer, whereas the edge layer also includes one or more network edge devices (NED). The edge layer in both systems is built using Network Function Virtualization (NFV) technology.

Figure 4. User-centric Edge-based IoT Security Architecture

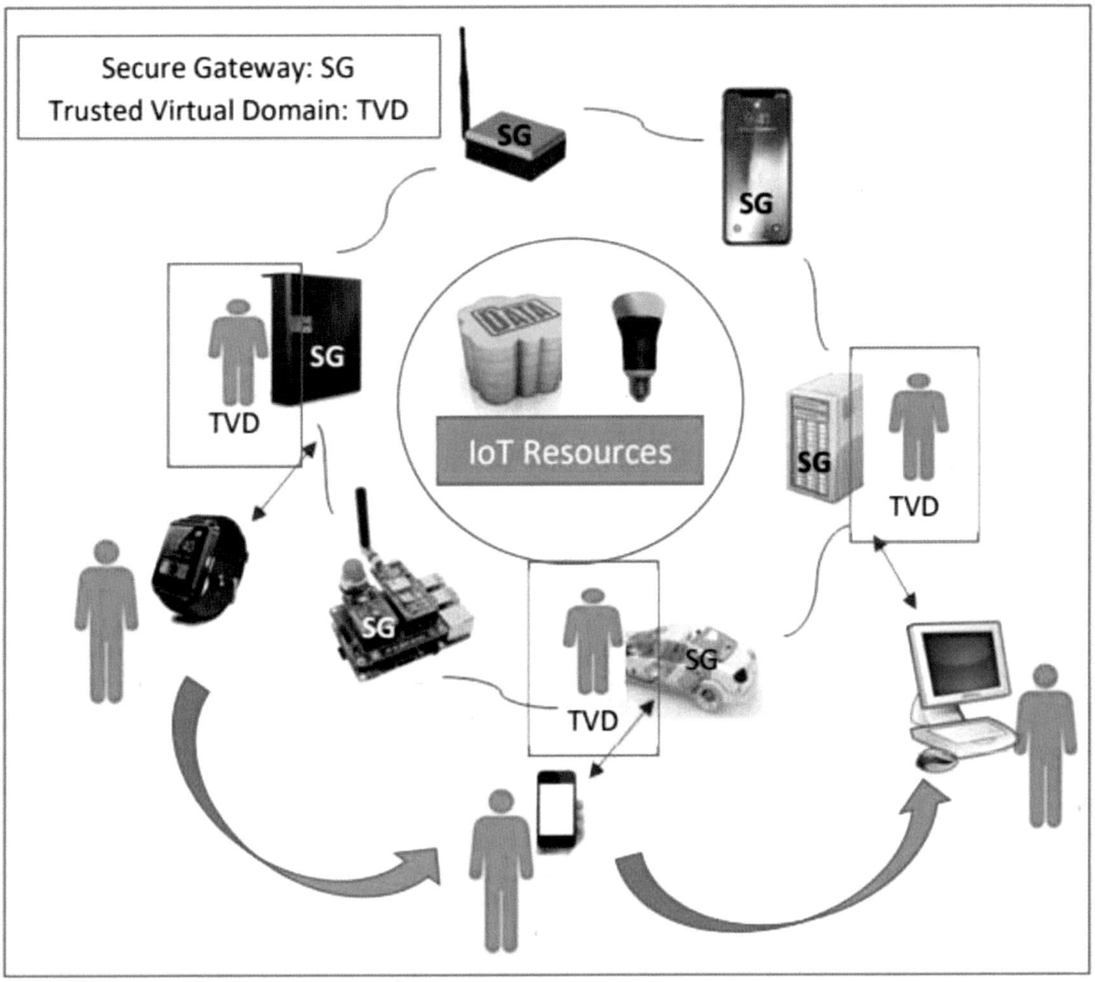

More specifically, every user plainly states what his security policy is. These policies are then converted into a collection of Personal Security Applications (PSAs), such as antivirus, firewalls, and content inspection tools, with the aid of Specification Policy Language and policy transformation mechanisms. A TVD is installed at a NED and functions as a logical container that holds user-specific PSAs. Users use the SECURED system to configure PSAs to the closest compatible NED. In order to establish confidence between the user and the SECURED system, remote attestation and verification mechanisms are used. The NFV orchestration system also aids in managing and controlling NEDs. In this manner, the edge controls the majority of user security requirements. A virtual mobile security architecture is given in a similar manner. The SAVC (security application virtual container), network enforcer, resource migrater, and orchestrator are its four main parts.

According to each user's individual security needs, SAVC contains a range of security solutions including firewalls, anti-phishing software, antivirus, etc. Each user's virtual private network is created by the network enforcer. Resource Migrator relocates the state of a certain SAVC to a place close to the user under orchestrator coordination. As a result, security concerns brought on by user mobility can be successfully handled.

Each IoT device must first register with the security profile controlling module in order to collect device-specific data and determine the security requirements unique to each device. The security of a separate IoT subsystem is then overseen by a security analysis module by means of the implementation of two tasks. One determines where to deploy the security functions while the other evaluates the security dependency for the IoT subsystem's registered devices. Based on each individual IoT device's resources and security profile, the protocol mapping module selects the proper security protocols from the protocol library. To further ensure the security of the physical system, the security simulation module models the effects of crucial instructions before they are actually carried out. Other parts perform tasks like hiding communication heterogeneity and organising various modules to cooperate.

For IoT applications, ReSIoT offers a reconfigurable security architecture. To offload the overhead of cryptographic calculations at IoT devices, the framework designs a security agent (SA), which can be a wireless router, a base station, or a gateway device. Therefore, sophisticated security techniques with high computational requirements will be used to safeguard the resource-constrained IoT devices in order to actualize the functions outlined in the aforementioned four ReSIoT components, the SAs collaborate to design a collection of reconfigurable security functions (RSFs) protocols. IoT security solutions can thus be built using a variety of complex and advanced cryptographic techniques, including attribute-based encryption and group signing.

Firewalls at the Edge Layer

Due to their resource limitations, the majority of IoT devices are unable to support firewalls or other robust security software. Additionally, if every IoT device has a firewall, managing a massive number of firewalls will be quite expensive given the volume of IoT devices. The most efficient and cost-effective firewalls are edge-based. A design for an edge-based firewall is shown in Figure 5. As shown in the picture, a set of flow policies are created from the firewall policies that IoT apps define. Following the identification and resolution of flow policy conflicts, a set of distributed firewall rules based on these policies is deployed at the edge. Later, all incoming and departing traffic is inspected against these regulations.

For the following benefits, placing the firewall at the edge layer is the best option. First, since there is just one conceptually centralised firewall, updating firewalls will be easier to administer. Second, an edge device may control an IoT subsystem in various IoT applications. As a result, the firewall can be set up to meet the subsystem's overall security requirements. Third, it can facilitate user mobility in the IoT system by allowing the edge layer to monitor user and end device movement and access credentials.

Then, we examine two firewall concepts based on edge computing, namely FLOWGUARD and a distributed firewall architecture at the network edge. The first uses virtual network function (VNF) technology, whereas the second uses software defined network (SDN) technology.

violation detection, Network state and configuration update and violation resolution are the three main function components of FLOWGUARD. The violation detection in FLOWGUARD traces the flow path to determine the original source and the end destination of each flow in the network in addition to checking each flow for violations as in conventional methodologies. Header Space Analysis (HSA) is intended to be used as the flow tracking technique. Violations are discovered based on the flow path and the firewall authorisation space. When implementing a new flow policy, a novel, all-encompassing violation resolution mechanism is built as part of the violation resolution process. The novel approach suggests flow rerouting and flow tagging as alternatives to outright rejecting new flows that might only partially contravene the flow regulation. dependency

Figure 5. Edge based Firewall

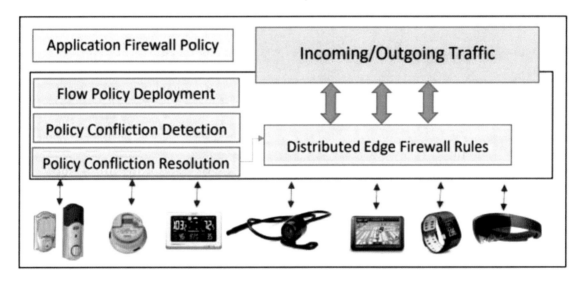

Figure 6. Distributed Intrusion Detection Systems based on Edge

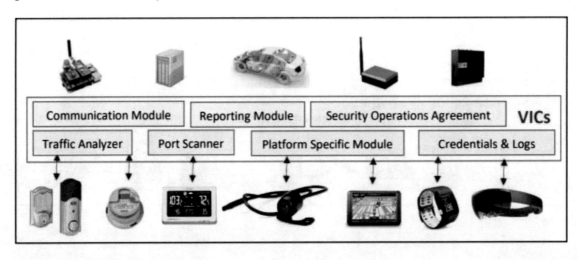

Figure 7. Virtual Immune System

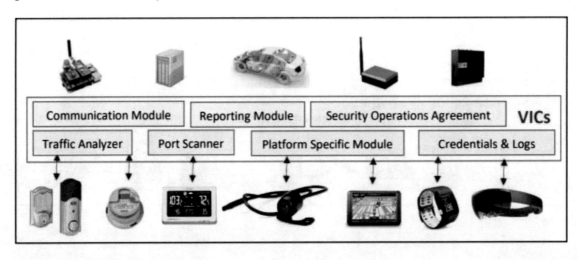

At the network edge, Markham and Payne describe a distributed firewall design. To enable centralised management at the edge layer of dispersed policy enforcement points for multiple devices, the design utilises a master/slave architecture. A policy server performs tasks such network connection group administration, audition, policy management, and user interface.

Edge Layer Intrusion Detection Systems (IDS)

In 2016, hackers breached a sizable number of IoT devices and utilised them to perform a Distributed DoS (DDoS) assault against many Dye Inc. DNS servers. The attack resulted in huge losses because it disrupted Internet service across a wide area. If a distributed intrusion detection system existed, it might be able to stop a DDoS attack in its tracks and lessen the damage it does. It is advantageous to construct intrusion detection techniques at the edge layer since there is a lot more information there. For better intrusion detection results, it might make use of cutting-edge machine learning techniques to relate data from various sources. It has the ability to respond to variations in attack patterns. The concepts shown below each try to identify intrusions in IoT systems at the edge layer.

Figure 6 shows a conceptual design for an edge-based intrusion detection system. The distributed traffic monitoring service in this configuration gathers real-time network traffic. At each edge device, intrusion detection algorithms are then executed. Moreover, traffic data from several edge devices is examined to perform collaborative intrusion detection. Finally, Platform Specific Module Credentials & Logs for Traffic Analyzer Port Scanner Reporting Module Communication Module VICs for Security Operations Agreements

In order to assess the consistency and security of the IoT infrastructure, Roman et al. propose a virtual immune system (VIS). Where as the virtual immune cells (VIC), and VIS kernel, are the two functional components of the virtual immune system as shown in Figure 7. They include a reporting module, a communication module and a security operations agreement module. A VIS orchestrator exists within the VIS Kernel and is responsible for configuring and deploying VICs in the edge infrastructure based on data gathered from a variety of sources, such as external threat intelligence feeds, internal system administrators and data gathered by VICs in the edge structure. The VICs perform platform-specific activities as well as communication port scanning and traffic analysis. They also maintain security operations level agreements, handle credentials, and store logs (SOLA).

SIOTOME is an example of a collaborative Edge-ISP architecture for identifying and isolating IoT security threats. In order to create effective and privacy-aware IoT security services, it merges the large scale perspective from the ISP with the granular understanding of each IoT device. By observing network traffic, the edge data collector in SIOTOME keeps track of IoT device activities. After then, the edge analyzer examines the information gathered to spot risks and assaults and alerts the edge controller when they are found. The network gateway is then set up by the edge controller to alter network traffic.

Additionally, SIOTOME uses defence techniques including network isolation to reduce the attack surface, the permitted network input and output, in addition to halt DDoS attempts and vulnerability scanning.

Figure 8. Multi segment Authentication in Edge Computing

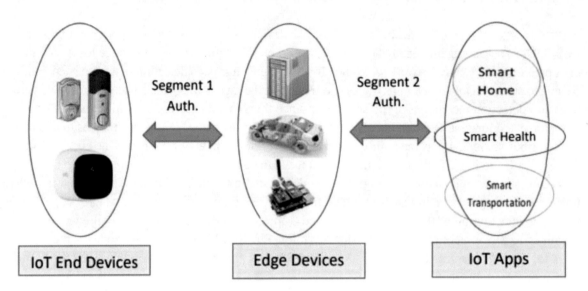

Authorization and Authentication Mechanisms Based on Edge Computing

Unauthorized access is currently the most common attack type against a control system, according to Trend Micro. Authentication and authorisation are essential security procedures to thwart many different sorts of assaults, such as DDoS attacks and unauthorised access. End-to-end security is also anticipated in the IoT system design based on authentication and authorisation procedures, although it is very challenging to achieve for a variety of reasons. First off, it is quite challenging to create end to end direct communication among two heterogeneous peers using mutual authentication as an example. Second, IoT end devices do not support many conventional authentication methods, such as those based on digital signatures. Various researchers develop authentication protocols based on edge that make use of multiple phase authentication with the assistance of the edge layer, as shown in Figure 8. The process of authentication is broken down into several phases, which includes the authentication among devices and edge layer and the authentication between the edge and a third party, which might be another end device, the cloud, or an IoT user. Different segments can employ specialised authentication techniques based on the traits of communication peers. The edge serves as a helpful man-in-the-middle in this scenario, assisting in the configuration of mutual authentication for heterogeneous devices. In addition, there is alternative way for the edge to act as the end devices in the authorisation and authentication process, namely when the end devices delegate certain tasks to the edge. Furthermore, multi-factor authentication is now conceivable in IoT systems since the edge has the capabilities to enable various authentication interfaces.

Privacy-preserving Designs Based on Edge Computing

IoT apps use a vast amount of sensitive and valuable data collected from numerous IoT devices. IoT customers anticipate strict privacy protection as a result of the deep integration of many IoT applications in to daily life. Different privacy goals, including differential privacy, and privacy preserving aggregation and k-anonymity, can be accomplished at the edge layer, a compact privacy preserving data aggregation approach (LPDA) is suggested. IoT devices communicate their locally handled sensing data to the edge node along with a MAC-message authentication code under this technique. After receiving the reports, the edge nodes compare the MAC value to verify the IoT end device's authenticity before producing an aggregated value for IoT applications. The suggested strategy addresses concerns with collecting hybrid IoT data, reducing the amount of communication, and filtering false data from IoT end device reports by utilising Chinese Remainder Theorem, homomorphic Paillier encryption, and one way hash chain techniques. In order to achieve the goal of privacy preservation, LPDA also uses differential privacy approaches.

PRIVACY-PRESERVATION FOR EDGE ENABLED IOT SERVICES USING AI

The two main categories of ML privacy protection techniques are training schemes and inference schemes. When protecting sensitive privacy data during the inference phase, privacy preserving training systems aim to apply encryption techniques to assure its security. A well-trained model often obtains the unorganized data given by the EN for inference in order to preserve inference strategies. The most popular encryption techniques are data obfuscation, anonymization, and cryptographic procedures. (J.chi et al., 2018) The overheads associated with computing and communication vary depending on the encryption mechanism, though. It makes it more difficult for ENs with limited resources to implement encryption mechanisms.

Lightweight AI Privacy Preserving Methods in ENs

The rapidly expanding IoT industry promotes "edge computing," a new computing paradigm that makes use of the computational and storage power of device nodes situated between a cloud data centre and terminal devices. EC brings data processing closer to the data sources than conventional cloud computing, which reduces the amount of data that must be transmitted to the data centre at the outset. Low latency real-time services are offered, and communication bandwidth utilisation is decreased. The privacy issues have received a lot of focus, both during module training and in work offloading methods. Traditional encryption techniques including data obfuscation, anonymization, and cryptographic procedures have all been asked in computer power and are being applied in cloud data centres.

1. *Preserving Privacy Using CNNs.*

The improved CNN inference module and LAYENT will be introduced in the context that follows. The earlier strategy enhances the fundamental framework so that the module is privacy conscious, while the later scheme employs the trained module to protect privacy.

LAYNET

A brand-new machine learning system that protects privacy is called LAYENT. LAYENT have accuracy up to 91% compared to other associated algorithms based on cloud computing, but it also effectively preserves privacy while incurring a little amount of computational overhead. The data will be disturbed before being transmitted to the possibly dangerous third party.

Revised CNN Inference Module

To identify the odd behaviour of the smart metres in the smart grid, an energy loss detection technique is developed. The revised convolutional neural network module is combined in the scheme. The CNN module is trained using the data produced by the smart metre, and after training, the trained module can identify aberrant data by drawing logical conclusions. The accuracy of the inference has increased to up to 92.67% thanks to the combination of the improved CNN module and the scheme.

2. *Privacy-Preservation Using DNNs.*

A deep learning framework called a deep neural network has been extensively used in fields like speech recognition, picture recognition, and natural language understanding. Large amounts of processing power must be used during the training of DNN modules. Two lightweight systems are used in the following context:

ObfNet. Before the inference data is sent to the backend, ObfNet- an obfuscation neural network strategy is suggested. A method called ObfNet makes data obfuscation for distant inference both light and unobtrusive. The minimal and discrete characters imply that ENs just need to create a tiny neural network and are not required to specify if the data are obscured. The installation of edge-enabled IoT has two problems. The separation of data sources and computing resources is one of them, and the privacy protection of inference models is another. These problems can be solved through remote inference. In remote interpretation, the data is transmitted to the backend, where it is processed, and the conclusions are then sent back. A lightweight neural network that can be used in ENs is ObfNet. The design of the training procedure is as follows. The backend joins the untrained ObfNet to the central InfNet-trained service inference model to create a focused DNN module.

Privacy Partition. An interactive network and a bipartite topological network make up the framework's basic structure, which makes privacy partition as a privacy-preserving framework for deep neural networks. An untrusted remote computing context and A trusted local computing context are the two partitions that make up a bipartite deep network topology, which is a neural network. A learning module will process the result of the most recent conversion in a trusted local computing context. The information that has been processed will next be fed into the first transformation layer in the context of remote computing. Privacy partition is an optional feature for some centralised deep learning frameworks under the edge network architecture. To protect their privacy, users can restrict access to the sensitive data stream. When ENs require the utilisation of distant services and computing, an interactive adversarial network offers a workable option. It can reduce the adversary's ability to learn input that is sensitive to privacy.

BLOCKCHAIN FOR AI BASED EDGE-ENABLED IOT SERVICES

A distributed algorithm is used to create and update data, transmit data among nodes by a peer to peer network, and maintain the stored data by a distributed archive in the blockchain, Additionally, it implements upper-layer application logic via smart contracts or automated script code. In brief, blockchain offers a novel method for protecting data transmission and preservation from assault or bug, as well as a decentralised environment. The solution to the most pressing security issues in IoT services is included in Part 1 by blockchain. The sharing of data resources, which occurs between mechanical devices and offers several communication options, is covered in Part 2 of the article. The increase in environmental efficiency based on IoT networks is covered in Part 3. In addition, Figure 3 depicts the section's hierarchical taxonomy, and Table 4 lists the research findings we address.

Blockchain for Security of IoT Services

Massive terminal devices will be installed in order to create an IoT network which can be used, and any device connected to the IoT network will be able to access data from the whole IoT network. The flaws of a single device cannot be avoided due to the sheer number of devices. Massive amounts of data from IoT services will leak if the device is compromised, which could have severe effects. Therefore, it becomes necessary to increase the security of IoT services. Because there are so many IoT devices, connecting them is not secure. As a result, it is simple for malicious individuals to steal the data that is sent between devices. Despite the fact that CAPTCHAs and other security measures exist, data protection is still limited. In order to address issues, blockchain technology and AI technologies have been developed.

Authentication Management and Access Control

Access control is to offer a collection of techniques for identifying, classifying, and hosting all system functions, classifying and categorizing all data, and then offering a straightforward and distinctive interface. In order to determine whether to grant access to the system's interface, authentication involves identifying the access using verification techniques like passwords. The user name and password combination for each device is used as identity identification in typical IoT services that do not use AI or blockchain. (Zhanyang Xu et.al, 2020) This method requires a lot of energy and is difficult to extend, so IP cameras can utilise it. By allowing a trustworthy third party organisation to grant the user access to numerous devices by authenticating their identity of a single device, single sign on protocols can make identity authentication simpler. Even while it can speed up the authentication process, if a user's account is compromised or one device malfunctions, it will have terrible consequences for the entire IoT system. The article makes a fresh design suggestion to address these issues. Users only need to validate their identities once on the blockchain (such as Ethereum) under this architecture before using the smart contract token to gain access to the system. When confirming identity, Smart Contact broadcasts the token, Ethereum address, Then the IoT service receives the package—which also contains the public key of user, IP address, and token—and verifies it. Blockchain may also be used to gather, store, and verify fingerprint data, which will help to overcome the current access authentication technology's falsification issue.

Reliability and Confidentiality of Data

IoT usage is expanding across several industries, including healthcare, banking, and agriculture. Different physical sensors are being used in the healthcare industry as part of the Internet of Things (IoT) to record bodily data that will assist doctors provide better patient care. These private information must be securely guarded.

In order to store IoT data securely, a crowdsourced approach using a blockchain is suggested by Xu et al. They create a blockchain-based mobile crowd sourcing architecture to protect the privacy and accuracy of player data. They produce service policies through better dynamic programming and density-based geographic grouping of applications with noise. In addition, they use decision-making using many criteria and simple additive weighting to evaluate the policies.

Edge-Enabled IoT Data Sharing using Block Chain

The IoT network is built on data, and as more data are collected, more accurate research findings and application development may be made. IoT data are currently gathered in a variety of industries, including agriculture, business, healthcare, and automatic driving. Because collecting repetitious data requires a lot of energy and time, it demonstrates that the sensors gathering various types of data are diverse and the database is held by several businesses, organisations, or governments. As a result, exchanging data from IoT services in the database can effectively assign the resource and lower unnecessary costs.

Massive data, a lack of trust in one another, heterogeneous devices, security issues, and a few other issues, however, create obstacles to secure data exchange. Blockchain becomes an excellent option when creating a platform for secure data sharing.

Efficiency of Edge-Enabled IoT Services using Block Chain

As previously mentioned in parts 1 and 2, the use of blockchain for IoT can efficiently certify the security of IoT services' data. However, as IoT services grow more popular, the demand for computing resources will inevitably outpace the capacity of the Internet, which will have an adverse effect on how effectively IoT services operate. If something like this occurs, it can cause data overload, service delays, and other problems. However, it is now impractical to just update the IoT devices' computational capabilities in order to address the core issue. Below, we present a few research findings from several fields that enhance the effectiveness of IoT services. To increase the effectiveness of the entire system, Khanji et al. talk about striking a balance between cache capacity and computing power and wanted a method using geometric programming to aggregate each IoT network data point and communicate information that could spread the cache of one device to other IoT devices.

CONCLUSION

With the growth of IoT, edge computing is developing as a key to the difficult and complex problems associated with handling lots of sensors and devices, as well as the resources needed to support them. In contrast to the cloud computing domain, edge computing will move data processing and storage to the network's "edge," close to the end users. Edge computing can thereby lessen traffic in order to lower IoT bandwidth requirements. In addition, edge computing can speed up response times for all real time IoT enabled applications compared to conventional cloud services by reducing transmission latency among edge or cloudlet servers and also end users. Additionally, the lifespan of nodes with restricted battery can be increased along with the lifespan of the whole IoT system by lowering the transmission cost of the load and moving the communication and computational overhead from nodes with restricted battery resources to nodes with important power resources.

REFERENCES

Ahmed, A., & Ahmed, E. (2016). A survey on mobile edge computing. *Proc. 10th Int. Conf. Intell. Syst. Control (ISCO),* 1-8.

Chi, J., Owusu, E., & Yin, X. (2018). Privacy partition: a privacy preserving framework for deep neural networks in edge networks. *Proceedings of the IEEE/ACM Symposium on Edge Computing (SEC),* 378–380. 10.1109/SEC.2018.00049

Du, P., & Nakao, A. (2016). Application specific mobile edge computing through network softwarization. *Proc. 5th IEEE Int. Conf. Cloud Netw. (Cloudnet),* 130-135. 10.1109/CloudNet.2016.54

Hsu, R., Lee, J., Quek, T., & Chen, J. (2018). Reconfigurable security: Edge-computing-based framework for iot. *IEEE Network, 32*(5), 92–99. doi:10.1109/MNET.2018.1700284

Salman, Elhajj, Kayssi, & Chehab. (2015). Edge computing enabling the Internet of Things. *Proc. IEEE 2ndWorld Forum Internet Things (WF-IoT),* 603-608.

Sha, K., Andrew Yang, T., & Wei, W. (2020). A survey of edge computing-based designs for IoT security. *Digital Communications and Networks, 6*(2), 195-202.

Sha, K., Wei, W., Yang, A., & Shi, W. (2016). Security in internet of things: Opportunities and challenges. *Proceedings of International Conference on Identification, Information & Knowledge in the Internet of Things (IIKI 2016).*

Shi, W., Cao, J., Zhang, Q., Li, Y., & Xu, L. (2016). Edge computing: Vision and challenges. *IEEE Internet of Things Journal, 3*(5), 637–646. doi:10.1109/JIOT.2016.2579198

Xu, Z., Liu, W., Huang, J., Yang, C., Lu, J., & Tan, H. (2020). Artificial Intelligence for Securing IoT Services in Edge Computing: A Survey. Security and Communication Networks. doi:10.1155/2020/8872586

Yu, W., Liang, F., He, X., Hatcher, W. G., Lu, C., Lin, J., & Yang, X. (2018). A Survey on the Edge Computing for the Internet of Things. *IEEE Access: Practical Innovations, Open Solutions, 6,* 6900–6919. doi:10.1109/ACCESS.2017.2778504

Chapter 9
Edge AI–Based Crowd Counting Application for Public Transport Stops

Hakki Soy

https://orcid.org/0000-0003-3938-0381

Necmettin Erbakan University, Turkey

ABSTRACT

Recently, the evolution of artificial intelligence has caused the emergence of smart systems exhibiting intelligent behavior like the human brain. Specifically, as a class of artificial intelligence methods, computer vision empowered with deep learning has tremendous promise for the accurate detection of crowds in real-time. In addition, the edge artificial intelligence approach allows for the development and deployment of artificial intelligence methods outside of the cloud. This study introduces the deep learning-based computer vision implementation to monitor public transport stops. The main aim is to determine the count of passengers through edge computing. The experimental study is realized with the popular YOLO object detector model on the Maixduino board developed for edge-based artificial intelligence (AI) applications with the internet of things (IoT). The experiments' results show that the obtained accuracy of crowd counting was found to be satisfactory.

INTRODUCTION

The United Nations (2018) reports that 68% of the world's population will live in urban areas by 2050. As a result of the urbanization trend that started with the industrial revolution and accelerated with the rise of citizens' living standards, the demand for natural resources is increasing day by day. The fascination with urban living is essentially due to better livelihood opportunities and easy access to cities' educational and medical services. At the point reached today, in the face of the uncontrolled increase in the population in cities, the only way to meet the needs in a sustainable way is to ensure the transition to smart cities with the help of information and communication technologies (ICTs). The ICT-enabled smart cities aim to create innovative services that help to make life better by rapidly responding to citi-

DOI: 10.4018/978-1-6684-6275-1.ch009

zens' requests. The main targets can be summarized as follows: to improve safety, reduce congestion, and minimize excessive consumption of finite resources (Bawany & Shamsi, 2015; Lonavath et al., 2017).

A smart city addresses the challenges of different applications, i.e., transportation management, public safety, street lighting, and waste management (McKinsey, 2018; OECD, 2019; Ismagilova et al., 2022). Among them, transportation management has special importance in smart cities, since it plays an influential role in shaping decisions that affect public safety, traffic congestion, resource efficiency, energy conservation, and fewer emissions. In a typical smart city, one of the biggest infrastructures is usually used for transportation and it may consist of multi-modal components that facilitate different transport options, such as cars, trucks, public transport (bus, tram, metro, train, and ferry), cycling, and walking. Smart transportation applications integrate independent transportation networks by connecting them into a single management platform and give the opportunity to intelligently control the traffic flows while optimizing the traffic signals (Shukla & Champaneria, 2017; Jawhar et al., 2018; Hanani et al., 2019).

During the last decade, traffic congestion has significantly increased in parallel with the increase in the number of vehicles. Therefore, the management of transportation systems has become increasingly difficult (Nguyen *et al.*, 2018). One of the most effective solutions to reduce traffic congestion is to encourage people to use public transportation in dense urban areas. On the other hand, especially due to the rapid increase in oil prices, the demand for the use of public transportation services has naturally increased in recent days. Public transportation means shared passenger-transport services, i.e., bus, tram (light rail), trolleybus (electrically powered bus), train, ferry, and metro. When the demand for public transportation increases, it becomes even more important to determine the crowding of bus/tram stops, metro stations, and even in-vehicles (De Weert & Gkiotsalitis, 2021). Smart cities have the ability to use technology to remotely monitor the number of passengers traveling by public transport. Based on the collected real-time crowd information, the Quality of Service (QoS) can be significantly improved by optimizing the timetables, service frequencies, and routes of public transportation vehicles. Consequently, smart (dynamic) public transportation management is an important part of smart cities to minimize the waiting time at stops and traveling time spent in traffic. More importantly, crowd monitoring shortens the dwell time, which refers to the time duration wherein public transport vehicles spend at a scheduled stop without moving (Franke et al., 2015; Khan et al., 2020).

The smart city trend introduces a variety of intelligent platforms consisting of distributed smart devices and decentralized decision-making systems that process real-time data. The provision of advanced applications in accordance with the smart city concept mainly depends on the use of ICTs, which enable people to access public services. ICTs refer to a wide range of technological tools that enable gathering, storing, analyzing, and sharing information through communications. When considering the communication part, the Internet of Things (IoT) comes to the fore and it allows to exchange of data between everyday objects, which are equipped with embedded electronics, mechanics, sensors, and actuators. Simply, IoT is an extensive network of connected devices, called 'things', which can be sensed or controlled remotely through the Internet. In light of evolving mobile technologies, the utilization of IoT in smart city services has a huge potential to change people's daily living habits for all social activities. Thanks to digitalized support systems, local governments and municipality authorities can provide efficient and optimal services to citizens. But, in parallel to the growing number of connected 'things', the digitalization of smart city operations can only be achieved when a huge amount of raw data is processed and analyzed (Zanella et al., 2014; Serrano, 2018; Cecaj et al., 2021; Salih & Younis, 2021).

Complementary to IoT, artificial intelligence (AI) and big data analytics are the key technologies to overcome the challenges of storing and analyzing massive volumes of data quickly (Allam & Dhunny,

2019). Conceptually, 'big data' term is a fancy catchphrase that refers to a huge amount of data gathered from a massive number of sources. A typical smart city is a real-world example of big data because it requires the collection of a lot of sensor data continuously (Khan et al., 2015; Bassoo et al., 2018). Unfortunately, the traditional statistical techniques are inadequate to handle the large scale of data clusters. At this point, AI can help us as a core enabler to identify hidden data patterns, correlations, anomalous behaviors, and meaningful insights (Kibria et al., 2018).

In fact, AI is an umbrella term that describes multi-dimensional technology powered by advanced tools for several purposes. Both machine learning (ML) and deep learning (DL) are the subsets of AI that enable faster evaluation of complex datasets (Campesato, 2020). ML allows machines to learn from datasets depending on previous experiences without being programmed by humans explicitly or assisted by expert knowledge. In this way, the machines can interpret data, acquire knowledge, and perform required actions like a human (Shalev-Shwartz & Ben-David, 2014). DL is a particular implementation of ML that can copy the learning processes of the human brain into machines. Actually, both ML and DL algorithms emulate human behavior through an artificial neural network (ANN), which is a computational model inspired by biological neurons in the brain cells. Unlike ML, DL refers to deep neural network implementation. Contrary to shallow neural networks with single or multiple neurons in a single layer, deep neural networks contain multiple neurons in multiple hidden layers that can process a large amount of data with higher accuracy. So, the DL method is more convenient to extract hierarchical representations from images and videos for feature detection. Parallel to rapid advances in embedded computing systems, it has a huge potential to achieve great success in computer vision tasks, i.e., face recognition as well as object detection, classification, and tracking (Goodfellow et al., 2016).

Up to recent years, AI algorithms have been run on cloud servers, because they need more computing power and storage capacity (Linthicum, 2017; Ballas et al., 2018). Nowadays, the concept of Artificial Intelligence of Things (AIoT) is emerging as a new trend in current literature to integrate the potential of IoT and AI technologies. In the AIoT ecosystem, the 'things' are equipped with 'embedded intelligence' besides sensing, computing, and communication capabilities. Therefore, AI-empowered things can learn from the generated data, make their own decisions, and even autonomously take actions on behalf of humans. Consequently, AIoT moves the computation closer to the source of data, enables intelligence on the edge of the network, and removes the need for cloud analytics platforms. In addition, the resulting 'edge AI' paradigm reduces the latency, bandwidth, and cost while guaranteeing higher security as compared to conventional cloud computing platforms. It should be emphasized that the realization of AI functionality depends on the computing capability of edge devices to process data and generate meaningful insights (Chen et al., 2020; Li et al., 2020; Zhang & Tao, 2021; Shadroo et al., 2022).

This chapter introduces the crowd monitoring application that can be implemented on public transport stops in a typical smart city. To realize the crowd monitoring function, the Maixduino board and onboard camera have been used as an edge AI platform. The motivation for the presented method comes from the challenges posed by real-world applications. Considering the well-known problems of passengers that use public transport (i.e., crowding at stops and on vehicles, delays, congestion), the presented edge AI platform monitors the crowding level and informs the public transport management center (PTMC) through its wireless connection features. Then, the timetables of public transportation are optimized, and/or service frequencies of public transport vehicles are dynamically modified by operators. Beyond that, the passengers can access updated public transport information using the mobile application on smart devices. In the same way, the passengers can be informed about overcrowded bus/tram stops and metro stations.

CROWD DETECTION FUNDAMENTALS

Crowd detection is essential functionality to ensure the efficient operation of public transport management in smart cities. To improve the passengers' comfort and satisfaction, it should be required to know the real-time crowding information both in vehicles as well as at the access infrastructure (e.g., bus/tram stops and metro stations). During the last decade, the advent of IoT solutions has empowered smart cities and real-time data collection has become a reality to implement more efficient ways of servicing sustainably. Clearly, IoT allows remote collection of sensory data to monitor the crowding in real-time or near real-time depending on the preferred communication technology. There is a wide range of wireless communication technologies with different capabilities. Considering the advantage of connecting a large number of 'things' over a large area, the smart city applications are mostly realized through wireless wide area networks (WWANs), i.e., mobile cellular networks (3G, 4G, and now 5G) as well as low power wide area networks (LPWANs) like LoRa and NB-IoT (Hammi et al., 2015; Cesana & Redondi, 2016; Jawhar et al., 2018). Although there are many wireless connectivity options available that can provide a solution for data transfer, the determination of the passenger crowd level is not so easy in public transportation services. Thus, the biggest challenge is to find and implement innovative solutions for crowd-level detection (Franke et al., 2015).

Crowd estimation helps to analyze the passengers' cumulative distribution and difficulties to give an appropriate service. There are a variety of sensing technologies that can be used for crowd estimation. According to their sensing functionalities, the existing technologies can be classified into two main categories, namely vision-based and non-vision-based (Irfan et al., 2016). The vision-based crowd-sensing can be achieved by using the captured image or sequence of images from optical/thermal cameras, Light Detection and Ranging (LiDAR), and Synthetic Aperture Radar (SAR) sensors. On the other hand, non-vision-based crowd-sensing can be realized by identifying the wireless signals from UWB, RFID, NFC, Bluetooth, Wi-Fi, LTE/5G, and GPS as well as the periodic readings of IR/PIR, pressure, and acoustic sensors. Considering the requirements of public transportation applications, optical cameras are becoming a more popular research topic in recent years, with the increase in studies on computer vision algorithms (Ballas et al., 2018; Singh et al., 2020).

In public transportation systems, a typical crowd can be characterized by several parameters, i.e., count, density, velocity, flow direction, turbulence, and pressure. Among them, count and density are mostly investigated parameters due to their efficient and simplistic implementation in vision-based crowd-monitoring applications (Singh et al., 2020).

- **Count:** Crowd counting is an essential method of learning the exact number of passengers waiting at a given bus/tram stop or metro station. There are two main approaches to counting the passengers in a given image (Khan et al., 2020).

  ○ In a detection-based approach, the object classifiers are trained to extract low-level features and detect parts of the human body. The detection-based approach demonstrates satisfactory performance for detecting the face or head in an image where all the passengers are visible clearly. But, it is not possible to count the exact number of passengers in highly congested images due to obscure people.

  ○ The regression-based approach estimates the statistical relationship between features of the human body and the count of passengers. As encountered in the detection-based approach, the performance of the regression-based approach gradually decreases when the density of the crowd increases in images. However, it can be said that the regression-based approach gives better performance than the detection-based approach when counting the passengers in highly crowded images.

With the advent of DL algorithms, traditional optical cameras have become 'smart' with image processing capabilities, which allows them to recognize objects by using characteristic patterns. But, still, object counting is a tedious and time-consuming task in image processing (Tong et al., 2019; Zhao et al., 2019).

- **Density:** Alternatively, by estimating the number of passengers per unit area, the crowd density parameter can be used to infer the count of passengers. Density estimation differs from crowd counting since it holds the number of passengers for each pixel as a fraction. Actually, density estimation is an approximation method for crowd counting by estimating the average number of pixels per segment classified as corresponding to a passenger in an image. The density estimation approach focuses on learning the mapping between the features in an input image and the actual crowding level. In the literature, there are various types of estimation methods that aim to generate a crowd distribution density map. Fundamentally, most of the existing crowd density estimation studies are based on the extraction of the background of the image (Singh et al., 2020).

DEEP LEARNING FOR CROWD DETECTION

Since the traditional vision-based methods remain insufficient to satisfy the expected performance requirements of crowd-counting applications, in recent years, many studies have been carried out using a convolutional neural network (CNN or ConvNet) to perform counting via density estimation (Ballas et al., 2018; Singh et al., 2020; Khan et al., 2020; Gouiaa et al., 2021). CNN is a deep neural network that is specially designed for object detection and classification problems. Similar to regular ANNs, a typical CNN is composed of a collection of neurons with learnable weights and biases. But thanks to the large number of layers containing many neurons, the CNNs mainly handle the inputs that have 2D input-data structures, i.e., images, texts, and time series (Huang & Le, 2021). As shown in Figure 1, a typical CNN architecture consists of an input layer, a certain number of convolutional layers, and pooling layers followed by a fully connected layer, and an output layer (Voulodimos et al., 2018; Bezdan & Džakula, 2019; Alzubaidi et al., 2021).

- In the input layer, the image is fed into the CNN in the form of an array of a matrix.
- In the convolutional layers, the mathematical convolution operation is performed with a filter matrix, known as a kernel. The kernel is responsible to create a two-dimensional array of numerical values that can be passed into the following layers, which gives the ability to learn the hidden patterns in an image. Thanks to the convolutions, the pixels in an image are interpreted as numerical values, and then the relevant patterns are identified. The obtained output image is the 2D feature map, which describes the low-level features (i.e., edges, corners, and lines) of the image. Clearly, a feature map is a convolved image generated from the original image with all the essential features by rejecting redundancy. To detect multiple features of the input image, multiple kernels can be

used in a convolution layer. In practice, the number of kernels is determined as powers of 2, e.g. 32, 64, 128, 512. More kernels allow more opportunities to investigate the input image in detail and learn more features from it. A typical CNN consists of multiple convolutional layers, which are stacked on top of one another. The input image is convolved with a set of kernels in a succession of multiple layers. The number of convolutional layers varies depending on the amount and complexity of the data. When multiple convolutional layers are used in a CNN, the output of one layer is exposed to further convolutions at the next convolutional layers. As the image is proceeding through the convolutional layers, a CNN is able to recognize more complex features of an input image.

- The pooling layers are used immediately after the convolutional layers. In the pooling layers, the size of the convolved feature map is reduced for each feature by decreasing the connections between layers. There are three different types of pooling operations (i.e., mean, maximum, or summation) that are used for pooling the feature map. The max-pooling downsizes an input by taking the largest element in each patch of the feature map. Mean-pooling calculates the average of the elements, while the total of the elements is computed in sum-pooling. The pooling layers connect the convolutional layers with the fully connected layer. It should be highlighted that the pooling layer is an essential step in CNN since it significantly reduces computation time and memory usage.

- A CNN breaks down the image into features, and analyzes them independently through convolution and pooling layers, respectively. Then, the obtained 3D matrix at the output of the last pooling layer is fed into one or more fully connected layer that makes the final classification decision. For that, firstly, the output of the pooling layer is flattened at the fully connected input layer and it is unrolled into a single vector. After that, it is forwarded to the following few layers of the feed-forward neural network that make up the fully connected layer. So, depending on the activation function (i.e., Sigmoid, ReLU, tanH, and softmax), the label prediction takes place and the final classification decision is taken about the target. Each activation function has a specific usage due to its unique advantages and disadvantages. While the sigmoid function is mainly used in binary image classification between two discrete classes, the softmax function is preferred in multi-class classification since it gives the probability distribution of target classes. Besides, the ReLU (Rectified Linear Units) and tanH (hyperbolic tangent) functions are available to use in a fully connected layer. In recent years, the ReLU function is gaining popularity due to its speed of convergence during the training of neural networks by suppressing all negative values at the output.

- Finally, the output layer gives the final probabilities for each label.

Figure 1. A typical CNN architecture for computer vision applications

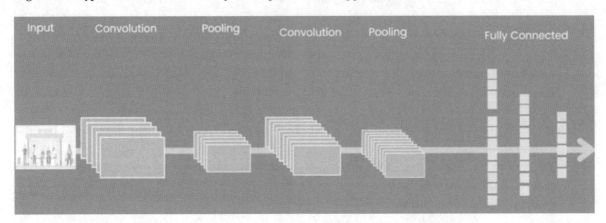

Today, CNNs are mostly employed in computer vision applications for visible image recognition tasks (Voulodimos et al., 2018). Although their performance has decreased slightly in overcrowded, the modern convolutional object detectors, like Region-based CNN (R-CNN) (Girshick et al., 2016), Fast R-CNN (Girshick, 2015), Faster R-CNN (Ren et al., 2017), Mask R-CNN (He et al., 2017), You Only Look Once (YOLO) (Redmon et al., 2016), and Single Shot Detection (SSD) (Liu et al., 2016), have pretty good detection accuracy in sparse scenes. A general object detector is usually composed of three sections, namely the backbone, detection neck, and detection head. The backbone is used for pre-training the object detector that can be thought of as a fully convolutional network (e.g., ResNet, DenseNet, VG-GNet). So, it helps to extract the feature maps from the image. Principally, the backbone is pre-trained on image classification datasets (i.e., ImageNet, MNIST, PASCAL VOC, CIFAR-10, CIFAR-100) and its effectiveness is demonstrated previously. The detection neck is a feature aggregator that collects, combines, and mixes features formed by lateral connections between the feature maps and then forwards them to the detection head. Lastly, the detection head is the object detection pipeline to predict the location of the bounding box and classify the objects. The detection head can be either two-stage (e.g., R-CNN) for sparse prediction or one-stage (e.g., YOLO) for dense prediction (Rodriguez-Conde et al., 2021; Bouraya & Belangour, 2021).

Two-stage detectors usually give better accuracy than one-stage detectors. The well-known two-stage detectors have been summarized as follows:

- R-CNN is a two-stage object detector, in which the detection progress is divided into generating candidate boxes and making predictions according to candidate boxes (Girshick et al., 2016).
- Fast R-CNN is an updated version of the R-CNN, which significantly speeds up the training and testing sessions (Girshick, 2015).
- Faster R-CNN is much faster than R-CNN and Fast R-CNN since the feature map is more effectively identified. In image segmentation, Faster R-CNN has two outputs for each object, i.e., class label and bounding-box offset (Ren et al., 2017).
- Mask R-CNN was developed on top of Faster R-CNN by adding an extra branch for predicting an object mask, called Region of Interest (RoI), besides the existing branch for bounding box recognition (He et al., 2017).

The two-stage detectors cannot meet the real-time operation requirements of practical applications in terms of detection speed. To immediately respond to real-time changes, the use of one-stage detectors can be considered. The popular one-stage detectors have been summarized as follows:

- YOLO is a one-stage object detector, which combines the region proposal and classification steps. Different from the two-stage object detectors, YOLO tries to solve the object detection task as a regression problem, and thus it is also called a regression-based object detector. Due to the simplicity of its network architecture, YOLO is extremely faster when compared with earlier two-stage object detectors (Redmon et al., 2016).
- SSD is another one-stage detector that encapsulates all computation in a single network. It calculates the scores for each object category in each bounding box and adjusts the coordinates to better match the shape of the object (Sultana et al., 2019).

Thanks to its enhanced learning capability that enables extracting the representations of objects, the YOLO algorithm has been widely used in object detection applications all around the world. Taking into account the shortcomings identified in practical applications, different YOLO algorithm versions were introduced from 2015 onwards, namely YOLO v1, YOLO v2, YOLO v3, YOLO v4, and now YOLO v5 (Wang et al., 2021, Srivastava et al., 2021). The characteristic features of different YOLO versions can be summarized as follows:

- YOLO v1 is a one-stage CNN architecture with twenty-four convolutional layers followed by two fully connected layers, which is inspired by GoogleNet. Basically, the YOLO v1 algorithm divides the image into a matrix of grid cells and each grid produces a number of bounding boxes with their confidence scores. The estimated confidence scores show the precision of the model about the bounding box containing an object. But, it has difficulty detecting and segregating small objects in images that appear in matrices, as each grid is constrained to detect only a single object. In crowd detection applications, this becomes a major problem since the surveillance cameras from a high perspective capture the people in the image with a small size. On the other hand, YOLO v1 predicts the bounding boxes using fully connected layers on top of convolutional feature extractors. According to that, the coordinates of the bounding boxes are predicted by fully connected layers. But, the accuracy of YOLO v1 is relatively low due to positioning errors in the prediction of bounding box coordinates. The later versions of YOLO focus on solving these problems and use more complex CNN models to extract features (Redmon et al., 2016).
- YOLO v2 (also known as YOLO9000) uses the DarkNet-19 model in its backbone, which consists of 19 convolution layers (added 11 more layers by YOLO v2) and 5 pooling layers using max-pooling operation. The batch normalization layers were added to all the convolutional layers. YOLO v2 also removes all fully connected layers and convolutional layers are used to predict the bounding boxes. While the YOLO v1 detects the coordinates of the bounding boxes, YOLO v2 is interested in the offsets of bounding boxes. Thanks to its customized CNN architecture, the YOLO v2 detector is faster and more robust than the YOLO v1. But, the YOLO v2 poses a challenge while detecting small objects due to the downsampling of an input image and losing fine-grained features (Redmon & Farhadi, 2017).
- YOLO v3 uses the DarkNet-53 model, which comprises 53 convolution layers (with 53 more layers for detection) trained on Imagenet. Its empowered architecture boasts of residual skip con-

nections, which help the activations propagate through deeper layers without gradient diminishing as well as an upsampling layer before the last layer. The most prominent feature is the multi-scale detection capability, which means that object detection is done by applying 1 x 1 detection kernels on feature maps of three different sizes at three different places. Although the YOLO V3 is more robust compared to YOLO v2, it runs a little slower due to more layers stacked onto its large architecture (Redmon & Farhadi, 2018).

- YOLO v4 uses the CSPDarknet-53 feature extractor model, in which the Cross Stage Partial (CSP) structure is integrated into the backbone to enhance the learning ability of CNN. The CSPDarknet-53 enhances the learning ability while reducing the amount of calculation. It consists of two parts, namely the main part and the skip connection part. The main part holds the original DarkNet-53 network structure, and additionally, multiple residual blocks are stacked onto it. The skip connection part is directly connected to a concat module of the network, which fuses the features from three different levels in the backbone. The skip connection is also connected to the main part. In YOLO v4, the spatial pyramid pooling (SPP) block is added to the CSPDarknet53 model to increase the receptive field and separates contextual features. Contrary to most of the accurate models that require many GPUs for training with a large mini-batch size, YOLO v4 promises an object detector that can be trained on a single GPU with a smaller mini-batch size. In order to simplify the training process, YOLO v4 exploits the bag of freebies (BoF) and several bag of specials (BoS). BoF refers to certain data augmentation techniques that change the training strategy to improve the accuracy of the detector without increasing the inference cost. Similarly, BoS refers to common plugin modules and post-processing methods that can significantly improve the accuracy of object detection although it slightly increases the inference cost (Bochkovskiy et al., 2020).

- As in YOLO v4, the latest member of the family released by Ultralytics, YOLO v5 uses the CSPDarknet-53 model. Despite that, it has also been updated with enhancements, i.e., novel mosaic data augmentation to the training pictures and auto-learning bounding box anchors. To remove the limitations of the DarkNet reference network, YOLO v5 is natively implemented in PyTorch, which is an open-source framework developed with the C and Lua programming languages. In this way, it becomes possible for developers to easily modify the network architecture and adapt the new modifications to deployment environments (Ultralytics, 2020). Actually, YOLO v5 can be considered as a re-implementation of YOLO v4 and it offers a group of object detection models, which are pre-trained on the Microsoft Common Objects in COntext (MS COCO) dataset (Lin et al., 2014). It should be noted that the YOLO v5 is extremely fast and more lightweight than the YOLO v4. Although it is still in the development phase and receives updates regularly, nowadays it is very popular due to its better detection ability to recognize and distinguish small objects (Kim et al., 2022).

Unfortunately, the realization of the convolutional object detection algorithms highly depends on high-performance hardware, which consists of a graphics processing unit (GPU) and an abundance of memory. For instance, the model size of YOLO v1 needs about 1 GB of memory, and it requires high-performance computing to run it. Whereas in many practical situations, the object detector algorithm should be run on embedded devices with constrained computation power and limited memory. In order to run the real-time object detection algorithms on the low-cost development boards, lighter versions of popular detectors have emerged and grown rapidly in recent years, i.e., MobileNet (Howard et al.,

2017), TensorFlow Lite (Louis et al., 2019), and Tiny YOLO. Among them, the Tiny YOLO detector has come to the fore due to its robust implementation. Tiny YOLO has a relatively small model size and it is suitable for use in memory-constrained edge devices. The trained Tiny YOLO model running on the CPU can be run on edge devices with almost no change to the code block. However, due to the compression of the model, the detection accuracy and the real-time performance are not the same when compared original YOLO model (Poon et al., 2022).

LITERATURE REVIEW

Crowd counting aims to estimate how many people are in a specific region of an image or a video stream. DL has a rich variety of algorithms that provide more accurate solutions for crowd-counting applications, compared to traditional methods. Therefore, many researchers contributed to the literature with various studies on the implementation of DL in crowd analysis and density estimation. When looking at the existing research studies, it is noteworthy that most of them have been focused on cloud-based solutions. The contents of some studies within the literature have been summarized as follows:

Zhang et al. (2015) proposed a CNN-based framework for cross-scene crowd counting to address the performance drops of the model when it is applied to an unseen scene. The proposed framework was trained by a switchable learning process both for crowd density and crowd count learning objectives, alternatively. The performance of the proposed framework was evaluated in three different datasets, namely the WorldExpo'10 crowd counting dataset created by authors, the UCSD pedestrian dataset, and the UCF CC 50 dataset. When compared to the global regression-based methods, the proposed CNN model outperformed them both for mean absolute error and mean squared error metrics.

Ilyas et al. (2019) introduced a detailed performance evaluation for the latest CNN-based crowd-counting techniques. As a background, the authors also discussed traditional crowd counting and image analysis techniques. The unique challenges of CNN-based crowd-counting applications (i.e., occlusion, clutter, irregular object distribution, non-uniform object scales, and inconstant perspective) were explained in detail. The advantages and limitations of basic CNN-based crowd-counting algorithms were summarized. Finally, the performance of selected algorithms was evaluated with a common mean absolute error performance metric.

Cenggoro (2019) presented a big picture of existing DL models for crowd-counting to accelerate the development of novel models for future works. The author gave detailed information about density map regression and prediction accuracy metrics. Also, the statistics of frequently used datasets (i.e., Shanghai Tech Part A and B, UCF_CC_50, and WorldExpo'10) were explained for benchmarking in crowd-counting studies. Lastly, CNN-based DL models were investigated under six different categories, i.e., scale-aware CNN, multi-tasking CNN, CNN with the local context, CNN with ensemble learning, generative adversarial networks (GAN) for crowd counting, and unsupervised/semi-supervised CNN.

Khan et al. (2020) reviewed the recent literature on crowd monitoring and localization by using deep CNN architecture. The authors also presented detailed descriptions of publicly available datasets, which contain the crowd videos and images. Beyond that, the crowd-monitoring approaches and related research fields were summarized to simplify the researchers' work for future studies.

Zhang et al. (2020) proposed a novel framework to improve the performance of crowd counting in dense scenes and obtaining accurate positions. The proposed framework includes two parts, namely fully CNN and peak confidence map (PCM). The CNN consists of backend and upsampling blocks that are used to encode the features of the input picture and the deconvolution layer to decode the feature information, respectively. The PCM offers an improvement over the density map to accurately predict the location of the person as well as the crowd count accurately. The experimental results on several datasets (Beijing-BRT, Mall, Shanghai Tech, and UCF_CC_50 datasets) showed the superiority of the proposed framework.

Gouiaa et al. (2021) reviewed the recent papers and provided a comprehensive survey of the CNN-based crowd-counting techniques. The reviewed studies were separated into different groups, i.e., detection-based, regression-based, and traditional density estimation-based approaches. The authors also investigated the recently published DL-based crowd density estimation approaches and datasets. Moreover, the potential applications of crowd counting were discussed by opening special parenthesis for images from unmanned aerial vehicles (UAV).

Xiang and Liu (2022) proposed a novel crowd density estimation method using the DL method. The authors mainly aim to develop a system that enables to detection of passenger flow in exhibition centers. For this purpose, they used the LR activation function to add nonlinear factors to the CNN. Besides, the dense blocks are derived from crowd density estimation to train the LR-CNN crowd density estimation model. According to the performance evaluation made with UCF_CC_50 and Shanghai Tech Part_A datasets, the proposed method improves the accuracy of crowd density estimation in exhibition centers.

Ardiansyah et al. (2022) proposed the CNN-based crowd detection warning system to maintain a distance of at least one meter due to the coronavirus (Covid-19). The proposed system was carried out using the NVIDIA Jetson Nano microcontroller as the computing hardware. In object detection, the OpenCV library, the Tiny YOLO v3 algorithm, and the Euclidean distance method were used to calculate the distance between persons. According to test results from the experimental study, the proposed warning system can detect persons with an accuracy rate of 92.79.

Up to date, in the majority of the crowd-counting applications, the edge AI-based DL implementation has largely been neglected. To fill this research gap, the main contribution of this study is to introduce an edge AI-based solution, which enables crowd counting at public transport stops.

MAIXDUINO EDGE AI PLATFORM FOR CROWD MONITORING

SiPEED is a Chinese company that produces several development boards based on different types of CPUs and FPGAs. SiPEED Maixduino RISC-V Kit is a development board to run AI algorithms at the edge, especially in AIoT applications. Maixduino RISC-V Kit includes a 2.4-inch TFT display, TF card slot, user buttons, and an OmniVision OV2640 camera module with a 2 Megapixel sensor and an f3.6mm lens. Figure 2 shows the SiPEED Maixduino RISC-V Kit with K210 KPU and OV2640 camera. Different than other SiPEED MAIX boards, the Maixduino was designed in an Arduino Uno form factor. Maixduino was mainly equipped with an onboard ESP32 module with ESP32-WROOM-32 chip and Kendryte series of K210 SoC neural network accelerator.

The ESP32 module from Espressif Systems works as a co-processor to support the communication tasks. ESP32-WROOM-32 is a 32-bit System on Chip (SoC) microcontroller with two processor cores clocked at 240 MHz. It essentially offers built-in Bluetooth (v4.2 BR/EDR and BLE) and Wi-Fi (802.11 b/g/n) networking capability. On the other side, the Kendryte K210 chip from Canaan Creative works as a Knowledge Processor Unit (KPU) to construct and execute neural networks. Canaan is a Chinese company that designs the Kendryte series of AI chips. Thanks to its integrated CNN accelerator, K210 speeds up the image processing process in computer vision applications. It can perform convolution (with 1x1 and 3x3 kernels), batch normalization, pooling (max, average), and activation function (sigmoid, ReLU) operations, which are extensively used in CNN computations. It supports more than twenty tensor operations (i.e., Conv2D, DepthwiseConv2D, MaxPool2D, Relu6) that are used in common CNN architectures (Trojan, 2020a).

Figure 2. The Maixduino board, OV2640 camera module, and K210 neural-network accelerator

Kendryte K210 is made using low-power silicon technology on a 28 nm process. As a powerful edge AI chip, K210 is powered by two 64-bit RISC-V CPU cores (each with a built-in independent FPU) that are clocked at 400 MHz (up to 800 MHz with overclocking), an audio accelerator (APU) for processing microphone array inputs up to 8 channels of audio input data, Fast Fourier Transform (FFT) Accelerator for high-performance complex FFT calculations (64-point, 128-point, 256-point or 512-point length), AES and SHA256 algorithm accelerators, low-power SRAM (6MiB of on-chip general-purpose and 2MiB of on-chip AI SRAM memory, a total of 8MiB), powerful DMA for superior data throughput and a total of 32 high-speed GPIO. Moreover, it has a wide range of peripheral units, i.e., DVP, JTAG, OTP, FPIOA, GPIO, UART, SPI, RTC, I2S, I2C, WDT, Timer, and PWM. At this point, it should be emphasized that since the RISC-V architecture can achieve the high performance and low power consumption needs at the same. So, K210 promises to better address the demands of high-end computer vision applications (consumes only 0.3W for 1 TOPS computing power) (Torres-Sanchez et al., 2020; Klippel et al., 2022).

SiPEED Maixduino can be programmed using C or Micropython programming languages. To create a project with a C source code, Arduino and PlatformIO can be used as an Integrated Development Environment (IDE). When using Micropython to program the Maixduino board, specialty IDEs (i.e., MaixPy, Thonny, and OpenMV) are also available. MicroPython is a high-level language for embedded devices, which significantly simplifies and accelerates all phases of ML and DL projects. It has many powerful libraries and also scripts are extensible with low-level C/C++ functions. Sipeed's MaixPy IDE is a clone of the OpenMV that can be used for comfortable handling of the Python script on MAIX boards. The serial terminal tool was integrated into the MaixPy IDE. It allows connecting to the board, editing and executing scripts on the computer, transferring the firmware to the board, as well as debugging functions. MaixPy IDE enables capturing the image from the camera in real-time and saving image files to the development board. In this way, spectral separation is performed and the captured image is separated into red, green, and blue colors (Trojan, 2020b, Dokic et al., 2021; Klippel et al., 2022).

Since the training of a typical CNN usually requires a large amount of computation power, the Kendryte K210 neural network accelerator should only be used for CNN inference computations on the edge device. MaixPy IDE supports only the model compilation with a K210-specific format model file, called kmodel. The neural network compiler, called NNcase, converts the model created with other popular frameworks (i.e., Keras, TensorFlow, Caffe, PyTorch) to the kmodel file with the (kmodel) extension. Although the current NNcase version (v1.7.1) generates kmodel v5 files, MaixPy IDE has no kmodel v5 support now, and it only supports up to kmodel v3/v4. To simplify the training stage, SiPEED also offers an online compilation service to customize the required functions. MaixHub is a cloud training platform for edge devices that can be used for online model training by only uploading data sets without writing any code (Dokic et al., 2021).

EXPERIMENTAL STUDY

Edge AI allows decision-making by thinking of an optimal solution, which maximizes resource efficiency in smart cities. This study introduces an edge AI-enabled DL approach to increase the comfort of passengers that are using public transport. The main aim is to remotely monitor the crowding level of the people at bus/tram stops through cameras and to optimize the timetables and service frequencies of public transport vehicles by informing the transport management center. Different from conventional cloud-based applications, the DL algorithm that detects the passengers waiting at the stop runs on the edge device. In this way, the crowding information about all the bus/tram stops used for public transport has been calculated in a decentralized manner. Due to its powerful neural network accelerator, the Maixduino board with an OV2640 camera has been used as an edge device. Also, the Sixfab tracking shield has been used to add cellular connectivity and GPS tracking ability to the Maixduino board. Figure 3 shows the test bed used in the experimental study. The Micropython language has been used for the model implementation and developed the required firmware. MaixPy IDE has been preferred due to the ability to debug the code blocks as well as provide support for file transfer. In order to show the practical validity of the Edge AI approach for public transportation management, the experimental study has been performed in Konya Province, Türkiye. Accordingly, some pilot bus and tram stops have been monitored through the proposed edge AI platform.

Figure 3. Edge AI test bed with Maixduino development board and Sixfab tracking shield

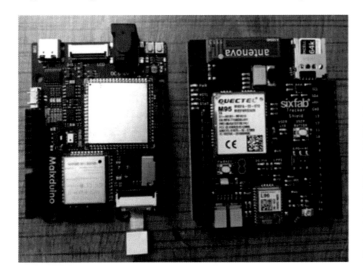

In the execution of the crowd-monitoring application, the main steps can be listed as follows:

1. Data collection and preparation: For the aim of training and testing the model again, a crowd image dataset has been created by mounting the Maixduino board at a distance from the bus/tram stop to capture the photos of the waiting passengers. While the dataset is created, the images have been captured from the video stream. So, the front view images have been stored with QVGA resolution (320 x 240 pixels) and RGB565 color. There are 840 photos available in the prepared data set, which are taken at different bus/tram stops and at different times of the day to provide diversity. So the dataset has been split into the train, test, and validation sets with the 80:20 ratio. In the prepared dataset, the count of passengers varies between 2 and 25 to differentiate the different crowding levels. Figure 4 shows the typical bus and tram stops that were studied in the experimental study.

Figure 4. The bus and tram stops that were studied to prepare the dataset for crowd monitoring

2. Determination of object detection model: In this study, the YOLO v3 model has been used for feature extraction and crowd detection by segregating humans from the background and identifying them with the help of bounding boxes. Figure 5 shows the network structure of the YOLO v3 model. There are some ready-to-use pre-trained models for the Maixduino board available in the GitHub repository (Aixier, 2022; Zhen8838, 2022; TonyZ1Min, 2022). It should be emphasized that the scope of this study is limited to the implementation of the existing reference model on the Maixduino board by training created dataset for the targeted application. On the contrary, the development of a novel CNN model and training it on the well-known dataset is out of the scope of this study.

Figure 5. The YOLO v3 network structure with the Darknet-53 backbone (Mao et al., 2019)

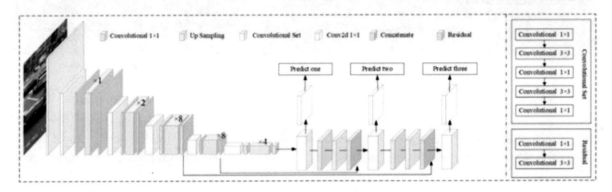

3. Model training: The pre-trained weights on the COCO dataset from the original YOLO v3 are optimized for crowd detection in bus/tram stops by iteratively processing the training images in the prepared dataset. The model has an accuracy of 84% on the training set.
4. Validation: The model has been improved by determining the optimum weights on a small part of the training dataset by tuning the parameters depending on the perceived errors, model bias, and spurious correlations. The model has an accuracy of 83% on the validation set.
5. Testing: The trained model's performance has been tested in terms of prediction accuracy by using a test set. It has been seen that the best-performing model's accuracy got saturated around at 79%. The obtained test accuracy was accepted as satisfactory.
6. Real-time crowd detection: After the training, validation, and testing stages, the weights of the YOLO v3 object detector are converted into the TensorFlow Lite file with (.tflite) extension, which is an open-source framework for inference on the edge devices. Maixduino supports TensorFlow Lite object detection model. But the MaixPy IDE supports only the kmodel files to store the neural network weights. So, the TensorFlow Lite file has been converted to the kmodel file through the NNcase compiler, which performs the compression and compilation. Then, both the model (.kmodel) and firmware (.bin) have been packaged into a single file with the (.kfpkg) extension. Lastly, the created package has been uploaded into the Maixduino board by using the kflash_gui flashing tool. While uploading the package, the firmware and model files are stored in different addresses, namely, the firmware is set to 0x000000 and the kmodel is set to 0x300000 (Trojan, 2020c).

All of the execution steps of the edge AI implementation were summarized in Figure 6.

Figure 6. The execution steps for edge AI implementation for crowd monitoring

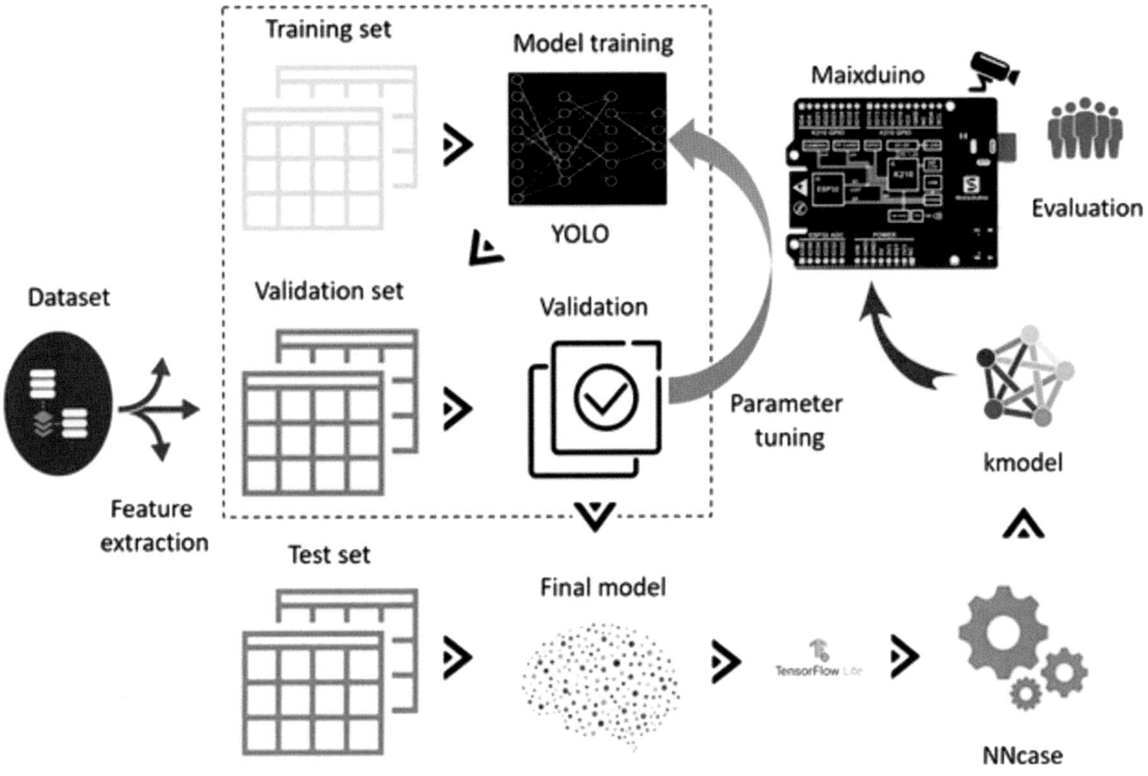

PERFORMANCE EVALUATION

The validity of the developed edge AI platform was verified by field tests on different bus/tram stops. When analyzing the results, the estimation accuracy was measured with the mean absolute error (MAE) performance metric, given as follows:

$$\text{MAE} = \frac{1}{N} \sum_{i=1}^{N} \left| n_i - \hat{n}_i \right|,$$

where N is the number of captured test images, n_i is the estimated count of passengers, and $\hat{n}_i$ is the true count of passengers for i th test image (Ilyas et al., 2019). As emphasized before, the count of passengers is restricted between 2 and 25, and the field tests were performed with a total of 125 images. The MAE value was obtained as 2.84 at the end of the performance evaluation. The obtained score was evaluated as satisfactory when considering that the study is carried out on the edge device.

According to the test results, the developed edge AI platform has superior detection performance for open-perspective images where passengers are clearly separated from each other. On the contrary, when the occlusion (closure) occurs due to two or more objects coming very close to each other and even merging, the performance of the developed edge AI platform is significantly degraded. It can be said that the error in the estimated passenger count increased for images with more than 15 passengers existing at the bus/tram stop. The conversion of the estimated passenger count to the density label (e.g. low, medium, and high) can be useful to interpret the current status of the bus/tram stops. Figure 7 and Figure 8 show the edge AI implementation for crowd monitoring at the tram stop and bus stop, respectively.

Figure 7. The edge AI implementation for crowd monitoring in public transportation tram stop

Figure 8. The edge AI implementation for crowd monitoring in public transportation bus stop

SOLUTIONS AND RECOMMENDATIONS

1. The OV2640 camera has uniform sensitivity to light across its field of vision. Although the trained model works pretty well in the daytime when all the people in crowding are visible clearly, its performance significantly decreases under unsatisfactory light conditions, especially in the nighttime. As a solution, it can be considered using thermal (infrared, IR) cameras, which can detect crowding in low-light environments, and even complete darkness. Because of the less sensitivity to the ambient lighting level and background color contrasts, thermal cameras have obvious advantages over traditional optical cameras.

2. In the application of crowd monitoring in public transportation, the optical cameras do not always allow us to accurately estimate the number of passengers due to obstructions in the camera's line of sight, non-uniform arrangement of passengers (clutter), and narrow viewing angle of the camera. Beyond that, poor light is an important problem, which is sourced from the shadowing effect depending on the sun's position and camera height. As a solution to those restrictions, it can be considered that the employment of multiple cameras for precise crowd detection with a multi-angle view.

CONCLUSION

Urbanization and the growth of the population in the cities cause overcrowding problems for citizens, especially in public places and services. It is inevitable to benefit from next-generation technologies to minimize the impact of urbanization-sourced problems. This study introduced an edge AI-based computer vision application to improve the comfort of passengers that use public transportation vehicles. In the proposed solution, the count of passengers at the bus/tram stops was estimated by using the DL method. Thanks to the edge AI-powered crowd monitoring approach, analysis of captured images can be made locally and quickly. Recently, due to the stringent protection regulations enforced by international data privacy laws, the placement of optical cameras is restricted to public areas. Contrary to cloud-based applications where many different users share the same physical storage, the edge computing approach promises much better privacy protection. Noteworthy that the proposed edge AI-based approach works independently from the storage of personal data on the cloud servers. Clearly, the collected images are processed on edge devices in real-time. Then the edge devices delete them without a store in the memory. On this basis, the proposed edge AI application may provide flexibility to enable the widespread use of optical camera-based crowd monitoring in public transport stops.

REFERENCES

Aixier. (2022). *K210-yolo3 model*. Retrieved July 27, 2022, from https://github.com/aixier/K210-yolo3

Allam, Z., & Dhunny, Z. A. (2019). On big data, artificial intelligence and smart cities. *Cities (London, England)*, *89*, 80–91. doi:10.1016/j.cities.2019.01.032

Alzubaidi, L., Zhang, J., Humaidi, A. J., Al-Dujaili, A., Duan, Y., Al-Shamma, O., Santamaría, J., Fadhel, M. A., Al-Amidie, M., & Farhan, L. (2021). Review of deep learning: Concepts, CNN architectures, challenges, applications, future directions. *Journal of Big Data*, *8*(1), 1–74. doi:10.118640537-021-00444-8 PMID:33816053

Ardiansyah, M. N., Kurniasari, M., Amien, M. D., Wijaya, D., & Setialana, P. (2022). Development of Crowd Detection Warning System Based on Deep Convolutional Neural Network using CCTV. *Journal of Engineering and Applied Technology*, *3*(1), 35–41. doi:10.21831/jeatech.v3i2.43771

Ballas, C., Marsden, M., Zhang, D., O'Connor, N. E., & Little, S. (2018). Performance of video processing at the edge for crowd-monitoring applications. *Proceedings of IEEE 4th World Forum on Internet of Things (WF-IoT)*. 10.1109/WF-IoT.2018.8355170

Bassoo, V., Ramnarain-Seetohul, V., Hurbungs, V., Fowdur, T. P., & Beeharry, Y. (2018). Big Data Analytics for Smart Cities. In N. Dey, A. Hassanien, C. Bhatt, A. Ashour, & S. Satapathy (Eds.), *Internet of Things and Big Data Analytics Toward Next-Generation Intelligence. Studies in Big Data* (Vol. 30, pp. 359–379). Springer.

Bawany, N. Z., & Shamsi, J. A. (2015). Smart City Architecture: Vision and Challenges. *International Journal of Advanced Computer Science and Applications*, *6*(11), 246–255.

Bezdan, T., & Džakula, N. B. (2019). Convolutional Neural Network Layers and Architectures. In *Proceedings of International Scientific Conference on Information Technology and Data Related Research (SINTEZA 2019)* (pp. 445-451). Academic Press.

Bochkovskiy, A., Wang, C.-Y., & Liao, H. Y. M. (2020). *YOLOv4: Optimal speed and accuracy of object detection*. Academic Press.

Bouraya, S., & Belangour, A. (2021). Object Detectors' Convolutional Neural Networks backbones: A review and a comparative study. *International Journal of Emerging Trends in Engineering Research*, *9*(11), 1379–1386. doi:10.30534/ijeter/2021/039112021

Campesato, O. (2020). *Artificial Intelligence, Machine Learning, and Deep Learning*. Mercury Learning & Information.

Cecaj, A., Lippi, M., Mamei, M., & Zambonelli, F. (2021). Sensing and Forecasting Crowd Distribution in Smart Cities: Potentials and Approaches. *IoT*, *2*(1), 33–49. doi:10.3390/iot2010003

Cenggoro, T. W. (2019). Deep Learning for Crowd Counting: A Survey. *Jurnal Emacs (Engineering, Mathematics and Computer Science)*, *1*(1), 17-28.

Cesana, M., & Redondi, A. E. C. (2016). IoT Communication Technologies for Smart Cities. In V. Angelakis, E. Tragos, H. C. Pöhls, A. Kapovits, & A. Bassi (Eds.), *Designing, Developing, and Facilitating Smart Cities: Urban Design to IoT Solutions* (pp. 139–162). Springer Cham.

Chen, C., Zhang, P., Zhang, H., Dai, J., Yi, Y., Zhang, H., & Zhang, Y. (2020). Deep Learning on Computational-Resource-Limited Platforms: A Survey. *Mobile Information Systems*, 1-19.

De Weert, Y., & Gkiotsalitis, K. (2021). A COVID-19 Public Transport Frequency Setting Model That Includes Short-Turning Options. *Future Transportation*, *1*(1), 3–20. doi:10.3390/futuretransp1010002

Dokic, K., Mikolcevic, H., & Radisic, B. (2021). *Inference speed comparison using convolutions in neural networks on various SoC hardware platforms using MicroPython.* RTA-CSIT.

Franke, T., Lukowicz, P., & Blanke, U. (2015). Smart crowds in smart cities: Real life, city scale deployments of a smartphone based participatory crowd management platform. *Journal of Internet Services and Applications*, 6(1), 1–19. doi:10.118613174-015-0040-6

Girshick, R. (2015). Fast R-CNN. In *Proceedings of IEEE International Conference on Computer Vision (ICCV)* (pp. 1440-1448). 10.1109/ICCV.2015.169

Girshick, R., Donahue, J., Darrell, T., & Malik, J. (2016). Region-based convolutional networks for accurate object detection and segmentation. *IEEE Transactions on Pattern Analysis and Machine Intelligence*, 38(1), 142–158. doi:10.1109/TPAMI.2015.2437384 PMID:26656583

Goodfellow, I., Bengio, Y., & Courville, A. (2016). *Deep Learning.* MIT Press.

Gouiaa, R., Akhloufi, M. A., & Shahbazi, M. (2021). Advances in Convolution Neural Networks Based Crowd Counting and Density Estimation. *Big Data Cognitive Computing*, 5(4), 1–21. doi:10.3390/bdcc5040050

Hammi, B., Khatoun, R., Zeadally, S., Fayad, A., & Khoukhi, L. (2018). IoT technologies for smart cities. *IET Networks*, 7(1), 1–13. doi:10.1049/iet-net.2017.0163

Hanani, F., Soulhi, A., & Saidi, R. (2019). Towards A Framework for Smart City Wireless Communication: Conclusions Drawn From Smart Transport Case Study. *Journal of Engineering and Applied Sciences (Asian Research Publishing Network)*, 14(8), 1601–1611.

He, K., Gkioxari, G., Dollár, P., & Girshick, R. (2017). Mask R-CNN. In *Proceedings of IEEE International Conference on Computer Vision (ICCV)* (pp. 2980-2988). 10.1109/ICCV.2017.322

Howard, A., Zhu, M., Chen, B., Kalenichenko, D., Wang, W., Weyand, T., Andreetto, M., & Adam, H. (2017). *Mobilenets: Efficient convolutional neural networks for mobile vision applications.* Academic Press.

Huang, S.-C., & Le, T.-H. (2021). Convolutional neural network architectures. In *Principles and Labs for Deep Learning* (pp. 201–217). Academic Press. doi:10.1016/B978-0-323-90198-7.00001-X

Ilyas, N., Shahzad, A., & Kim, K. (2019). Convolutional-Neural Network-Based Image Crowd Counting: Review, Categorization, Analysis, and Performance Evaluation. *Sensors (Basel)*, 20(1), 1–33. doi:10.339020010043 PMID:31861734

Irfan, M., Marcenaro, L., & Tokarchuk, L. (2016). Crowd analysis using visual and non-visual sensors, a survey. In *Proceedings of IEEE Global Conference on Signal and Information Processing (GlobalSIP)* (pp. 1249-1254). 10.1109/GlobalSIP.2016.7906041

Ismagilova, E., Hughes, L., Rana, N. P., & Dwivedi, Y. K. (2022). Security, Privacy and Risks within Smart Cities: Literature Review and Development of a Smart City Interaction Framework. *Information Systems Frontiers*, 24(2), 393–414. doi:10.100710796-020-10044-1 PMID:32837262

Jawhar, I., Mohamed, N., & Al-Jaroodi, J. (2018). Networking architectures and protocols for smart city systems. *Journal of Internet Services and Applications*, *9*(1), 1–16. doi:10.118613174-018-0097-0

Khan, A., Shah, J. A., Kadir, K., Albattah, W., & Khan, F. (2020). Crowd Monitoring and Localization Using Deep Convolutional Neural Network: A Review. *Applied Sciences (Basel, Switzerland)*, *10*(14), 1–17. doi:10.3390/app10144781

Khan, K., Albattah, W., Khan, R. U., Qamar, A. M., & Nayab, D. (2020). Advances and Trends in Real Time Visual Crowd Analysis. *Sensors (Basel)*, *20*(18), 1–28. doi:10.339020185073 PMID:32906659

Khan, N. A., Nebel, J.-C., Khaddaj, S., & Brujic-Okretic, V. (2020). Scalable System for Smart Urban Transport Management. *Journal of Advanced Transportation*, *2020*, 1–13. doi:10.1155/2020/8894705

Khan, Z., Anjum, A., Soomro, K., & Tahir, M. A. (2015). Towards cloud based big data analytics for smart future cities. *Journal of Cloud Computing: Advances. Systems*, *4*(2), 1–11.

Kibria, M. G., Nguyen, K., Villardi, G. P., Zhao, O., Ishizu, K., & Kojima, F. (2018). Big Data Analytics, Machine Learning, and Artificial Intelligence in Next-Generation Wireless Networks. *IEEE Access: Practical Innovations, Open Solutions*, *6*, 32328–32338. doi:10.1109/ACCESS.2018.2837692

Kim, J.-H., Kim, N., Park, Y. W., & Won, C. S. (2022). Object Detection and Classification Based on YOLO-V5 with Improved Maritime Dataset. *Journal of Marine Science and Engineering*, *10*(3), 1–14. doi:10.3390/jmse10030377

Klippel, E., Oliveira, R. A. R., Maslov, D., Bianchi, A. G. C., Delabrida, S. E., & Garrocho, C. T. B. (2022). Embedded Edge Artificial Intelligence for Longitudinal Rip Detection in Conveyor Belt Applied at the Industrial Mining Environment. *SN Computer Science*, *3*(4), 1–6. doi:10.100742979-022-01169-y

Li, E., Zeng, L., Zhou, Z., & Chen, X. (2020). Edge AI: On-Demand Accelerating Deep Neural Network Inference via Edge Computing. *IEEE Transactions on Wireless Communications*, *19*(1), 447–457. doi:10.1109/TWC.2019.2946140

Lin, T.-Y., Maire, M., Belongie, S., Bourdev, L., & Girshick, R. (2014). Microsoft COCO: common objects in context. In *Proceedings of European Conference on Computer Vision (ECCV)* (pp. 740-755). Academic Press.

Linthicum, D. S. (2017). Making Sense of AI in Public Clouds. *IEEE Cloud Computing*, *4*(6), 70–72. doi:10.1109/MCC.2018.1081067

Liu, W., Anguelov, D., Erhan, D., Szegedy, C., Reed, S., Fu, C.-Y., & Berg, A. C. (2016). SSD: Single Shot MultiBox Detector. In *Proceedings of European Conference on Computer Vision (ECCV 2016)* (pp. 21–37). 10.1007/978-3-319-46448-0_2

Lonavath, A. K., Virugu, K., Kumar, V. S., & Naik, D. K. (2017). Evolution of Smart City Concept and its Economic Performance: A Study of Cities in Telangana State of India. *International Journal of Research in Geography*, *3*(4), 84–99.

Louis, M. S., Azad, Z., Delshadtehrani, L., Gupta, S., Warden, P., Reddi, V. J., & Joshi, A. (2019). Towards Deep Learning using TensorFlow Lite on RISC-V. In *Third Workshop on Computer Architecture Research with RISC-V (CARRV)* (pp. 1-6). Academic Press.

Mao, Q.-C., Sun, H.-M., Liu, Y.-B., & Jia, R.-S. (2019). Mini-YOLOv3: Real-Time Object Detector for Embedded Applications. *IEEE Access: Practical Innovations, Open Solutions, 7,* 133529–133538. doi:10.1109/ACCESS.2019.2941547

McKinsey Global Institute. (2018). *Smart Cities: Digital Solutions for a More Livable Future.* Author.

Nguyen, D.-B., Dow, C.-R., & Hwang, S.-F. (2018). An Efficient Traffic Congestion Monitoring System on Internet of Vehicles. *Wireless Communications and Mobile Computing, 2018,* 1–17. doi:10.1155/2018/9136813

OECD. (2019). *Enhancing the contribution of digitalisation to the smart cities of the future.* OECD.

Poon, Y.-S., Lin, C.-C., Liu, Y.-H., & Fan, C.-P. (2022). YOLO-Based Deep Learning Design for In-Cabin Monitoring System with Fisheye-Lens Camera. *Proceedings of IEEE International Conference on Consumer Electronics (ICCE).* 10.1109/ICCE53296.2022.9730235

Redmon, J., Divvala, S., Girshick, R., & Farhadi, A. (2016). You Only Look Once: Unified, Real-Time Object Detection. In *Proceedings of IEEE Conference on Computer Vision and Pattern Recognition (CVPR)* (pp. 779-788). 10.1109/CVPR.2016.91

Redmon, J., & Farhadi, A. (2017). YOLO9000: better, faster, stronger. In *Proceedings of IEEE Conference on Computer Vision and Pattern Recognition (CVPR)* (pp. 7263-7271). IEEE.

Redmon, J., & Farhadi, A. (2018). *YOLOv3: An incremental improvement.* Academic Press.

Ren, S., He, K., Girshick, R., & Sun, J. (2017). Faster R-CNN: Towards Real-Time Object Detection with Region Proposal Networks. *IEEE Transactions on Pattern Analysis and Machine Intelligence, 39*(6), 1137–1149. doi:10.1109/TPAMI.2016.2577031 PMID:27295650

Rodriguez-Conde, I., Campos, C., & Fdez-Riverola, F. (2021). Optimized convolutional neural network architectures for efficient on-device vision-based object detection. *Neural Computing & Applications, 34*(13), 10469–10501. doi:10.100700521-021-06830-w

Salih, T. A., & Younis, N. K. (2021). Designing an Intelligent Real-Time Public Transportation Monitoring System Based on IoT. *Open Access Library Journal, 8*(10), 1–14. doi:10.4236/oalib.1107985

Serrano, W. (2018). Digital Systems in Smart City and Infrastructure: Digital as a Service. *Smart Cities, 1*(1), 134–154. doi:10.3390martcities1010008

Shadroo, S., Rahmani, A. M., & Rezaee, A. (2022). Survey on the application of deep learning in the Internet of Things. *Telecommunication Systems, 79*(4), 601–627. doi:10.100711235-021-00870-2

Shalev-Shwartz, S., & Ben-David, S. (2014). *Understanding Machine Learning: From Theory to Algorithms.* Cambridge University Press. doi:10.1017/CBO9781107298019

Shukla, S. N., & Champaneria, T. A. (2017). Survey of various data collection ways for smart transportation domain of smart city. *Proceedings of International Conference on I-SMAC (IoT in Social, Mobile, Analytics and Cloud) (I-SMAC).* 10.1109/I-SMAC.2017.8058265

Singh, U., Determe, J.-F., Horlin, F., & De Doncker, P. (2020). Crowd Monitoring: State-of-the-Art and Future Directions. *IETE Technical Review, 38*(6), 578–594. doi:10.1080/02564602.2020.1803152

Srivastava, S., Divekar, A. V., Anilkumar, C., Naik, I., Kulkarni, V., & Pattabiraman, V. (2021). Comparative analysis of deep learning image detection algorithms. *Journal of Big Data*, *8*(1), 1–27. doi:10.118640537-021-00434-w

Sultana, F., Sufian, A., & Dutta, P. (2019). Review of Object Detection Algorithms using CNN. *Proceedings of 2nd International Conference on Communication, Devices and Computing (ICCDC 2019)*.

Tong, M., Fan, L., Nan, H., & Zhao, Y. (2019). Smart Camera Aware Crowd Counting via Multiple Task Fractional Stride Deep Learning. *Sensors (Basel)*, *19*(6), 1–14. doi:10.339019061346 PMID:30889874

TonyZ1Min. (2022). *YOLO for K210*. Retrieved July 27, 2022, from https://github.com/TonyZ1Min/yolo-for-k210

Torres-Sanchez, E., Alastruey-Benede, J., & Torres-Moreno, E. (2020). Developing an AI IoT application with open software on a RISC-V SoC. In *Proceedings of XXXV Conference on Design of Circuits and Integrated Systems (DCIS)* (pp. 1-6). 10.1109/DCIS51330.2020.9268645

Trojan, W. (2020a, May). Artificial Intelligence for Beginners (1): Object recognition using the Maixduino board. *Elektor Magazine*, 12-17.

Trojan, W. (2020b, July). Artificial Intelligence for Beginners (2): Neural networks with Linux and Python. *Elektor Magazine*, 110-114.

Trojan, W. (2020c, Sept.). Artificial Intelligence for Beginners (3): A stand-alone neural network. *Elektor Magazine*, September & October 2020,44-49.

Ultralytics. (2020). *YOLO-v5*. Retrieved July 27, 2022, from https://github.com/ultralytics/yolov5

United Nations. (2018). The World's *Cities*. Author.

Voulodimos, A., Doulamis, N., Doulamis, A., & Protopapadakis, E. (2018). Deep Learning for Computer Vision: A Brief Review. *Computational Intelligence and Neuroscience*, *2018*, 1–13. doi:10.1155/2018/7068349 PMID:29487619

Wang, R., Wang, Z., Xu, Z., Wang, C., Li, Q., Zhang, Y., & Li, H. (2021). A Real-Time Object Detector for Autonomous Vehicles Based on YOLOv4. *Computational Intelligence and Neuroscience*, *2021*, 1–11. doi:10.1155/2021/9218137 PMID:34925498

Xiang, J., & Liu, N. (2022). Crowd Density Estimation Method Using Deep Learning for Passenger Flow Detection System in Exhibition Center. *Scientific Programming*, *2022*, 1–9. doi:10.1155/2022/1990951

Zanella, A., Bui, N., Castellani, A., Vangelista, L., & Zorzi, M. (2014). Internet of Things for Smart Cities. *IEEE Internet of Things Journal*, *1*(1), 22–32. doi:10.1109/JIOT.2014.2306328

Zhang, C., Li, H., Wang, X., & Yang, X. (2015). Cross-scene Crowd Counting via Deep Convolutional Neural Networks. In *Proceedings of IEEE Conference on Computer Vision and Pattern Recognition (CVPR)* (pp. 833-841). 10.1109/CVPR.2015.7298684

Zhang, J., Chen, S., Tian, S., Gong, W., Cai, G., & Wang, Y. (2021). A Crowd Counting Framework Combining with Crowd Location. *Journal of Advanced Transportation*, *2021*, 1–14. doi:10.1155/2021/6664281

Zhang, J., & Tao, D. (2021). Empowering Things with Intelligence: A Survey of the Progress, Challenges, and Opportunities in Artificial Intelligence of Things. *IEEE Internet of Things Journal, 8*(10), 7789–7817. doi:10.1109/JIOT.2020.3039359

Zhao, Z.-Q., Zheng, P., Xu, S.-T., & Wu, X. (2019). Object Detection with Deep Learning: A Review. *IEEE Transactions on Neural Networks and Learning Systems, 30*(11), 3212–3232. doi:10.1109/TNNLS.2018.2876865 PMID:30703038

Zhen8838. (2022). *K210 Yolo framework*. Retrieved July 27, 2022, from https://github.com/zhen8838/K210_Yolo_framework

Chapter 10
Patient Behavioral Analysis With Smart Healthcare and IoT

Sanjay Rajendra Mate

 https://orcid.org/0000-0002-3960-259X

Sangam University, India & Bhilwara and Government Polytechnic Daman (Gujarat Technological University), India

Renuka Suryawanshi

MIT World Peace University, India

Manjusha Taur

Canadian Imperial Bank of Commerce, Canada

Kishor S. Wagh

 https://orcid.org/0000-0002-0309-0705

All India Shri Shivaji Memorial Society's Institute of Information Technology, India

ABSTRACT

Consider a person with total mental capacity and an active lifestyle who can now not communicate or connect with the world around them due to a severe motor impairment to being locked into their body. Assume the person cannot notify their caregiver when uncomfortable or in distress. Caregivers dealing with locked-in patients must currently rely on their instincts, troubleshooting skills, and standard operating procedures to offer the best care possible. And with these safeguards in place, patients continue to suffer from needless rashes, illnesses, and deaths that should have been avoided. Modern technologies could significantly change this outcome and are being under-utilized in such healthcare environments. This chapter explores patient behavioral analysis with smart healthcare and IoT.

DOI: 10.4018/978-1-6684-6275-1.ch010

INTRODUCTION

Integrating these advances into robust healthcare monitoring and communication systems could dramatically improve the quality of life for patients with locked-in syndrome. The purpose of this research is to analyze brain diseases using the Internet of Things. A machine learning model advances brain-computer interface (BCI) signal processing and shows the potential to improve the capabilities of mobile Internet of Things (IoT) devices. The device provides caregivers with up-to-date and relevant telemetry, enabling rapid intervention in the event of an emergency or emergencies. This allows for more credible accountability and improves data collection for the development of care. The device allows locked-in patients to interact with caregivers through a keyword-selection key interface.

Figure 1. Healthcare Information and Communication Technologies (ICT)

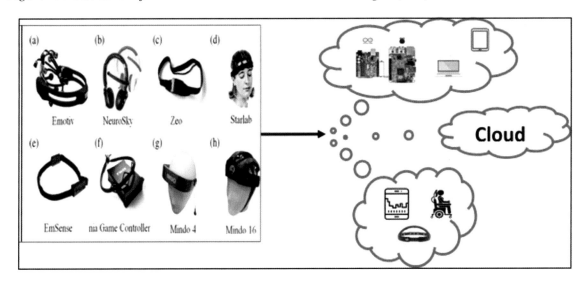

For several years, the healthcare industry has been implementing and deploying information and communication technologies (ICT) for successful healthcare administration, diagnosis, monitoring and controlling can be seen in Figure 1. Information and communication technology (ICT) helps a variety of health care professionals consult and advise patients, and also enables communication with far-flung resources. Most health care professionals can offer treatment or prescribe medication after physically interacting with a patient on an examination table. If doctors and medical professionals have infrastructure concerns, they can also take advantage of advances in information and communication technology (ICT) to see patients remotely. Recent advances in Information and Communication Technology (ICT) and the emergence of the Internet of Things (IoT) are creating new opportunities for research and discovery across all industries, including medicine and healthcare. For this reason, as per Mate (2020) hospitals have started using mobile devices for connectivity, leveraging the Internet of Things (IoT) and merging with small sensor nodes like Wi-Fi. Remote diagnosis is also possible and essential for some diseases such as Covid-19. ICT helps in remote monitoring too. As healthcare infrastructure advances, there is a greater emphasis on innovative systems for improving patients' lives with disabilities. In addition, the governments of such regions fund the welfare of their people, providing great opportunities for BCI's research and development (R&D) activities. As per Attallah et.al. (2020), Patients with chronic diseases such as Alzheimer's disease, Parkinson's disease, and epilepsy represent a high demand for BCI technology.

Furthermore, the high prevalence of neurodegenerative disorders drives global demand for brain-computer interface (BCI) technology during the forecast period. Non-invasive BCIs are poised to alter how we interact with our devices (smartphones and computers). Brain-machine interfaces enable us to monitor our gadgets with our minds, allowing people with disabilities to drive robotic prostheses with their thoughts. Berbano et.al. (2017), Aside from healthcare, brain-machine interface applications include controlling connected (IoT) devices like smart door locks directly through the brain, eliminating the need for a go-between like a virtual assistant, and many more.

BCI technology, Rashidy et.al. (2021) which allows non-muscular adjustment of technology and devices, has been used by researchers to bridge the contact gap. Non-invasive BCI studies are commonly used, allowing patients to indicate anxiety and critical contacts (yes/no) in a variety of scenarios. On the other hand, according to Alhussein et.al. (2018) non-invasive BCI has some drawbacks: B. Expensive facilities, painful long-term wear and tear, restricted mobility. Combine non-invasive BCI signals and IoT devices with ML models to improve caregiver skills by bridging communication gaps and enabling complex responses to patient needs. On the one hand, BCI provides accurate medical signals and intuition data. On the other hand, for comfort reasons, patients do not wear the BCI system indefinitely. Comfort Reasons with multiple sensors and ML models solves mobility and offers versatile support, 24/7 data monitoring and early detection of unstable conditions.

Another recent trend is the use of more compact and affordable IoT devices to improve healthcare services and aid patient recovery. For example, researchers are currently using his IoT devices in combination with his ML models in the fight against COVID-19. The scientist used his Raspberry Pi4's image recognition model and an infrared camera to identify feverish individuals, greatly improving case detection efforts. Additionally, engineers are adding to the already extensive list of accessories that extend the capabilities of IoT devices. Persistent infections are physical or dysfunctional behaviors such as hypertension, diabetes, cardiovascular disease, obesity, and stroke. These diseases are responsible for most of the threats to human well-being and have since accounted for more than 66% of all deaths worldwide. As the population grows, the advantage of persistent infections expands. Clinic boundaries are not required for all patients. Additionally, ongoing problems require special attention at home to address the patient's issues and plan treatment. Additionally, according to Rashidy (2021) most parents and families lack the necessary time and skills, compromising patient satisfaction.

E-wellbeing framework execution (for instance, distant patient observing (RPM), electronic wellbeing record (EHR) frameworks, versatile wellbeing (m-wellbeing), telemedicine, e-visits, e-meetings, etc.) is getting progressively applicable. Such frameworks permit ceaseless observing, conclusion, forecast, and treatment. Accordingly, Rashidy (2021), they add to bring down medical care costs while urging patients to approach their day-by-day lives while their fundamental signs are consistently observed. Besides, these frameworks permit doctors to arrive at patients whenever, not simply while in a medical clinic. As per Suryawanshi (2020), Patient consideration (PM) programs assist patients with learning their indications and medicines, assisting them with living autonomously and improving their satisfaction. In clinics, PM frameworks are significant; for instance, they might be utilized to rate patient's dependent on their incapacities, permitting clinics to focus on essential patient considerations. The Internet of Things (IoT) is a bleeding-edge innovation that empowers all items to get shrewd. The Internet of Things enormously affects various areas, with a fascinating clinical space. IoT can consociate sensors, gadgets, and patients without requiring human mediation through distant observing frameworks. A small body region organization (WBAN) is the Internet of Things (IoT). It is a remote sensor network that interfaces sensors on a patient's body to the organization, empowering distant checking of the patient's vital signs. A WBAN is a little organization of sensors in the clinical field that incorporates a heartbeat oximeter, spinners, a spirometer, a worldwide situating framework (GPS), and electroencephalography. Numerous clinical information focuses are assembled ceaselessly from patients, permitting doctors to be checked progressively utilizing a scope of interior and outside sensors. As per Rashidy (2021), next are the fundamental strides in creating PMs: (1) Data assortment: Vital signs are constantly checked using intrusive and non-obtrusive procedures. This move is utilized to acquire crucial signs like EEG, ECG, pulse, and pulse. Instruments are being used to gather logical factors, for example, temperature and pulse notwithstanding vital signs (room temperature, pressure, and so forth) (2) Data move and capacity: All information is collected and sent to the cloud for investigation, arranging, and handling.

The purpose of this chapter is to share recent advances in healthcare using brain computer interface technology. Using brain computer interface, we can collect all different types of brain waves. The device can be used to analyze data and provide input to microcontrollers for various purposes, such as treating Alzheimer's Disease, brain malformations, brain tumors, cerebellar disorders, and confusion.

RELATED WORK

Many researchers have revealed that poor nursing performance suffered from ignorance and high prices within the healthcare system.Therefore, many studies have planned solutions to address tactical problems using the IoT alongside skill enhancement as per Pradhan (2021), cooperative perception, and auto-triggered management according to Suryawanshi (2020), to optimize efficiency and impairment through explicit mishandling of non-invasive BCI signals and IoT period information.Others are taking advantage of newer technology and using cloud-based remote health services to make care more efficient. Griggs et al. are willing to use good blockchain-based contracts to facilitate secure analysis and management of medical sensors. The study by Bibani et al.found that a diet with high levels of saturated fat and cholesterol was associated with an increased risk of heart disease. Show us a hybrid cloud and fog platform that can be used to supply remote care. However, such styles need the information transferred and shared on the public internet in order to be successful.

There is a lot of healthcare information out there in the form of visuals, and sometimes it has important information about human survival alongside it. Table 1 shows recent work related to EEG and ECG while table 2 shows EEG signal range for delta, theta, alpha, gamma, beta etc. Analyzing healthcare data is a very important task, as it can save human lives and help to restore characteristics of life.Sarkar and others projected a design for buildings that can be used for IoT and bestowed a unified syntax for data about healthcare. Many researchers support ideas or cause public processing, and come up with new answers to mine the vast unstructured biomedical written material to support therapeutic analysis. As a model, Jiang et al. provided the most advanced, sophisticated individuals with a wealth of information in a healthcare system in visual form, connecting an accompanying detachable wrist sensor via a mobile phone to view the wearer's well-being. Hossain et al. state that the use of social media can have a positive effect on people's mental health.There is a need for a healthcare data foundation that utilizes voice pathology estimation (VPA). This would allow for accurate and consistent health data tracking.

Although everything that happened seemed to support a different model or design from the norm in the domain of prediction, in the end, the data seemed to support the standard model or design.In comparison, our approach seeks to combine BCIs signals and wearable IoT symbol data to mitigate error in identifying problems, be dramatic at first detection of ailments, provide better forecasting, and use healthcare cost-effectively and smoothly .

Table 1. Review of related work in ECG and EEG

Authors & Year	Datasets	Physiological Signals Sr.	Technique (s)	Results
Bekolay et.al. (2018)	"Training set" and "Testing_Words" words spelling asks 4 participants.	Electrooculography (EOG) and Electroencephalography (EEG)	Classifier - Linear Discriminant Analysis (LDA)	Evaluated the physiological hybrid signal P300-based speller introducing the half checkerboard (HCBP).
Berbano et al. (2017)	EEG (Subject dependent)	Experimented on 8 males and 9 females performed a stroop color-word test to induce mental stress.	87.37%	Highlighted the division of subjects in an emotional, mental, physical, and unstressed state
Vikrant Doma (2020)	ECG (Subject dependent)	Electrocardiogram (ECG) data were acquired from 16 subjects at a time of examination and after the winter holiday.	93% KNN, SVM	Intense stress and weak stress samples correlated in autonomic reactivity differentiation
Shon D. et.al. (2019)	ECG, electrodermal activity(EDA) and EEG (Subject dependent)	15 healthy participants, 8 males, and 7 females mean age 40.8 9.5 years, participated using wearable sensor devices measured signals (HRV, EDA, EEG).	SVM, LDA, KNN	Enhancement in features extraction and classification algorithms for stress models in real scenarios. It assists in identifying stress in a real-life environment
Xia et al. (2019)	EEG (Subject dependent)	Seventeen healthy participants participated in EEG recording with 32 channels.	DWT, SVM	EEG results indicate the impact of acute stress ion the frontal and parietal head area. Especially in theta, alpha and gamma frequency bands.

Table 2. EEG Signal Range

Delta	0.5 to 4	Normal person (0)
Theta	4 to 8	
Alpha	8 to 13	
Beta	13 to 30	
Gamma	30 to 54	Abnormal person (1)

Brain-Computer Interface (BCI)

The cerebrum PC interface (BCI) is a mechanism for catching, either wired or remotely, the neural elements of the human mind and sending them to outer gadgets to help people in speaking with their current circumstances without the utilization of PCs. their actual capacity is the essential point of this present area's advancements is to help. As per Vaibhaw (2020), individuals who have neurological inabilities have complete control of their lives. They have a practical cerebrum, yet they can't handle their bodies because of neuronal harm. This type of BCI can improve their satisfaction altogether.

As shown in Figure 2, the BCI is customized to perceive the electromagnetic waveforms created by neural exercises in the cerebrum and afterward unravel them to choose the individual's motivation, so it can interpret those examples into orders that it can ship off the machine to do activities for the individual's benefit, like turning a wheelchair, killing lights, or getting a book.

As per Vaibhaw (2020), The accompanying measures are typically remembered for BCI: signal obtaining, preprocessing, or signal improvement, including extraction and order. The reviewed signals are then taken care of as contributions to the control gadgets.

Figure 2. Brain-Computer Interface

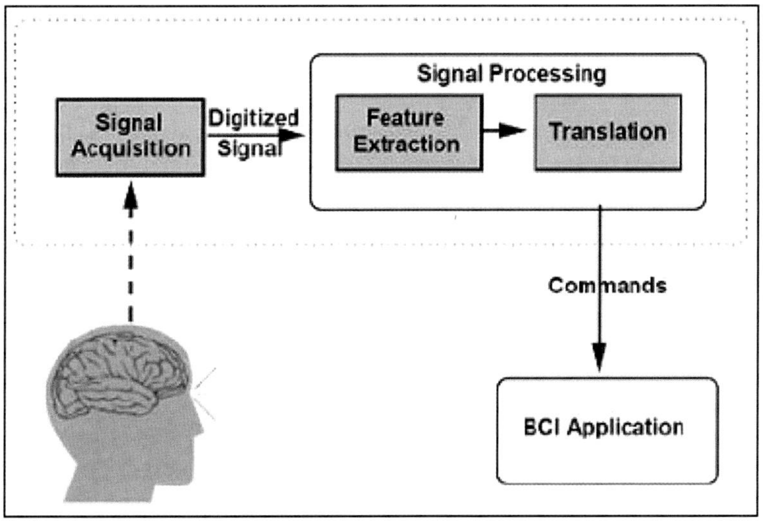

EEG Stands for Electroencephalography

By placing anodes on the scalp, electroencephalography, also known as EEG, is a non-invasive method for measuring the electromagnetic thought signal generated by brain activity. This is the main reason why this kind of recording is so common. As per Vaibhaw et.al. (2020), the signal captured by this technology is weak because it should pass through the brain, skull, and multiple layers of tissues beneath the scalp. According to Alhussein et.al. (2018), it is less ridiculous than CT checking and is also employed to assess brain issues. The cathodes connected to the speakers, the simple-to-advanced converter, and the capacity unit make up the EEG recording framework. As per Vaibhaw et.al. (2020), Brain motivations are ingested by terminals, improved by an enhancer, converted to computerized signals by a basic to advanced converter, and then recorded and produced by an advanced converter.

The basically discovered delta signal in infants dynamically decreases as they develop and has a recurrence of less than 4 Hz. These negative effects are more noticeable in adults. According to Biswal et.al. (2013), These symptoms are quite unusual in a cognizant adult and may indicate a neurological issue when they occur when they are in a deep sleep. According to Alhussein et.al. (2018) Theta waves occur and repeat between 4 and 7 hertz. The majority of young people are familiar with these types of waves. Children and gentle waves show a conscious person. The waves connected to fixation are these. The optical area of the brain is where alpha waves, which have a repetition frequency of 812 Hz, are discovered according to Berbano et.al. (2017). These waves are influenced by mental effort, as per Attallah et.al. (2020).

Alpha waves: The recurrence frequency of beta waves is around 1230 Hz. As per Vathalani et.al. (2017), They can also be found in the center and frontal projections of the mind. These waves are commonly associated with thought and motor activity, as per Grtiggs et.al. (2009)]. Gamma waves, which have a 30100 Hz recurrence, are connected to particular engine capacity. According to tests, gamma waves and engine activity are associated during maximum muscle constriction, and gamma waves are replaced by beta waves during powerless withdrawals, as per Yangui et.al. (2016). Since gamma waves are impacted by external noise, they are normally not used in EEG. In spite of this, as they provide information at a higher goal than beta and alpha waves, research into their use in BCI is ongoing.

The recurrence frequency of beta waves is around 1230 Hz. They can also be found in the center and frontal projections of the mind. As per Vathalani et.al. (2017), these waves are commonly associated with thought and motor activity Griggs (2009). Gamma waves, which have a 30100 Hz recurrence, are connected to particular engine capacity. According to Yangui et.al. (2016) the tests of gamma waves and engine activity are associated during maximum muscle constriction, and gamma waves are replaced by beta waves during powerless withdrawals. According to Vathalani et.al. (2017), Since gamma waves are impacted by external noise, they are normally not used in EEG. However, as they provide information at a higher goal than beta and alpha waves, research into their use in BCI is ongoing.

DEVELOPMENT PROCEDURE of BCI

EEG Recording

Signals may be collected invasively (via direct contact with the cortex) or non-invasively (via indirect contact with the cortex) (contact only from the skin). In both cases, electrodes are positioned in the regions where, depending on the BCI method, EEG signals are extracted. Some preprocessing is considered in this acquisition stage, such as notch filters and band pass filters to remove the EEG in the desired frequency band.

It is essential to use a sensitive electrode device connected to the surface of the head to extract high-quality EEG signals. In EEG signal acquisition, two types of electrode headsets are used. They are gel-based electrodes as opposed to dry-based electrodes.

The 10-20 System of Electrode Placement is a technique used to depict the area of scalp anodes. These scalp anodes are utilized to record the electroencephalogram (EEG) using a machine called an electroencephalograph. Each point on figure 3 to one side shows a potential cathode position.

Figure 3. 10–20 system (EEG)

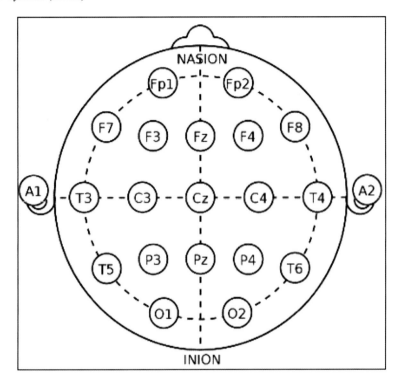

Dataset

EEG comprises a broad group of data collection and examination methods utilized in the industry to assess the inside qualities of the part, segment, or framework without causing harm. Among the available methods, EEG uses the stressed and unstressed state of a child and this method consists of pre-processing, EEG band separation, EEG band selection, EEG feature extraction, Stress detection and proves to be reliable and feasible. The EEG data is recorded at 512 Hz frequency. In this dataset, the down-sampled (128 Hz) and filtered (4 to 45 Hz) pre- processed EEG dataset is used. The 32 electrodes Fp1, AF3, F3, F7, FC5, FC1, C3, T7, CP5, CP1, P3, P7, PO3, O1, Oz, Pz, Fp2, AF4, Fz, F4, F8, FC6, FC2, Cz, C4, T8, CP6, CP2, P4, P8, PO4, and O2 are positioned according to the international 10-20 system. An electrode interfacing with neural tissue is critical to propelling determination and treatments for the neurological issues, just as giving point by point data about the neural signals

Signal Preprocessing after Extraction

Preprocessing was used to enhance the characteristics of the captured signals. The raw signals were first filtered with a band pass filter to exclude frequencies in the alpha (0-14Hz) and beta (14-30Hz) ranges etc. The filtered frequency signals were then further preprocessed to remove artifacts. Such as eye blinks are more visible in EEG signals with Motor Imagery features as per Lee (2019). Table 3 shows a sample of brain emotion data collected using NeuroSky single channel Device and analyzed brain state according to voltage received. By taking the general average, these standard features can be omitted. A preprocessing software tool is developed after applying filters and preprocessing methods to visualize the EEG signals electrode by an electrode.

Table 3. Sample Brain emotion data collected using NuroSky Device

Sr No	Attention	Meditation	Blink Strength	Delta	Theta	Alpha	Beta	Gamma	Avg	Out come
1	48	20	47	4.263574	14.12051	6.234082	12.825	22.39409	21.85466	0
2	48	20	47	4.263574	14.12051	6.234082	12.825	22.39409	21.85466	0
3	48	20	47	4.263574	14.12051	6.234082	12.825	22.39409	21.85466	0
4	48	20	47	4.263574	14.12051	6.234082	12.825	22.39409	21.85466	0
5	48	20	47	4.263574	14.12051	6.234082	12.825	22.39409	21.85466	0
6	48	20	47	4.263574	14.12051	6.234082	12.825	22.39409	21.85466	0
7	48	20	47	4.263574	14.12051	6.234082	12.825	22.39409	21.85466	0
8	48	20	47	4.263574	14.12051	6.234082	12.825	22.39409	21.85466	0
9	48	20	47	4.263574	14.12051	6.234082	12.825	22.39409	21.85466	0
10	48	20	47	4.263574	14.12051	6.234082	12.825	22.39409	21.85466	0
11	48	20	47	4.263574	14.12051	6.234082	12.825	22.39409	21.85466	0
12	48	20	47	4.263574	14.12051	6.234082	12.825	22.39409	21.85466	0
13	48	20	47	4.263574	14.12051	6.234082	12.825	22.39409	21.85466	0
14	48	20	47	4.263574	14.12051	6.234082	12.825	22.39409	21.85466	0
15	48	20	47	4.263574	14.12051	6.234082	12.825	22.39409	21.85466	0

Extraction and Selection of Features:

A cycle of dimensionality reduction known as "feature extraction" reduces an underlying organization of unprocessed data to more manageable groups for processing. Numerous aspects that call for a significant number of registering assets to measure are a characteristic of these enormous informational indexes.

It is possible to efficiently understand the highlights by removing the relevant information or qualities from the sign using a process called feature extraction. It is a charitable cycle to interpret an information signal after that. The data that was extracted reflects the physiology and living systems of the action occurring inside the brain. It required a sizable amount of memory or a special calculation to study the data because it contained numerous components in a wide arrangement of information. Figure 4 illustrates an extraction

Figure 4. Feature extraction process

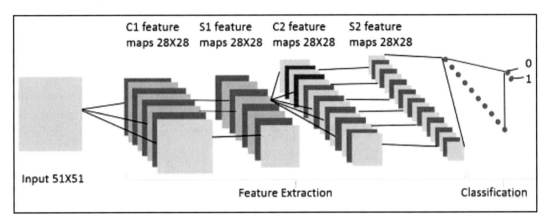

Each and every highlight has been tested using the EEG data collecting. It is thought that aftereffects vary greatly from one element to another. Highlight selection provides less information, which makes the order framework less confusing and improves AI computations.

Analyze the Principal Components

A linear transformation technique called PCA is used to transform correlated data into uncorrelated data. A list of components is created using the supplied data and arranged in descending order according to their variance. According to Lee (2019), the input data is then projected onto an Eigen space with k dimensions and k eigenvectors. The covariance matrix is used in the computation of eigenvectors. PCA may not always ensure accurate classification since the discriminating function could not be present in the set of the greatest principle components. On the other hand, because it recognizes artifacts and reconstructs the signal without the noise, it is quite effective at removing noise from data, according to Griggs (2009).

Analysis of Independent Components

Without understanding the meaning of the sign, free part examination (ICA) breaks the inconsistent message down into its components. As per Lee (2019), it functions under the assumption that the selected signal is a composite of numerous individual indicators from various exercises. The component of an information vector is determined by the number of sources, whereas the component of a yield vector is determined by the number of information channels considered.

The Wavelet Transforms

A well-known numerical strategy for information extraction is wavelet change as per Rashidy (2021). As per Vaibhaw (2020), wavelet change can be utilized to productively examine nonstationary flags because of its effortlessness in characterizing a sign's time-recurrence.

Wavelets are numerical capacities that gap information into various recurrence parts over a brief time frame length, making them valuable for signal investigation in both the recurrence and time spaces.

Estimating states of being with sharp spikes and discontinuities outflanks the conventional Fourier change technique.

FT simply shows the various recurrence substances and disregards the recurrence's circumstance. Transient Fourier change was subsequently used to tackle the issue that FT was having by breaking the sign into progressive time terms and afterward applying FT. As per Vaibhaw (2020), this brought about an expanded worldly goal yet diminished recurrence goal. These issues are tended to by wavelet change.

For a similitude between the sign and the foreordained waveform, consistent wavelet change (CWT) is undifferentiated from the format coordinating on coordination with the channel.

CWT enjoys an upper hand over MF because of the extraordinary property of wavelet change, which disintegrates the sign in both recurrence and time spaces. Constant wavelet change adds a great deal of adaptability and excess to the signal since it investigates it at countless frequencies. The discrete wavelet change was created, which investigates and decays the sign into just discrete qualities.

THE NEURAL NETWORK'S TRAINING

In the wake of preprocessing, the information was taken care of in the organization for preparation. The organization structure that is utilized for all preparation is the Multilayer Perceptron Network (MLP). The Neural Network comprises M hidden layers and X info neurons, and Y yield neurons. Force backpropagation, otherwise called backpropagation, is a showing of learning rules. Some datasets were all around prepared for energy backpropagation, while others were just easily prepared for backpropagation. For all arranging, the Sigmoid exchange work was utilized.

Classification

Grouping is a significant assignment of EEG signals. It can work depending on the element extraction. The highlights esteem are info, and it can anticipate the class for classifier technique. A classifier has various boundaries that should be learned from preparing information. The learned classifier is a model of the relationship between the highlights and the classes.

For instance, if the information includes x of a class: y, the model of classifier work y = x(n) can foresee new occurrences. These examples are not utilized in preparing information. Those removed information from EEG datasets were then ordered utilizing linear and nonlinear classifiers to examine better classifiers for EEG information arrangement. These are depicted beneath in a word. With the help of trained classifier data, classification is used to categorize test data. Sensitivity, specificity, accuracy, F-measured, kappa index, Mathew's correlation coefficient (MCC), Precision, Area under the curve (AUC), and other performance assessment matrices have all been utilized.

Before becoming a command for an application and before users receive feedback on whether or not a certain mental order was identified, these EEG features are assessed.

While great work is being done to provide modes of operation that don't require calibration, most BCIs now employ off-line calibration because it's necessary to produce a dependable system. The best features from several EEG channels are selected at this point once the classification algorithm has been calibrated. a user-provided training data collection

Since EEG signals are very user-specific, the majority of BCI devices in use today are calibrated specifically for each user. This training data set includes EEG signals that were recorded as the user repeatedly carried out each relevant mental task as directed.

The BCI closed-loop classifies the users' EEG patterns based on EEG features using classification algorithms, also referred to as classifiers.

Classifier Based on k-Nearest Neighbors

The k-closest neighbor classifiers (k-NNCs) work with the understanding that connected highlights in a component space with different information focuses structure of a diverse group. The classifier utilizes k-closest neighbors to characterize similarities between test information and highlights of each class, each in turn. A huge worth of k can help limit the probability of blunders; however, it can likewise build vulnerability, so the worth of k is picked to best match the condition. As per Vaibhaw (2020), the closest k neighbors are masterminded in sliding requests of nearness. The loads between joins are utilized. k-NNC isn't broadly utilized in BCI because of its high affectability.

Analyze Linear Discriminant Feature

Direct discriminant examination (LDA) is broadly used to sort designs into two gatherings; nonetheless, it tends to be reached out to group numerous examples.

In order to identify the classes, LDA encourages a variety of straight segregation work that takes on a few hyperplanes in the component space. LDA expects that all groupings are directly detachable. As per Vaibhaw (2020), if there are two classes, the LDA creates one hyperplane and transfers the data onto it to strengthen the division of the two classifications. This hyperplane is created simultaneously while considering two boundaries.

Machine Learning with Support Vectors

The assistance vector machine (SVM) functions similarly to direct discriminant analysis. Similar to LDA, a hyperplane or group of hyperplanes is created to divide the component vectors into different classes; however, it chooses the hyperplane that is located the farthest from the preparation tests.

By arranging input data into high-dimensional space, SVM determines the hyperplane with the best edge in accordance with Cover's hypothesis. According to Cover's hypothesis and Vaibhaw (2020), a perplexing order problem projected into high-dimensional nonlinear space is bound to be more distinct than one projected into low-dimensional nonlinear space.

With the aid of part work, nonlinear SVM can coexist with a nonlinear choice limit, increasing its adaptability. SVM is widely used in

Artificial Neural Network (ANN)

The assistance vector machine (SVM) functions similarly to direct discriminant analysis. A hyperplane or group of hyperplanes is created to divide the component vectors into different classes, similar to how LDA does. However, this method chooses the hyperplane that is farthest from the closest tests being prepared.

By arranging input data into high-dimensional space, SVM determines the hyperplane with the best edge in accordance with Cover's hypothesis. According to Cover's hypothesis, a perplexing order problem projected into high-dimensional nonlinear space is bound to be more distinct than one projected into low-dimensional nonlinear space. With the aid of part work, nonlinear SVM can coexist with a nonlinear choice limit, increasing its adaptability. The use of SVM in BCI systems is widespread.

THE ARCHITECTURE OF HEALTHCARE IOT

IoT frameworks are presently fitted with sensors that can take care of issues similar to the human mind because of late advancements in sensor innovation and artificial consciousness. As per Prashan et.al. (2021), In an IoT setting, psychological calculation helps investigate covered-up designs in vast amounts of information. Besides, it upgrades a sensor's capacity to handle medical care information and react to its environmental factors naturally. All sensors in an intelligent IoT network work together with other smart gadgets, as per Pradhan (2021). The joining of psychological figuring into an IoT framework permits medical care suppliers to all be more likely to screen patient information and give sufficient therapy. As per Pradhan et.al. (2021), EEG-based savvy medical services are observing a framework that utilizes intellectual processing to evaluate the patient's obsessive condition. The EEG information, related to other sensor information like discourse, movement, body development, and looks, was utilized to survey a patient's condition. It likewise accommodates clinical help with the instance of pathogenic infections. Accordint to Pradhan et al. (2021) proposed a psychological information move framework that can distinguish, screen, and dissect patient wellbeing information. Since the patient is in critical condition, as seen in Figure 5, the information on the patient is sent with the greatest urgency. Because of the expanding significance of the brain in contemporary society, the research of brain functions has become a frequent subject in the medical industry. According to Suryawanshi (2020), Consider their tension in human life to get the basic explanation for these circumstances.

Figure 5. Internet of Things (IoT)– cloud-based savvy medical care framework

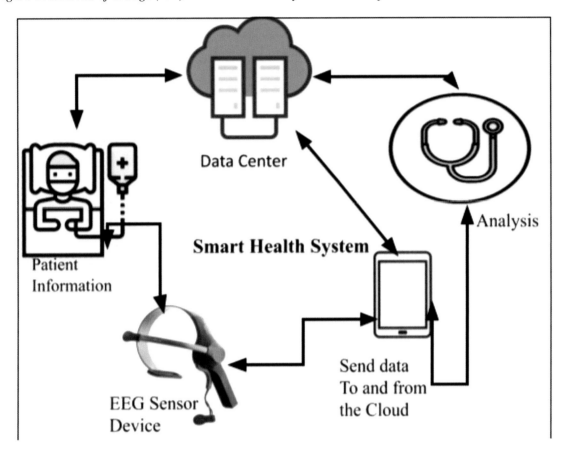

As shown in Figure 6, Collecting raw data, analyzing patient behavior using biomedical smart sensors and analysis will improve healthcare performance. According to Alhussein (2018), Cloud-based psychological Internet of Things (IoT)– based shrewd medical care framework that speaks with savvy gadgets, sensors, and other medical services partners, settles on educated choices dependent on a patient's state and offers ideal, minimal expense, and open medical care administrations.

The first step that we must perform is signal collecting using bio-medical signals employing biosensors such as EEG, ECG, EOG, and EMG. When collecting various biomedical signals, it is necessary to concentrate on feature extraction, feature selection, and artefact elimination. We can collect biomedical signals utilizing a Bluetooth device and an appropriate microcontroller. Nowadays, raspberry pi and Arduino microcontrollers are famous and easy to use. According to the program, we can gather real-time bio signals and access, process, and control them from any location using the internet.

This example will look at an EEG signal that we may gather with any portable EEG device, such as the Neurosky Mind wave 2. And the received signal can be shared or sent over the cloud, allowing us to analyze the data and assist the patient remotely.

Figure 6. Receiver Section

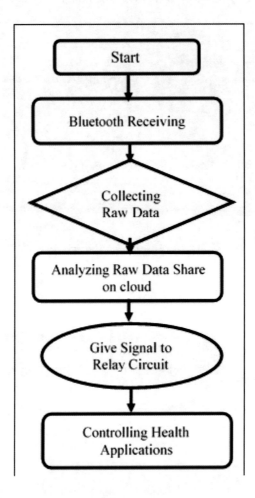

Receivers' portion of the framework The Neurosky MindWave is a system that displays electrical signals produced by cerebral activity in the brain, according to the MindWave Headset from Neurosky. As per Alhussein et.al. (2018), formally reworded a headband, an ear clip, and a sensor arm with an EEG cathode that rests on the forehead above the eye make up this headwear system. A Bluetooth-specific device is included with the Neurosky MindWave. It can then transfer its unfinished data to another Bluetooth-enabled PC as per Alhussein et.al. (2018).

Crude indications, the EEG power spectrum, meters for meditation and attention, flicker recognition, and on-head identification are used to measure the Mind Wave. As per Alhussein et.al. (2018), the EEG power scale stores information about a client's brain waves such as Delta, Theta, Alpha, Beta, and Gamma, just like meters for Attention and Meditation that measure how successfully the client is engaging in either activity. By interpreting the electrical sign and using computations to get readings on a scale from 0 to 100, this value is obtained.

Therefore, real-time bio signals of patients can be recorded, processed, or evaluated with the aid of the internet of things.

Difficulties, Limitations, and Future Scope

A significant amount of mechanical innovation has recently been used in the medical services industry to address medical care-related issues. According to Pradhan (2021), with access to medical care administrations at the touch of a button, this has a significant influence official paraphrase. By leveraging innovative systems management techniques, dispersed computing, and intelligent sensors, IoT has successfully disrupted the market for medical services. Alhussein (2018), IoT has its own set of obstacles and challenges, just like any other technology, where future studies might focus on it.

Normalization

Many manufacturers offer a diverse range of products in the medical services sector. The majority of these things promise that they will comply with industry-standard plan norms and conventions. In any case, there is a lack of authenticity. As a result, Pradahan (2021), the establishment of a dedicated gathering appropriate for standardizing these Healthcare IoT gadgets based on correspondence protocols, data total, and entrance interfaces is essential. The approval and standardization of electronic clinical records captured by Healthcare IoT devices should also be carefully considered, as per Alhussein et.al. (2018).

Information Privacy and Security

The continuous checking rule has been altered by the usage of distributed computing. In any case, this has made networks for medical services more susceptible to hackers. According to Pradhan et.al. (2021), this could lead to the misuse of private patient information, which could affect the course of therapy. official paraphrase in order to safeguard an IoT architecture against this terrible attack, numerous safeguards should be taken during the planning process. According to Pradhan et.al. (2021), Healthcare IoT network's clinical and detecting devices should configure and use personality confirmation, secure booting, adaptability to internal failure, board approval, whitelisting, secret word assurance, and secure matching conventions to thwart attacks.

Furthermore, network conventions such as Wi-Fi, Bluetooth, and ZigBee should be used in connection with trustworthy direction plans and message integrity checking procedures. Because IoT is a network in which every client is linked to the worker, every flaw in IoT security administrations jeopardies the patient's safety. This could be remedied Pradhan et.al. (2021), by integrating refined and dependable calculations and cryptographic techniques into a more secure environment.

Nonstop Monitoring

Long-term patient monitoring is required in many medical care contexts, such as chronic illnesses, heart infections, and more. As per Pradhan et.al. (2021), the IoT framework should be able to do effective ongoing checking in such circumstances.

Ecological Impact

The development of a Healthcare IoT framework necessitates the incorporation of numerous biological sensors as well as semiconductor-rich devices. Earth metals and other hazardous synthetic chemicals are routinely used in assembly and manufacturing. This could have a harmful impact on the climate. As a result, an appropriate administrative body should be established to monitor and control sensor fabrication. Furthermore, more research should be conducted to develop biodegradable sensors.

CONCLUSION

The IoT plan for medical services was examined from a variety of angles in the momentum study. The design of a HealthCare IoT framework, its elements, and the linkages between these segments are all carefully examined in this paper. Additionally, this research frequently appears in healthcare initiatives that have looked into IoT-based innovations. These concepts have helped medical professionals observe and diagnose a range of ailments, calculate a range of wellness metrics, and deliver demonstration offices in remote locations.

Due to this, the medical services industry has moved away from a clinic-based paradigm and toward a framework that is more understanding-based. We also talked about the various Healthcare IoT measures and their most recent trends. Investigations have also been made into the challenges and issues that the design, development, and deployment of the Healthcare IoT framework raised. The foundation of upcoming development and exploratory goals will be established by these issues. Users who need to start their research and establish a foothold in the industry have also been accommodated with comprehensive up-to-date data regarding healthcare IoT devices.

REFERENCES

Abdelrazek, S., El-Rashidy, N., El-Sappagh, S., Islam, S. R. M., & El-Bakry, H. (2021). Mobile health in remote patient monitoring for chronic diseases: Principles, trends, and challenges. *Diagnostics (Basel)*, *11*(4), 607. doi:10.3390/diagnostics11040607 PMID:33805471

Attallah, O. (2020). An effective mental stress state detection and evaluation system using minimum number of frontal brain electrodes. *Diagnostics (Basel)*, *10*(5), 292. doi:10.3390/diagnostics10050292 PMID:32397517

Bekolay, T., Bergstra, J., DeWolf, T., Eliasmith, C., Hunsberger, E., Rasmussen, D., & Stewart, T. C. (2014). Nengo: A Python tool for building large-scale functional brain models. *Frontiers in Neuroinformatics*, *7*, 48. doi:10.3389/fninf.2013.00048 PMID:24431999

Berbano, A. E. U., Pengson, H. N. V., Prado, S. V., Razon, C. G. V., & Tungcul, K. C. G. (2017, September). Classification of stress into emotional, mental, physical and no stress using electroencephalogram signal analysis. In *2017 IEEE International Conference on Signal and Image Processing Applications (ICSIPA)* (pp. 11-14). IEEE. 10.1109/ICSIPA.2017.8120571

Bibani, O., Glitho, R. H., Hadj-Alouane, N. B., Morrow, M. J., Polakos, P. A., Ravindran, P., & Yangui, S., (2016, June). A platform as-a-service for hybrid cloud/fog environments. In *2016 IEEE international symposium on local and metropolitan area networks (LANMAN)* (pp. 1-7). IEEE.

Biswal, B., Biswal, M. K., Dash, P. K., & Mishra, S. (2013). Power quality event characterization using support vector machine and optimization using advanced immune algorithm. *Neurocomputing, 103,* 75–86. doi:10.1016/j.neucom.2012.08.031

Cho, A., Lee, H., Whang, M., & Lee, S. (2019). Vision-Based Measurement of Heart Rate from Ballista cardio graphic Head Movements Using Unsupervised Clustering. *Sensors (Basel), 19*(15), 3263. doi:10.339019153263 PMID:31344939

Doma, V., & Pirouz, M. (2020). A comparative analysis of machine learning methods for emotion recognition using EEG and peripheral physiological signals. *Journal of Big Data, 7*(1), 1–21. doi:10.118640537-020-00289-7

Huan, G., Liu, G., Liu, J., Zhang, D., & Zhu, X. (2009, December). A hybrid FES rehabilitation system based on CPG and BCI technology for locomotion: A preliminary study. In *International Conference on Intelligent Robotics and Applications* (pp. 1073-1084). Springer.

Malik, A. S., Subhani, A. R., & Xia, L. (2019). A physiological signal-based method for early mental-stress detection. In *Cyber-Enabled Intelligence* (pp. 259–289). Taylor & Francis.

Muhammad, G., Alhussein, M., Hossain, M. S., & Amin, S. U. (2018). Cognitive IoT-Cloud Integration for Smart Healthcare: Case Study for Epileptic Seizure Detection and Monitoring. *Mobile Networks and Applications, 23*(6), 1624–1635. doi:10.100711036-018-1113-0

Pradhan, Pal, & Bhattacharyya. (2021). IoT-Based Applications in Healthcare Devices. *Journal of Healthcare Engineering.* doi:10.1155/2021/6632599

Sanjay & Renuka. (2020). Smart Healthcare using Internet of Things (IoT) for Remote Diagnosis of Covid-19 Patients. *i-Manager's Journal on Software Engineering, 15*(2), 15-24. Doi:10.26634/jse.15.2.18075

Sarraf, Pattnaik, & Vaibhaw. (2020). *Brain-computer interfaces and their applications, An Industrial IoT Approach for Pharmaceutical Industry Growth.* Elsevier. doi:10.1016/B978-0-12-821326-1.00002-4

Shon, D., Im, K., Jang, B., Kim, J. M., Lim, D. S., & Park, J. H. (2018). Emotional Stress State Detection Using Genetic Algorithm-Based Feature Selection on EEG Signals. *International Journal of Environmental Research and Public Health, 15*(11), 2461. doi:10.3390/ijerph15112461 PMID:30400575

Suryawanshi & Vanjale. (2020). Optimum analysis of brain activities by using classification and learning techniques. *International Journal of Advanced Science and Technology, 29*(7).

Vathalani, Sathaye, & Peshattiwar. (2017). Anti-Oxidant Potential of Methanolic Extract Of Trigonella Foenum, Trachyspermum Copticum, Nigella Sativa And Their Combination In 1:1:1 Ratio. *International Journal of Pharmaceutical Sciences and Research, 8*(4).

Zhao, C., Min, G., Winkley, J., Yang, L. T., Jiang, P., & Munnoch, R. (2016). An Intelligent Information Forwarder for Healthcare Big Data Systems with Distributed Wearable Sensors. *IEEE Systems Journal, 10*(3), 1147–1159. doi:10.1109/JSYST.2014.2308324

Chapter 11

Deep Learning Neural Networks for Online Monitoring of the Combustion Process From Flame Colour in Thermal Power Plants

Sujatha Kesavan

Dr. MGR Educational and Research Institute, India

Latha B.

Dr. MGR Educational and Research Institute, India

Sivanand R.

Dr. MGR Educational and Research Institute, India

Tamilselvi C.

Dr. MGR Educational and Research Institute, India

Rengammal Sankari B.

Dr. MGR Educational and Research Institute, India

Krishnaveni S.

Dr. MGR Educational and Research Institute, India

ABSTRACT

The combustion quality determination in power station boilers is of great importance to avoid air pollution. Complete combustion minimizes the exit of NOx, SOx, CO, and CO_2 emissions, also ensuring the consistency in load generation in thermal power plants. This chapter proposes a novel hybrid algorithm, called black widow optimization algorithm with mayfly optimization algorithm (BWO-MA), for solving global optimization problems. In this chapter, an effort is made to develop BWO-MA with artificial neural networks (ANN)-based diagnostic model for onset detection of incomplete combustion. Comparison has been done with existing machine learning methods with the proposed BWO-MA-based ANN architecture to accommodate the greater performance. The comprehensive analysis showed that the proposed achieved splendid state-of-the-art performance.

DOI: 10.4018/978-1-6684-6275-1.ch011

INTRODUCTION

The boilers are steam generators which convert pre-heated water into super heated steam. This high pressure super heated steam drives the turbine connected to the generator to produce electric power (Gang Lu, 2007). Thermal Power Plant (TPP) – Expansion-I at Neyveli Lignite Corporation (NLC) has two units with generation capacity of 210MW each. The boiler height is 90m and the complete firing of coal is finished within 42m. Furnace is located at the 18th metre of the boiler. Initially, heavy oil is for initial firing and subsequently the firing is enhanced by using lignite as the fuel whose calorific value is 2350 kCal/kg and fired at a rate of 189 to 230 t/hr. The burners and the flame detectors are arranged laterally. It includes six mills to crush the coal so that it becomes fine powder. The coal is also pre-heated so that it is used as the pulverized coal (G. Lu, 2009).

Existing Vs Proposed Flame Monitoring System

The present scenario at NLC consists of an infrared camcorder, automatically positioned and surrounded by a water cooled envelope, operated by a servomotor. The video captured by the camera is displayed on the CRT monitor is used for identifying the ON/OFF flame status to prevent the explosion of boiler (Pu Han, 2006). The over loading of the furnace without a flame status tracker causes the boiler to explode and is perilous (M.G. Abdul Rahman, 2004). Figure 2 shows the schematic for existing and proposed flame tracker at NLC using AI methods. An additional device is needed to send the flame video to the laptop and Cannon video splitter was used to extract the frames from flame video (Ross J. Quinlan, 1992).

BACKGROUND

ANN is a computational model that is designed in a way that the human brain analyses and processes information. It is based on Artificial Intelligent (AI) and connects various processing elements; each is similar to a single node. ANN is comprised of interconnected processing components which are called neurons (M. Kanevski, 2002). All nodes take various signals based on the internal weight as an input and produce a single output. The generated output is the input for another neuron. The architecture of ANN is categorized into different layers such as input layer, various hidden layer, and output layer as in Figure 1. The input layer accepts the input and processes it. The output layer provides the final output. The mathematical function is performed in the hidden layers and it doesn't have any direct interaction with the user (Enrique Teruela, 2005).

ANN is capable to adapt its configuration based on the internal or external data that runs over the network during the learning process. ANN has the ability to mitigate the error, possibility of recalling, and provides a high-speed data (Jay D. Martin, 2004). Therefore, it is utilized to solve the complex problem like prediction and classification. ANN has been applicable for various filed such as prediction, character recognition and data forecasting etc., ANN learning can be either supervised or unsupervised. Supervised training is one of the common neural networks training which is accomplished by providing set of sample data with the expected outcome from every sample to the neural network (Sujatha, K, 2018). Unsupervised training is as same as supervised training the only difference is it does not provide the expected outcome to the neural network. These unsupervised training is occurred when the neural network classify the input into numerous groups (Sujatha, K, 2011).

Figure 1. Basic structure of ANN

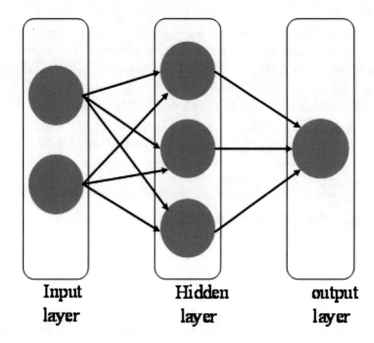

Input	Hidden	output
layer	layer	layer

MATERIALS AND METHODS

Mayfly Optimization

The main perception of the MFO technique is stimulated from the behavior of mayfly especially from the mating process of a mayfly. The mayfly belongs to the Ephemeroptera order which is one kind of primitive group of insects called Balaenoptera. The name of mayfly is derived from the event that they appear mainly in the UK in May month. This optimization technique depends on the PSO and comprises the advantage of PSO, GA, and FA. Adolescent mayflies are visible to the naked eye after completing the hatching. An adult mayfly exists only one or two days, until achieving the ultimate goal of breeding. The male attracts the female by assembling swarms, few meters above the water, and perform a nuptial dance. The female fly enters the swarm and mates with a male. This mating process exists for a few seconds. After completing the mating process, the female mayfly drops the eggs onto the surface of the water and the process goes on. The feasible solution to the problem is denoted by each mayfly position in the search. At first, two sets of mayflies are generated randomly which contain the female and male populations. The swarm is gathered by the movement of the male mayfly that indicates the male mayfly position. Whereas the female mayfly does not gather the swarm but they fly to the male for the breeding process. Selection of parents is done through the male and female populations. Parent selection is the same way as the female attracts the male. The selection is either done in a random process or by their fitness value. At last, the finest female breed with the finest male mayfly and the process goes on.

Male Mayflies' Movement

The male mayflies gathering in swarm indicates each male mayfly location based on its own knowledge or by its neighbour flies. Consider, the current position of the fly is a_m^i m in the search space at time step i. The position of the flies is varied based on the addition of velocity v_m^{i+1} to the current position. This is given in the below Equations (1) to (3).

$$a_m^{i+1} = a_m^i + v_m^{i+1} \tag{1}$$

Moreover, the velocity of the male mayfly m is evaluated as follows

$$v_{mn}^{i+1} = v_{mn}^i + \propto_1 e^{-\beta r_p^2} \left(pbest_{mn} - a_{mn}^i \right) + \propto_2 e^{-\beta r_g^2} \left(gbest_n - a_{mn}^i \right) \tag{2}$$

Where, v_{mn}^i indicates mayfly velocity, $pbest_m$ is the best position of the mayfly, $\propto_1, \propto_2$ are positive attractive constant which is utilized to scale the contribution of cognitive and social component. r_p and r_g is the cartesian distance between the a_m and $pbest_m$ as well as a_m and $gbest$ respectively. These distances are evaluated as follows

$$a_m - A_m = \sqrt{\sum_{n=1}^{j} \left(a_{mn} - A_{mn} \right)^2} \tag{3}$$

Where, a_{mn} indicates the nth element of mayfly m, A_m is equal to the $pbest_m$ and $gbest$.

Female Mayflies' Movement

The female mayflies fly in the direction of male for the breeding process. Consider b_m^i as the current position of the female mayfly m in the search space at time step i. The position of the flies is varied based on the addition of velocity v_m^{i+1} to the current position. Whereas, the attraction process is performed in random. Therefore, this process is modelled as deterministic process based on the fitness function that is the best male will attract the best female then the second-best male attracts the second-best female and so on. Subsequently, the minimization problem is taken into account and its velocities are evaluated as follows in Equation (4).

$$v_{mn}^{i+1} = \begin{cases} v_{mn}^i + \propto_2 e^{-\beta r_{mf}^2} \left(a_{mn}^i - b_{mn}^i \right), & if\ f\left(b_t\right) > f\left(a_t\right) \\ v_{mn}^i + fl * r, & if\ f\left(b_t\right) \leq f\left(a_t\right) \end{cases} \tag{4}$$

Where, r_m indicates the cartesian distance between the female and male mayfly, fl indicate the coefficient of the random walk therefore the value of r ranges from [-1,1]. v_{mn}^i is the velocity of female fly m in dimension $n=1,...,x$ at time step 'i'.

Mating of Mayfly

The mating process of two mayflies is indicated by the crossover operator. In the mating process, the parent is selected from either the male or female population. The male attracts the female based on the parent selection process. Normally, the selection process is carried out either at random or based on a fitness function. In the end, the best female breeds with the best male, then the second-best female breeds with the second-best male, and so on. The outcome of the crossover is two offspring which are produced as follows in Equation (5) and (6).

$$\text{Offspring1} = L*M+(1-L)*F \tag{5}$$

$$\text{Offspring2} = L*F+(1-L)*M \tag{6}$$

Where, M and F indicate the male and female parent, 'L' indicates the random value within a particular range. The initial velocities of the offspring are fixed as zero.

Black Widow Optimization

Based upon the concept of the black widow spider, BWO (Black widow optimization) has been obtained. The black widow mostly has the character of nocturnal, where the female spider remains blind during the day whereas at the night time the female spins the web. Moreover, the female one spends most of her life in the same web where it resides initially. Usually, the female spider starts the mating, by the continuous process of this the female leaves certain spots in the net with the liquid called a pheromone to captivate the male spiders. The bizarre thing here is that once the mating has been completed, the female one eats the male spider and saved the egg to the egg sack. Once the egg hatches and offspring have been formed and it's ready for sibling cannibalism, then again there is a chance of the child cannibalism where the child consumes its mother in case of lacking in fitness.

The first one is sexual-based cannibalism where the female eats her husband after mating with respect to the fitness value. The second is sibling cannibalism where the healthy spider eats its weaker siblings. As per the cannibalism rate, the concept is utilized. The fittest young ones are alive in the population and others are discarded from it. This is called sibling cannibalism. Third is child cannibalism where the child eats its mother in case of the weaker values.

The female spider lays the eggs in the socks after the 11 days of the gestation period, the offspring have been formed and the same is ready for sibling cannibalism. In this, the young strong spider eats their weakest sibling. The Black widow spider lives together for seven days for the maternal web, this time the sibling cannibalism has happened often. The density-dependent cannibalism decides the size of the population this might be significant in the black widow populations where the mother even consumes the young spiders in a short period. The remaining living spiders are considered the fittest young spiders. So based on this black spider concept, the BWO (Black Widow Optimization) is achieved.

Mathematical Evaluation

Based on the random initial population of black widows, the black widow optimization process has been started. This type of randomly generated population encompasses the female and male black widows for the offspring formation. The starting population of the black widow is expressed in Equation (7) to (9).

$$X_{N,d} = [x_{1,1}, x_{1,2}, x_{1,3}, \ldots, x_{1,d}] \tag{7}$$

Where the number of the decision variable is d, the population of the black widow is $X_{N,d}$, then the upper bound population is ub then the population number is N.

The $(X_{N,d})$ is useful in minimizing or maximizing the core function and is denoted by effective solution population as follows,

$$\text{Objective Function} = f(N,d) \tag{8}$$

In the proposed BWO model, various predefined parameters are specified such as Q_{pt}, Q_e, R_P, R_E, Ω_{ts}, Ω_{es}, Ω_{er}, Ωs_r which are defined in the previous sections. These parameters are used to indicate the upper and lower bounds of P_e and P_s.

Upper bound of P_e is $P_{e\,max}$, lower bound of P_e is $\dfrac{Q_E - P_{pt}\Omega_{ts}}{\Omega_{es}}$, upper bound of P_s is $\dfrac{Q_P - P_{e.max}\Omega_{er}}{\Omega_{es}}$,

upper bound of P_s is $\dfrac{Q_P - \left(Q_E - P_{pt}\Omega_{ts}\right)\Omega_{er} / \Omega_{es}}{\Omega_{sr}}$ and the lower bound of P_s is $\dfrac{Q_P - P_{e.max}\Omega_{er}}{\Omega_{sr}}$.

Mutation is the next step of the black widow optimization. The mutation rate is used for the selection of young spider. A small random value is added to a selected young spider for mutation process.

For the mutation process, smaller randomly generated values are incorporated with a selected young sibling spider.

$$Z_{k,d} = Y_{k,d} + \alpha \tag{9}$$

Where $Z_{k,d}$ is the mutated population of black widows, Here, the randomly generated muted value is α, then the randomly selected number is k and the younger spider which is selected randomly is $Yk_{,d}$. This work has two partitions: The first part is a rudimentary part, in which image pre-processing and segmentation have been implemented to increase the image and mitigate the noise. The feature selection & classification have occurred in the second portion. Figure 3 shows the proposed methodology.

Figure 2. Proposed Architecture for combustion quality analysis from flame gas

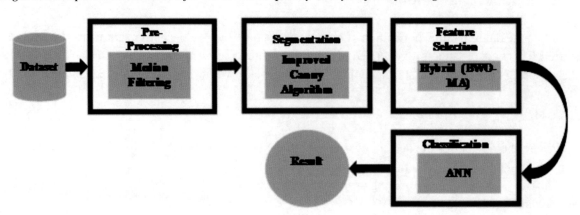

The flame image classification and identification approach have four various phases: pre-processing, segmentation, feature selection & classification. The first stage is preprocessing, where the plant images are composed and employed with the preprocessing stage, where the filtering approach (median filtering) has been performed. The filtering process usually helps to get rid of unwanted noise from the input image, then to enhance the contrast of the image, the histogram equalization has been performed. Once the preprocessing gets completed, by using the improvised canny algorithm, segmentation of the plant images has performed. Once the image is segmentation process is completed then segmentation output goes to the feature selection process. As a novel contribution to the feature selection, a hybrid algorithm called a Black Widow Optimization Algorithm with Mayfly Optimization Algorithm (BWO-MA), for solving global optimization problems. The main reason is that the mayflies mutated to enhance the exploration ability of the algorithm. Once the feature selection process is complete then output is sent to the classification process. A combined (BWO-MA) with Artificial Neural Networks (ANN) based diagnostic model for earlier diagnosis of incomplete combustion conditions. The proposed method is to extract an automatic set of features for classifying and identification of plant diseases. The proposed method has high efficiency in improving classification accuracy.

Pre-Processing the Flame Images

It's utilized for preprocessing as it changes the intensity of the image to enhance the contrast of the plant image. Let's assume In^{im} as input image with the matrix of $j_R \times j_S$ integer pixel lies among 0 and 1, and then, INV are defined as the possible count of intensity values. The maximum value taken usually is 256. In eq (10), the NHS histogram of In^{HE} with a bin possible intensity is mentioned. Moreover, the term $he = 0,1,\ldots,INV-1$ with a bin possible intensity is explained in Equation (11).

$$NHS = \frac{number\ of\ pixels\ with\ density\ he}{total\ number\ of\ pixels} \qquad (10)$$

$$In^{HE} = floor\left[\left(INV - 1\right)\sum_{he=0}^{In^{im}}NHS\right] \tag{11}$$

From the above equation, *floor()* usually rounds the values to the closer integer value. As a result, the histogram makes even the In^{HE} flame image to a median filter for the removal of the noise. Though the filter removes the noise, it retains its pixel whether it's high or low but it enhances the edges of the plant images. This median filter is nonlinear. The major idea of the filter is it replaces the noisy pixel with the median value of the nearest pixel which is sorted out based on the grey level flame images. The result In^{MF} is given based on Equation (12) when the median filter is implemented for the input flame image In^{HE}.

$$In^{MF}\left(a,b\right) = med\left\{In^{HE}\left(a - x, b - y\right)u, x \in H\right\} \tag{12}$$

The median filtered images and the original filter is denoted by In^{MF}, In^{HE} in the Equation (12) and then H is denoted as the two-dimensional mask. As a result of this, the final preprocessed image is In^{MF}. And this step is moved further into the segmentation phase.

Flame Image Segmentation Model Using Improved Canny Algorithm

Flame image segmentation using Otsu is a method that creates the separability of the resultant classes maximum to automatically determine the thresholds. Its basic ideas are according to the grey characteristics of flame images, the image is separated into background and foreground, making their variances of inter-class maximum, finally obtaining the optimal thresholds. For an $M{\times}N$ flame image $I(x,y)$, the segmented threshold of foreground and background represents as T, the rate of the foreground is $\omega 1$, its average value is $u1$; the rate of background is $\omega 2$, and the average value is $u2$, the mean of the image is u, the variance of the inter-class is g. Then we can get the following formulas as in Equation (13) to (20)

$$\omega_1 = \frac{N_1}{M \times N} \tag{13}$$

$$\omega_2 = \frac{N_2}{M \times N} \tag{14}$$

$$N_1 + N_2 = M{\times}N \tag{15}$$

$$\omega 1_{\times}\omega 2_{=} 1 \tag{16}$$

$$u = u1_{\times}\omega 1 +_{u}2 +_{\omega}2 \tag{17}$$

$$g = \omega1 \times (u-u1)2_+ \omega^2 \times (u-u2)2 \qquad (18)$$

$$g = \omega1 \times \omega2 \times (u1 - u_2)2 \qquad (19)$$

Finally, by implementing the traversed method which attains the threshold that makes g maximum, and the optimal threshold is T. As the highest threshold of T, and the low threshold can be got as:

$$Th = k \times T1 \qquad (20)$$

Where k is a constant, k's default value is considered to be 2.

Flame Image Feature Selection Using Hybrid Black Widow Optimization Algorithm with Mayfly Optimization Algorithm (BWO-MA)

Flame image classification involves feature selection performed a hybrid Black Widow Optimization Algorithm with Mayfly Optimization Algorithm (BWO-MA) to determine the combustion quality. The description of each methodology is given below: As a novel contribution to the feature extraction, a hybrid algorithm called Black Widow Optimization Algorithm with Mayfly Optimization Algorithm (BWO-MA), for solving global optimization problems. To improve the exploration capability of the algorithm, the main reason is considered to be the mayflies transformation which mainly combines the black widow mutation mechanism of the BWO with the mutated behaviors of the MA, thus greatly enhancing increasing the local searching and global searching ability of the algorithm.

Initial Population

BWO (Black Widow Optimization algorithm), the population is initially executed randomly, where two types of populations require such as male and female. Based on this initialization offspring are generated for the future generation. In this process, the computation of fitness value is significant; the fitness function is denoted as f at a widow. The following (Equation (21) and (22)) shows a mathematical representation of the black widow spider's initial population.

$$X_{N,d} = \begin{bmatrix} x_{1,1} & x_{1,2} & x_{1,3} \dots\dots x_{1,d} \\ x_{2,1} & x_{2,2} & x_{2,3} \dots\dots x_{2,d} \\ & x_{N,1} & x_{N,2} & x_{N,3} \dots x_{N,d} \end{bmatrix} \qquad (21)$$

$$lb \le X_i \le ub$$

Here, N indicates the size of the population, the black spider population is $x_{N,d}$, the problem's number of the decision variable is d, then the upper bound & lower bound of the population is ub,lb respectively. The eq (21) represents the effective solution populations $x_{N,d}$ are useful in reducing or increasing the objective function.

$$\text{RMSE} = \frac{1}{n}\sum_{i=1}^{n} w_i \left(t_i - \hat{t_i}\right)^2 \tag{22}$$

N - No of samples

t_i- True sample value

$\hat{t_i}$ - Corresponds to the predictive value

The procreate is helpful to generate offsprings as in Equation (23) and (24)

x1 and x2 → Parents

y1 and y2 → Offspring

$$y_1 = \mu \times x1 + (1 - \mu) \times x2 \tag{23}$$

$$y2 = \mu \times x2 + (1 - \mu) \times x1 \tag{24}$$

'i' and 'j' can be represented in the range of 1 to N

μ can be determined in the random range of 0 and 1.

Cannibalism and Mutation

Cannibalism can be executed by three types such as sexual cannibalism, Child cannibalism, and sibling cannibalism.

To develop exploration capability, the newly formed offspring are evolved, as described below, a normally generated random number gets added to the variable of the offspring as in Equation (25)

$$offspring_n^{'} = offspring_n + k \tag{25}$$

Where normally distributed random value is k.

Convergence

A three-stop condition could be taken just like the other evolutionary algorithms, which are: i) an already defined total of iterations. ii) for several iterations, there are no changes in the fitness value of the optimal widow which is an observant iii) reached the specific level of accuracy.

Pseudo-Code of the Hybrid (BWO-MA) Algorithm

Input: Max- num of iterations, No of cannibalism rate, procreate rate to num. of reproduction is "nr", mutation rate

Output: Objective function's –RMSE,

//Initialization

The initial population of black widow spiders

Each population is a D-dimensional array

1. Fitness value (RMSE) evaluation until termination reached
2. Determine nr and find the best solution in pop1(population 1)

// Cannibalism& procreating

3. For i=1 to nr do
4. from pop1, two solutions are selected randomly as parents;
5. By using equation 12, generate D children;
6. Destroy the father;
7. Based on the cannibalism rate, destroy some of the children (new achieved solutions);
8. Save the remaining solutions into pop2;
9. End for

// Mutation

10. Offspring mutation
11. Replace worst mayflies with the best new offspring created by utilizing equation (16)

// Updating

12. Update the population
13. Return the best solution from pop;
14. The obtained best solution is given into the ANN classifier
15. The performance is evaluated to prove the best classifier.
16. Stop

Flame Image Classification Using (BWO-MA) with ANN

For the wider range of information processing, an ANN (Artificial Neural Network) is utilized which is a softer computing technique. This technique acts as the weighted graph where nodes are considered as the artificial neurons and then the directed edges among neurons are taken to be the weights. This network is defined into two types: One is a recurrent network and the other one is a feed forward network. Recurrent networks are dynamic whereas feed forward networks are static by nature. This produces output as one set and not in a sequential manner for the provided inputs. As a result of this, the multilayer neural networks were executed successfully in the decision support systems for inferring the combustion quality and flue gas emissions.

Figure 3. ANN structure for predicting Combustion Quality from flame image

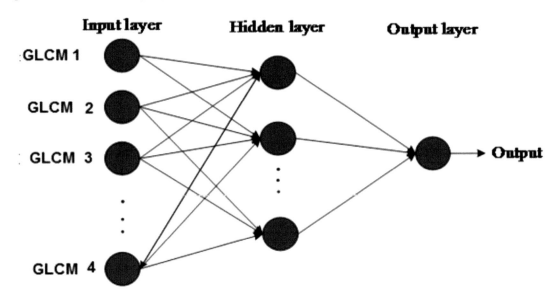

In MLP (Multilayer Perceptron) multiple layers of the neurons have existed, but the three of the minimum layers are the input layer, hidden layer, and one output layer. Here the output layer is responsible for the results. With the nonlinear activation function, every neuron in the other layers is acted as the computational component which except from the input layer. The objective of the neural network is whenever the data exists in the input layer the neurons are calculated consecutively then the result is attained at each output neuron. The output of the neural network denoted the suitable classes for the input. Along with weight values, each of the neurons in the hidden layers and the inputs is associated with other neurons of the very next layer. To sum up the threshold and calculate the weighted inputs, the hidden layer's inputs are responsible. The MLP structure with input, hidden and output layer structure is demonstrated in Figure 3. The elements of the datasets are in the input layer. The hidden layer secures the not linearly separated data, finally, the desired results are provided by the output layer. In the weight function, a threshold node gets included in the input layer. By executing the sigmoid function, the result's sums accomplished the activity of the neurons. In eq (26) the entire process is explained.

$$p_j = \sum_{i=1}^{n} w_{j,i} x_i + \theta_j, m_j = f_j\left(p_j\right) \tag{26}$$

Where p_j is assumed to be the linear input combination of x_1, x_2, x_n, and θj consider as the threshold, then w$j_{,i}$ is the connectivity between the neuron j and the input xi also, the activation function here is jt^h neuron and mj as the output. As described in the eq (27) sigmoid function is the general choice for activation function.

$$f\left(t\right) = \frac{1}{1+e^{-t}} \tag{27}$$

For the training of MLP, the backpropagation method has been utilized which is a method of gradient descent method used in the adoption of weights. From the pseudorandom sequence generator, all of the (weight vector) is being created with smaller random values. However, this process can take many steps to train the network, and then the adjusted weights are calculated at every step. To overcome the above-mentioned problems, a (BWO-MA) based approach is utilized to compute the optimal value of the weight and threshold functions, because (BWO-MA) have the capability to determine weight parallel and finding the optimal solutions.

Hyper-Parameter Tuning With (BWO-MA)

Hyper-parameters selection is significant process of machine learning performance improvement; therefore, appropriate technique should consider for enhancing the tuning process. Thus, the reason, an incorporation of effective optimization makes tremendous impact in the performance of machine learning. Here, a hybrid meta-heuristic algorithm is considered including Black Widow Optimization Algorithm with Mayfly Optimization Algorithm (BWO-MA). Moreover, t*he* BWO-MA *approach* to solve optimization problems of selecting and tuning hyper-parameters makes huge difference than other optimizations. The enhancement of the exploration ability of the machine learning algorithm was the reason for the selection of the BWO-MA. As the discussion in the previous section, ANN performance is improved by tuning the parameters of ANN with the *BWO-MA* strategy. One input layer, one hidden layer, and one output layer are the parameters utilized in this work to predict the identification of combustion quality from flame images.

RESULTS AND DISCUSSION

Flame Image Description

The flame images are gathered from boiler at the thermal power plant. Initially the flame video is recorded using infra-red cameras placed tangentially at various locations of the boiler to track the fire ball during the light up of the boiler. The flame video is divided into frames. Each frame corresponds to the color image of the flame pertaining to complete and incomplete combustion. The size of each frame is 47x35, from which a square image extraction is done. A set of 39 flame images are categorized as complete and incomplete combustion. The existing and the proposed intelligent flame monitoring system is illustrated in Figure 4.

The data set (Figure 5) contains 3 visual features such as color, area of the flame and intensity. Furthermore, the effectiveness of this online flame monitoring system is validated by comparing the evaluation metrics of the proposed approach with the existing approaches. The evaluation metrics are computed by the confusion matrix attained from the experimental outcomes. For flame image analysis, Accuracy, Precision, Recall, F1_score and specificity are taken as an evaluation metrics.

Table 1. Measurement of parameters corresponding to each group of images

Class	NOx mg/Nm3	CO ppm	CO2 Nm3/hr	SOx Nm3/hr	Flame Temperature in (deg Celsius)	Air/fuel ratio (No units)	Combustion conditions
1	70	100 to 120	1000	70	1250	Ratio is 4:1, 890 t/hr-air, 182 t/hr-lignite	Complete Combustion
2	200	300	7000	200	300	Ratio is 2:1, 230 t/hr- lignite, 400 t/hr - air	Incomplete combustion

The experimental process is carried out in MATLAB 2020-Ra version along with computer window 10 PRO with 8 GB RAM, Intel ® core (TM) i3-6098P CPU @ 3.60 GHz. MATLAB code was utilized to construct and train the ANN framework and find the hyper parameters by the hybridization of black widow optimization and mayfly algorithm. Hence, a rule of thumb can be used to find the centre as the mean of each class, the distance among input patterns and the centres as in Figure 6.

Figure 4. Existing Vs Proposed Set up

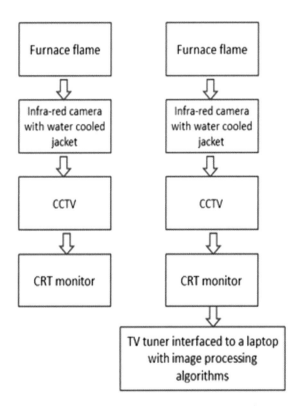

Figure 5. Flame images-complete and incomplete combustion

The features extracted involve the GLCM (Grey level co-occurrence matrix) values recoded in Table 2. In this work, Machine learning technique is incorporated with the meta-heuristic algorithms namely Artificial neural network (ANN) with hybrid mayfly and black widow optimization algorithm (BWO-MA) to effectively recognize the hand gesture. The evaluation metrics results have shown better performance of the proposed ANN with BWO-MA approach. Furthermore, different fish images are taken as an input from the open source dataset to classify the flame images based on combustion quality.

Table 2. GLCM values for the flame images

No.	GLCM 1	GLCM 2
1	-0.3984	0.7183
2	-0.3826	-0.1149
3	-0.3434	0.0248
4	-0.3016	0.1389
5	-0.2445	0.0354
6	-0.1749	0.0458
7	-0.1165	0.1589
8	-0.0778	0.1823
9	-0.0552	0.1387
10	-0.0424	0.0331
11	-0.0302	-0.0095
12	-0.0200	0.0168
13	-0.0079	-0.0340
14	0.0041	-0.0864
15	0.0190	-0.1157
16	0.0362	-0.1382
17	0.0550	-0.1758
18	0.0745	-0.1794
19	0.0949	-0.2394
20	0.1129	-0.2624
21	0.1283	-0.2643
22	0.1455	-0.1811
23	0.1593	-0.1028
24	0.1704	-0.0939
25	0.1823	-0.0732
26	0.1910	-0.0780
27	0.1990	-0.0160
28	0.2071	0.0124
29	0.2132	0.0045
30	0.2192	0.0638

Figure 6. Variation of the features corresponding to combustion category

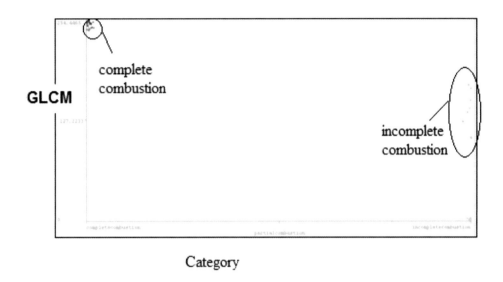

Category

The testing was done and the results are also validated. Totally 38 flame images were taken for testing. The values of True Positive (TP), Recall and Precision are '1' for the classification by the ANN with BWO-MA. On the other hand, the values of False Positive (FP) are '0' is shown in Figures 7, 8, 9 and 10. The comparison chart in Figure 11 shows that the images were classified based on their combustion quality, NOx, CO2, CO and SOx emissions. The TP, recall and precision values are nearly '1'for all the two categories by ANN with BWO-MA algorithm.

Figure 7. True Positive for various algorithms during testing

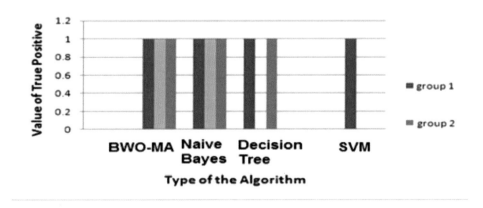

Figure 8. False Positive for various algorithms during testing

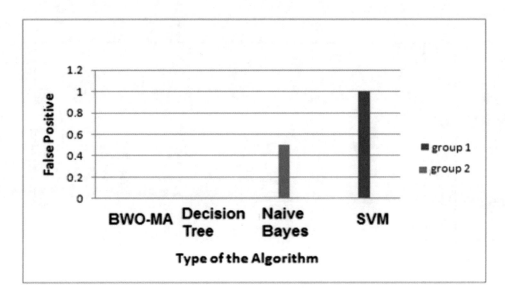

Figure 9. Precision for various algorithms during testing

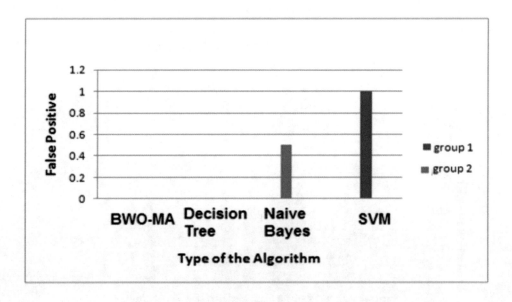

Figure 10. Recall for various algorithms during testing

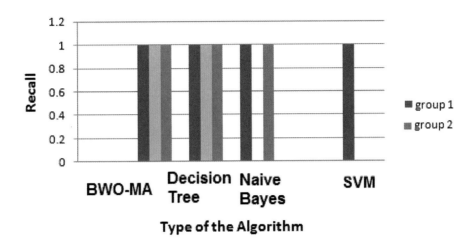

Table 3. Distribution of Flame images for training and testing

Group	Number of images for training	Number of images for testing
1	10	9
2	10	9
Total	20	18

The GLCM 1 and GLCM 2 values obtained after processing the 38 images from group 1 and group 2 are given in Table 2. The centres are calculated based on the 2D vector of all the 38 flame images (Figure 11). The triangular points show group 2 and square points represent group 1. The common centre for group 2 and group 1 are indicated. The distance between these two common centres are large and ther is no overlapping of centres from either group that indicates, the images of complete combustion and incomplete combustion are distinct. Testing of image to know the complete combustion or incomplete combustion is done with final weights obtained. Testing results indicate only 31 images were correctly classified out of 38 images which indicate 81.58% classification (Figure 12).

Figure 11. Centres for group 1 and group 2 flame images

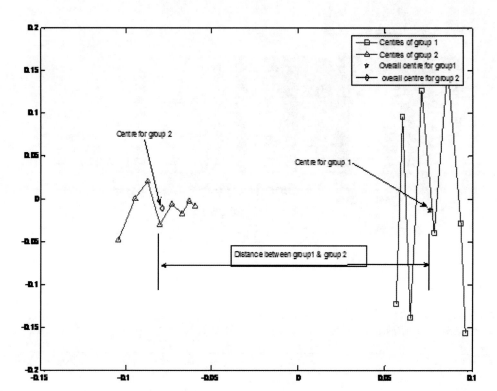

Figure 12. Target outputs and tested outputs of the flame images

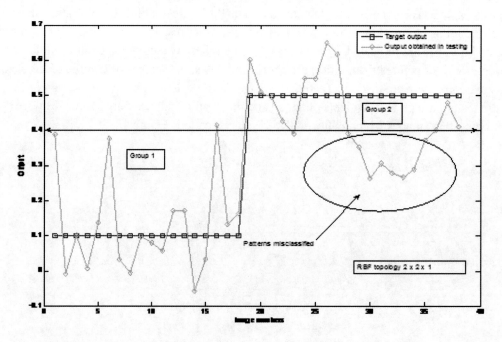

CONCLUSION

Thus, the automation of combustion quality was done by analysing the flame images for a power station boiler. The features were extracted and reduced using SVM, Naive Bayes, Decision tree and ANN with BWO-MA algorithms. The True Positive (TP) for BWO-MA is '1' for all the two categories of combustion whereas for the other two algorithms the TP value is '0'. The False Positive (FP) for BWO-MA is '0' whereas for the other algorithms it has the maximum value. The precision and recall values for all the two categories by BWO-MA is '1' whereas for the other algorithms it is very much less than 1 or even '0' nearly. This states that monitoring and control of combustion quality in power station boilers can be done successfully using intelligent techniques like SVM, Decision Tree, Navie Bayes and BWO-MA for identification of complete and incomplete combustion. Testing results indicate only 31 images were correctly classified out of 38 images which indicate 81.58% classification. Classification performance can be further improved by further preprocessing of the acquired images.

REFERENCES

Abdul Rahman, M.G., Gibbins, J.R, & Forrest, A.K. (2004). *Combustion in Power Station Boilers –Advanced Monitoring Using Imaging.* Imperial College of Science, Technology, and Medicine.

Gilabert, Lu, & Yan. (2005). Three dimensional visualisation and reconstruction of the luminosity distribution of a flame using digital imaging. *Techniques, Sensors & Their Applications,* 167–171.

Han, Zhang, Zhen, & Wang. (2006). Boiler Flame Image Classification Based on Hidden Markov Model. *IEEE ISIE,* 9-12.

Kanevski, M., Pozdnukhov, A., Canu, S., & Maignan, M. (2002). Advanced Spatial Data Analysis and Modelling with Support Vector Machines. *International Journal of Fuzzy Systems,* 606–615.

Lu & Yan. (2009). Advanced Monitoring and Characterization of combustion flames. *20th annual meeting and meeting of the Advanced Power Generation Division,* 1-25.

Lu, Yan, Cornwell, Whitehouse, & Riley. (2007). *Impact of co-firing coal and biomass on flame characteristics and stability.* Academic Press.

Martin. (2004). On the Use of Kriging Models to Approximate Deterministic Computer Models. *Proceedings International Design Engineering Technical Conferences and Computers and Information in Engineering Conference.*

Quinlan, R. J. (1992). Learning with Continuous Classes. *5th Australian Joint Conference on Artificial Intelligence,* 343-348.

Sujatha, K., Bhavani, N. P. G., Cao, S.-Q., & Ram Kumar, K. S. (2018). Soft sensor for flame temperature measurement and IoT based monitoring in power plants. *Materials Today: Proceedings, 5*(4), 10755–10762. doi:10.1016/j.matpr.2017.12.359

Sujatha, K., & Pappa, N. (2011). Combustion Quality Monitoring in PS Boilers Using Discriminant RBF. *ISA Transactions, 2*(7), 2623–263.

Tan, C. K., Wilcox, S. J., Ward, J., & Lewitt, M. (2003). Monitoring near burner slag deposition with a hybrid neural network system. *Measurement Science & Technology, 14*(7), 232–236. doi:10.1088/0957-0233/14/7/332

Teruela, E., Cortésb, C., Díezb, L. I., & Arauzob, I. (2005). Monitoring and Prediction of fouling in coal-fired utility boilers using Neural Networks. *Chemical Engineering Science, 60*(18), 5035–5048. doi:10.1016/j.ces.2005.04.029

Chapter 12
Analysis of Political and Ideological Systems in Education With Lightweight Deep Learning

Angela Diaz-Cadena
University of Guayaquil, Ecuador

Miguel Botto-Tobar
iD https://orcid.org/0000-0001-7494-5224
Eindhoven University of Technology, The Netherlands

ABSTRACT

As China's population grows, the country places a greater focus on the value of cultural education. A successful instructional approach includes ideological and political content within the context of cultural training. Students would do well to observe the facial expressions used by their lecturers in class to completely appreciate the themes being discussed and the strategies being used. A group of high school seniors from a Shanghai high school will take part in experimental research to determine the model's viability. The objective is to assess the effectiveness of education in the classroom is to conduct a poll with students and instructors to get a sense of their thoughts on the topic. More than half of the student body prefers competitions and lectures to other sorts of intellectual and political involvement in the classroom. This model's expression recognition accuracy is more than 2.9% greater than that of other models, and the model's improvement effect is incredible. The authors also investigated the influence of including experimentation in the quality evaluation process.

DOI: 10.4018/978-1-6684-6275-1.ch012

INTRODUCTION

China's overall investment in this business has expanded because of the Chinese government's recent decision to prioritize education (Yu et al., 2016). This is an important phase in a person's growth since they have the most opportunities to learn and improve during their senior year of high school (Furtak et al., 2017). However, throughout the formative years of China's educational system, examination-centered education has been the norm. Cultural knowledge is transmitted in the classroom without regard to the existence of other components of knowledge transfer. If this practice is permitted to continue, pupils will have an advantage in theory but a deficit in real-world experience. Children's sentiments and concerns may be overlooked, which can be harmful to their development and health (Jin & Martin, 2019). This is detrimental to a child's growth and health. This eventually led to the establishment of the "ideological and political course." In terms of students' viewpoints on political and ideological concerns, it exposes them to hot media themes and disseminates cultural information, all with the purpose of getting them more interested in the learning process. When this way of teaching is used, students are more likely to be fully involved in the learning process, which helps them grow in general. The use of computer technology and questionnaires, as well as other methods of data collection, can help determine whether a particular educational style is successful. The notion of analyzing massive volumes of data on the quality of English instruction supplied to university students to arrive at exceedingly plausible conclusions. This was done to identify the top English language schools. When tested, the model achieved an accuracy rate of 90.22 percent in the processing and evaluation of large datasets (Guo & Yu, 2020). As a result, the model is a trustworthy predictor of the educational program's quality. Several other critical technologies might be utilised to include data mining technology in the evaluation system for teaching ideological and political courses. This would be beneficial to both students and instructors. A data mining method and a set of indicators can be employed to analyse the performance of a teacher's lessons (Lv, 2021). This makes evaluating the effectiveness of a teacher's instruction straightforward (Su et al., 2021). An analytic hierarchy technique to assess the efficiency of ideological and political teaching in university-level English classrooms in the age of big data. This strategy was developed in response to the increase in data volumes. The goal of this method is to assess training quality in a range of professional scenarios. The strategy is designed to take advantage of the opportunities given by the big data era. The existing approach for measuring the effectiveness of IPE contains considerable distortions because of shoddy data processing. They created the IPE efficacy evaluation methodology after doing extensive data mining research. Data mining clustering was successfully used to accomplish the cleaning and preprocessing of the actual effect of IPE. It turned out that the model's data processing abilities were much better than those of the earlier model (Zhang & Meng, 2021).

However, just a few studies have been conducted to investigate the efficiency of education that incorporates ideological and political content into cultural courses. Many studies have been conducted to date using technological devices to measure the success of school intellectual and political education(IPE). The expressions on the students' faces in class will reveal whether they are familiar with the topic being taught and the manner of instruction used by their teachers. The use of technology that identifies expressions in educational contexts allows for a more objective assessment of the effects of training. The real-time data collection on children's expressions uses equipment that is already in the classroom. This data can then be used to investigate the impact of conventional cultural teaching as well as ideological and political education within the curriculum. This document begins with a thorough explanation of the various influential theories and makes them available for your review. Furthermore, it describes the specific steps that must be followed to build the model. After that, a series of experiments and a questionnaire are done to find out if this type of IPE in a Shanghai high school curriculum is useful or not.

BACKGROUND

Children must gain a deeper awareness of the world in which they live, but they must also acquire the mental capacity to reflect on their own lives, the beliefs they have, and the world in which they live. Putting all your eggs in the basket of a single teacher or class, on the other hand, will not generate the desired results (Poorchangizi et al., 2019). The "Course Ideological and Political Integration (CIP)" theory proposes a novel approach to dealing with these challenges (Robinson, 2020), with the purpose of supporting students in building moral character and boosting their intelligence in all aspects of their lives. Using an educational technique known as CIP, concepts from the field of international and public education are included in the curriculum of a wide range of academic fields. Furthermore, it can help pupils establish proper concepts and morality, laying the groundwork for their general development (Lim & Apple, 2018). The two key CIP defining traits are depicted in Figure 1. These characteristics have philosophical underpinnings that are concealed beneath the surface.

Figure 1. Characteristics of the CIP

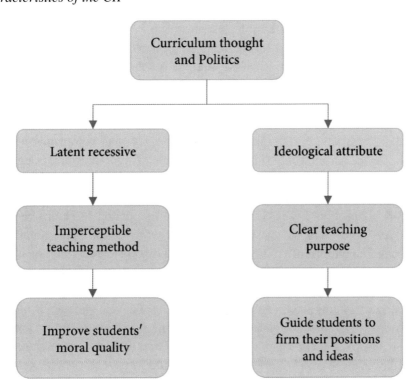

Figure 1 depicts a few of the odd elements utilised to construct the CIP. As a result, it appears that IPE is taught individually in a range of topic areas rather than as a critical ideological and political issue for students. This is done to avoid exposing students to too much information in the classroom that has blatantly ideological or political connotations. If teachers apply political and ideological principles and concepts in the classroom, pupils may be more susceptible to ideological training, which is good for the students' overall development (Gou et al., 2021). As a direct result of the manifest nature of this ideology, CIP can steer students toward the formation of a steadfast political stance and tenacity, both of which are required for the development of accurate conceptions and, ultimately, a robust personality. Both CIP characteristics are required, and they work well together. This educational strategy includes general education, cultural transfer, and ideological instruction. The students' excitement can be brought out to its fullest, which can help them grow in a healthy way.

Given that everything included inside it can communicate with one another, the intelligent Internet of Things may be viewed as a type of communication between various sensing systems via the Internet and sensor networks. Finally, the sensor network will allow for efficient data transfer, processing, and trading in accordance with a set of rules. Because of this, we will be able to monitor and manage how things are connected to one another. Given the enormous impact that the intelligent Internet of Things will have on students' educational experiences, it is critical to develop a framework for analyzing ideological and political education as well as undertake research on coping strategies. The primary objectives of this article are to (1) investigate the current situation of ideological and political education, (2) propose a technique for analyzing it, and (3) propose remedies based on that evaluation. The data for this inquiry was gathered via a questionnaire. According to experimental results, most college students (about 64%) favor the concept of ideological and political education, and the recommended ideologies and political education methodologies are extremely feasible. Instead of being an isolated event, the rise of the internet of things is a natural result of a certain moment in human history. This is the fourth major technological shift in human history. Although definitions of the Internet of Things fluctuate significantly at each level, their essential structure cannot be isolated from the broader value of the Internet of Things. The initial concept behind the "Internet of Things" was a network of things that could be individually identified using specific signals and other data transfer mechanisms. In line with the terms of the communication agreement, any device may be linked to the Internet, and the information transmission number may be used to identify the device. Users would subsequently be able to communicate throughout the network. For example, identifying signals in the Internet of Things' intelligent interface identification network adhere to specified standards. These IDs are seamlessly included into the data architecture to provide a successful network connection. It was later proposed that the Internet of Things be implemented as a network in which every object is linked to every other object in the network. This conclusion was feasible based on this concept. The Internet of Things (IoT) is frequently considered a continuation of the Internet since it is built on the infrastructure of pre-existing computers and other devices. The collaboration of sensor, RFID, and Internet technologies aids in the growth of the Internet. The Internet, at its most basic, acts as a means for linking items and transferring information. The real and the virtual are mixing right now. Sensor networks, RFID, mobile Internet, the cloud, and fuzzy identification are just some of the technologies that make up the backbone of the Internet of Things, which aims to automatically identify, link, and intelligently analyze data from a wide range of products. This article provides a high-level summary of the concepts underpinning the Internet of Things. The IoT is the process of connecting many sensing devices to each other through data exchange over the Internet and sensor networks.

ENHANCED VERSION OF CONVOLUTION NEURAL NETWORK (CNN) USED AS THE FOUNDATION FOR A MODEL TO EVALUATE THE QUALITY OF INSTRUCTION

Students' behaviour and expressions are frequently utilised to evaluate a teacher's instruction. Students' facial expressions indicate that they are paying attention to what and how their lecturers educate them. Using facial expression recognition in the classroom can help us learn more about how children learn and how to teach them.

Convolution Neural Network (CNN)

Most discriminative deep structures, such as CNN, reduce data preprocessing. It's utilised in computer vision and natural language processing (Zou, 2022) (Sakalle et al., 2022), so it's a good example of a deep learning approach. Because CNNs are designed after the human eye, they can learn both supervised and unsupervised. Sakale et al., 2022) may extract grid-like topological information with little processing due to sparse layer connections and shared hidden convolution kernel parameters (Sakalle et al., 2022). CNN is divided into three layers: convolutional, convex, and linked. The pooling layer minimises the magnitude of the parameters, while the convolution layer captures local and global input data attributes. The convolution layer does this. At the completely linked layer, all sub-layer parameters can be mapped to a new coordinate system. This maximises efficiency as well as accuracy (Khan et al., 2020).

CNN's ability to learn representations enables it to comprehend the fundamental foundations of the data, which is a significant benefit even after the structure and number of parameters of a model have been optimised. The early convolutional layers of a CNN may be able to catch up on local variables such as picture texture. Having this expertise is likely to make it easier to recognise photographs. One of CNN's applications. A larger receptive field is used in deep convolutional layer deep learning (Lindsay, 2021). This enables the learning of abstract attributes such as object size and orientation. It means that the convolution kernel's pixel-weighting approach considers information about the picture's content. The two-dimensional kernel extent is represented by the activation function, denoted by the offset, a convolution kernel parameter that determines the relative importance of separate pixels

It's Plausible to Argue That CNN Has Been More Useful to Society Over The Last Few Decades

The recurrent linear unit (ReLu) is the chosen activation mechanism for many distinct types of CNNs (ReLU). Training on this model is much faster than training on traditional sigmoids (Wang et al., 2018). The asymmetry of ReLU is an excellent example of this. Possibly. Real-world network models will lose some of their usefulness and realism (Alhassan & Zainon, 2021). A PReLU function is preferred over a ReLU function. The phrase "parameterized ReLU," or PReLU, refers to a specific use of ReLU that employs them. The graph below shows a comparison and contrast of the two sets of data.

Figure 2. The ReLU function, which comprises (a) the ReLU function and (b) the PReLU function, will be the primary topic of discussion throughout this article

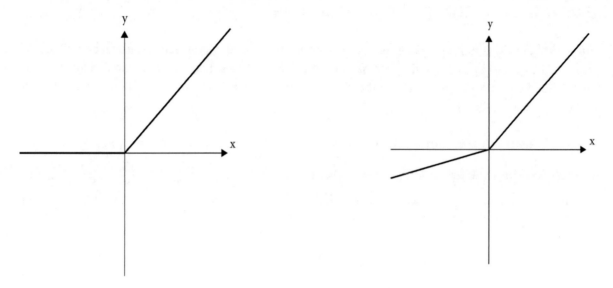

When a positive input value is given, the graph generated by the PReLU function looks like the graph produced by the ReLU function. Gradient expansion and disappearance When a positive input value is given, the graph generated by the PReLU function looks like the graph produced by the ReLU function. are reduced as a result, as shown in figure 2a. PReLU's gradient parameter is zero when the input value is negative, figure 2b shows PReLu. It increases model validity and eliminates the fading problem of negative area neurons (Thakur et al., 2020; Abu Alfeilat et al., 2019). The channel receives function input. The slope coefficient is negative. When this requirement is met, PReLU and ReLU can collaborate. Back-propagation can optimise PReLU in conjunction with other model layers.

THE PROPOSED METHOD

CNN's dependability improves in tandem with its coverage, deep CNNs feature many weight components. These requirements necessitate suitable equipment (Kashyap, 2019). Face-recognition technology is increasingly available in mobile and embedded devices. These computers lack the processing power required for deep CNN. A newer, more effective CNN model has been released. Stochastic gradient descent can be used to find the optimal values for the PReLU function and model parameters. Data may be made more intelligible and comprehensible by reducing its dimensionality via principal component analysis (PCA). This processing method, which keeps only the most important information and throws away the rest, greatly improves the accuracy and speed. This decreases training loss and improves model accuracy. The graph depicts an example loss function. What factors influence one's learning rate? This parameter controls how frequently the weight is changed, which affects model accuracy. The random sample size and the true value of a random group Principal component analysis is a prominent method for reducing dimensionality. By merging data from two sets of variables that are already connected in some manner, it is feasible to construct a new set of linear variables that are unrelated to the two original sets (Tiwari et al., 2018) (Kashyap, 2019) (Kashyap, 2018). This can be done in some cases by merging two sets of variables that are linked in some way. The fundamental building blocks are varieties that have undergone a variety of changes. Throughout its history, PCA has gone through each of its four distinct phases. The normalised data is then saved in a matrix known as X. Each row of this matrix contains a data vector, a new index value, and information about the overall number of indicators and data volume. The graphic depicts the subject in detail and with great precision. As indicated, the covariance matrix Y is constructed. Identifying the intersection of the eigenvectors is simple because this is an ordered real symmetric matrix with real eigenvalues. Eigenvalues and unit eigenvectors are now computed.

Figure 3. The Primary Actions of the PCA

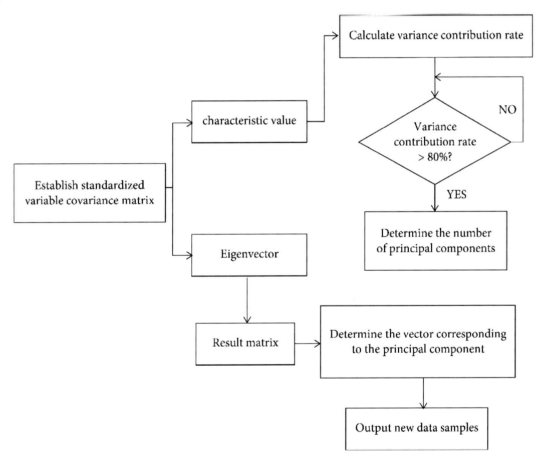

If there are p main components, the coefficients of the newly created principal component index Bm, which corresponds to the original index vector Am, are organised in decreasing order as 1, 2,... p eigenvectors. When there is only one major component, the coefficients show no discernible pattern. There are two techniques for selecting a candidate. If is greater than 80%, the number of major component indicators chosen equals the number of indicators. The primary components are chosen in the second step by producing a transformation matrix with a unit eigenvector. The number of appropriate eigenvalues for each fundamental component represents it. Figure 3 displays the key stages of PCA.

Figure 4. Depicts the Lightweight CNN Model That Has Been Changed

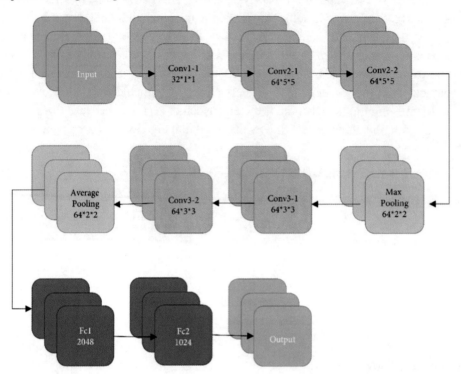

Figure 4 An overview of the improved version of the fundamental CNN model, a 10-layer model, is depicted in Figure 4. There are five convolutional layers in a neural network. Layers include convolutional, max-pooling, and average pooling. These responsibilities are handled by the PReLU operation. The pooling layers reduce the number of parameters as well as the size of the image. If you want your model's output to be as accurate as humanly possible, you must use the totally connected layer (Salih Hasan et al., 2021) (Lee & Kang, 2019) (Eng et al., 2019). The Softmax output layer is the final but most critical layer. This page provides a sorted index of all integrated attributes that are currently accessible. Figure 5 is accessible to you if you want more proof.

Figure 5. Depicts the Process of Creating a Convolutional Neural Network Model

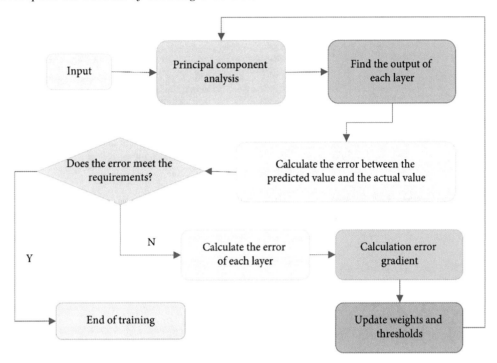

Figure 5 shows how to improve a CNN model's performance while using fewer resources and how to improve it. It depicts the process's training and start-up steps. You must first load the principal photo collection before you can index the expressions stored inside it. The dataset should be separated into two sections: inspection and training. Then, for a neural network model, a picture of a key feature component is found and changed.

DEVELOPING A QUESTIONNAIRE TO EVALUATE CURRENT CIP TEACHING METHODS

To investigate cultural, ideological, and political training, face expression recognition models were built using a modified version of CNN. Understanding the instructional environment is crucial for measuring teaching quality successfully (Kusuma et al., 2020). (Nair & Bhagat, 2021). This method of assessing teaching quality can be combined with others to improve both the mode and quality of education. Surveys are used to assess CIP training (Nair et al., 2022). Shanghai high school students participated in the study. Only 118 of the 120 questionnaires distributed to participants were returned (115 of which were found to be legitimate). Each of these three dimensions includes one question, for a total of seven, as seen in Figure 6.

Figure 6. The Specific Content of The Questionnaire

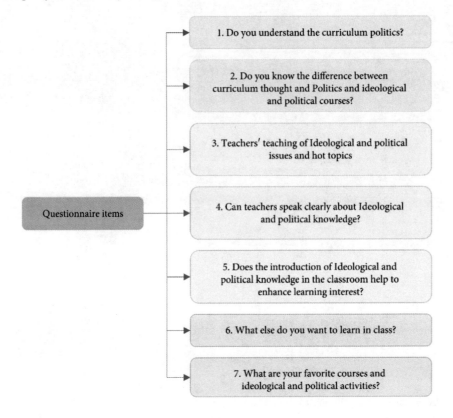

The three most important factors to consider in this situation are: first, how students feel about their professors' ideological or political understanding; second, teachers' pedagogical practices; and third, what students hope to gain from their instructors. What do students think of their professors' political or ideological expertise? Questions 1 and 2 are about this. What do students think of their teachers' ideological and political knowledge?

DATASET

The facial expressions of 118 responders reveal fury, derision, and disgust. The Jaffe dataset contains 213 256-by-256-pixel still images depicting one neutral facial mood and six basic facial expressions. The Jaffe dataset contains unique perspectives on a variety of topics. Because of this, experimenting with this dataset is tough. Fer-2013 was created from web video face expression photos. It consists of 35,887 grayscale 48x48 photographs with seven expression descriptors. The magnitude of this dataset makes evaluating it challenging. Using a 7:3 sample ratio, 70% of each dataset is used for training, while 30% is used for model validation.

RESULTS

A test called accuracy is utilized to compare the regular CNN to the improved CNN. The lightweight CNN model proposed has been shown to be successful in actual trials (Nair et al., 2022). Furthermore, the label recognition results are displayed, including a count of the number of samples that have been correctly labeled (Agrawal et al., 2022). This enables calculation. The total number of samples with both a label and a result of recognition. Column "Recognition Results" The value increases the model's recognition of facial expressions. The learning rate parameter is a modifiable component that can affect the accuracy of the model's predictions. Prior to the start of the randomized trial, the model's learning rate will be changed, and the importance of the Jaffe data set will be enhanced. This educational milestone requires between 0.001 and 0.002 years of study. There might be up to 400 different courses offered.

Figure 7. This figure depicts the outcomes of a survey in which respondents were asked about their level of CIP knowledge. The data is separated into two categories: (a) responses to the questionnaire's first question, and (b) responses to the questionnaire's second question. The purpose of the survey was to establish how familiar students were with CIP

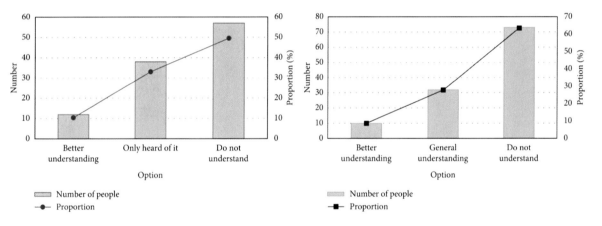

Figure 8. (a-c) The Findings of a Poll Conducted Among Students to Assess the Influence of Their Professors' Lectures on Ideological and Political Topics Are Published Here

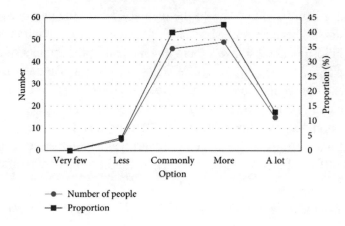

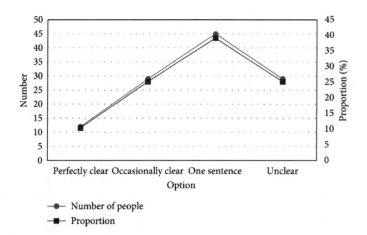

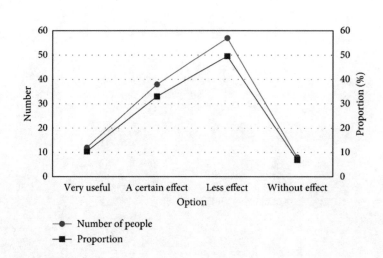

Figure 9. Here is a summary of some possible inferences based on the study on the goals that students had for various teaching approaches. The students' responses to Questions 9(a) and 9(b) of the survey served as the foundation for these findings

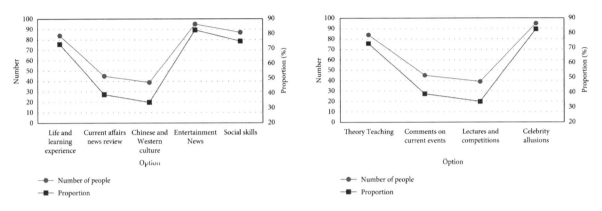

Figure 7a responses to the questionnaire's first question, and Figure 7b shows responses to the questionnaire's second question. The purpose of the survey was to establish how familiar students were with CIP and the class could even explain how the CIP differs from other political and ideological perspectives. This is a major reason why the CIP-supported educational paradigm has yet to expand throughout the region. Teachers can help students understand CIP. This will assist pupils in adjusting to the new teaching technique and promote their growth. Figure 8 depicts the findings of a survey about the ideological and political understanding of students' professors. Figure 8a, figure 8b, and figure 8c depict how students will learn about current events and politics in class. CIP received great feedback from the children who took part. The students' responses to Questions shown in figure 9a and figure 9b of the survey served as the foundation for these findings. Most professors are unable to communicate these concepts to their students, student learning is limited. At a certain point, educational institutions should prioritize providing teachers with specialized training to assist them in teaching political and ideological concepts to students. Figure 9 depicts the survey findings on the educational approach students expect from their instructors. In addition to cultural awareness, Figure 9 children want to learn about entertainment news, life skills, and the learning process. This demonstrates that children are ready to learn. Students are more willing to attend CIP lectures and competitions because of the program. According to a recent poll, classroom techniques are not diverse enough, do not provide students with real-world context, and do not allow teachers to share their own experiences and knowledge. As a result, these elements require extra attention.

MODEL TRAINING RESULTS

As shown in Figure 10, the recommended lightweight CNN model performed well when trained on the datascts.

Figure 10. (a-c) The model was trained using the Ck+, Jaffe, and fFer-2013 datasets, and the following are the results

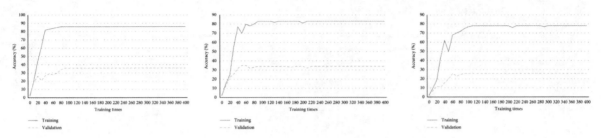

As shown in Figure 10, after 80 rounds of training using the Ck+ dataset, the model's identification accuracy increased from 80% to 86%, as shown in Figure 10a, figure 10b and 10c. After training on the Jaffe dataset, which had 90 different training samples, our recognition accuracy was 83%. This was completed after training with this dataset because of the size and intricacy of Fer-2013. When 110 training pieces were used, the system's recognition accuracy was 78 percent. The general performance, speed, and accuracy have all improved.

Figure 11. Depicts the Effect That a Neural Network's Learning Rate Has on Its Overall Performance

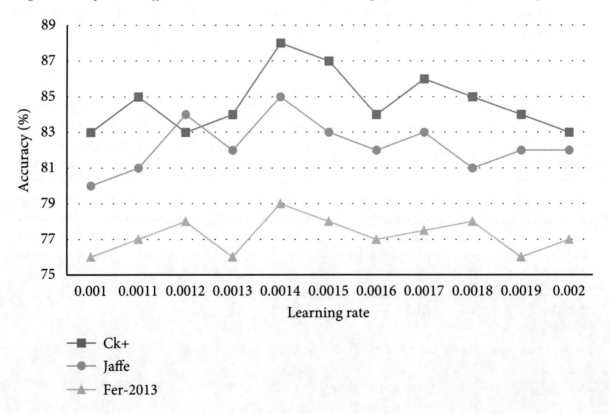

Figure 11 depicts the influence of the learning rate on total neural network performance. It controls how fast model parameters are adjusted during training. When learning rates are excessively high, parameters will bounce around the minimal value, making it difficult to choose the best response. When a model's learning rate is too slow, additional iterations and processing are required, resulting in overfitting. The model has an accuracy of 0.0014 in detecting people's emotions only by looking at their faces. The model is presently learning at a 0.0014 pace.

Figure 12. Depicts How Well Enhanced CNN, Improved CNN, And Lightweight Performed. Across Three Datasets, CNN Recognised the Subject's Expression

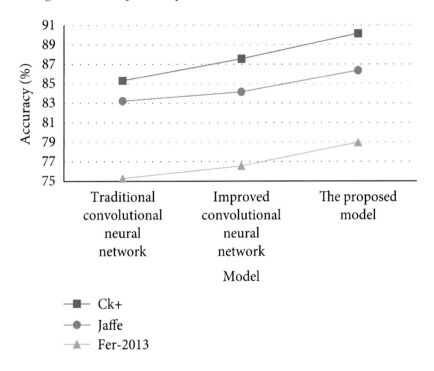

The models in Figure 12 that included all three datasets were the most accurate at identifying facial emotions. CNN has a recognition rate of 81.28 percent. CNN has a recognition rate of 82.76 percent; identification accuracy is 85.17 percent on average. The enhanced lightweight CNN model outperforms standard and upgraded CNNs by 4.8 and 2.9 percent on Ck+, Jaffe, and Fer-2013, respectively. The lightweight CNN model has been improved and is more efficient. Model development is astounding. The model can be used in the classroom to recognize students' facial expressions. The results of the recognition tests could show how well the students understand the training and how CIP teaches.

CONCLUSION

In the past, subjective surveys were used to assess teaching quality. To evaluate the training effect, an updated, lightweight CNN model will be used. The expressions of the students will be examined. A questionnaire survey and an experiment were conducted to better understand CIP instruction in a Shanghai high school. CIP education in schools needs to be improved. Most instructors are politically and ideologically inept. It's bad for kids who don't grasp CIP. Simple teaching methods do not generate enough excitement in the classroom. The accuracy of the standard CNN is 4.8 percentage points higher than that of the enhanced CNN. Model enhancements are critical. This method examines the model's effectiveness using a publicly available dataset. This strategy must be used in the classroom before undertaking field research. These findings can be used to compare traditional cultural instruction versus CIP instruction.

REFERENCES

Abu Alfeilat, H. A., Hassanat, A. B. A., Lasassmeh, O., Tarawneh, A. S., Alhasanat, M. B., Eyal Salman, H. S., & Prasath, V. B. S. (2019). Effects of distance measure choice on k-nearest neighbor Classifier Performance: A Review. *Big Data*, *7*(4), 221–248. doi:10.1089/big.2018.0175 PMID:31411491

Agrawal, M., Kumar Shukla, P., Nair, R., Nayyar, A., & Masud, M. (2022). Stock prediction based on technical indicators using Deep Learning Model. *Computers, Materials & Continua*, *70*(1), 287–304. doi:10.32604/cmc.2022.014637

Alhassan, A. M., & Zainon, W. M. (2021). Brain tumor classification in magnetic resonance image using hard swish-based RELU activation function-convolutional neural network. *Neural Computing & Applications*, *33*(15), 9075–9087. doi:10.100700521-020-05671-3

Eng, S. K., Ali, H., Cheah, A. Y., & Chong, Y. F. (2019). Facial expression recognition in Jaffe and KDEF datasets using histogram of oriented gradients and support vector machine. *IOP Conference Series. Materials Science and Engineering*, *705*(1), 012031. doi:10.1088/1757-899X/705/1/012031

Furtak, E. M., Circi, R., & Heredia, S. C. (2017). Exploring alignment among learning progressions, teacher-designed formative assessment tasks, and student growth: Results of a four-year study. *Applied Measurement in Education*, *31*(2), 143–156. doi:10.1080/08957347.2017.1408624

Gou, C., Zhou, D., & Li, H. (2021). The research and exploration of "curriculum including ideology and politics" in the financial practical talent cultivation with the core of moral education: Taking the major of Finance and Economics in Sichuan University of Arts and Science as an example. *Creative Education*, *12*(04), 809–816. doi:10.4236/ce.2021.124057

Guo, J., & Yu, S. (2020). Retracted: Evaluation model of college English teaching quality based on Big Data Analysis. *IOP Conference Series. Materials Science and Engineering*, *750*(1), 012077. doi:10.1088/1757-899X/750/1/012077

Jin, J., & Martin, R. (2019). Exploring the past to navigate the future: Examining histories of higher dance education in China in an internationalized context. *Research in Dance Education*, *20*(2), 225–240. doi:10.1080/14647893.2019.1566304

Kashyap, R. (2018). Object boundary detection through robust active contour based method with global information. *International Journal of Image Mining*, *3*(1), 22. doi:10.1504/IJIM.2018.093008

Kashyap, R. (2019). Big Data Analytics challenges and solutions. *Big Data Analytics for Intelligent Healthcare Management*, 19–41. doi:10.1016/b978-0-12-818146-1.00002-7

Kashyap, R. (2019). Machine learning for internet of things. *Advances in Wireless Technologies and Telecommunication*, 57–83. doi:10.4018/978-1-5225-7458-3.ch003

Khan, A., Sohail, A., Zahoora, U., & Qureshi, A. S. (2020). A survey of the recent architectures of deep convolutional Neural Networks. *Artificial Intelligence Review*, *53*(8), 5455–5516. doi:10.100710462-020-09825-6

Kusuma, G. P., Jonathan, J., & Lim, A. P. (2020). Emotion recognition on FER-2013 face images using fine-tuned VGG-16. *Advances in Science. Technology and Engineering Systems Journal*, *5*(6), 315–322. doi:10.25046/aj050638

Lee, H.-S., & Kang, B.-Y. (2019). Continuous emotion estimation of facial expressions on Jaffe and CK+ datasets for Human–Robot Interaction. *Intelligent Service Robotics*, *13*(1), 15–27. doi:10.100711370-019-00301-x

Lim, L., & Apple, M. W. (2018). The Politics of Curriculum Reforms in Asia: Inter-referencing discourses of power, culture and knowledge. *Curriculum Inquiry*, *48*(2), 139–148. doi:10.1080/0362678 4.2018.1448532

Lindsay, G. W. (2021). Convolutional Neural Networks as a model of the visual system: Past, present, and future. *Journal of Cognitive Neuroscience*, *33*(10), 2017–2031. doi:10.1162/jocn_a_01544 PMID:32027584

Lv, X. (2021). A quality evaluation scheme for curriculum in ideological and political education based on Data Mining. *2021 13th International Conference on Measuring Technology and Mechatronics Automation (ICMTMA)*. doi:10.1109/icmtma52658.2021.00149

Nair, R., & Bhagat, A. (2021). An introduction to clustering algorithms in Big Data. Encyclopedia of Information Science and Technology, Fifth Edition, 559–576. doi:10.4018/978-1-7998-3479-3.ch040

Nair, R., Sharma, P., & Sharma, T. (2022). Optimizing the performance of IOT using FPGA as compared to GPU. *International Journal of Grid and High Performance Computing*, *14*(1), 1–15. doi:10.4018/ IJGHPC.301580

Nair, R., Soni, M., Bajpai, B., Dhiman, G., & Sagayam, K. M. (2022). Predicting the death rate around the world due to COVID-19 using regression analysis. *International Journal of Swarm Intelligence Research*, *13*(2), 1–13. doi:10.4018/IJSIR.287545

Poorchangizi, B., Borhani, F., Abbaszadeh, A., Mirzaee, M., & Farokhzadian, J. (2019). The importance of professional values from nursing students' perspective. *BMC Nursing*, *18*(1), 26. Advance online publication. doi:10.118612912-019-0351-1 PMID:31312111

Robinson, R. P. (2020). Until the Revolution: Analyzing the politics, pedagogy, and curriculum of the Oakland Community School. Espacio. *Tiempo y Educación*, *7*(1), 181–203. doi:10.14516/ete.273

Sakalle, A., Tomar, P., Bhardwaj, H., & Alim, M. A. (2022). A modified LSTM framework for analyzing COVID-19 effect on emotion and mental health during pandemic using the EEG signals. *Journal of Healthcare Engineering, 2022*, 1–8. doi:10.1155/2022/8412430 PMID:35281542

Sakalle, A., Tomar, P., Bhardwaj, H., Iqbal, A., Sakalle, M., Bhardwaj, A., & Ibrahim, W. (2022). Genetic programming-based feature selection for emotion classification using EEG Signal. *Journal of Healthcare Engineering, 2022*, 1–6. doi:10.1155/2022/8362091 PMID:35299691

Salih Hasan, B. M., & Abdulazeez, A. M. (2021). A review of principal component analysis algorithm for dimensionality reduction. *Journal of Soft Computing and Data Mining, 2*(1). Advance online publication. doi:10.30880/jscdm.2021.02.01.003

Su, S., Qu, W., Wu, Y., & Yang, Z. (2021). Intelligent evaluation scheme of ideological and Political Education Quality of College English course based on AHP under the background of Big Data. *2021 6th International Conference on Smart Grid and Electrical Automation (ICSGEA)*. doi:10.1109/icsgea53208.2021.00123

Thakur, R. S., Yadav, R. N., & Gupta, L. (2020). Prelu and edge-aware filter-based image denoiser using Convolutional Neural Network. *IET Image Processing, 14*(15), 3869–3879. doi:10.1049/iet-ipr.2020.0717

Tiwari, S., Gupta, R. K., & Kashyap, R. (2018). To enhance web response time using agglomerative clustering technique for web navigation recommendation. *Advances in Intelligent Systems and Computing*, 659–672. doi:10.1007/978-981-10-8055-5_59

Wang, S.-H., Muhammad, K., Hong, J., Sangaiah, A. K., & Zhang, Y.-D. (2018). Alcoholism identification via convolutional neural network based on parametric relu, dropout, and batch normalization. *Neural Computing & Applications, 32*(3), 665–680. doi:10.100700521-018-3924-0

Yu, S., Chen, B., Levesque-Bristol, C., & Vansteenkiste, M. (2016). Chinese education examined via the lens of self-determination. *Educational Psychology Review, 30*(1), 177–214. doi:10.100710648-016-9395-x

Zhang, J., & Meng, G. (2021). *Evaluation model of practical effect of ideological and political education based on Deep Data Mining. In 2021 Global Reliability and Prognostics and Health Management.* PHM-Nanjing. doi:10.1109/phm-nanjing52125.2021.9612831

Zou, Q. (2022). Exploring the education reform of architectural drawing and drafting under the background of curriculum ideology and politics. *Journal of Contemporary Educational Research, 6*(3), 40–48. doi:10.26689/jcer.v6i3.3790

Chapter 13
Comparative Analysis of Feature Selection Methods for Detection of Android Malware

Meghna Dhalaria
Jaypee University of Information Technology, India

Ekta Gandotra
Jaypee University of Information Technology, India

Deepak Gupta
 https://orcid.org/0000-0002-1547-196X
Jaypee University of Information Technology, India

ABSTRACT

Over the past few years, Android has been found to be the most prevalent operating system. The increase in the adoption of Android by users has led to many security issues. The amount of malware targeting Android has significantly increased. Due to the increase in the amount of malware, their detection and classification have become a major issues. Currently, the detection techniques comprise static and dynamic malware analysis. This chapter presents a comparative study of various feature selection methods through machine learning classifiers for Android malware classification. The study examines the features acquired through static malware analysis (such as command strings, permissions, intents, and API calls), and various feature selection techniques are employed to find suitable features for classifying malware to carry out the comparative analysis. The experimental results illustrate that the gain ratio feature selection approach selects relevant features for the classification of Android malware and provides an accuracy of 97.74%.

DOI: 10.4018/978-1-6684-6275-1.ch013

INTRODUCTION

In the current era, there is an increase in the usage of smartphones in our day-to-day lives. A Lot of users use these smartphones due to the various functionalities they are providing like emailing, gaming, watching videos, banking etc. There are various operating systems (OS) available in the market such as Windows, iOS, Android, BlackBerry etc. Among these, Android is found to be the most prevalent one. Android is a mobile OS based on Linux kernel specifically built for touchscreen devices such as tablets and smartphones etc. It is established in 2005 by Google (Android Developers, 2011). Unfortunately, the renown of these devices has resulted in an increasing level of cybercrimes. Malware is considered the major issue with respect to security threats. It refers to distinct forms of intrusive software such as worms, rootkits, backdoors and trojan horses etc. They perform malicious activities like extracting unauthorized personal information, destruct the information or gain access to a device etc. In various attack scenarios, an attacker can exploit Android's vulnerabilities and compromise a user. In one scenario, a Trojan app might provide cool HD wallpapers in the foreground, while secretly collecting private information from users' phones, such as contacts. A wallpapers app will require INTERNET permission in order to download wallpapers. Unsuspecting users may not check permission requests and accidentally grant READ_CONTACTS permission. The attacker can use this data for monetary gain and/or propagation of malware. Another scenario involves an attacker draining a victim's smartphone's battery life by overusing resource-consuming services like radio, GPS, etc. to kill their smartphone.

According to the worldwide Statista report, Android is turned out to be a leading mobile OS with 74.13% of market share by December 2019 (Statista: Mobile operating systems market share, 2020). The increase in the use of Android resulted in the increase of malware. In 2020, McAfee stated that there is 121 million total and 49 million new malware are discovered (McAfee Lab: Threat Predictions Report, 2020).

The increasing use of Android applications (apps) lured attackers to build complex and sophisticated malware which is difficult to analyze. The earlier signature-based approach was extensively used for identifying malware. This method extracts patterns from the fishy files matching with the malware signature database for malware detection (Kouliaridis et al., 2020; Aslan and Samet, 2020). The major constraint of this method is that it cannot detect unknown malware (i.e. zero-day). Machine learning (ML) techniques are now being used by researchers to detect Android malware. These methods allow computers to think and make predictions. Static and dynamic malware analysis features can be used by machine learning approaches to classify apps (Memon and Anwar, 2015, Dhalaria and Gandotra, 2021a; Dhalaria and Gandotra, 2020a; Dhalaria and Gandotra, 2022; Dhalaria and Gandotra, 2020b; Dhalaria and Gandotra, 2021b).

Static malware analysis investigates the app by investigating its source code. The major constraint of this approach is that it is unable to examine the obfuscation code (Barrera et al., 2010; Singla et al., 2015). But this limitation is overwhelmed by dynamic malware analysis which monitors the activities of an app by executing it in a sandbox (virtual environment). The major constraint of this approach is that it needs more time and resources and cannot explore all execution paths (Gandotra et al., 2014). A more number of features degrade the accuracy of the classification models and may increase the complexity of the model. So to overcome this problem, different feature selection techniques are used. These techniques help in selecting appropriate features for the purpose of classification. Moreover, it also reduces the model building time.

In this chapter, we use various feature selection and ML methods to classify Android apps. A comparative analysis of feature selection and ML algorithms is carried out to finalize the method/technique that provides the best results for detecting Android malware. Experiments are performed on a dataset of real Android apps consisting of various features. The contributions of the chapter are as follows:

1. Prepared the binary malware classification dataset using static malware analysis.
2. Various feature selection methods are employed on the created dataset to select a relevant set of features for the detection of malware.
3. Comparative analysis of feature selection and ML algorithms is carried out to select the best techniques.

The remaining chapter is arranged as follows: Section 2 provides the existing literature survey. Section 3 describes the methodology used in this chapter. The findings are presented and described in section 4. At last, section 5 concludes the chapter.

LITERATURE REVIEW

This section presents the work associated with the identification and classification of Android malware using ML techniques.

(Coronado-De-Alba et al., 2016) examined different feature selection techniques to categorize the Android apps. The findings demonstrate that the accuracy obtained without feature selection, chi-square and relief feature selection approach was 97.53%, 97.51% and 97.43% respectively. (Deepa et al., 2015) presented an approach for malware identification through the feature selection technique. They employed different classifiers for identifying apps as either benign or malware. The consequences show that the accuracy obtained by J48 and Adaboost was 88.75% with 600 variables. (Zhao et al., 2015) presented a tool named feature extraction and selection tool (FEST). They also proposed an algorithm to select the best features for characterizing the apps as malware or benign. (Talha et al., 2015) introduced a system i.e. APK Auditor that used a static analyzer to distinguish and categorize the apps as goodware or malware. The experimental outcomes indicate that the specificity and detection rate acquired by the system were 0.925 and 88%. (Sheen et al., 2015) suggested a technique in regard to multi-feature collaborative decision fusion to detect malware effectively. They utilize different characteristics like permissions and API calls to provide better detection efficiency. The outcomes suggest that their technique provides the best performance than state of the art approaches. (Peiravian et al., 2013) suggested a framework on the basis of static features. They used permissions and API calls for detecting malicious apps. Bagging, Decision tree (DT) and support vector machine (SVM) are employed to classify the apps. The outcomes indicate that SVM provides better accuracy i.e. 95.7% for detecting malware. (Du et al., 2015) presented a novel multisource method to identify Android malware by focusing on static features. They employed the dempster-shafer technique to fuse these sources of information. The outcomes demonstrate that false positive rate (FPR) and accuracy obtained by the algorithm were 1.9 and 97% respectively. (Yerima et al., 2015) employed the information gain feature selection technique on the malware dataset, which comprises 179 features. They employed random forest (RF) for the detection of malware. The accuracy obtained by RF was 97.5%. (Kim et al., 2018) presented a multimodal framework that relies on deep learning for malware detection. They examined the importance of features based on the proposed approach.

Furthermore, they compared their framework with the existing deep learning based frameworks based on the deep learning approach. (Wang et al., 2014) investigated the risk of the apps while considering permissions as a feature. The authors used three feature ranking techniques i.e. correlation coefficient, T-test and mutual information. They also utilized the principal component analysis (PCA) and forward selection method to identify the risk. The outcomes show that their detector gives a 94.62% detection rate with FPR of 0.6. (Dhalaria et al., 2019) compared different ML and ensemble learning techniques to detect malware. The consequences demonstrate that the stacking approach is best for detecting malware. (Gandotra et al., 2016a) used both static and dynamic features for identifying zero-day malware. The approach is tested and verified on a real-world corpus of malicious apps. The findings demonstrate that the combination of both static and dynamic features provided better accuracy. It also showed that the process of selecting significant features can improve the detection rate as well as the time for building the model. (Gupta et al., 2020) designed two approaches on the basis of big data and ensemble learning for better detection of malware. The first approach relies on ensemble learning and the second approach selected the best set of classifiers for stacking. The experimental outcomes illustrated that the proposed approach is much effective in detecting malware. (Dhalaria and Gandotra, 2021c) have made malware datasets based on both malware analysis approaches. The authors build the datasets in order to help researchers for developing new algorithms or techniques for better identifying malware. The results demonstrated that the hybrid approach improves the detection as compared to the single individual approach. Table 1 illustrates the comparative study of malware detection and classification techniques.

Table 1. Comparative study of malware detection and classification techniques

Authors	Features extracted	Data source		Feature selection technique used	ML technique used	Results
		Benign	Malware			
Coronado-De-Alba et al., 2016	Hardware components, permissions, intents	Google Play Store, Drebin and Third party Store	765	1531	Chi-Square and Relief	RF and Random Committee	Accuracy-97.56%
Deepa et al., 2015	Opcode, methods and strings	Aapsapk, Contagiomobile	758	612	CFS, Goodman kruskals, IG	Adaboost, NB, Ibk, J48, RF, SVM	Accuracy-88.75%
Zhao et al., 2015	Permissions, intents, IP And URL, API calls	Drebin and Google Play Store	3986	3986	Chi-Squared, IG, FrequenSel	K-NN and SVM	Accuracy-97.8%
Talha et al., 2015	Permissions	Contagio mobile, Genome Project, Drebin, Play store	1853	6909	---	Designed APK Auditor	Accuracy- 88%
Sheen et al., 2015	Permissions and API calls	Genome project	904	1073	Chi-Square, Relief and IG	NB, DT, Decision stump, SVM and Random tree	F-measure- 0.988
Peiravian et al., 2013	Permissions and API calls	Genome Project, Android market and Google Play Store	1250	1260	---	SVM, Bagging and DT	Accuracy-96.88%
Yerima et al., 2015	Permissions, app attributes	McAfee's internal Repository	3938	2925	IG	RF and Simple logistic	Accuracy-97.5%
Kim et al., 2018	Permission, Strings, API calls, Shared library function opcode and Method opcode	VirusShare, Malgenome Project and Google Play Store	19,747	13,075	---	Multimodal Neural Network	Accuracy- 98%
Wang et al., 2014	Permissions	Mal-com 1 and Mal-com 2 from antivirus companies and Google Play Store	315794	29216	Mutual information, correlation coefficient and t-test	SVM, RF and DT	Accuracy-94.62%
Alazab, 2020	API calls	Androzoo, Malshare, contagio mobile and Play store	19000	17915	Chi-square and ANOVA	NB, SVM, K-NN, RF, Adaboost, J48, simple logistic, JRip, LR and Random Committee	Accuracy-98.1%.

RF- Random Forest, NB- Naive Bayes, K-NN- K-Nearest Neighbor, LR- Logistic Regression, CFS- Correlation feature selection and IG- Information Gain

This chapter compares various feature selection methods and ML classifiers to detect Android malicious apps.

METHODOLOGY USED

This section explains the methodology used to carry out a comparative study of feature selection methods and ML algorithms to detect Android malicious apps. We employed different feature selection and ML techniques to finalize the best approach. We first gathered the Android apps. These are then scanned using the Avira antivirus (AV) (Avira (accessed April, 2019)) tool. After this, the feature extraction process is carried out to extract static features using a self-developed script that makes use of various tools like AXMLprinter2 (AXMLPrinter2 (accessed April, 2019)), string (Gandotra et al., 2016b) and Baksmali Disassembler (Enck et al., 2011). The features extracted using these tools are command strings, permissions, API calls and intents. The feature selection techniques such as information gain (IG), ReliefF, correlation feature selection (CFS) and Gain Ratio (GR) are used to select the relevant features. The feature vector table is built from the chosen feature set and provides an input to the different classifiers such as

K-NN, NB, SVM and RF. The proposed architecture is demonstrated in figure1and the methodology is explained in the following subsection.

Figure 1. Methodology Used

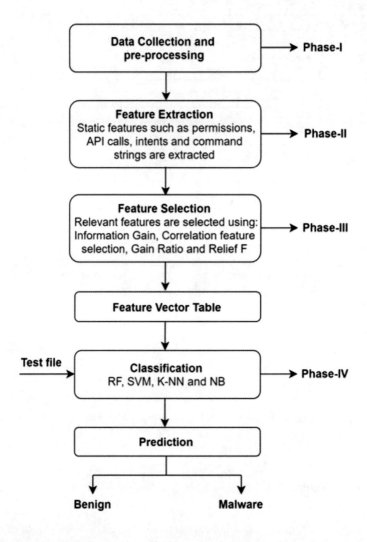

Data Collection and Pre-Processing (Phase-I)

A total of 4400 Android apps have been gathered from different sources like virusshare (Virusshare (accessed March, 2019)), apkpure (Apkpure (accessed March, 2019)) and apkmirror (APKMirror (accessed March, 2019)). The Android malicious apps are gathered from virusshare and benign apps are gathered from apkpure and apkmirror. These apps are then scanned using the Avira AV tool to eradicate the duplicate apps and label the apps accordingly.

Feature Extraction (Phase-II)

Android file format is saved in the Android application package (.apk) extension. A python script is developed using various tools like AXMLprinter2, string and Baksmali Disassembler for extracting the features from these files. The features extracted using these tools are command strings, permissions, API calls and intents. 277 permissions and 22 intents are mined using AXMLPrinter2, 6 command strings are extracted using string tool and 47 API calls are mined using baksmali disassembler. The Android apps have yielded 352 static features in all. Figure 2 demonstrates the extraction process of static features.

Figure 2. Feature extraction process

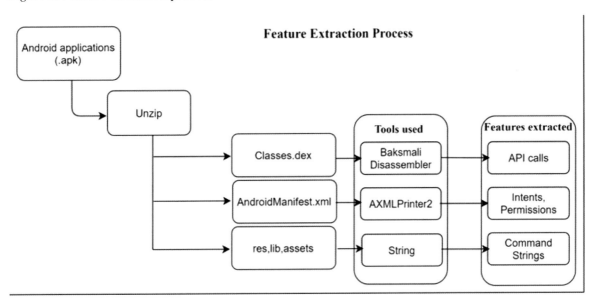

Feature selection (Phase-III)

This sub-section discusses various feature selection techniques employed for identifying the malware. Feature selection is also referred to as dimensionality reduction. It is used to eliminate noise and irrelevant features (Chizi and Maimon, 2009; Han et al., 2022). Four feature selection approaches such as IG, CFS, GR and ReliefF are employed using the ranking method to rank the features in accordance with their weights. Then the features are sorted according to rank. These features are provided as input to the forward selection approach to reduce the model's complexity of the model and train the classifiers faster. Forward selection is an iterative approach in which the system begins with no features in the model. In every iteration, it continues adding the feature to the model until the new addition of feature does not enhance the performance of the model. In the end, we obtained an optimal set of features. The description of the feature selection techniques used in this work is given as follows:

Information Gain

It is considered one of the most significant feature selection techniques. It uses the concept of information theory (Liu et al., 2003). It computes the information, an attribute provides about the target label. It uses entropy to calculate the uniformity of samples and also calculates the IG of an attribute which is computed as shown in equation (1)

$$IG = H(Y) - H(Y,F) \tag{1}$$

Where $H(Y)$ is the entropy of the dataset *(Y)* with z classes. It is computed as given in equation (2)

$$H\left(Y\right) = \sum_{j=1}^{z} - p_j log_2 p_j \tag{2}$$

Here p_j is the probability of class j in the dataset *Y*. $H(Y,F)$ is the entropy of the dataset with respect to attribute *F*. It is calculated as shown in equation (3)

$$H\left(Y,F\right) = \sum_{p \in F} P\left(z\right) H\left(z\right) \tag{3}$$

Here p demonstrates the possible values of the feature *F*. The more the IG of a specific attribute, the more significant the feature is. Figure 3 illustrates the top 10 static features based on the IG feature selection technique.

Figure 3. Top 10 static features based on IG

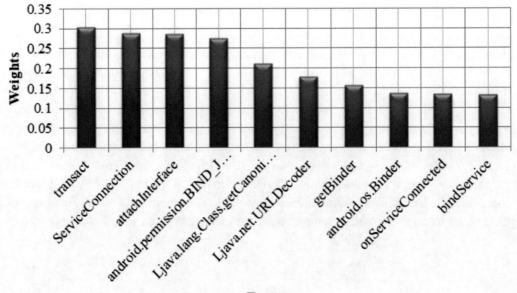

Correlation feature selection (CFS)

It is a heuristic-based method. In this method, if a feature has a high correlation to class label then that feature is considered to be the best feature (Hall, 2000). It is computed as in equation (4)

$$M = \frac{k \times r_{cf}}{\sqrt{k + k \times (k-1) \times r_{ff}}} \tag{4}$$

Where M stands for heuristic merit, r_{cf} represents the average attribute to attribute correlations, k symbolizes the number of attributes and r_{ff} symbolizes the average attributes to class correlations. Figure 4 illustrates the top 10 static features based on the CFS technique.

Figure 4. Top 10 static features based on CFS

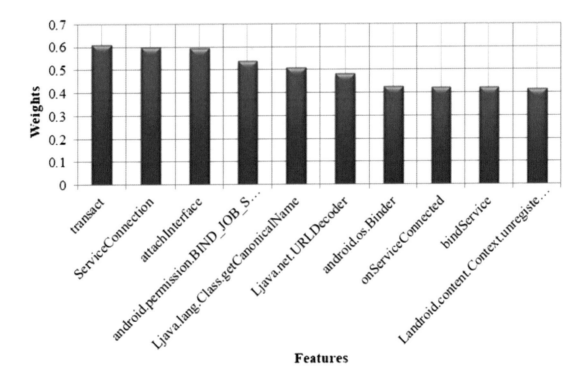

Gain ratio

It is the modification of IG that minimizes its bias. It overwhelms the problem of IG by considering the number of branches that will result before making the split (Han, 2022). It corrects the IG by considering the information of split into account. It adapts to overcome the bias. The GR for specific attribute F is calculated as given in equation (5)

$$GR = \frac{Gain\left(F\right)}{Split\,info\left(F\right)} \tag{5}$$

Where *Split info* of dataset *(Y)* with z classes are calculated as given in equation (6)

$$Split\,info_F\left(Y\right) = \sum_{j=1}^{z} \frac{\left|Y_j\right|}{\left|Y\right|} \times log\left(\frac{\left|Y_j\right|}{\left|Y\right|}\right) \tag{6}$$

Figure 5 illustrates the top 10 static features based on the GR feature selection technique.

Figure 5. Top 10 static features based on GR

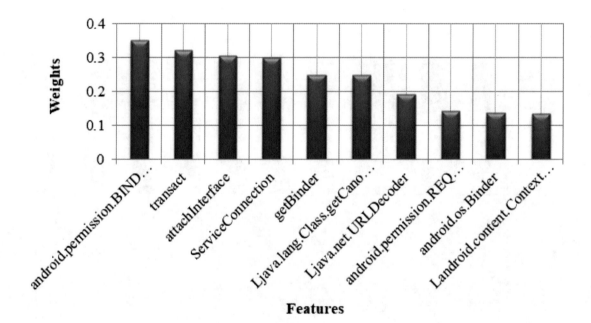

ReliefF

It is the extended version of the relief technique. The weights of every attribute are computed through the difference between two conditional probabilistic approaches. These two approaches are the nearest miss and the nearest hit approach. The main difference between reliefF and relief is that reliefF utilizes Manhattan distance and relief utilizes Euclidean distance (Robnik-Šikonja, M and Kononenko, 2003). Figure 6 illustrates the top 10 static features based on the ReliefF feature selection technique.

Figure 6. Top 10 features based on ReliefF

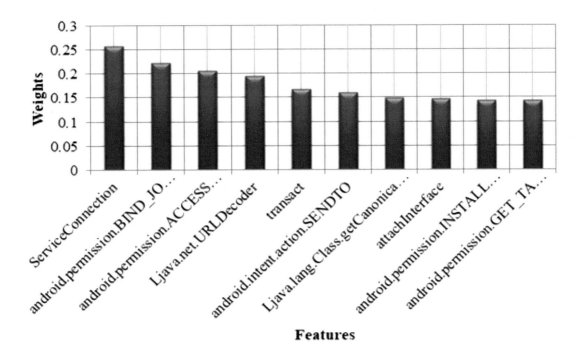

The main goal of phase-III is to determine the best feature selection technique that can be used to improve the results of the classifiers. After applying these feature selection approaches, the feature vector table is built from the chosen feature sets and is used as an input to the different classifiers.

Figure 7. Effect of number of features on accuracy for different feature selection methods

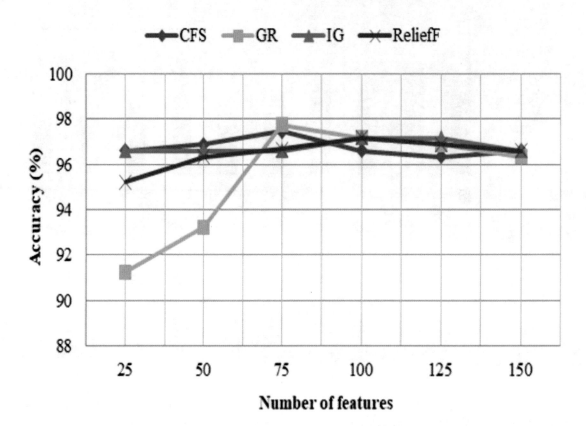

Figure 7 illustrates the effect of a number of features on accuracy for different feature selection methods using the forward selection approach. For all four feature selection techniques used, we get the optimal results with 75 features. These selected features are used to carry out the further experimental work.

Classification (Phase-IV)

ML is used in many areas such as image detection or text identification (Ghosh et al. 2021; Rajasoundaran et al., 2021; Rawat et al., 2022). In this chapter, several ML classifiers are used for malware classification. The four classifiers i.e. K-NN, SVM, RF and NB are employed for classification. A summary of these classifiers are discussed below:

SVM- It forms a hyperplane for classifying the data. For less generalization and confidence error, the hyperplane must be chosen by a margin this leads to the distance closest to training data objects in any class as much higher as possible. SVM is resistant to overfitting even in the high dimensional variable (Keerthi and Gilbert, 2002).

K-NN- It classifies the unknown instances on the basis of the class of the instances nearest to it in the training set by calculating the distance between the training observations and the unknown observations. K-NN is also called a lazy learner (Shakhnarovich et al., 2006).

RF- It can be used to solve problems involving both multiclass and binary classification. It creates distinct decision trees. The integration of all trees results in RF and provides high accuracy. RF takes less training time and doesn't cause the problem of overfitting. It classifies the new instances using the concept of majority voting (Liaw and Wiener, 2002).

NB- It is based on the Bayes rule of conditional probability. It takes advantage of all the variables present in the data and examines them separately as they are independent of one another (Domingos and Pazzani, 1997).

Performance Metrics

The classifier's performance is examined through performance metrics which are described below:

Different evaluation parameters like recall, Matthews's correlation coefficient (MCC), FPR, precision, AUC (Area Under Curve), f-measure and accuracy are used to assess the classifiers' performance (Gupta and Rani, 2018).

Accuracy: It is calculated as (in equation (7)) the number of apps that are correctly classified divided by the total number of observations.

$$Accuracy = \frac{t_p + t_n}{t_p + t_n + f_p + f_n} \times 100 \tag{7}$$

Where $f_p, f_n, t_p,$ and t_n stands for false positive, false negative, true positive and true negative respectively.

Recall: It is computed as (in equation (8)) the number of malware apps that are correctly classified divided by the number of malware apps that are correctly and incorrectly classified as benign apps.

$$Recall = \frac{t_p}{t_p + f_n} \tag{8}$$

FPR: It is calculated as (in equation (9)) the number of malware apps that are incorrectly classified divided by false positive and true negative.

$$FPR = \frac{f_p}{f_p + t_n} \tag{9}$$

Precision or Positive Predictive value (PPV): It is calculated as (in equation (10)) the malware apps that are correctly classified to the number of true cases.

$$Precision = \frac{t_p}{t_p + f_p} \tag{10}$$

F-measure: It is also known as F-score. It measures both precision and recall in a single measurement as shown in equation (11)

$$F - measure = \frac{2 \times \left(Recall \times precision\right)}{Recall + precision} \tag{11}$$

MCC: It is utilized to calculate the trait of binary classification problems. It is calculated using equation (12)

$$MCC = \frac{t_p \times t_n - f_p \times f_n}{\sqrt{\left(t_p + f_n\right)\left(t_p + f_p\right)\left(t_n + f_p\right)\left(t_n + f_n\right)}} \tag{12}$$

AUC: It refers to "Area Under the Curve". It offers a consistent level of performance throughout all feasible classification thresholds.

EXPERIMENTAL SETUP AND RESULTS

This section describes the experimental setup and results based on static features. Different techniques are used which are run on python 3.7 under Intel Core i5 processor, 64 bit with 8GB RAM. The complete dataset is divided into two parts: a training set and test set. 90% of the data is utilized as a training set and 10% is utilized as a test set. We employed fivefold cross-validation in the training phase, which splits the dataset into five subsets and the hold-out approach is repeated five times. Every time one subset is used for the testing and the rest four subsets are used for the training. The outcomes from these folds are then averaged to generate a single evaluation. When the model is created, we supply the test set to test the performance of the model. Table 2 and Table 3 show the results obtained using IG feature selection approach on training and testing data respectively.

Table 2. Training set results of different classifiers based on IG feature selection approach

Base Classifiers	Recall	FPR	PPV	F-measure	AUC	MCC	Accuracy (%)
K-NN	0.954	0.045	0.955	0.954	0.978	0.909	95.39
SVM	0.942	0.058	0.942	0.942	0.942	0.884	94.17
RF	0.965	0.035	0.965	0.965	0.993	0.930	**96.49**
NB	0.865	0.133	0.868	0.865	0.948	0.734	86.52

Table 3. Test set results of different classifiers based on IG feature selection approach

Base Classifiers	Recall	FPR	PPV	F-measure	AUC	MCC	Accuracy (%)
K-NN	0.946	0.054	0.947	0.946	0.971	0.893	94.64
SVM	0.927	0.074	0.927	0.927	0.927	0.854	92.67
RF	0.966	0.034	0.966	0.966	0.990	0.932	**96.61**
NB	0.817	0.183	0.817	0.817	0.892	0.634	81.69

RF achieves the highest classification accuracy based on the IG feature selection approach. The accuracy obtained by RF for training and testing data is 96.49% and 96.61% respectively. NB provides the minimum accuracy for both training and testing data. Table 4 and Table 5 show the results obtained using the CFS feature selection approach on training and testing data respectively.

Table 4. Training set results of different classifiers based on CFS feature selection approach

Base Classifiers	Recall	FPR	PPV	F-measure	AUC	MCC	Accuracy (%)
K-NN	0.955	0.044	0.956	0.955	0.978	0.911	95.48
SVM	0.939	0.060	0.939	0.939	0.939	0.879	93.92
RF	0.966	0.034	0.966	0.966	0.993	0.931	**96.55**
NB	0.865	0.134	0.868	0.865	0.948	0.733	86.49

Table 5. Test set results of different classifiers based on CFS feature selection approach

Base Classifiers	Recall	FPR	PPV	F-measure	AUC	MCC	Accuracy (%)
K-NN	0.946	0.054	0.947	0.946	0.978	0.893	94.64
SVM	0.915	0.085	0.916	0.915	0.915	0.831	91.54
RF	0.975	0.025	0.975	0.975	0.993	0.949	**97.46**
NB	0.817	0.183	0.817	0.817	0.893	0.634	81.69

RF achieves the highest classification accuracy based on the CFS feature selection approach. The accuracy obtained by RF for training and testing data is 96.55% and 97.46% respectively. NB provides the minimum accuracy for both training and testing data. Table 6 and Table 7 show the results obtained using the GR feature selection approach on training and testing data respectively.

Table 6. Training set results of different classifiers based on GR feature selection approach

Base Classifiers	Recall	FPR	PPV	F-measure	AUC	MCC	Accuracy (%)
K-NN	0.928	0.072	0.928	0.928	0.978	0.856	92.79
SVM	0.908	0.090	0.912	0.908	0.909	0.820	90.82
RF	0.937	0.063	0.937	0.937	0.985	0.874	**93.70**
NB	0.857	0.141	0.862	0.856	0.936	0.719	85.68

Table 7. Test set results of different classifiers based on GR feature selection approach

Base Classifiers	Recall	FPR	PPV	F-measure	AUC	MCC	Accuracy (%)
K-NN	0.969	0.031	0.969	0.969	0.987	0.938	96.90
SVM	0.927	0.072	0.932	0.927	0.928	0.859	92.67
RF	0.977	0.023	0.977	0.977	0.991	0.955	**97.74**
NB	0.825	0.173	0.828	0.825	0.894	0.654	82.53

RF achieves the highest classification accuracy based on the GR feature selection approach. The accuracy obtained by RF for training and testing data is 93.70% and 97.74% respectively. NB provides the minimum accuracy for both training and testing data. Table 8 and Table 9 show the results obtained using the ReliefF feature selection approach on training and testing data respectively.

Table 8. Training set results of different classifiers based on ReliefF feature selection approach

Base Classifiers	Recall	FPR	PPV	F-measure	AUC	MCC	Accuracy (%)
K-NN	0.960	0.040	0.960	0.960	0.982	0.920	95.95
SVM	0.946	0.054	0.946	0.946	0.946	0.892	94.61
RF	0.967	0.033	0.967	0.967	0.994	0.934	**96.67**
NB	0.860	0.138	0.864	0.860	0.946	0.724	86.02

Table 9. Test set results of different classifiers based on ReliefF feature selection approach

Base Classifiers	Recall	FPR	PPV	F-measure	AUC	MCC	Accuracy (%)
K-NN	0.952	0.048	0.952	0.952	0.972	0.905	95.21
SVM	0.913	0.088	0.913	0.913	0.912	0.826	91.26
RF	0.969	0.031	0.969	0.969	0.994	0.938	**96.90**
NB	0.797	0.204	0.798	0.797	0.883	0.595	79.71

RF achieves the highest classification accuracy based on the ReliefF feature selection approach. The accuracy obtained by RF for training and testing data is 96.67% and 96.90% respectively. NB provides the minimum accuracy for both training and testing data.

From the experimental results, it is found that among all the classifiers, RF is superior in classifying the Android malware. Table 10 demonstrates the comparative analysis of test set results of RF classifiers based on different feature selection approaches. It shows that RF provides the best results for the GR feature selection method.

Table 10. Test set results of RF classifiers based on different feature selection approach

Base Classifiers	Recall	FPR	PPV	F-measure	AUC	MCC	Accuracy (%)
IG	0.966	0.034	0.966	0.966	0.990	0.932	96.61
CFS	0.975	0.025	0.975	0.975	0.993	0.949	97.46
GR	0.977	0.023	0.977	0.977	0.991	0.955	**97.74**
ReliefF	0.969	0.031	0.969	0.969	0.994	0.938	96.90

Figure 8. Comparison of feature selection methods based on different classifiers

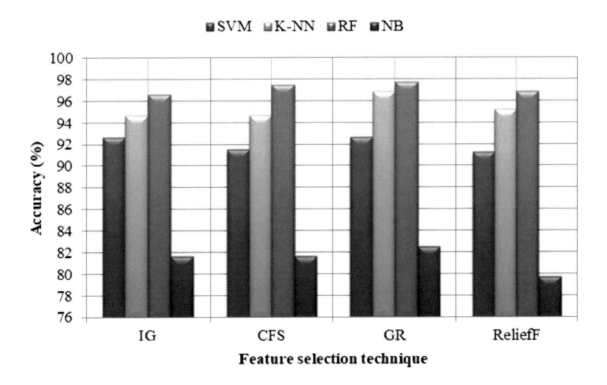

Figure 8 illustrates the comparison of feature selection methods for different classifiers based on accuracy. It demonstrates that RF gives the highest accuracy of 97.74% for the GR feature selection method.

Figure 9. Comparison of feature selection methods based on different classifiers

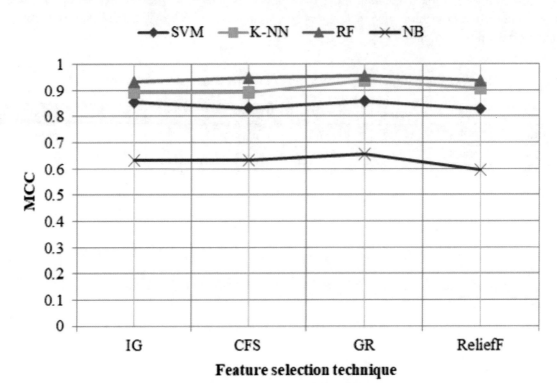

Figure 9 illustrates the comparison of feature selection methods for different classifiers based on MCC. It demonstrates that RF gives the highest MCC of 0.955 for the GR feature selection method.

CONCLUSION AND FUTURE WORK

This chapter presented a comparative study of various feature selection methods and machine learning algorithms for Android malware detection and classification. Different static features like command strings, permissions, intents and API calls are extracted using static malware analysis to carry out a comparative analysis. From the experimental results, it is found that with all feature selection methods, RF performed better than all other machine learning algorithms for Android malware detection. Further, it is concluded that the GR feature selection technique is best suited to our dataset for selecting the appropriate feature set. The GR feature selection technique along with RF provides the highest accuracy of 97.74% for Android malware detection. The presented method described here could potentially be used in the future to construct an Android malware detection tool that addresses the constraints of the mobile device environment, particularly in terms of memory, storage and power consumption. Furthermore, we will focus on the detection of Android apps using big data tools and deep learning techniques.

REFERENCES

Alazab, M. (2020). Automated malware detection in mobile app stores based on robust feature generation. *Electronics (Basel)*, *9*(3), 435. doi:10.3390/electronics9030435

Android Developers. (2011). *What is Android?* Author.

APKMirror. (2019). https://www.apkmirror.com/

Apkpure. (2019). https://apkpure.com/

Aslan, Ö. A., & Samet, R. (2020). A comprehensive review on malware detection approaches. *IEEE Access: Practical Innovations, Open Solutions*, *8*, 6249–6271. doi:10.1109/ACCESS.2019.2963724

Avira. (2019). https://www.avira.com/

AXMLPrinter2. (2019). https://code.google.com/archive/p/android4me/downloads

Barrera, D., Kayacik, H. G., Van Oorschot, P. C., & Somayaji, A. (2010). A methodology for empirical analysis of permission-based security models and its application to android. In *Proceedings of the 17th ACM conference on Computer and communications security* (pp. 73-84). 10.1145/1866307.1866317

Chizi, B., & Maimon, O. (2009). Dimension reduction and feature selection. In *Data mining and knowledge discovery handbook* (pp. 83–100). Springer. doi:10.1007/978-0-387-09823-4_5

Coronado-De-Alba, L. D., Rodríguez-Mota, A., & Escamilla-Ambrosio, P. J. (2016). Feature selection and ensemble of classifiers for Android malware detection. In *2016 8th IEEE Latin-American Conference on Communications (LATINCOM)* (pp. 1-6). IEEE. 10.1109/LATINCOM.2016.7811605

Deepa, K., Radhamani, G., & Vinod, P. (2015). Investigation of feature selection methods for android malware analysis. *Procedia Computer Science*, *46*, 841–848. doi:10.1016/j.procs.2015.02.153

Dhalaria, M., & Gandotra, E. (2020a). Android malware detection using chi-square feature selection and ensemble learning method. In *2020 Sixth International Conference on Parallel, Distributed and Grid Computing (PDGC)* (pp. 36-41). IEEE. 10.1109/PDGC50313.2020.9315818

Dhalaria, M., & Gandotra, E. (2020b). A framework for detection of android malware using static features. In *2020 IEEE 17th India Council International Conference (INDICON)* (pp. 1-7). IEEE. 10.1109/INDICON49873.2020.9342511

Dhalaria, M., & Gandotra, E. (2021a). Android malware detection techniques: A literature review. *Recent Patents on Engineering*, *15*(2), 225–245. doi:10.2174/1872212114999200710143847

Dhalaria, M., & Gandotra, E. (2021b). CSForest: An approach for imbalanced family classification of android malicious applications. *International Journal of Information Technology*, *13*(3), 1059–1071. doi:10.100741870-021-00661-7

Dhalaria, M., & Gandotra, E. (2021c). *A hybrid approach for android malware detection and family classification*. Academic Press.

Dhalaria, M., & Gandotra, E. (2022). Risk Detection of Android Applications Using Static Permissions. In *Advances in Data Computing, Communication and Security* (pp. 591–600). Springer. doi:10.1007/978-981-16-8403-6_54

Dhalaria, M., Gandotra, E., & Saha, S. (2019). Comparative analysis of ensemble methods for classification of android malicious applications. In *International Conference on Advances in Computing and Data Sciences* (pp. 370-380). Springer. 10.1007/978-981-13-9939-8_33

Domingos, P., & Pazzani, M. (1997). On the optimality of the simple Bayesian classifier under zero-one loss. *Machine Learning*, *29*(2), 103–130. doi:10.1023/A:1007413511361

Du, Y., Wang, X., & Wang, J. (2015). A static Android malicious code detection method based on multi-source fusion. *Security and Communication Networks*, *8*(17), 3238–3246. doi:10.1002ec.1248

Enck, W., Octeau, D., McDaniel, P. D., & Chaudhuri, S. (2011). A study of android application security. In USENIX security symposium (Vol. 2, No. 2). USENIX.

Gandotra, E., Bansal, D., & Sofat, S. (2014). Malware analysis and classification: A survey. *Journal of Information Security*.

Gandotra, E., Bansal, D., & Sofat, S. (2016a). Zero-day malware detection. In *2016 Sixth international symposium on embedded computing and system design (ISED)* (pp. 171-175). IEEE. 10.1109/ISED.2016.7977076

Gandotra, E., Bansal, D., & Sofat, S. (2016b). Tools & techniques for malware analysis and classification. *International Journal of Next-Generation Computing*, 176-197.

Ghosh, U., Alazab, M., Bashir, A. K., & Pathan, A. S. K. (Eds.). (2021). *Deep Learning for Internet of Things Infrastructure*. CRC Press. doi:10.1201/9781003032175

Gupta, D., & Rani, R. (2018). Big data framework for zero-day malware detection. *Cybernetics and Systems*, *49*(2), 103–121. doi:10.1080/01969722.2018.1429835

Gupta, D., & Rani, R. (2020). Improving malware detection using big data and ensemble learning. *Computers & Electrical Engineering*, *86*, 106729. doi:10.1016/j.compeleceng.2020.106729

Hall, M. A. (2000). *Correlation-based feature selection of discrete and numeric class machine learning*. Academic Press.

Han, J., Pei, J., & Tong, H. (2022). *Data mining: concepts and techniques*. Morgan Kaufmann.

Keerthi, S. S., & Gilbert, E. G. (2002). Convergence of a generalized SMO algorithm for SVM classifier design. *Machine Learning*, *46*(1), 351–360. doi:10.1023/A:1012431217818

Kim, T., Kang, B., Rho, M., Sezer, S., & Im, E. G. (2018). A multimodal deep learning method for android malware detection using various features. *IEEE Transactions on Information Forensics and Security*, *14*(3), 773–788. doi:10.1109/TIFS.2018.2866319

Kouliaridis, V., Barmpatsalou, K., Kambourakis, G., & Chen, S. (2020). A survey on mobile malware detection techniques. *IEICE Transactions on Information and Systems*, *103*(2), 204–211. doi:10.1587/transinf.2019INI0003

Liaw, A., & Wiener, M. (2002). Classification and regression by randomForest. *R News*, *2*(3), 18–22.

Liu, T., Liu, S., Chen, Z., & Ma, W. Y. (2003). An evaluation on feature selection for text clustering. In *Proceedings of the 20th international conference on machine learning (ICML-03)* (pp. 488-495). Academic Press.

McAfee Labs. (2020). *Threat Predictions Report*. McAfee Labs.

Memon, A. M., & Anwar, A. (2015). Colluding apps: Tomorrow's mobile malware threat. *IEEE Security and Privacy*, *13*(6), 77–81. doi:10.1109/MSP.2015.143

Peiravian, N., & Zhu, X. (2013). Machine learning for android malware detection using permission and api calls. In *2013 IEEE 25th international conference on tools with artificial intelligence* (pp. 300-305). IEEE. 10.1109/ICTAI.2013.53

Rajasoundaran, S., Prabu, A. V., Routray, S., Kumar, S. S., Malla, P. P., Maloji, S., & Ghosh, U. (2021). Machine learning based deep job exploration and secure transactions in virtual private cloud systems. *Computers & Security*, *109*, 102379. doi:10.1016/j.cose.2021.102379

Rawat, S., Srinivasan, A., Ravi, V., & Ghosh, U. (2022). Intrusion detection systems using classical machine learning techniques vs integrated unsupervised feature learning and deep neural network. *Internet Technology Letters*, *5*(1), e232. doi:10.1002/itl2.232

Robnik-Šikonja, M., & Kononenko, I. (2003). Theoretical and empirical analysis of ReliefF and RReliefF. *Machine Learning*, *53*(1), 23–69. doi:10.1023/A:1025667309714

Shakhnarovich, G., Darrell, T., & Indyk, P. (2006). *Nearest-neighbor methods in learning and vision: theory and practice*. Neural Information, Processing. doi:10.7551/mitpress/4908.001.0001

Sheen, S., Anitha, R., & Natarajan, V. (2015). Android based malware detection using a multifeature collaborative decision fusion approach. *Neurocomputing*, *151*, 905–912. doi:10.1016/j.neucom.2014.10.004

Singla, S., Gandotra, E., Bansal, D., & Sofat, S. (2015). Detecting and classifying morphed malwares: A survey. *International Journal of Computers and Applications*, *122*(10).

Statista: Mobile operating systems market share. (2020). https://www.statista.com/statistics/272698/global-market-sha re-held-by-mobile-operating-systems-since-2009/

Talha, K. A., Alper, D. I., & Aydin, C. (2015). APK Auditor: Permission-based Android malware detection system. *Digital Investigation*, *13*, 1–14. doi:10.1016/j.diin.2015.01.001

Virusshare. (2019). https://virusshare.com/

Wang, W., Wang, X., Feng, D., Liu, J., Han, Z., & Zhang, X. (2014). Exploring permission-induced risk in android applications for malicious application detection. *IEEE Transactions on Information Forensics and Security*, *9*(11), 1869–1882. doi:10.1109/TIFS.2014.2353996

Yerima, S. Y., Sezer, S., & Muttik, I. (2015). High accuracy android malware detection using ensemble learning. *IET Information Security*, *9*(6), 313–320. doi:10.1049/iet-ifs.2014.0099

Zhao, K., Zhang, D., Su, X., & Li, W. (2015). *Fest: A feature extraction and selection tool for Android malware detection. In 2015 IEEE symposium on computers and communication (ISCC)*. IEEE.

Chapter 14
Applications of Internet of Things With Deep Learning

Jyoti R. Munavalli

(iD) https://orcid.org/0000-0002-0811-1499

BNM Institute of Technology, Visvesvaraya Technological University, India

Bindu S.

BNM Institute of Technology, Visvesvaraya Technological University, India

Yasha Jyothi M. Shirur

(iD) https://orcid.org/0000-0001-8966-1312

BNM Institute of Technology, Visvesvaraya Technological University, India

ABSTRACT

In recent times, it is observed that many technologies converge to result into efficient systems. Among others, internet of things has wide applications. IoT is a collective network of devices that collect data, compute, communicate, and act accordingly. The data surge has resulted in various kinds of data analytics for which machine learning and deep learning are extensively used. IoT collects data in real time and processes this data. Deep learning mechanism has a potential to make IoT systems efficient. The deep learning in IoT is the disruptive innovation that leads to various smart things. This chapter highlights the prominent applications in which deep learning has blended with IoT and discusses the applications like smart cities, smart homes, smart farms, smart supply chain management, and smart healthcare. The chapter concludes with a discussion on the challenges and limitations of the IoT infrastructure.

INTRODUCTION

Internet of Things (IoT) is a very popular and an efficient technology that connects the world together. It connects the physical world to the digital world. The recent evolution or innovations have seen different disruptive technologies like Artificial Intelligence (AI) playing a prominent role in the well-being of humans as well as in the future of mankind.

DOI: 10.4018/978-1-6684-6275-1.ch014

Industry 4.0 has given the necessary push to the process advancements that are needed in industries to work better or more efficiently. There is an interconnection between additive manufacturing, cloud computing, cyber security, big data analytics, autonomous robots, IoT, Artificial Intelligence and Augmented Reality. When all these are well connected, it results in today's much expected digital transformation. The massive growth in big data has fueled the rise in the number of IoT applications.

Machine learning is a field that helps the machine/models to learn from previous data. To learn, the models require huge data. Machine learning helps to extract the features and classify the output based on the understanding of the user. There are certain minute features that might be overseen to include in the machine learning model. So, a deep learning model extracts all the possible features and classifies based on those multiple features, thus improving the accuracy of classification. Whether machine learning or deep learning, both require huge data sets as inputs.

Smart systems are standalone systems that combine data sensing and actuation to analyze a situation and help to take informed decisions. Figure 1 shows the relation between the IoT and deep learning. The IoT devices like types of sensors and edge devices generate huge amount of data continuously in real time. This data forms the input to deep learning models. The more the data is made available by IoT devices, the accurate the recognition, prediction and image retrieval is offered by deep learning models. This provides valuable insights for decision making in business. As stated, IoT and DL are vital technological trends in the recent time (Saleem and Chishti 2021).

Figure 1. Relation between IoT and Deep Learning

Different deep learning architectures like Convolutional Neural Network (CNN), Recurrent Neural Network (RNN), Auto-Encoder (AE), Generative Adversarial Network (GAN), Restricted Boltzmann Machine (RBM) and Deep Belief Network (DBN) are used in IoT applications. CNNs can classify, detect and predict images and text data and are used in image recognition tasks. CNN detects important features from data without manual intervention. RNN is used in applications that are based on time-series problems, prediction problems, image description generation, etc. RNNs are the only networks that have internal memory because of which it can store records and identify pattern in it. AEs are unsupervised learning techniques that are trained to eliminate noise from signals and these are used in image compression and denoising. GANs are used in video prediction, generating image datasets, human faces. Cartoon characters, 3D object generation etc. RBMs help in reduction of dimensionality, classification and regression.

These are used for recommendation engines, pattern recognition and radar target recognition. DBNs are used in applications where CNN are used like recognition of images and speech, sequences of videos and data on mocap. DBN are computationally less costly (Saleem and Chishti 2021).

In this chapter, we focus on IoT applications where deep learning techniques are used. We highlight the way, IoT and deep learning together are shaping the future of mankind. We discuss the applications like smart cities, smart homes, smart farming, smart supply chain management and smart healthcare. We conclude with the challenges faced in IoT.

SMART CITIES

According to Statistics, 56.61% of the world's population will live in urban areas and it's predicted that it will increase by 68% by 2050. The statistics also reveal that more than 90% of the world's urban population growth will occur in Asia and Africa between 2021 and 2050. This unbelievable increase in population growth will lead to multiple problems in urban areas to which the solution is a smart city enabled by IoT. A smart city is a collection of billions of smart devices that senses, collects or gathers and transmit information over a network spread across a wide city. To ease out the livelihood of the people living in urban areas, these smart devices share data and coordinate accordingly. To promote development in the economic, infrastructure and environment, the solutions must focus on developing the cities of the future that optimize the public assets digitally. Figure 2 shows the areas where the IoT solutions are provided to build smart cities:

Figure 2. IoT Solutions provided to Build Smart Cities

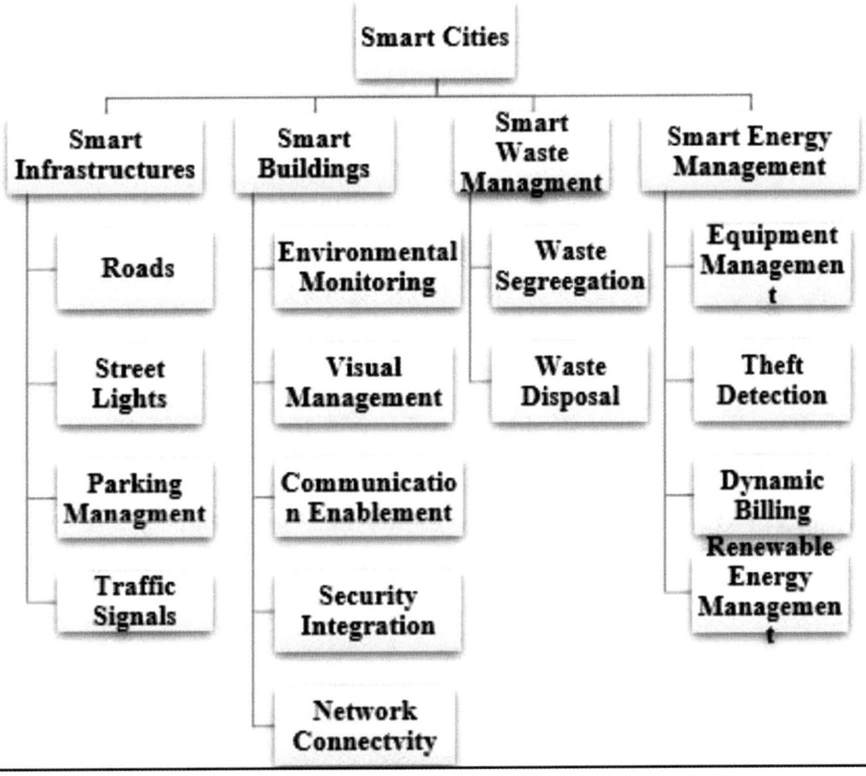

In smart cities, usage of deep learning methods finds importance in multiple areas. Nowadays it is used to detect violent and dangerous situations, suicide prevention in public places, crowd disaster avoidance, automated weapons, it also finds major role in traffic monitoring to detect the rule violations, roadside surveillance and vacant parking lot. In recent days when infectious disease Covid-19 caused by the SARS-CoV-2 virus hit the global the deep learning is also used to find the social distance and mask detection.

SMART INFRASTRUCTURE

Smart Roads

The advancement and development in the smart roads' technology demand zero percent fatality due to road accidents and provide efficient transport with added advantages. Smart roads are built considering multiple aspects such as energy harvesting (Papagiannakis, Dessouky et al. 2016, Toh Chai K. 2020), the automatic weighting of the loads carried by vehicles (Toh Chai K. 2020), smart interaction between moving vehicles to ease the traffic conditions (Guerrieri 2021), smart street light enabled roads (Dizon and Pranggono 2022), fast emergency rescue equipped roads and vehicle speed monitoring system (Yan, Wang et al. 2021). The incorporation of these features enables smart transportation which ultimately leads to the development of smart cities. These kinds of roads will support the safe mobility of mankind and also produce electricity that could be used to light up the streetlights at night. The applications built on IoT, Artificial Intelligence and Machine Learning encourages the smart roads to work in the required manner and transform society to live in a better environment.

Smart Lights

Smart lights may be used in multiple places to ensure proper lighting based on the requirement to ease out the operations carried out at that place. Smart lights are used on roads as streetlights, at home, at warehouses, at railway stations, bus stations and where ever the crowd is available (Kumar, Raut et al. 2022). The smart lights have to work in multiple scenarios, they can either be turned ON or OFF based on the sunlight intensity. These lights operate smartly and change their intensity depending on the number of people present inside the room or premises (Amirkhani, Garcia-Hansen et al. 2017).

Smart Parking Management

Urban areas are witnessing an increase in the number of vehicles and at the same time there is scarcity of space. This issue needs to be addressed and the way to overcome this problem is through smart parking, an IoT based solution. Many researchers and companies are coming up with multiple solutions to address this issue. The solution provided should be easy for anyone to use and preferably cost effective. Additionally, it should have the features like showing the location of the empty parking space and help to locate the vehicle when the owner of the vehicle is back. Automation of bill generation avoids human intervention and people can get away with the problem and nuisance of waiting period for billing. If the developed prototypes incorporate the capability of Artificial Intelligence and Machine Learning in studying the pattern of the parking system, then it will enhance the features of the product. This solution not only provides easy parking in places with a huge crowd but also saves time for vehicle owners and drivers. At the same time, it is possible to reduce fuel consumption and avoid unnecessary emission of poisonous carbon monoxide gas that affects the breathing of the human being in the crowded area especially in the market place and shopping malls (Assim and Al-Omary 2020, Saleem, Siddiqui et al. 2020).

Smart Traffic Signals

A lot of research work has been carried out on the optimization of traffic signals. The efficient usage of traffic signals will always have a major role in the smooth transportation of passengers and goods from one place to another place. Traffic signals enabled with IoT and Artificial Intelligence provide a better solution for monitoring real time traffic and changing the signals dynamically based on the real time conditions of the roads and the movement of vehicles (Sarrab, Pulparambil et al. 2020). Such adaptive traffic management systems help the ambulances to reach the hospitals or patients during emergency situations thus saving patients' life. The control of the lights may be local or centralized. It is also possible to make it automatic based on the condition of traffic to change the time allocated for each of the roads connected to that traffic signal. Adaptation of the suggested techniques makes better management of the vehicle on the roads.

SMART BUILDINGS

The building will be considered as smart when it is automated and make life easy for the person or people who live in it. Nowadays, most of malls, hospitals, educational institutes, corporate offices and apartments are automated for monitoring multiple parameters and send alerts to the concerned persons or a team in advance, so that the appropriate measures can be taken to overcome the damages caused in the later stage due to unawareness. The buildings are considered to be smart if it is possible to measure the crucial or critical parameters. The components used to measure the parameters are as shown in Figure 3.

Figure 3. Critical Components in IoT enabled Smart Buildings

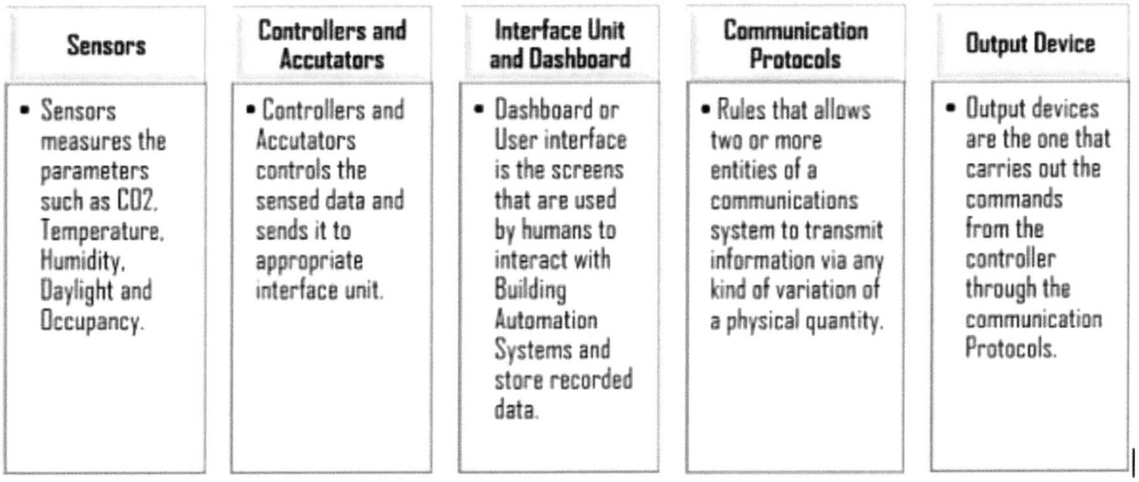

Sensors	Controllers and Accutators	Interface Unit and Dashboard	Communication Protocols	Output Device
• Sensors measures the parameters such as CO2, Temperature, Humidity, Daylight and Occupancy.	• Controllers and Accutators controls the sensed data and sends it to appropriate interface unit.	• Dashboard or User interface is the screens that are used by humans to interact with Building Automation Systems and store recorded data.	• Rules that allows two or more entities of a communications system to transmit information via any kind of variation of a physical quantity.	• Output devices are the one that carries out the commands from the controller through the communication Protocols.

The important five senses of an intelligent building need to be considered for designing a smart and intelligent buildings and this is depicted in Figure 4.

Figure 4. Five Senses of Smart and Intelligent Building

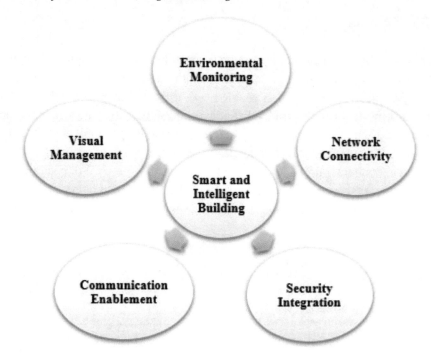

Environmental Monitoring

Environmental monitoring in the smart buildings is a continuous process which demands accurate values in order to take the necessary measures to overcome the issues related to parameters crossing their maximum or minimum limits. There are multiple methods available in the literature, and a spatial correlation of data analysis using the Gaussian Process is one of the techniques. In this process, it is possible to simulate the required environment in Berkeley Lab and observed that the results obtained are very impressive (Zhang, Duan et al. 2019). The other technique used is sensing the parameters are statistically modelled by spatio-temporal non-parametric Gaussian processes to provide humans more comfort and control energy consumption efficiently, multiple other techniques are explored by the researchers and compared with the existing technique to improve the performance of the monitoring system (Nguyen, Hu et al. 2017).

Visual Management

Visual Management is the most important factor in smart building design. It provides information about the intruder by continuously monitoring the surveillance area. The high-resolution cameras have to be placed in a position where the visibility of the required area is maximum. For providing a sufficient amount of information reasonable numbers of cameras need to be placed. After capturing the images and videos, five stages of processing are carried out as shown in Figure 5. This will help to monitor the building and overcome issues related to theft and illegal activities carried out in common places of the building premises.

Figure 5. Stages of Visual management in IoT enabled Smart Building

Network Connectivity and Communication Enablement

Network Connectivity is another important term which is essential in intelligent building design. It poses multiple challenges, since the communication is heterogenous in nature and needs a proper solution for better connectivity between the devices in IoT. Figure 6 shows the communication network connectivity available in the IoT system used on the smart building for better communication between the devices existing in the system.

Figure 6. Connectivity between the IoT Enabled Devices

- PLC – Power Line Communication
- PoE – Power over Ethernet
- RFID – Radio-Frequency Identification
- NFC – Near-Field Communication
- BLE - Bluetooth Low-Energy

- IPv6 – Internet Protocol Version 6
- 6LoWPAN – IPv6 over Low power Wireless Personal Area Network
- CoAP – Radio-Frequency Identification
- MQTT – Message Queuing Telemetry Transport

Security Integration

The smart and intelligent building integrated with multiple devices is vulnerable to multiple threats. All the devices have to be protected with proper security when used in buildings where the maintenance of data confidentiality is very high. There are multiple techniques available in the literature which are integrated with the design to provide the necessary security. The techniques which are implemented and tested in some of the buildings are "Building Energy management Open-Source Software (BEMOSS)" and "SAFIR: Secure access framework for IoT-enabled services" (Hernández-Ramos, Moreno et al. 2015, Rathinavel, Pipattanasomporn et al. 2017). In smart building constructions, machine learning is used in specific phases of building's life-cycle. The energy efficiency can be improved by integrating adaptability solutions provided by the researcher at the HVAC control and electricity usage (Alanne and Sierla 2022).

SMART WASTE MANAGEMENT

The population growth in urban areas is increasing exponentially as a result there is a huge generation of waste like dry waste, wet waste, medical waste and electronic waste. Waste management is one of the critical parameters considered in smart cities since segregation and disposal of waste is a major concern to keep the urban areas neat and hygienic. The classification of waste can be made on the basis of matter (Solid, Liquid and Air Emissions), degrading feature (Bio-degradable and non-Biodegradable), environmental impact (Hazardous and Non-Hazardous) and source of generation (Household, Industrial, Radioactive, Electronic, Medical and Nuclear).

In literature, mutiple techniques are available for segregation of wastes like wet waste, dry waste and metallic waste. These techniques make use of sensors and aurdino controller with conveyor belt without the interference of human effort (T. S. Arulananth 2021). But this type is not sufficient for complex waste segregation, the smart technology involvement in this makes the job much easier. The researchers are working on cloud based waste segregation, which is considered as one of the recent techniques used (Aazam, St-Hilaire et al. 2016). For better management of the waste, along with the segregation, proper measure from the authoritive agency has to be taken for the disposal of it. The organic waste generated can be used for agriculture farming which avoids the use of hazardous chemical fertilizers.

Smart Energy Management

It involves efficient energy production and distribution. The factors like renewable energy management, dynamic billing, equipment management and theft detection make it smart and intelligent. There are multiple sources of energy generation which involve hydroelectricity power, geothermal energy, solar energy, wind energy, hydrogen energy, fossil fuel energy, tidal energy, wave energy, biomass energy and nuclear power. It is the right time to concentrate on renewable energy, since energy consumption is not matching with energy generation. Unless energy is generated using different methods and used smartly for various applications, it will become difficult to balance between the generation and usage of it.

The Government is also encouraging this activity by giving subsidies to the people who are installing solar panels on their building to generate the solar energy. If generated energy is excess then through power grid lines it can be also returned to the electricity board for which they will get the amount based on the units returned.

The dynamic billing and payment gateway enabled by the electricity board makes the usage much easier for the customers. Multiple techniques are used to detect energy theft out of which energy auditing and regular meter testing has helped to reduce this activity to certain extent. The Green energy management is the best solution for energy management, it will be supported by intelligence system to operate the smart grids, homes and industries. It works efficiently with edge computing devices which are based on real-time energy management via server supervisor based on cloud data (Han, Muhammad et al. 2021). In order to make human life easier most of the jobs are performed automatically. The automatic system will be composed of multiple electrical and electronic gadgets to support the recent technology due to which there will be heavy demand of the energy. There are multiple deep learning algorithms or methods used by the system to predict the electricity consumption, to name few are re-current neural network (RNN), Long term memory (LSTM) and gated recurrent unit (GRU). To increase the prediction accuracy, hyperparameter tuning is preferred one (Palak, Revati et al. 2021).

Smart Homes

Home automation refers to Domotics, derived from Latin "Domus" meaning home. This intends to add security and comfort to the owners by providing the flexibility of controlling the devices using smartphones or other interfaces (Gurjar 2017). Several generations have evolved and the latest technological advancements in home automation are the Zwave protocols used for device-to-device communication and ZigBee wireless network protocols is a low power standard used in IoT networks which operate on the IEEE 802.15. 4 standards also in unlicensed bands operating in 2.4 GHz, 900 MHz, and 868 MHz whereas Z-Wave operate with 908.42 MHz. Z-Wave is prone to interfere with Wi-Fi so it uses a low radio frequency band to avoid interference especially if the home network is operated at 2.4 GHz. Also, it is important to note that a Zigbee operated device will not communicate with Z-Waves operated device and vice versa. Zigbee and Z-Wave signals have the capability to hop around the gadgets at home without the need to have a connection to Wi-Fi however; it can access the internet through the central hub. Zigbee uses the IEEE 802.15.4 standard physical radio specification whereas the Z-Wave can propagate up to 100 meters in the open air. The buildings have a tendency to attenuate the signals which could reduce the range. So, it is preferable to have the Z-Wave device placed approximately every 30 feet apart or even much closer to achieve maximum efficiency. The Z-Wave signal can hop roughly 600 feet, and Z-Wave networks can be linked together for even larger deployments. Home automation is beneficial for several reasons so as to control the home appliances and domestic features by local area network or by remote control. Real-time decision-making provides a framework for using Artificial Intelligence which deals with different intelligent home automation systems and technologies (Tien 2017). A protocol used in smart homes for device-to-device communication with each other can share information and can control functions of the other connected devices but it has to use the same network as that of its central hub. For example, Alexa supports several communication protocols used in home automation devices including Z-Wave and ZigBee.

The next generation uses Artificial Intelligence algorithms to control devices in home automation as in Amazon Echo or the Nest Learning Thermostat. The Amazon Echo connects to the Alexa service which is voice-based intelligent control which responds and acts only when the word 'Alexa" is used. However, the word Alexa could also be replaced with other words as well such as "Amazon", "Echo", "Computer" etc. (Stoops 2002). It has several voice-based controls such as requests for playing the music of choice, programming the wish list or to-do list, and also provides real-time information such as weather forecasting or traffic flows etc. Alexa can only interact with Wi-Fi or with ZigBee in the case of Echo Plus. A compatible hub can connect to all home assistive devices including Google Assistant on smartphones which work with Z-Wave which is similar to Google Home that work on Zigbee as well.

The Nest Learning Thermostat is the first thermostat that learns what temperature a user wants at different times of the day and then builds a schedule accordingly. The Echo Nest work is an intelligent music and data platform that works on text and audio contents of recorded music (Xu, Zeng et al. 2019). The difference is the fact that Alexa is the software, located in Amazon Servers, and the Echo devices are the hardware, which allows to access Alexa, in simple words, Alexa is the virtual assistant that answers any questions you have Then it makes your requests happen. On the other side, the Echo devices, are the official devices Amazon launched. They come as 'Alexa enabled devices', to allow every user free access to Alexa.

The later generation belongs to a class of devices such as robots, addressed as a buddy—robots which are capable of interacting with humans as does Rovio and Rumba. They are the first of its kind robots which can socialize and interact with humans and is capable of protecting family members as well (Richert, Shehadeh et al. 2016). BUDDY provides family assistance such as monitoring the homes, and can interact with smart devices to keep the children occupied and can entertain them. Rovio, a remote-controlled camera on wheels uses Wi-Fi to capture pictures for security purposes. The camera housed on wheels can also be adjusted to different angles which also has been fitted with a microphone, speaker, and LED lights for illumination which can be accessed through a computer or a smart phone from anywhere and can explore home or office with streaming audio and video. While on a holiday trip, Rovio can be programmed to move around the house and take pictures and send it to the owner while Roomba is a vacuum cleaner that can automatically guide itself and move around the house and clean by collecting the dirt.

In general, home automation has a centralized control system that can control electronics, appliances, and security systems (Javale, Mohsin et al. 2013). The basic block diagram of the home automation system is shown in Figure 7. It uses Wi-Fi technology and consists of a web server having a system core to control and monitor the interfacing modules used in homes providing suitable interfaces to sensors and actuators used for home automation. Similar technology could be used for server web-based applications which connected to the internet to provide remote access using a compatible web browser.

Figure 7. Basic block diagram used in home automation system

Need for Automation System

Nowadays, smart homes are preferred for comfort with all the luxury to lead a better quality of life and also provide security against theft and intrusion. Home automation involves having a single controller with monitoring the appliances used for entertainment such as audio, video, and home theatre, for lighting, and for other purposes such as sensing parameters of humidity, temperature, gas, fire detection, etc (El-Basioni, Mohamed et al. 2014) and for security and emergency systems. They highlight the need for automation of domestic appliances as elderly, handicapped patients, and people with disabilities can benefit and become independent to a large extent. Self-management boosts their confidence and avoids them from getting into depression. In fact, the cost of living becomes more economical than supervised medical assistants. The existing control system is difficult to manage and to operate individual remotes specific to the appliance.

An extensive survey was carried out on the increasing elderly population and highlights the need for a smart system for home automation (Navod Neranjan Thilakarathne 2020). They have proposed a wireless system controlled by remote where physical challenged or handicapped and even disabled elderly people can operate the required devices without being in the vicinity of the control point. In this work, a local control is still used along with additional controls supported using XBEE communication transceivers. The system also caters to the needs of the blind person by interfacing with braille keys using customized laser-engraved backlit buttons. A CNN deep learning model which has enhanced security of their houses was reported to detect intruders in the home, especially where handicapped elderly lived (Taiwo, Ezugwu et al. 2022). AI &AR based home automation has become popular nowadays which can detect gas leakage and give an alert with a voice note and also turns ON the exhaust automatically (Natarajan, Saideep et al. 2020).

Smart home control systems are not new but have lacked people's attention. Smart homes for example in the United Kingdom are an integrated technology with services through home networking. They have incorporated communication networks connecting to electrical appliances and services, which can be monitored and controlled remotely. On the other hand, the systems are reliable and consume low power. Some domestic appliances in homes which could be controlled are switching ON or OFF electronic gadgets such as refrigerators, television, washing/cleaning and cooking appliances, as well as appliances such as motors, and pumps (Ranjbar 2012). It can also govern the HVAC (Heating, Ventilation, and Air Conditioning) systems and fans. It also controls lamps by providing control on intensity suiting the ambience for different occasions. It can also control the window blinds and curtains having the capability to block natural light. It can also be used in alert systems detecting smoke, fire, or gas and even controls intrusion devices differentiating pets from intruders. Smart control systems can detect vibrations and predict earthquakes using 3D accelerometer sensors (Sandeep Sony 2019). Smart home automation incorporates low power techniques and also supports solar and wind-based systems to reduce pollution. Smart devices are capable of measuring irregular heartbeats, respiration rate and blood pressure in case of emergency (Tewary, Chakraborty et al. 2016).

The authors in (Taiwo, Ezugwu et al. 2022) have reported a system using Deep Learning Convolutional Neural Networks (DL-CNN) that is used to train and recognize different kinds of voice commands. Speech recognition system controls several electronic devices connected to the system and had 100% success rate in room conditions with background intensity of 24dB (silent).

In another work, the authors reported on an automated system that controls lighting, temperature, multimedia systems, and appliances where IoT is used to connect tocommon infrastructure (Jaihar, Lingayat et al. 2020, Taiwo, Ezugwu et al. 2022). A home automation system controls multiple devices connected to a centralized server. These devices are controlled remotely by a user through a tablet or a mobile application. Smart home systems can also predict future action so as to minimize user interaction based on emotions. Gesture recognition is used in smart homes for interactions. Conventional gesture recognition systems demand dedicated infrastructure such as wearable and other devices leading to high costs for implementation. The authors proposed Free Gesture, a device-free gesture recognition scheme capable of identifying common gestures using deep learning techniques by using Wi-Fi enabled IoT devices. An adaptive deep learning model is used to predict usage of lights (Peng, Li et al. 2020).

Smart homes with modern infrastructure are becoming a mandatory requirement where universal controllers are used to operate several appliances through voice-based commands. The same concept is also extended to Autonomous vehicles which are capable of doing its specific job safe and successfully. Vehicle automation geared up initially with buses and trucks and later on extended to the supermarket for stocking and unloading. Today research towards autonomous vehicles has accelerated and managed to bring autonomous vehicles on roads. All TESLA make products are planning towards the launch of self-driven vehicles equipped with all necessary electronics to provide comfort, safety and security. Autonomous vehicles are embedded with sensors, cameras laser scanners and GPS trackers for systematic control of the vehicle. Overall, autonomous vehicles provide a platform for researchers with multidisciplinary areas to collaborate in research and development.

SMART FARMING

UN Food and Agriculture Organization predicts that the world will need to produce 70% more food in 2050. The decrease in the agricultural lands and depletion of natural resources enables to enhance farm yield as a critical requirement to meet the food requirement. Another major issue that needs to be addressed is agricultural labour in most of the countries has declined and the shifting structure of the agricultural workforce. As a result of this, the adoption of smart farming with internet connectivity finds major role to play and address the issued to the above-mentioned facts to reduce the need for manual labour. IOT solutions majorly concentrate to help the farmers to fill the supply gap by enhancing the better yield of the crop which in-turn increases the profit and as a bonus protects the environment by addressing global warming.

Crop Management

Study based on the climate conditions and nature of the soil will help to understand the type of crop to grow to better yield. The techniques like image processing, data analysis based on the sensors used to monitor the health of the soil and environment will also help for smart agriculture. The nutrients measurement using android on regular basis makes crop management easier for the farmers.

Livestock Management

To enhance the quantity and quality of livestock products, the adoption of livestock technology is extremely important. If this technology is adopted by the farmers, then it helps to protect the health of costumer and the environment and at the same time it increases the profit of the farmer (Guntoro, Hoang et al. 2019).

The deep learning plays an important role in finding the plant disease at the early stage and deficiency in the nutrients, so that it can be taken care to increase the yield by spraying medicines in the affected area or by providing the sufficient nutrients. It will be also helpful to detect the weed, landcover over the period (Ünal 2020).

SMART SUPPLY CHAIN MANAGEMENT (SCM)

Supply chain/Logistics management in real time in any industry is a challenging task. It deals with the flow of goods, raw materials and services between people or places. With most of the things going digital, SCM also upgraded its processes and its flow. The supplies like raw materials, goods and products are tagged with various sensors. These sensors generate a huge amount of data in real time. This data, in turn is used by deep learning models to extract a pattern to take informed decisions or in prediction modeling. The data from IoT devices are generally passed on to the cloud and computed. This results in a latency. Fog devices/computing are used to minimize the latency (Pandit, Mir et al. 2020).

Below are few of the areas in which deep learning is applied to achieve optimized inventory, improved planning and efficiency, and increased service levels.

- Autonomous Planning and scheduling
- Demand and supply management
- Sensing Market situations
- Customer behavior

Task scheduling is an important aspect of SCM that needs to be performed in real time. This requires the computational latency to be low. The authors in (Pandit, Mir et al. 2020) proposed a two-level neural network; the first convolutional layer identifies the possibility of data stream analysis. In the second level, a reinforcement module schedules all the possible tasks thereby reducing the computational latency. The hidden layer in the CNN convolutes the input. Reinforcement learning (RL module) is used to maximize the rewards so that the tasks are scheduled in an optimized way. RL have been used in many Industry 4.0 applications to solve complex optimization problems (Kegyes, Süle et al. 2021).

Along with different kinds of sensors, RFID technology that is also used in IoT is used to improve transportation and distribution. Logistics tracking is the most important aspects of SCM. It helps from manufacturing to delivery of goods while identifying the bottlenecks in the process. The increasing demand has put a lot of pressure on supply chains due to a shortage of resources and workers. The items in the inventory system are tagged with sensors. This offers visibility of the items and can be monitored in real time. Deep learning algorithms are used to make supply chain management efficient. Based on the previous data collected, future inventory is predicted. Inventory management and its optimization using deep learning apply long short-term memory theory where deep inventory management is transformed to time series and then back propagation is applied. It was observed in a study that applying deep learning methods reduced about 25% of inventory cost (Deng and Liu 2021). To maintain efficient inventory in real time, the trends in demand need to be known. So, consumer behavior is tracked based on the data collected from IoT sensors. The behavior is monitored by parameters like shopping experience at various points in the store, biometric data and also facial expressions (Generosi, Ceccacci et al. 2018). Along with retail stores, even retail websites collect and analyze the behavior of customers. The aggregation of data from several IoT devices is used to predict customer requirements. The Internet of Behaviors deals with understanding of the data and promoting new products. Data regarding the consumption timelines and product categories is analyzed. From these statistics, Deep Neural Network models are developed. The rDNN model is an extension of the DNN model that considers unbalanced data effectively. rDNN models reduce training costs and reduce any redundancies in data samples (Javaid, Haleem et al. 2021, Zhang, Wang et al. 2022).

SMART HEALTHCARE

Over the last decade, healthcare services have transitioned from smart healthcare to Intelligent healthcare. The data is collected by the IoT devices like sensors, cameras and actuators and Machine learning and deep learning methods/algorithms are applied for performing data analysis (Bolhasani, Mohseni et al. 2021, Ahamed, Bhatt et al. 2022). The use of Information technology in healthcare has resulted in positive outcomes (Kruse C 2018). Now this aggregated real time patient data through IoT technologies changes healthcare into intelligent healthcare. Healthcare has many facets of IoT applications. Widely, it can be classified into four application sectors.

Figure 8. Sectors of IoT applications in healthcare

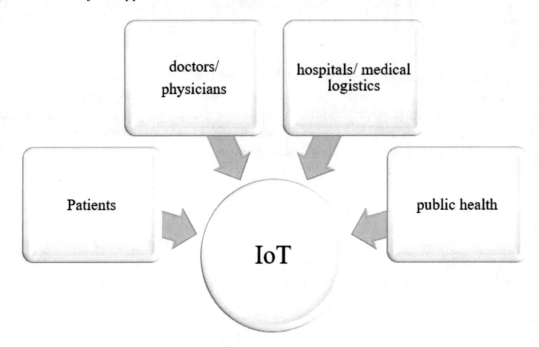

IoT usage has been in different sectors of healthcare (Figure 8) like for patients (Yao, Bi et al. 2018), doctors/ physicians, hospitals, medical logistics and public health/community (Yao, Bi et al. 2018). For patients, there are areas such as assisted healthcare, personalized healthcare, preventive healthcare through wearables and critical care. For hospitals, there are outpatient clinics and data analytics, for doctors/physicians there are imaging and diagnostics. And genomics for public health. Healthcare IoT is also referred to as Medical IoT (M-IoT).

The ageing population requires more health services (Jyoti R. Munavalli 2014). The remote monitoring system reduces the length of hospital stay and also prevents readmissions. This not only reduces hospital cost but also improves treatment outcomes. A deep learning-based monitoring system does not require wearable sensors and vision-based methods instead it uses a camera to capture the body movements continuously in real time and the posture is detected through the captured image. This way of monitoring does not require additional devices on patients rather a camera situated at a distance will do the job effectively with 94% of accuracy. CNN methods are used in extracting the features and data mining techniques for analysis (Ahmed, Jeon et al. 2021).

EHR/EMR – Electronic Health Records/electronic medical records are patient records in digital form. EHR/EMR data were analyzed using statistical models and machine learning algorithms for developing prediction models but currently deep learning provides more insight into the data (Shickel, Tighe et al. 2018, Xiao, Choi et al. 2018, Ayala Solares, Diletta Raimondi et al. 2020). There are tools like Deepr, Deep patient, Med2Vec and Doctor AI that are based on CNN and RNN for extracting more number of features (Caroprese, Veltri et al. 2018). The EMR of patients could be used for extracting a lot of direct information and also decode the patterns, if any. A study extracted two datasets: hypertension, and medical diagnosis and treatment prescription from the EMR using a deep model (modified CNN). It showed that a few unknown concepts/information were revealed about the patients (Liang, Zhang et al. 2014). EMRs when analyzed precisely, help in operations management/control of outpatient clinics like minimizing the cycle time and waiting time, and improving resource utilization (Dachyar and Nattaya 2020, Munavalli, Rao et al. 2020, Munavalli, Boersma et al. 2021). The applications of analytics on EMR data are not only limited to this but it also aides in the layout design of the outpatient clinic (J R Munavalli 2021, Munavalli, Rao et al. 2022).

Medical images like MRI are substantially used in the diagnosis of disease in cardiology, pathology, ophthalmology, dermatology, lungs and respiratory. Deep learning models extract the features and learn automatically. In medical images, CNN is a powerful way to learn images as well as structured data. Various CNN architectures like AlexNet, VGG, ResNet, DenseNet, SENets, YOLO etc are used for deep learning implementation. These methods are implemented in TensorFlow and Keras (Lundervold and Lundervold 2019, Aggarwal, Sounderajah et al. 2021, Esteva, Chou et al. 2021). The classification and segmentation of medical images result in prediction of the disease and its growth. Based on these predictions, the treatment courses are decided to cure the diseases. The fundus camera is used to capture the retina image. Further, image classification using CNN model is performed to detect diabetic retinopathy and glaucoma. The segmentation of medical images, particularly the MRI analysis, shows an early diagnosis of Alzheimer's disease, schizophrenia, Parkinson's syndrome and Dementia. The medical images also reveal the cancers like gastric, breast, skin etc (Cai, Gao et al. 2020). Most recently, the coronavirus (covid-19) detection based on x-ray, CT scan and MRI was done by implementing deep learning techniques. The spread distribution, prediction of infection spread in the community, transmission rate and outbreak prediction were also identified using deep learning architectures (Bhattacharya, Reddy Maddikunta et al. 2021). Proactive healthcare is better than reactive healthcare and IoT aides in developing such systems. Three layers, namely the sensing layer, the analysis layer and the cloud layer were proposed. Temperature sensor, motion and audio sensors, O_2 sensor, heart rate sensor, EEG, ECG and travel history were used in the sensing layer. The analysis layer deployed machine learning models to classify if the patient is covid positive or not. Various health parameters are collected and analyzed through data mining techniques in real time by putting all the collected data on a cloud. To detect the covid-19 suspect in real time, machine learning as well as neural networks were applied. That resulted in 95% accuracy (Mir, Jamwal et al. 2022).

Genomic, a study of genes, predicts, diagnose and provides personalized and precise treatments. Data science concepts are applied to genomics where powerful statistical and computational methods are used to decode hidden information or hidden patterns or unknown correlations in DNA. When genomic data is integrated with EHR, the clinical decision making to select the patient treatment becomes effective (Devi and Rizvi 2020). With the huge kind of data that genomics is involved with, DL methods give much required high computation power and additionally, DL uses data in their raw form (Yusuf Aleshinloye and Steve 2021).

Now a days, people wear smart bands or smart watches (also referred as wearables) that help in monitoring the body vitals in real time. The case study was conducted on an athlete. The wearable devices captured the data such as blood pressure, temperature, heart rate, oxygen levels and many more vitals. These data are sent to the cloud where deep learning methodologies are applied to identify or detect any abnormalities, and early detection of diseases or predictions result in early prevention. Back propagation was implemented for hidden layer of the DNN model. Multiple hidden layers were implemented to improve model accuracy and this results in model complexity, increase in computation cost and overfitting. Principal Component Analysis (PCA) was used for dimensionality reduction and Gradient Descent (GD) algorithm was implemented for optimization (Wu, Liu et al. 2021). These kinds of devices monitor patient fall detection, hearing impairment, sitting, standing, walking, running, Glucose monitoring, heartrate monitoring, hand hygiene monitoring, depression and mood monitoring, and Parkinson's disease monitoring (Hamid, Goyal et al. 2021, Zhang, Li et al. 2022). The real time monitoring of patients helps in predicting the risks of heart failure and its survival chances. The acquired data was classified into alive and deceased and respective features are extracted. These extracted features are compared with new patient data. Based on the trained data, risks of the heart failure is predicted. Multilayer Perceptron (MLP) model was implemented where 13 clinical features were extracted and the study used a batch size of 256 and 25 epochs. The architecture consisted a total of eight layers (1 input-6 hidden-1 output) with sigmoid function. Another model CNN was implemented with total of eight layers (2 convolutional-0.5 dropout value-2 max-pooling-2 dense layers) using ReLU as an activation function. RNN and LSTM were also implemented for heart failure prediction using the same data. CNN predicted with accuracy of 92.8% (Umer, Sadiq et al. 2022). It is interesting to know that the wearables/sensors are mounted on the soldier's uniform and their health is monitored as soldiers work in extreme environmental conditions like desert, mountains, sub-zero degrees and forests (Usharani, Rajmohan et al. 2022).

Figure 9. Wearable workflow

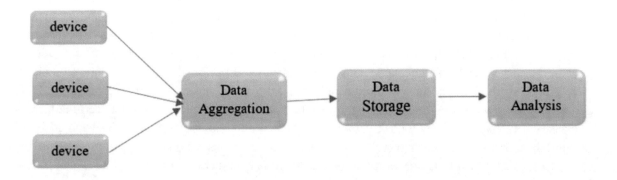

Figure 9 shows the process involved from capturing the data to analysis. All the devices like sensors and actuators capture the data in real time. These data are collected together and are preprocessed means they are integrated and correlation among them is identified. This data is stored in the cloud and later analysis of this data is carried out. Cloud computing means the computing is performed in the cloud where edge and fog computing in IoT is computations are performed in the edge devices (Greco, Percannella et al. 2020).

Deep learning is also applied in managing consumables in ICUs. A CNN architecture is used to classify and recognize the consumables and get it refilled on time. A bot named consumabot, an optical recognition system was developed based on CNN - MobileNet in Tensorflow. The system was trained to identify 20 different materials in ICU (Peine, Hallawa et al. 2019). During emergency situations, most of the time the doctors in the emergency department do not have access to the patient data. The IoT based devices collect the patient vitals in the ambulance and transmit them or the doctor will have access to this data during treatment. This will fasten the treatment process without unnecessary delays (Edoh 2019).

CHALLENGES AND LIMITATIONS

As it is seen, more companies are adopting IoT solutions because of which we see a greater number of devices being connected. The future generation networks require reliable as well as cost effective communication networks. The intelligence that is brought in with deep learning into IoT infrastructure, definitely benefits the stake holders like providers, consumers and users. This offers a lot of opportunities to be explored and solutions to be tapped (Zikria, Afzal et al. 2020).

The amount of data the IoT devices collect is massive and is of a different variety. Data aggregation of a variety of data and their sources is a challenging task. Along with that, the reduction in noise that is either captured while sensing or while transmitting, is another issue that needs to be addressed.

The rate at which the data is been captured and stored requires very good bandwidth. All these are a continuous process and also cost a lot. Connectivity is also a challenge in implementing IoT solutions.

The amount of data either needs to be processed at the edge (devices) or in the cloud that requires lot of computations based on the prediction models that are applied. Powerful computations are required for applying deep learning techniques on IoT networks or data.

Security or privacy is another concern in terms of IoT deployment. As data is captured in all possible forms, contents or permission has to be taken by its owners. Any cyber-attacks on these data intensive networks would result in a compromise in privacy. So additional layer has to be there for encryption that will provide the security for the data in the network (Hussain, Hussain et al. 2020, Yue, Li et al. 2021).

Artificial Neural Network, Convolutional Neural Network, Recurrent Neural Network, Autoencoders are the existing DL architectures (Thilagam, Beno et al. 2022). With further modifications, enhancement of classical models, deep hybrid architecture will improve the capabilities of this methodology and also accuracy. Addressing the challenges and limitations of IoT infrastructure, we see huge potential in IoT networks with deep learning techniques for the future growth.

REFERENCES

Aazam, M., St-Hilaire, M., Lung, C., & Lambadaris, I. (2016). Cloud-based smart waste management for smart cities. *2016 IEEE 21st International Workshop on Computer Aided Modelling and Design of Communication Links and Networks (CAMAD)*, 188-193.

Aggarwal, R., Sounderajah, V., & Martin, G. (2021). Diagnostic accuracy of deep learning in medical imaging: A systematic review and meta-analysis. *NPJ Digit. Med.*, *4*, 65. doi:10.103841746-021-00438-z PMID:33828217

Ahamed, S., Bhatt, P., Sultanuddin, S., Walia, R., Haque, M. A., & Inayath Ahamed, S. B. (2022). An Intelligent IoT enabled Health Care Surveillance using Machine Learning. *2022 International Conference on Advances in Computing, Communication and Applied Informatics (ACCAI)*, 1-5. 10.1109/ACCAI53970.2022.9752648

Ahmed, I., Jeon, G., & Piccialli, F. (2021). A Deep-Learning-Based Smart Healthcare System for Patient's Discomfort Detection at the Edge of Internet of Things. *IEEE Internet of Things Journal*, *8*(13), 10318–10326. doi:10.1109/JIOT.2021.3052067

Amirkhani, M., Garcia-Hansen, V., Isoardi, G., & Allan, A. (2017). An Energy Efficient Lighting Design Strategy to Enhance Visual Comfort in Offices with Windows. *Energies*, *10*(8), 1126. doi:10.3390/en10081126

Arulananth, T. S., Baskar, M., Divya Sree, R., Sai Teja, P., & Santhosh Kumar, T. (2021). Smart garbage segregation for the smart city management systems. *AIP Conference Proceedings*, *2317*, 020044. doi:10.1063/5.0036617

Assim, M., & Al-Omary, A. (2020). A survey of IoT-based smart parking systems in smart cities. *3rd Smart Cities Symposium (SCS 2020)*.

Ayala Solares, J. R., Diletta Raimondi, F. E., Zhu, Y., Rahimian, F., Canoy, D., Tran, J., Pinho Gomes, A. C., Payberah, A. H., Zottoli, M., Nazarzadeh, M., Conrad, N., Rahimi, K., & Salimi-Khorshidi, G. (2020). Deep learning for electronic health records: A comparative review of multiple deep neural architectures. *Journal of Biomedical Informatics*, *101*, 103337. doi:10.1016/j.jbi.2019.103337 PMID:31916973

Benjamin, S., & Patrick, J. (2018). Deep EHR: A Survey of Recent Advances in Deep Learning Techniques for Electronic Health Record (EHR) Analysis. *IEEE Journal of Biomedical and Health Informatics*, *22*(5), 1589–1604. doi:10.1109/JBHI.2017.2767063 PMID:29989977

Bhattacharya, S., Reddy Maddikunta, P. K., Pham, Q. V., Gadekallu, T. R., & Krishnan, S. (2021). Deep learning and medical image processing for coronavirus (COVID-19) pandemic: A survey. *Sustainable Cities and Society*, *65*, 102589. doi:10.1016/j.scs.2020.102589 PMID:33169099

Bolhasani, H., Mohseni, M., & Rahmani, A. M. (2021). Deep learning applications for IoT in health care: A systematic review. *Informatics in Medicine Unlocked*, *23*, 100550. doi:10.1016/j.imu.2021.100550

Cai, L., Gao, J., & Zhao, D. (2020). A review of the application of deep learning in medical image classification and segmentation. *Annals of Translational Medicine*, *8*(11), 713. doi:10.21037/atm.2020.02.44 PMID:32617333

Caroprese, L., Veltri, P., Vocaturo, E., & Zumpano, E. (2018). Deep Learning Techniques for Electronic Health Record Analysis. *9th International Conference on Information, Intelligence, Systems and Applications (IISA)*. 10.1109/IISA.2018.8633647

Dachyar, M., & Nattaya, N. (2020). *Collaborating Internet of Things (IoT) and Electronic Medical Record (EMR) to Reduce Healthcare Waiting time. Outpatient Cardiology Service Case: A BPR Approach*. Atlantis Press. doi:10.2991/aebmr.k.200606.014

Deng, C., & Liu, Y. (2021). A Deep Learning-Based Inventory Management and Demand Prediction Optimization Method for Anomaly Detection. *Wireless Communications and Mobile Computing*, *2021*, 9969357. doi:10.1155/2021/9969357

Devi, G., & Rizvi, S. A. M. (2020). Integration of Genomic Data with EHR Using IoT. *2nd International Conference on Advances in Computing, Communication Control and Networking (ICACCCN).* 10.1109/ICACCCN51052.2020.9362968

Dizon, E., & Pranggono, B. (2022). Smart streetlights in Smart City: A case study of Sheffield. *Journal of Ambient Intelligence and Humanized Computing, 13*(4), 2045–2060. doi:10.100712652-021-02970-y

Edoh, T. O. (2019). *Internet of Things in Emergency Medical Care and Services.* Medical Internet of Things (m-IoT) - Enabling Technologies and Emerging Applications.

El-Basioni, B.M., Mohamed, S., El-kader, A., & Eissa, H.S. (2014). *Independent Living for Persons with Disabilities and Elderly People Using Smart Home Technology.* Academic Press.

Esteva, A., Chou, K., & Yeung, S. (2021). Deep learning-enabled medical computer vision. *NPJ Digit. Med., 4*, 5. doi:10.103841746-020-00376-2 PMID:33420381

Generosi, A., Ceccacci, S., & Mengoni, M. (2018). A deep learning-based system to track and analyze customer behavior in retail store. *2018 IEEE 8th International Conference on Consumer Electronics - Berlin (ICCE-Berlin).*

Greco, L., Percannella, G., Ritrovato, P., Tortorella, F., & Vento, M. (2020). Trends in IoT based solutions for health care: Moving AI to the edge. *Pattern Recognition Letters, 135*, 346–353. doi:10.1016/j.patrec.2020.05.016 PMID:32406416

Guerrieri, M. (2021). Smart Roads Geometric Design Criteria and Capacity Estimation Based on AV and CAV Emerging Technologies. A Case Study in the Trans-European Transport Network. *International Journal of Intelligent Transportation Systems Research, 19*(2), 429–440. doi:10.100713177-021-00255-4

Guntoro, B., Hoang, Q. N., & A'yun, A. Q. (2019). Dynamic Responses of Livestock Farmers to Smart Farming. *IOP Conference Series: Earth and Environmental Science, 372*(1), 012042. 10.1088/1755-1315/372/1/012042

Gurjar, N. N. (2017). Security Sensors for Protection in Smart Homes Using IoT. *International Journal of Advance Research, Ideas and Innovations in Technology, 2*(4).

Hamid, D. S. B. A., Goyal, S. B., & Ghosh, A. (2021). Application of Deep Learning with Wearable IoT in Healthcare Sector. *2021 IEEE 6th International Conference on Computing, Communication and Automation (ICCCA).*

Han, T., Muhammad, K., Hussain, T., Lloret, J., & Baik, S. W. (2021). An Efficient Deep Learning Framework for Intelligent Energy Management in IoT Networks. *IEEE Internet of Things Journal, 8*(5), 3170–3179. doi:10.1109/JIOT.2020.3013306

Hobbs, F., & Stoops, N. (2002). *Demographic Trends in the 20th Century.* United States Census Bureau. CENSR-4. https://www.census.gov/prod/2002pubs/censr-4.pdf

Hussain, F., Hussain, R., Hassan, S. A., & Hossain, E. (2020). Machine Learning in IoT Security: Current Solutions and Future Challenges. *IEEE Communications Surveys and Tutorials, 22*(3), 1686–1721. doi:10.1109/COMST.2020.2986444

Jaihar, J., Lingayat, N., Vijaybhai, P. S., Venkatesh, G., & Upla, K. P. (2020). Smart Home Automation Using Machine Learning Algorithms. *2020 International Conference for Emerging Technology (INCET).* 10.1109/INCET49848.2020.9154007

Javaid, M., Haleem, A., Singh, R. P., Rab, S., & Suman, R. (2021). Internet of Behaviours (IoB) and its role in customer services. *Sensors International, 2,* 100122. doi:10.1016/j.sintl.2021.100122

Javale, D., Mohsin, M., Nandanwar, S. & Shingate, M. (2013). Home automation and security system using Android ADK. *International Journal of Electronics Communication and Computer Technology, 3*(2), 382-385.

Kegyes, T., Süle, Z., & Abonyi, J. (2021). The Applicability of Reinforcement Learning Methods in the Development of Industry 4.0 Applications. *Complexity, 2021,* 7179374. doi:10.1155/2021/7179374

Kruse, C. S. & Beane, A. (2018). Health Information Technology Continues to Show Positive Effect on Medical Outcomes: Systematic Review. *J Med Internet Res 2018, 20*(2).

Kumar, S., Raut, R. D., Priyadarshinee, P., & Narkhede, B. E. (2022). Exploring warehouse management practices for adoption of IoT-blockchain. *Supply Chain Forum: An International Journal,* 1-16. 10.1080/16258312.2022.2082852

Liang, Z., Zhang, G., Huang, J. X., & Hu, Q. V. (2014). Deep learning for healthcare decision making with EMRs. *2014 IEEE International Conference on Bioinformatics and Biomedicine (BIBM).* 10.1109/BIBM.2014.6999219

Lundervold, A. S., & Lundervold, A. (2019). An overview of deep learning in medical imaging focusing on MRI. *Zeitschrift fur Medizinische Physik, 29*(2), 102–127. doi:10.1016/j.zemedi.2018.11.002 PMID:30553609

Mir, M. H., Jamwal, S., Mehbodniya, A., Garg, T., Iqbal, U., & Samori, I. A. (2022). IoT-Enabled Framework for Early Detection and Prediction of COVID-19 Suspects by Leveraging Machine Learning in Cloud. *Journal of Healthcare Engineering, 2022,* 7713939. doi:10.1155/2022/7713939 PMID:35432824

Munavalli, J. R., Merode, F., Rao, S.V., & Srinivas, A. (2014). Healthcare of India: Today and Tomorrow. *International Journal of Innovative Research and Development, 3*(2), 350–356.

Munavalli, J. R., Boersma, H. J., Rao, S. V., & van Merode, G. G. (2021). *Real-Time Capacity Management and Patient Flow Optimization in Hospitals Using AI Methods. Artificial Intelligence and Data Mining in Healthcare.* Springer International Publishing.

Munavalli, J. R., Rao, S. V., Aravind, S., & van Merode, G. G. (2021). Workflow-based Adaptive Layout Design to Improve the Patient Flow in the Outpatient Clinics. *Annals of the Romanian Society for Cell Biology, 25*(3), 8249–8257.

Munavalli, J. R., Rao, S. V., Srinivasan, A., & van Merode, F. (2022). Dynamic Layout Design Optimization to Improve Patient Flow in Outpatient Clinics Using Genetic Algorithms. *Algorithms, 15*(3), 85. doi:10.3390/a15030085

Munavalli, J. R., Rao, S. V., Srinivasan, A., & van Merode, G. G. (2020). An intelligent real-time scheduler for out-patient clinics: A multi-agent system model. *Health Informatics Journal*, 26(4), 2383–2406. doi:10.1177/1460458220905380 PMID:32081068

Natarajan, A., Saideep, A., & Reddy, K. S. (2020). Artificial Intelligence and Augmented Reality driven Home Automation. *2020 International Conference on Electronics and Sustainable Communication Systems (ICESC)*. 10.1109/ICESC48915.2020.9155916

Nguyen, L., Hu, G., & Spanos, C. J. (2017). Spatio-temporal environmental monitoring for smart buildings. *2017 13th IEEE International Conference on Control & Automation (ICCA)*.

Palak, M., Revati, G., & Sheikh, A. (2021). Smart Building Energy Management using Deep Learning Based Predictions. *2021 North American Power Symposium (NAPS)*. 10.1109/NAPS52732.2021.9654262

Pandit, M. K., Mir, R. N., & Chishti, M. A. (2020). Adaptive task scheduling in IoT using reinforcement learning. *Int. J. Intell. Comput. Cybern.*, 13(3), 261–282. doi:10.1108/IJICC-03-2020-0021

Papagiannakis, A. T., Dessouky, S., Montoya, A., & Roshani, H. (2016). Energy Harvesting from Roadways. *Procedia Computer Science*, 83, 758–765. doi:10.1016/j.procs.2016.04.164

Peine, A., Hallawa, A., Schöffski, O., Dartmann, G., Fazlic, L. B., Schmeink, A., Marx, G., & Martin, L. (2019). A Deep Learning Approach for Managing Medical Consumable Materials in Intensive Care Units via Convolutional Neural Networks: Technical Proof-of-Concept Study. *JMIR Medical Informatics*, 7(4), e14806. doi:10.2196/14806 PMID:31603430

Peng, Z., Li, X., & Yan, F. (2020). An Adaptive Deep Learning Model for Smart Home Autonomous System. *2020 International Conference on Intelligent Transportation, Big Data & Smart City (ICITBS)*. 10.1109/ICITBS49701.2020.00156

Ramos, J. L., Cano, M. V., Bernabé, J. B., Carrillo, D. G., & Gómez-Skarmeta, A. F. (2015). SAFIR: Secure access framework for IoT-enabled services on smart buildings. *Journal of Computer and System Sciences*, 81(8), 1452–1463. doi:10.1016/j.jcss.2014.12.021

Ranjbar, M., & Ghanbary, A. (Eds.). (2012). *Implications of ICT for Society and Individual. Technologies for Enhancing Pedagogy, Engagement and Empowerment in Education: Creating Learning-Friendly Environments*. IGI Global.

Rathinavel, K., Pipattanasomporn, M., Kuzlu, M., & Rahman, S. (2017). *Security concerns and countermeasures in IoT-integrated smart buildings. In 2017 IEEE Power & Energy Society Innovative Smart Grid Technologies Conference*. ISGT.

Richert, A., Shehadeh, M. A., Müller, S. L., Schröder, S., & Jeschke, S. (2016). Socializing with robots: Human-robot interactions within a virtual environment. *2016 IEEE Workshop on Advanced Robotics and its Social Impacts (ARSO)*. 10.1109/ARSO.2016.7736255

Saleem, A. A., Siddiqui, H. U. R., Shafique, R., Haider, A., & Ali, M. (2020). A Review on Smart IOT Based Parking System. In R. Ghazali, N. Nawi, M. Deris, & J. Abawajy (Eds.), *Recent Advances on Soft Computing and Data Mining. SCDM 2020. Advances in Intelligent Systems and Computing* (Vol. 978). Springer. doi:10.1007/978-3-030-36056-6_26

Saleem, T. J., & Chishti, M. A. (2021). Deep learning for the internet of things: Potential benefits and use-cases. *Digital Communications and Networks*, 7(4), 526–542. doi:10.1016/j.dcan.2020.12.002

Sony, S., Laventure, S., & Sadhu, A. (2019). A literature review of next-generation smart sensing technology in structural health monitoring. *Structural Control and Health Monitoring*, 26(3), e2321. doi:10.1002tc.2321

Taiwo,O., Ezugwu, A. E., Oyelade, O. N. & Almutairi, M.S. (2022). Enhanced Intelligent Smart Home Control and Security System Based on Deep Learning Model. *Wireless Communications and Mobile Computing*. doi:10.1155/2022/9307961

Tewary, S. (2016). A novel approach towards designing a wearable Smart Health Monitoring System measuring the vital parameters and emergency situations in real-time and providing the necessary medical care through telemedicine. *2016 IEEE Students' Conference on Electrical, Electronics and Computer Science (SCEECS)*, 1-8. doi: 10.1109/SCEECS.2016.7509332

Thilagam, K. (2022) Secure IoT Healthcare Architecture with Deep Learning-Based Access Control System. *Journal of Nanomaterials*. doi:. doi:10.1155/2022/2638613

Thilakarathne, N. N., Kagita, M. K., & Gadekallu, T. R. (2020). The Role of the Internet of Things in Health Care: A Systematic and Comprehensive Study. *International Journal of Engineering and Management Research*, 10(4), 2394–6962. doi:10.31033/ijemr.10.4.22

Tien, J.M. (2017). Internet of Things, Real-Time Decision Making, and Artificial Intelligence. *Ann. Data. Sci.*, 4, 149–178. doi:. doi:10.1007/s40745-017-0112-5

Toh, C. K., Sanguesa, J. A., Cano, J. C., & Martinez, F. J. (2020). Advances in smart roads for future smart cities. *Proceedings. Mathematical, Physical, and Engineering Sciences, 476*(2233), 20190439. doi:. doi:10.1098/rspa.2019.0439

Umer, M., Sadiq, S., Karamti, H., Karamti, W., Majeed, R., & Nappi, M. (2022). IoT Based Smart Monitoring of Patients' with Acute Heart Failure. *Sensors (Basel)*, 22(7), 2431. doi:10.339022072431 PMID:35408045

Unal, Z. (2020). Smart Farming Becomes Even Smarter with Deep Learning—A Bibliographical Analysis. *IEEE Access: Practical Innovations, Open Solutions*, 8, 105587–105609. doi:10.1109/ACCESS.2020.3000175

Usharani, S., Rajmohan, R., Bala, P. M., Saravanan, D., Agalya, P., & Raman, D. R. (2022). Integrated Implementation of Hybrid Deep Learning Models and IoT Sensors for Analyzing Solider Health and Emergency Monitoring. *2022 International Conference on Smart Technologies and Systems for Next Generation Computing (ICSTSN)*, 1-6. 10.1109/ICSTSN53084.2022.9761332

Wu, X., Liu, C., & Wang, L. (2021). *Internet of things-enabled real-time health monitoring system using deep learning. Neural Comput & Applic*. doi:10.100700521-021-06440-6

Xiao, C., Choi, E., & Sun, J. (2018, October 1). Opportunities and challenges in developing deep learning models using electronic health records data: A systematic review. *Journal of the American Medical Informatics Association*, 25(10), 1419–1428. doi:10.1093/jamia/ocy068 PMID:29893864

Xu, R., Zeng, Q., Zhu, L., Chi, H., Du, X., & Guizani, M. (2019). Privacy Leakage in Smart Homes and Its Mitigation: IFTTT as a Case Study. *IEEE Access : Practical Innovations, Open Solutions, 7*, 63457–63471. doi:10.1109/ACCESS.2019.2911202

Yan, L., Wang, P., Yang, J., Hu, Y., Han, Y. & Yao, J. (2021) Refined Path Planning for Emergency Rescue Vehicles on Congested Urban Arterial Roads via Reinforcement Learning Approach. *Journal of Advanced Transportation*. doi:. doi:10.1155/2021/8772688

Yao, Z. J., Bi, J., & Chen, Y. X. (2018). Applying Deep Learning to Individual and Community Health Monitoring Data: A Survey. *Int. J. Autom. Comput., 15*(6), 643–655. doi:10.100711633-018-1136-9

Yue, Y., Li, S., Legg, P. & Li, F. (2021). Deep Learning-Based Security Behaviour Analysis in IoT Environments: A Survey. *Security and Communication Networks*. doi:. doi:10.1155/2021/8873195

Yusuf, A. A., & Adeshina, S. A. (2021). Deep Learning Methodologies for Genomic Data Prediction: Review. *JAIMS, 2*(1-2), 1-11. Available from: http://www.oapublishing-jaims.com/jaims/article/view/61

Zhang, Q., Duan, R., Wang, J., & Cui, Y. (2019). Smart building environment monitoring based on Gaussian Process. *2019 International Conference on Control, Automation and Information Sciences (ICCAIS)*, 1-6. 10.1109/ICCAIS46528.2019.9074549

Zhang, S., Li, Y., Zhang, S., Shahabi, F., Xia, S., Deng, Y., & Alshurafa, N. (2022). Alshurafa N. Deep Learning in Human Activity Recognition with Wearable Sensors: A Review on Advances. *Sensors (Basel), 22*(4), 1476. doi:10.339022041476 PMID:35214377

Zhang, Y., Wang, A. & Hu, W. (2002). Deep Learning-Based Consumer Behavior Analysis and Application Research. *Wireless Communications and Mobile Computing*. doi:. doi:10.1155/2022/4268982

Zikria, Y. B., Afzal, M. K., Kim, S. W., Marin, A., & Guizani, M. (2020). Deep learning for intelligent IoT: Opportunities, challenges and solutions. *Computer Communications, 164*, 50–53. doi:10.1016/j.comcom.2020.08.017

Compilation of References

Barrow, P. (2016). Security in Cloud Computing for Service Delivery Models: Challenges and Solutions. *Int. Journal of Engineering Research and Applications, 6*(4), 76-85. http://www.ijera.com

Han, T., Hao, K., Tang, X. S., Wang, T., & Liu, X. (2022, June). A Compressed Sensing Network for Acquiring Human Pressure Information. *IEEE Transactions on Cognitive and Developmental Systems, 14*(2), 388–402. doi:10.1109/TCDS.2020.3041422

Amazon. (2016). *AWS GovCloud (US) user guide.* Amazon.

Hung, L. L. (2022). Intelligent Sensing for Internet of Things Systems. *Journal of Internet Technology, 23*(1), 185–191.

Intelligence, S. C. B. (2008). National Intelligence Council: Disruptive Technologies Global Trands 2025. *SRI Consulting Business Intelligence*, (Appendix), F-2.

Joung, H.-A., Ballard, Z. S., Wu, J., Tseng, D. K., Teshome, H., Zhang, L., Horn, E. J., Arnaboldi, P. M., Dattwyler, R. J., Garner, O. B., Di Carlo, D., & Ozcan, A. (2020). Point-of-care serodiagnostic test for early-stage Lyme disease using a multiplexed paper-based immunoassay and machine learning. *ACS Nano, 14*(1), 229–240. doi:10.1021/acsnano.9b08151 PMID:31849225

Kanjo, E., Younis, E., & Ang, C. S. (2019). Deep Learning Analysis of Mobile Physiological, Environmental and Location Sensor Data for Emotion Detection. *Information Fusion, 49*, 46–56. doi:10.1016/j.inffus.2018.09.001

Kolias, C., Kambourakis, G., Stavrou, A., & Gritzalis, S. (2015). Intrusion detection in 802.11 networks: Empirical evaluation of threats and a public dataset. *IEEE Communications Surveys and Tutorials, 18*(1), 184–208. doi:10.1109/COMST.2015.2402161

Amazon. (2022). *Amazon AWS lambada function.* Amazon. https://aws.amazon.com/lambda/features/

Koroniotis, N., Moustafa, N., Sitnikova, E., & Turnbull, B. (2019). Towards the development of realistic botnet dataset in the internet of things for network forensic analytics: Bot-iot dataset. *Future Generation Computer Systems, 100*, 779–796. doi:10.1016/j.future.2019.05.041

Maa, L., Liuc, Y., Zhanga, X., Yed, Y., Yind, G., & Johnson, B. A. (2019). Deep learning in remote sensing applications: A meta-analysis and review. *ISPRS Journal of Photogrammetry and Remote Sensing, 152*, 166–177. doi:10.1016/j.isprsjprs.2019.04.015

Li, C., Wang, Y., Zhang, X., Gao, H., Yang, Y., & Wang, J. (2019). Deep Belief Network for Spectral–Spatial Classification of Hyperspectral Remote Sensor Data. *Sensors (Basel), 19*(1), 204. doi:10.339019010204 PMID:30626030

Citrix. (2022). Hybrid cloud. *Citrix.* https://www.citrix.com/en-in/glossary/what-is-hybrid-cloud.html#:~:text=Hybrid%20cloud%20is%20a%20solution,as%20needs%20and%20costs%20fluctuate

Li, D., Yu, R., Song, C., Jia, G., & Zhou, X. (2020) Distributed computing framework of intelligent sensor network for electric power internet of things. *9th Joint International Information Technology and Artificial Intelligence Conference (ITAIC)*, pp. 68-71, 10.1109/ITAIC49862.2020.9338769

Angenent-Mari, N. M., Garruss, A. S., Soenksen, L. R., Church, G., & Collins, J. J. (2020). A deep learning approach to programmable RNA switches. *Nature Communications*, *11*(1), 5057. doi:10.103841467-020-18677-1 PMID:33028812

Litjens, G., Kooi, T., Bejnordi, B. E., Setio, A. A. A., Ciompi, F., Ghafoorian, M., & Sanchez, C. I. (2017). A survey on deep learning in medical image analysis. *Medical Image Analysis*, *42*, 60–88. doi:10.1016/j.media.2017.07.005 PMID:28778026

Ma, X., Yao, T., Hu, M., Dong, Y., Liu, W., Wang, F., & Liu, J. (2019). A Survey on Deep Learning Empowered IoT Applications. *IEEE Access : Practical Innovations, Open Solutions*, *7*, 181721–181732. doi:10.1109/ACCESS.2019.2958962

Al-Fedaghi, S. (n.d.). Experimentation with personal identifiable information. Abdul Aziz Rashid Al-Azmi College of Engineering and Petroleum, Kuwait University.

Manyika, J., Chui, M., Bughin, J., Dobbs, R., Bisson, P., & Marrs, A. (2013). *Disruptive technologies: Advances that will transform life, business, and the global economy,* (Vol. 180). McKinsey Global Institute.

Mekruksavanich, S. (2021). Jitpattanakul,(2019), A. LSTM Networks Using Smartphone Data for Sensor-Based Human Activity Recognition in Smart Homes. *Sensors (Basel)*, *21*, 1636. doi:10.339021051636 PMID:33652697

Best practices for PII compliance in Amazon Connect. (n.d.). https://docs.aws.amazon.com/connect/latest/adminguide/compliance-validation-best-practices-PII.html

Hassan, M., Alam, G. R., Uddin, Z., Huda, S., Almogren, A., & Fortino, G. (2019). Human emotion recognition using deep belief network architecture. *Information Fusion, 51*, 10-18. doi:10.1016/j.inffus.2018.10.00

AWS services in scope by compliance program. (n.d.). https://aws.amazon.com/compliance/services-in-scope/

Moustafa, N., & Slay, J. (2015, November). UNSW-NB15: a comprehensive data set for network intrusion detection systems (UNSW-NB15 network data set). In *military communications and information systems conference (MilCIS)*, (pp. 1-6). IEEE.

Otebolaku A, Enamamu T, Alfoudi A, Ikpehai A, Marchang J, Lee GM,(2020). Deep Sensing: Inertial and Ambient Sensing for Activity Context Recognition Using Deep Convolutional Neural Networks. *Sensors (Basel), 20*(13), 3803. . doi:10.3390/s20133803

Cloud Security tools: CASB, CWPP and CSPM, Use Cases, for cloud security to success at scale, why do you need to use automation? Explained and Explored. (n.d.). https://www.linkedin.com/pulse/cloud-security-tools-casb-cwp-cspmuse-cases-success-praveen/

Qun-Xiong, Z., Kun-Rui, H., Zhong-Sheng, C., Zi-Shu, G., Yuan, X., & Yan-Lin, H.(2021),Novel virtual sample generation using conditional GAN for developing soft sensor with small data. *Engineering Applications of Artificial Intelligence, 106*. doi:10.1016/j.engappai.2021.104497

Ranieri,C,M., MacLeod S., Dragone M., Vargas PA., Romero RAF,.(2021) Activity Recognition for Ambient Assisted Living with Videos, Inertial Units and Ambient Sensors. *Sensors (Basel), 21*(3), 768. . doi:10.3390/s21030768

Şeker. M., Özerdem, M.S. (2019). Autoencoders Based Deep Learning Approach for Focal-Nonfocal EEG Classification Problem. *Innovations in Intelligent Systems and Applications Conference (ASYU),* pp. 1-4, 10.1109/ASYU48272.2019.8946412

Awais, M., Chiari, L., Ihlen, E.A.F., Helbostad, J.L., Palmerini, L.(2021) Classical Machine Learning Versus Deep Learning for the Older Adults Free-Living Activity Classification. doi:10.3390/s21144669

Sah, D. K., Nguyen, T. N., Cengiz, K., Dumba, B., & Kumar, V. (2022). Load-balance scheduling for intelligent sensors deployment in industrial internet of things. *Cluster Computing*, *25*(3), 1715–1727. doi:10.100710586-021-03316-1

Suthaharan, S., Alzahrani, M., Rajasegarar, S., Leckie, C., & Palaniswami, M. (2010, December). Labelled data collection for anomaly detection in wireless sensor networks. In *sixth international conference on intelligent sensors, sensor networks and information processing*, (pp. 269-274). IEEE 10.1109/ISSNIP.2010.5706782

Sharafaldin, I., Lashkari, A. H., & Ghorbani, A. A. (2018). Toward generating a new intrusion detection dataset and intrusion traffic characterization. *ICISSp*, *1*, 108–116. doi:10.5220/0006639801080116

Shaheen, A., Waheed, U. B., Fehler, M., Sokol, L., & Hanafy, S. (2021). GroningenNet(2021), Deep Learning for Low-Magnitude Earthquake Detection on a Multi-Level Sensor Network. *Sensors (Basel)*, *21*(23), 8080. doi:10.339021238080 PMID:34884084

Shi, Q., Zhang, Z., He, T., Sun, Z., Wang, B., Feng, Y., Shan, X., Salam, B., & Lee, C. (2020). Deep learning enabled smart mats as a scalable foor monitoring system. *Nature Communications*, *11*(1), 4609. doi:10.103841467-020-18471-z PMID:32929087

Sivanathan, A., Gharakheili, H. H., Loi, F., Radford, A., Wijenayake, C., Vishwanath, A., & Sivaraman, V. (2018). Classifying IoT devices in smart environments using network traffic characteristics. *IEEE Transactions on Mobile Computing*, *18*(8), 1745–1759. doi:10.1109/TMC.2018.2866249

Namuduri, S., Narayanan, B. N., Venkata, S. P. D., Burton, L., & Bhansali, S. (2020). Review—Deep Learning Methods for Sensor Based Predictive Maintenance and Future Perspectives for Electrochemical Sensors. *Journal of the Electrochemical Society*, *167*(3), 037552. doi:10.1149/1945-7111/ab67a8

Cloud security standards: What to expect and what to negotiate version 2.0. (n.d.). https://www.omg.org/cloud/deliverables/CSCC-Cloud-Security-Standards-What-to-Expect-and-What-to-Negotiate.pdf

Saleem, T. J., & Chishti, M. A. (2021). Deep learning for the internet of things: Potential benefits and use-cases. *Digital Communications and Networks*, *7*(4), 526–542. doi:10.1016/j.dcan.2020.12.002

Tavallaee, M., Bagheri, E., Lu, W., & Ghorbani, A. A. (2009, July). A detailed analysis of the KDD CUP 99 data set. In *symposium on computational intelligence for security and defense applications*, (pp. 1-6). IEEE.

Chinnaiyan, R., & Balachandar, S. (2018a). Reliable digital twin for connected footballer. *Lecture Notes on Data Engineering and Communications Technologies, Springer International conference on Computer Networks and Inventive Communication Technologies (ICCNCT - 2018)*.

Tawsif, K., Nor Azlina Ab. Aziz, J. Emerson Raja, J. Hossen, Jesmeen M. Z. H. (. (2022). A Systematic Thematic Review on Emotion Recognition System Using Physiological Signals. *Data Acquisition and Methodology*. doi:10.28991/ESJ-2022-06-05-017

Awin, F. A., Alginahi, Y. M., Abdel-Raheem, E., & Tepe, K. (2019). Technical issues on cognitive radio-based Internet of Things systems: A survey. *IEEE Access : Practical Innovations, Open Solutions*, *7*, 97887–97908. doi:10.1109/ACCESS.2019.2929915

Chinnaiyan, R., & Balachandar, S. (2018b). Centralized reliability and security management of data in Internet of things (IoT) with rule builder. *Lecture Notes on Data Engineering and Communications Technologies, Springer International conference on Computer Networks and Inventive Communication Technologies (ICCNCT - 2018)*.

Vaccari, I., Orani, V., Paglialonga, A., Cambiaso, E., & Mongelli, M. A. (2021). Generative Adversarial Network (GAN) Technique for Internet of Medical Things Data. *Sensors (Basel), 2021*(21), 3726. doi:10.339021113726 PMID:34071944

Wei, H., Jafari, R., & Kehtarnavaz, N. (2019, August 24). Fusion of Video and Inertial Sensing for Deep Learning-Based Human Action Recognition. *Sensors (Basel), 19*(17), 3680. doi:10.339019173680 PMID:31450609

Yen, C. T., Liao, J. X., & Huang, Y. K. (2021, December 11). Feature Fusion of a Deep-Learning Algorithm into Wearable Sensor Devices for Human Activity Recognition. *Sensors (Basel), 21*(24), 8294. doi:10.339021248294 PMID:34960388

Younis, E., Zaki, S. M., Kanjo, E., & Houssein, E. H. (2022). Evaluating Ensemble Learning Methods for Multi-Modal Emotion Recognition Using Sensor Data Fusion. *Sensors (Basel), 2022*(22), 5611. doi:10.339022155611 PMID:35957167

Ballard, Z., Brown, C., Madni, A. M., & Ozcan, A. (2021). Machine learning and computation-enabled intelligent sensor design. *Nature Machine Intelligence, 3*(7), 556–565. doi:10.103842256-021-00360-9

Chinnaiyan, R. (2022a). Smart vehicle tracking system using Internet of things. *International Journal of Scientific Research in Science and Technology, 9*(2), 351–355.

Chinnaiyan, R. (2022b). Intelligent hospital monitoring system using Internet of things. *International Journal of All Research Education and Scientific Methods, 10*(4).

Balachandar, S., & Chinnaiyan, R. (2018a). A reliable troubleshooting Model for IoT devices with sensors and voice based chatbot application. *International Journal for Research in Applied Science & Engineering Technology.*

Balachandar, S., & Chinnaiyan, R. (n.d.). A reliable agnostic data compression model between edge and cloud IOT platform. *International Journal of Computer Engineering and Applications, 12*(1), 139–143.

Bao, Z., Zhao, J., Huang, P., Yong, S., & Wang, X. (2021, June 28). A Deep Learning-Based Electromagnetic Signal for Earthquake Magnitude Prediction. *Sensors (Basel), 21*(13), 4434. doi:10.339021134434 PMID:34203508

Balachandar, S., & Chinnaiyan, R. (2020). *Reliable admin framework of drones and IOT sensors in agriculture farmstead using blockchain and Smart contracts BDET.* Academic Press.

Balachander, S., & Chinnaiyan, R. (2019). Internet of Things based Agro based Monitoring using Drones with Block Chain. *ICICCS.*

Balachander, S., & Chinnaiyan, R. (2018b). Internet of Things based Reliable Real–Time Disease Monitoring of Poultry Farming Imagery Analytics. ICCBI.

Cao, J., Li, W., Wang, Q., & Yu, M. (2018). A Sensor-Based Human Activity Recognition System via Restricted Boltzmann Machine and Extended Space Forest. In G. Fortino, A. Ali, M. Pathan, A. Guerrieri, & G. Di Fatta (Eds.), Lecture Notes in Computer Science: Vol. 10794. *Internet and Distributed Computing Systems. IDCS 2017.* Springer., doi:10.1007/978-3-319-97795-9_8

Casagrande, F. D., Tørresen, J., & Zouganeli, E. (2018) Sensor Event Prediction using Recurrent Neural Network in Smart Homes for Older Adults. *International Conference on Intelligent Systems (IS),* pp. 662-668, 10.1109/IS.2018.8710467

Chen, F., Deng, P., Wan, J., Zhang, D., Vasilakos, A. V., & Rong, X. (2015). Data mining for the internet of things: Literature review and challenges. *International Journal of Distributed Sensor Networks, 11*(8), 431047. doi:10.1155/2015/431047

Golestani, N., & Moghaddam, M. (2020). Human activity recognition using magnetic induction-based motion signals and deep recurrent neural networks. *Nature Communications, 11*(1), 1551. doi:10.103841467-020-15086-2 PMID:32214095

Hamza, A., Gharakheili, H. H., Benson, T. A., & Sivaraman, V. (2019, April). Detecting volumetric attacks on lot devices via sdn-based monitoring of mud activity. In *Proceedings of the 2019 ACM Symposium on SDN Research,* (pp. 36-48). 10.1145/3314148.3314352

Aazam, M., St-Hilaire, M., Lung, C., & Lambadaris, I. (2016). Cloud-based smart waste management for smart cities. *2016 IEEE 21st International Workshop on Computer Aided Modelling and Design of Communication Links and Networks (CAMAD),* 188-193.

Abdelrazek, S., El-Rashidy, N., El-Sappagh, S., Islam, S. R. M., & El-Bakry, H. (2021). Mobile health in remote patient monitoring for chronic diseases: Principles, trends, and challenges. *Diagnostics (Basel), 11*(4), 607. doi:10.3390/diagnostics11040607 PMID:33805471

Abdou, M., Mohammed, R., Hosny, Z., Essam, M., Zaki, M., Hassan, M., & Mostafa, H. (2019, December). End-to-end crash avoidance deep IoT-based solution. In *31st International Conference on Microelectronics (ICM),* (pp. 103-107). IEEE. 10.1109/ICM48031.2019.9021613

Abdul Rahman, M.G., Gibbins, J.R, & Forrest, A.K. (2004). *Combustion in Power Station Boilers –Advanced Monitoring Using Imaging.* Imperial College of Science, Technology, and Medicine.

Abie, H. (2019, May). Cognitive cybersecurity for CPS-IoT enabled healthcare ecosystems. In *13th International Symposium on Medical Information and Communication Technology (ISMICT),* (pp. 1-6). IEEE.

Aboubakar, M., Kellil, M., & Roux, P. (2021). A review of IoT network management: Current status and perspectives. *Journal of King Saud University-Computer and Information Sciences.*

Abu Alfeilat, H. A., Hassanat, A. B. A., Lasassmeh, O., Tarawneh, A. S., Alhasanat, M. B., Eyal Salman, H. S., & Prasath, V. B. S. (2019). Effects of distance measure choice on k-nearest neighbor Classifier Performance: A Review. *Big Data, 7*(4), 221–248. doi:10.1089/big.2018.0175 PMID:31411491

Aggarwal, R., Sounderajah, V., & Martin, G. (2021). Diagnostic accuracy of deep learning in medical imaging: A systematic review and meta-analysis. *NPJ Digit. Med., 4,* 65. doi:10.103841746-021-00438-z PMID:33828217

Agrawal, M., Kumar Shukla, P., Nair, R., Nayyar, A., & Masud, M. (2022). Stock prediction based on technical indicators using Deep Learning Model. *Computers, Materials & Continua, 70*(1), 287–304. doi:10.32604/cmc.2022.014637

Ahamed, S., Bhatt, P., Sultanuddin, S., Walia, R., Haque, M. A., & Inayath Ahamed, S. B. (2022). An Intelligent IoT enabled Health Care Surveillance using Machine Learning. *2022 International Conference on Advances in Computing, Communication and Applied Informatics (ACCAI),* 1-5. 10.1109/ACCAI53970.2022.9752648

Ahmed, A., & Ahmed, E. (2016). A survey on mobile edge computing. *Proc. 10th Int. Conf. Intell. Syst. Control (ISCO),* 1-8.

Ahmed, I., Jeon, G., & Piccialli, F. (2021). A Deep-Learning-Based Smart Healthcare System for Patient's Discomfort Detection at the Edge of Internet of Things. *IEEE Internet of Things Journal, 8*(13), 10318–10326. doi:10.1109/JIOT.2021.3052067

Aixier. (2022). *K210-yolo3 model.* Retrieved July 27, 2022, from https://github.com/aixier/K210-yolo3

Al-Ali, A. R., Zualkernan, I. A., Rashid, M., Gupta, R., & Alikarar, M. (2017). A smart home energy management system using IoT and big data analytics approach. *IEEE Transactions on Consumer Electronics, 63*(4), 426–434. doi:10.1109/TCE.2017.015014

Alavizadeh, H., Jang-Jaccard, J. (2022), Deep Q-Learning Based inforcement Learning Approach for Network Intrusion Detection. *Computers,* pp.11-41 doi:10.3390/computers11030041

Alazab, M. (2020). Automated malware detection in mobile app stores based on robust feature generation. *Electronics (Basel), 9*(3), 435. doi:10.3390/electronics9030435

Alazab, M., Manogaran, G., & Montenegro-Marin, C. E. (2022). Trust management for internet of things using cloud computing and security in smart cities. *Cluster Computing, 25*(3), 1765–1777. doi:10.100710586-021-03427-9

Alhassan, A. M., & Zainon, W. M. (2021). Brain tumor classification in magnetic resonance image using hard swish-based RELU activation function-convolutional neural network. *Neural Computing & Applications, 33*(15), 9075–9087. doi:10.100700521-020-05671-3

Allam, Z., & Dhunny, Z. A. (2019). On big data, artificial intelligence and smart cities. *Cities (London, England), 89*, 80–91. doi:10.1016/j.cities.2019.01.032

Almusaylim, Z. A., Alhumam, A., & Jhanjhi, N. Z. (2020). Proposing a secure RPL based internet of things routing protocol: A review. *Ad Hoc Networks, 101*, 102096. doi:10.1016/j.adhoc.2020.102096

Al-Turjman, F., Ever, E., Zikria, Y. B., Kim, S. W., & Elmahgoubi, A. (2019). SAHCI: Scheduling approach for heterogeneous content-centric IoT applications. *IEEE Access : Practical Innovations, Open Solutions, 7*, 80342–80349. doi:10.1109/ACCESS.2019.2923203

Alzubaidi, L., Zhang, J., Humaidi, A. J., Al-Dujaili, A., Duan, Y., Al-Shamma, O., Santamaría, J., Fadhel, M. A., Al-Amidie, M., & Farhan, L. (2021). Review of deep learning: Concepts, CNN architectures, challenges, applications, future directions. *Journal of Big Data, 8*(1), 1–74. doi:10.118640537-021-00444-8 PMID:33816053

Amanullah, M. A., Habeeb, R. A. A., Nasaruddin, F. H., Gani, A., Ahmed, E., Nainar, A. S. M., & Imran, M. (2020). Deep learning and big data technologies for IoT security. *Computer Communications, 151*, 495–517. doi:10.1016/j.comcom.2020.01.016

Amirkhani, M., Garcia-Hansen, V., Isoardi, G., & Allan, A. (2017). An Energy Efficient Lighting Design Strategy to Enhance Visual Comfort in Offices with Windows. *Energies, 10*(8), 1126. doi:10.3390/en10081126

Amuthan, N. (2022). *Smart Surveillance System with Facial Recognition and Image-Processing Approach using AI.* 202241013636.

Andrade, R. O., & Yoo, S. G. (2019). Cognitive security: A comprehensive study of cognitive science in cybersecurity. *Journal of Information Security and Applications, 48*, 102352. doi:10.1016/j.jisa.2019.06.008

Android Developers. (2011). *What is Android?* Author.

Ansari, M. S., Bartos, V., & Lee, B. (2022). GRU-based deep learning approach for network alert prediction. *FGCS, 128*, 235–247.

APKMirror. (2019). https://www.apkmirror.com/

Apkpure. (2019). https://apkpure.com/

Ardiansyah, M. N., Kurniasari, M., Amien, M. D., Wijaya, D., & Setialana, P. (2022). Development of Crowd Detection Warning System Based on Deep Convolutional Neural Network using CCTV. *Journal of Engineering and Applied Technology, 3*(1), 35–41. doi:10.21831/jeatech.v3i2.43771

Arulananth, T. S., Baskar, M., Divya Sree, R., Sai Teja, P., & Santhosh Kumar, T. (2021). Smart garbage segregation for the smart city management systems. *AIP Conference Proceedings, 2317*, 020044. doi:10.1063/5.0036617

Aslan, Ö. A., & Samet, R. (2020). A comprehensive review on malware detection approaches. *IEEE Access: Practical Innovations, Open Solutions, 8*, 6249–6271. doi:10.1109/ACCESS.2019.2963724

Assim, M., & Al-Omary, A. (2020). A survey of IoT-based smart parking systems in smart cities. *3rd Smart Cities Symposium (SCS 2020).*

Attallah, O. (2020). An effective mental stress state detection and evaluation system using minimum number of frontal brain electrodes. *Diagnostics (Basel), 10*(5), 292. doi:10.3390/diagnostics10050292 PMID:32397517

Avira. (2019). https://www.avira.com/

AXMLPrinter2. (2019). https://code.google.com/archive/p/android4me/downloads

Ayala Solares, J. R., Diletta Raimondi, F. E., Zhu, Y., Rahimian, F., Canoy, D., Tran, J., Pinho Gomes, A. C., Payberah, A. H., Zottoli, M., Nazarzadeh, M., Conrad, N., Rahimi, K., & Salimi-Khorshidi, G. (2020). Deep learning for electronic health records: A comparative review of multiple deep neural architectures. *Journal of Biomedical Informatics, 101,* 103337. doi:10.1016/j.jbi.2019.103337 PMID:31916973

Ayei, E., Ibor, F. A., Olusoji, B., & Okunoye, O. E. (2020). Conceptualisation of Cyberattack prediction with deep learning. *Cybersecurity, 3,* 14. doi:10.118642400-020-00053-7

Babu, M. H., Vinayakumar, R., & Soman, K. P. (2018), A short review on applications of deep learning for cyber security.

Ballas, C., Marsden, M., Zhang, D., O'Connor, N. E., & Little, S. (2018). Performance of video processing at the edge for crowd-monitoring applications. *Proceedings of IEEE 4th World Forum on Internet of Things (WF-IoT).* 10.1109/WF-IoT.2018.8355170

Barrera, D., Kayacik, H. G., Van Oorschot, P. C., & Somayaji, A. (2010). A methodology for empirical analysis of permission-based security models and its application to android. In *Proceedings of the 17th ACM conference on Computer and communications security* (pp. 73-84). 10.1145/1866307.1866317

Bassoo, V., Ramnarain-Seetohul, V., Hurbungs, V., Fowdur, T. P., & Beeharry, Y. (2018). Big Data Analytics for Smart Cities. In N. Dey, A. Hassanien, C. Bhatt, A. Ashour, & S. Satapathy (Eds.), *Internet of Things and Big Data Analytics Toward Next-Generation Intelligence. Studies in Big Data* (Vol. 30, pp. 359–379). Springer.

Basumallik, S., Ma, R., & Eftekharnejad, S. (2019). *Packet-data anomaly detection in PMU-based state estimator using convolutional neural network. Int. J. Elec- tric.* Power Energy System.

Bawany, N. Z., & Shamsi, J. A. (2015). Smart City Architecture: Vision and Challenges. *International Journal of Advanced Computer Science and Applications, 6*(11), 246–255.

Bekolay, T., Bergstra, J., DeWolf, T., Eliasmith, C., Hunsberger, E., Rasmussen, D., & Stewart, T. C. (2014). Nengo: A Python tool for building large-scale functional brain models. *Frontiers in Neuroinformatics, 7,* 48. doi:10.3389/fninf.2013.00048 PMID:24431999

Benjamin, S., & Patrick, J. (2018). Deep EHR: A Survey of Recent Advances in Deep Learning Techniques for Electronic Health Record (EHR) Analysis. *IEEE Journal of Biomedical and Health Informatics, 22*(5), 1589–1604. doi:10.1109/JBHI.2017.2767063 PMID:29989977

Berbano, A. E. U., Pengson, H. N. V., Prado, S. V., Razon, C. G. V., & Tungcul, K. C. G. (2017, September). Classification of stress into emotional, mental, physical and no stress using electroencephalogram signal analysis. In *2017 IEEE International Conference on Signal and Image Processing Applications (ICSIPA)* (pp. 11-14). IEEE. 10.1109/ICSIPA.2017.8120571

Bezdan, T., & Džakula, N. B. (2019). Convolutional Neural Network Layers and Architectures. In *Proceedings of International Scientific Conference on Information Technology and Data Related Research (SINTEZA 2019)* (pp. 445-451). Academic Press.

Bhattacharya, S., Reddy Maddikunta, P. K., Pham, Q. V., Gadekallu, T. R., & Krishnan, S. (2021). Deep learning and medical image processing for coronavirus (COVID-19) pandemic: A survey. *Sustainable Cities and Society*, *65*, 102589. doi:10.1016/j.scs.2020.102589 PMID:33169099

Bhuvaneswari, T., Hossen, J., Amir Hamzah, N. A., Velrajkumar, P., & Hong Jack, O. (2020). Internet of things (IOT) based Smart Garbage Monitoring System. *Indonesian Journal of Electrical Engineering and Computer Science*, *20*(2), 736. doi:10.11591/ijeecs.v20.i2.pp736-743

Bibani, O., Glitho, R. H., Hadj-Alouane, N. B., Morrow, M. J., Polakos, P. A., Ravindran, P., & Yangui, S., (2016, June). A platform as-a-service for hybrid cloud/fog environments. In *2016 IEEE international symposium on local and metropolitan area networks (LANMAN)* (pp. 1-7). IEEE.

Biswal, B., Biswal, M. K., Dash, P. K., & Mishra, S. (2013). Power quality event characterization using support vector machine and optimization using advanced immune algorithm. *Neurocomputing*, *103*, 75–86. doi:10.1016/j.neucom.2012.08.031

Bochkovskiy, A., Wang, C.-Y., & Liao, H. Y. M. (2020). *YOLOv4: Optimal speed and accuracy of object detection*. Academic Press.

Bolhasani, H., Mohseni, M., & Rahmani, A. M. (2021). Deep learning applications for IoT in health care: A systematic review. *Informatics in Medicine Unlocked*, *23*, 100550. doi:10.1016/j.imu.2021.100550

Bouraya, S., & Belangour, A. (2021). Object Detectors' Convolutional Neural Networks backbones: A review and a comparative study. *International Journal of Emerging Trends in Engineering Research*, *9*(11), 1379–1386. doi:10.30534/ijeter/2021/039112021

Buczak, A. L., & Guven, E. (2016). A survey of data mining and machine learning methods for cyber security intrusion detection. *IEEE Communications Surveys and Tutorials*, *18*(2), 1153–1176. doi:10.1109/COMST.2015.2494502

Cai, L., Gao, J., & Zhao, D. (2020). A review of the application of deep learning in medical image classification and segmentation. *Annals of Translational Medicine*, *8*(11), 713. doi:10.21037/atm.2020.02.44 PMID:32617333

Campesato, O. (2020). *Artificial Intelligence, Machine Learning, and Deep Learning*. Mercury Learning & Information.

Caroprese, L., Veltri, P., Vocaturo, E., & Zumpano, E. (2018). Deep Learning Techniques for Electronic Health Record Analysis. *9th International Conference on Information, Intelligence, Systems and Applications (IISA)*. 10.1109/IISA.2018.8633647

Cecaj, A., Lippi, M., Mamei, M., & Zambonelli, F. (2021). Sensing and Forecasting Crowd Distribution in Smart Cities: Potentials and Approaches. *IoT*, *2*(1), 33–49. doi:10.3390/iot2010003

Cenggoro, T. W. (2019). Deep Learning for Crowd Counting: A Survey. *Jurnal Emacs (Engineering, Mathematics and Computer Science)*, *1*(1), 17-28.

Cesana, M., & Redondi, A. E. C. (2016). IoT Communication Technologies for Smart Cities. In V. Angelakis, E. Tragos, H. C. Pöhls, A. Kapovits, & A. Bassi (Eds.), *Designing, Developing, and Facilitating Smart Cities: Urban Design to IoT Solutions* (pp. 139–162). Springer Cham.

Chen, C., Zhang, P., Zhang, H., Dai, J., Yi, Y., Zhang, H., & Zhang, Y. (2020). Deep Learning on Computational-Resource-Limited Platforms: A Survey. *Mobile Information Systems*, 1-19.

Cheng, R. W., Rong, F. X., Lee, S. J., & Chie, H. L. (2018). Network intrusion detection using equality constrained-optimization-based extreme learning machines. *Knowledge-Based Systems*, *147*, 68–80. doi:10.1016/j.knosys.2018.02.015

Chen, J., Wang, Y., & Wang, X. (2012). On-demand security architecture for cloud computing. *Computer, 45*(7), 73–78. doi:10.1109/MC.2012.120

Chi, J., Owusu, E., & Yin, X. (2018). Privacy partition: a privacy preserving framework for deep neural networks in edge networks. *Proceedings of the IEEE/ACM Symposium on Edge Computing (SEC),* 378–380. 10.1109/SEC.2018.00049

Chizi, B., & Maimon, O. (2009). Dimension reduction and feature selection. In *Data mining and knowledge discovery handbook* (pp. 83–100). Springer. doi:10.1007/978-0-387-09823-4_5

Cho, A., Lee, H., Whang, M., & Lee, S. (2019). Vision-Based Measurement of Heart Rate from Ballista cardio graphic Head Movements Using Unsupervised Clustering. *Sensors (Basel), 19*(15), 3263. doi:10.339019153263 PMID:31344939

Cloudian (2020, August 11). *Eight Storage Requirements for AI and Deep Learning.* https://cloudian.com/resource/data-sheets/eight-storage-requirements-artificial-intelligence-deep-learning/

Cordero, C. G., Hauke, S., Mühlhäuser, M., & Fischer, M. (2016), Analysing flow-based anomaly intrusion detection using replicator neural networks. In: *14th Annual Conference on Privacy, Security and Trust (PST).* IEEE, pp. 317–24

Coronado-De-Alba, L. D., Rodríguez-Mota, A., & Escamilla-Ambrosio, P. J. (2016). Feature selection and ensemble of classifiers for Android malware detection. In *2016 8th IEEE Latin-American Conference on Communications (LATIN-COM)* (pp. 1-6). IEEE. 10.1109/LATINCOM.2016.7811605

Dachyar, M., & Nattaya, N. (2020). *Collaborating Internet of Things (IoT) and Electronic Medical Record (EMR) to Reduce Healthcare Waiting time. Outpatient Cardiology Service Case: A BPR Approach.* Atlantis Press. doi:10.2991/aebmr.k.200606.014

Daniel, S. (2019). A Survey of Deep Learning Methods for Cyber Security. *Information, 10*(4), 122. doi:10.3390/info10040122

De Weert, Y., & Gkiotsalitis, K. (2021). A COVID-19 Public Transport Frequency Setting Model That Includes Short-Turning Options. *Future Transportation, 1*(1), 3–20. doi:10.3390/futuretransp1010002

Deepa, K., Radhamani, G., & Vinod, P. (2015). Investigation of feature selection methods for android malware analysis. *Procedia Computer Science, 46*, 841–848. doi:10.1016/j.procs.2015.02.153

Deepa, P., Rashmita Khilar. (2021). A Report on Voice Recognition System: Techniques,Methodologies and Challenges using Deep Neural Network, 2021 Innovations in Power and Advanced Computing Technologies (i-PACT), Qasem Abu-Hajira, Saleh Zein-Sabatto(2020), An Efficient Deep-Learning-Based Detection and Classification System for Cyber-Attacks in IoT Communication Networks. *Electronics (Basel), 9*, 2152. doi:10.3390/electronics9122152

Deng, C., & Liu, Y. (2021). A Deep Learning-Based Inventory Management and Demand Prediction Optimization Method for Anomaly Detection. *Wireless Communications and Mobile Computing, 2021*, 9969357. doi:10.1155/2021/9969357

Devi, G., & Rizvi, S. A. M. (2020). Integration of Genomic Data with EHR Using IoT. *2nd International Conference on Advances in Computing, Communication Control and Networking (ICACCCN).* 10.1109/ICACCCN51052.2020.9362968

Dhalaria, M., & Gandotra, E. (2020b). A framework for detection of android malware using static features. In *2020 IEEE 17th India Council International Conference (INDICON)* (pp. 1-7). IEEE. 10.1109/INDICON49873.2020.9342511

Dhalaria, M., & Gandotra, E. (2021c). *A hybrid approach for android malware detection and family classification.* Academic Press.

Dhalaria, M., & Gandotra, E. (2020a). Android malware detection using chi-square feature selection and ensemble learning method. In *2020 Sixth International Conference on Parallel, Distributed and Grid Computing (PDGC)* (pp. 36-41). IEEE. 10.1109/PDGC50313.2020.9315818

Dhalaria, M., & Gandotra, E. (2021a). Android malware detection techniques: A literature review. *Recent Patents on Engineering*, *15*(2), 225–245. doi:10.2174/1872212114999200710143847

Dhalaria, M., & Gandotra, E. (2021b). CSForest: An approach for imbalanced family classification of android malicious applications. *International Journal of Information Technology*, *13*(3), 1059–1071. doi:10.100741870-021-00661-7

Dhalaria, M., & Gandotra, E. (2022). Risk Detection of Android Applications Using Static Permissions. In *Advances in Data Computing, Communication and Security* (pp. 591–600). Springer. doi:10.1007/978-981-16-8403-6_54

Dhalaria, M., Gandotra, E., & Saha, S. (2019). Comparative analysis of ensemble methods for classification of android malicious applications. In *International Conference on Advances in Computing and Data Sciences* (pp. 370-380). Springer. 10.1007/978-981-13-9939-8_33

Dizon, E., & Pranggono, B. (2022). Smart streetlights in Smart City: A case study of Sheffield. *Journal of Ambient Intelligence and Humanized Computing*, *13*(4), 2045–2060. doi:10.100712652-021-02970-y

Dmaa (2022). Distributed-deep-learning-algorithm-for-wavelength-analysis. *Business Insider*. https://www.businessinsider.com/dmaa-distributed-deep-learning-algorithm-for-wavelength-analysis

Dokic, K., Mikolcevic, H., & Radisic, B. (2021). *Inference speed comparison using convolutions in neural networks on various SoC hardware platforms using MicroPython*. RTA-CSIT.

Doma, V., & Pirouz, M. (2020). A comparative analysis of machine learning methods for emotion recognition using EEG and peripheral physiological signals. *Journal of Big Data*, *7*(1), 1–21. doi:10.118640537-020-00289-7

Domingos, P., & Pazzani, M. (1997). On the optimality of the simple Bayesian classifier under zero-one loss. *Machine Learning*, *29*(2), 103–130. doi:10.1023/A:1007413511361

Du, P., & Nakao, A. (2016). Application specific mobile edge computing through network softwarization. *Proc. 5th IEEE Int. Conf. Cloud Netw. (Cloudnet)*, 130-135. 10.1109/CloudNet.2016.54

Du, Y., Wang, X., & Wang, J. (2015). A static Android malicious code detection method based on multi-source fusion. *Security and Communication Networks*, *8*(17), 3238–3246. doi:10.1002ec.1248

Edoh, T. O. (2019). *Internet of Things in Emergency Medical Care and Services*. Medical Internet of Things (m-IoT) - Enabling Technologies and Emerging Applications.

El-Basioni, B.M., Mohamed, S., El-kader, A., & Eissa, H.S. (2014). *Independent Living for Persons with Disabilities and Elderly People Using Smart Home Technology*. Academic Press.

Enck, W., Octeau, D., McDaniel, P. D., & Chaudhuri, S. (2011). A study of android application security. In USENIX security symposium (Vol. 2, No. 2). USENIX.

Eng, S. K., Ali, H., Cheah, A. Y., & Chong, Y. F. (2019). Facial expression recognition in Jaffe and KDEF datasets using histogram of oriented gradients and support vector machine. *IOP Conference Series. Materials Science and Engineering*, *705*(1), 012031. doi:10.1088/1757-899X/705/1/012031

Esteva, A., Chou, K., & Yeung, S. (2021). Deep learning-enabled medical computer vision. *NPJ Digit. Med.*, *4*, 5. doi:10.103841746-020-00376-2 PMID:33420381

Ferdowsi, A., & Saad, W. (2018). Deep learning for signal authentication and security in massive internet-of-things systems. *IEEE Transactions on Communications, 67*(2), 1371–1387. doi:10.1109/TCOMM.2018.2878025

Ferrag, M. A., Maglaras, L., Moschoyiannis, S., & Janicke, H. (2020). Deep learning for cyber security intrusion detection: Approaches, datasets, and comparative study. *Journal of Information Security and Applications, 50.*

Filali, A., Nour, B., Cherkaoui, S., & Kobbane, A. (2022). *Communication and Computation O-RAN Resource Slicing for URLLC Services Using Deep Reinforcement Learning.* arXiv preprint arXiv:2202.06439.

Fiore, U., Palmieri, F., Castiglione, A., & De Santis, A. (2013). Network anomaly detection with the restricted Boltzmann machine. *Neurocomputing, 122*, 13–23. doi:10.1016/j.neucom.2012.11.050

Fortino, G., Guerrieri, A., Savaglio, C., & Spezzano, G. (2022). A Review of internet of things Platforms through the IoT-A Reference Architecture. In *International Symposium on Intelligent and Distributed Computing,* (pp. 25-34). Springer, Cham. 10.1007/978-3-030-96627-0_3

Franke, T., Lukowicz, P., & Blanke, U. (2015). Smart crowds in smart cities: Real life, city scale deployments of a smartphone based participatory crowd management platform. *Journal of Internet Services and Applications, 6*(1), 1–19. doi:10.118613174-015-0040-6

Furtak, E. M., Circi, R., & Heredia, S. C. (2017). Exploring alignment among learning progressions, teacher-designed formative assessment tasks, and student growth: Results of a four-year study. *Applied Measurement in Education, 31*(2), 143–156. doi:10.1080/08957347.2017.1408624

Gai, K., & Qiu, M. (2018). Optimal resource allocation using reinforcement learning for IoT content-centric services. *Applied Soft Computing, 70*, 12–21. doi:10.1016/j.asoc.2018.03.056

Gandotra, E., Bansal, D., & Sofat, S. (2014). Malware analysis and classification: A survey. *Journal of Information Security.*

Gandotra, E., Bansal, D., & Sofat, S. (2016a). Zero-day malware detection. In *2016 Sixth international symposium on embedded computing and system design (ISED)* (pp. 171-175). IEEE. 10.1109/ISED.2016.7977076

Gandotra, E., Bansal, D., & Sofat, S. (2016b). Tools & techniques for malware analysis and classification. *International Journal of Next-Generation Computing*, 176-197.

Generosi, A., Ceccacci, S., & Mengoni, M. (2018). A deep learning-based system to track and analyze customer behavior in retail store. *2018 IEEE 8th International Conference on Consumer Electronics - Berlin (ICCE-Berlin).*

Ghosh, U., Alazab, M., Bashir, A. K., & Pathan, A. S. K. (Eds.). (2021). *Deep Learning for Internet of Things Infrastructure.* CRC Press. doi:10.1201/9781003032175

Gilabert, Lu, & Yan. (2005). Three dimensional visualisation and reconstruction of the luminosity distribution of a flame using digital imaging. *Techniques, Sensors & Their Applications,* 167–171.

Girshick, R. (2015). Fast R-CNN. In *Proceedings of IEEE International Conference on Computer Vision (ICCV)* (pp. 1440-1448). 10.1109/ICCV.2015.169

Girshick, R., Donahue, J., Darrell, T., & Malik, J. (2016). Region-based convolutional networks for accurate object detection and segmentation. *IEEE Transactions on Pattern Analysis and Machine Intelligence, 38*(1), 142–158. doi:10.1109/TPAMI.2015.2437384 PMID:26656583

Goodfellow, I., Bengio, Y., & Courville, A. (2016). *Deep Learning.* MIT Press.

Gou, C., Zhou, D., & Li, H. (2021). The research and exploration of "curriculum including ideology and politics" in the financial practical talent cultivation with the core of moral education: Taking the major of Finance and Economics in Sichuan University of Arts and Science as an example. *Creative Education, 12*(04), 809–816. doi:10.4236/ce.2021.124057

Gouiaa, R., Akhloufi, M. A., & Shahbazi, M. (2021). Advances in Convolution Neural Networks Based Crowd Counting and Density Estimation. *Big Data Cognitive Computing, 5*(4), 1–21. doi:10.3390/bdcc5040050

Greco, L., Percannella, G., Ritrovato, P., Tortorella, F., & Vento, M. (2020). Trends in IoT based solutions for health care: Moving AI to the edge. *Pattern Recognition Letters, 135*, 346–353. doi:10.1016/j.patrec.2020.05.016 PMID:32406416

Greenstadt, R., & Beal, J. (2008, October). Cognitive security for personal devices. In *Proceedings of the 1st ACM workshop on Workshop on AISec*, (pp. 27-30). 10.1145/1456377.1456383

Grobauer, B., Walloschek, T., & Stocker, E. (2010). Understanding cloud computing vulnerabilities. *IEEE Security and Privacy, 9*(2), 50–57. doi:10.1109/MSP.2010.115

Guerrieri, M. (2021). Smart Roads Geometric Design Criteria and Capacity Estimation Based on AV and CAV Emerging Technologies. A Case Study in the Trans-European Transport Network. *International Journal of Intelligent Transportation Systems Research, 19*(2), 429–440. doi:10.100713177-021-00255-4

Guntoro, B., Hoang, Q. N., & A'yun, A. Q. (2019). Dynamic Responses of Livestock Farmers to Smart Farming. *IOP Conference Series: Earth and Environmental Science, 372*(1), 012042. 10.1088/1755-1315/372/1/012042

Guo, X., Lin, H., Li, Z., & Peng, M. (2019). Deep-reinforcement-learning-based QoS-aware secure routing for SDN-IoT. *IEEE Internet of Things Journal, 7*(7), 6242-6251.

Guo, J., & Yu, S. (2020). Retracted: Evaluation model of college English teaching quality based on Big Data Analysis. *IOP Conference Series. Materials Science and Engineering, 750*(1), 012077. doi:10.1088/1757-899X/750/1/012077

Gupta, C., Johri, I., Srinivasan, K., Hu, Y. C., Qaisar, S. M., & Huang, K. Y. (2022). A Systematic Review on Machine Learning and Deep Learning Models for Electronic Information Security in Mobile Networks. *Sensors (Basel), 22*(5), 2017. doi:10.339022052017 PMID:35271163

Gupta, D., & Rani, R. (2018). Big data framework for zero-day malware detection. *Cybernetics and Systems, 49*(2), 103–121. doi:10.1080/01969722.2018.1429835

Gupta, D., & Rani, R. (2020). Improving malware detection using big data and ensemble learning. *Computers & Electrical Engineering, 86*, 106729. doi:10.1016/j.compeleceng.2020.106729

Gurjar, N. N. (2017). Security Sensors for Protection in Smart Homes Using IoT. *International Journal of Advance Research, Ideas and Innovations in Technology, 2*(4).

Habeeb, F., Szydlo, T., Kowalski, L., Noor, A., Thakker, D., Morgan, G., & Ranjan, R. (2022). Dynamic Data Streams for Time-Critical IoT Systems in Energy-Aware IoT Devices Using Reinforcement Learning. *Sensors (Basel), 22*(6), 2375. doi:10.339022062375 PMID:35336544

Haghi Kashani, M., Rahmani, A. M., & Jafari Navimipour, N. (2020). Quality of service-aware approaches in fog computing. *International Journal of Communication Systems, 33*(8), e4340. doi:10.1002/dac.4340

Hall, M. A. (2000). *Correlation-based feature selection of discrete and numeric class machine learning*. Academic Press.

Hamid, D. S. B. A., Goyal, S. B., & Ghosh, A. (2021). Application of Deep Learning with Wearable IoT in Healthcare Sector. *2021 IEEE 6th International Conference on Computing, Communication and Automation (ICCCA)*.

Hammi, B., Khatoun, R., Zeadally, S., Fayad, A., & Khoukhi, L. (2018). IoT technologies for smart cities. *IET Networks, 7*(1), 1–13. doi:10.1049/iet-net.2017.0163

Han, Zhang, Zhen, & Wang. (2006). Boiler Flame Image Classification Based on Hidden Markov Model. *IEEE ISIE*, 9-12.

Hanani, F., Soulhi, A., & Saidi, R. (2019). Towards A Framework for Smart City Wireless Communication: Conclusions Drawn From Smart Transport Case Study. *Journal of Engineering and Applied Sciences (Asian Research Publishing Network), 14*(8), 1601–1611.

Han, J., Pei, J., & Tong, H. (2022). *Data mining: concepts and techniques*. Morgan Kaufmann.

Han, T., Muhammad, K., Hussain, T., Lloret, J., & Baik, S. W. (2021). An Efficient Deep Learning Framework for Intelligent Energy Management in IoT Networks. *IEEE Internet of Things Journal, 8*(5), 3170–3179. doi:10.1109/JIOT.2020.3013306

Harnik, D., Pinkas, B., & Shulman-Peleg, A. (2010). Side channels in cloud services: Deduplication in cloud storage. *IEEE Security and Privacy, 8*(6), 40–47. doi:10.1109/MSP.2010.187

Haykin, S., Fuster, J. M., Findlay, D., & Feng, S. (2017). Cognitive risk control for physical systems. *IEEE Access : Practical Innovations, Open Solutions, 5*, 14664–14679. doi:10.1109/ACCESS.2017.2726439

He, K., Gkioxari, G., Dollár, P., & Girshick, R. (2017). Mask R-CNN. In *Proceedings of IEEE International Conference on Computer Vision (ICCV)* (pp. 2980-2988). 10.1109/ICCV.2017.322

Hobbs, F., & Stoops, N. (2002). *Demographic Trends in the 20th Century*. United States Census Bureau. CENSR-4. https://www.census.gov/prod/2002pubs/censr-4.pdf

Howard, A., Zhu, M., Chen, B., Kalenichenko, D., Wang, W., Weyand, T., Andreetto, M., & Adam, H. (2017). *Mobilenets: Efficient convolutional neural networks for mobile vision applications*. Academic Press.

Hsu, R., Lee, J., Quek, T., & Chen, J. (2018). Reconfigurable security: Edge-computing-based framework for iot. *IEEE Network, 32*(5), 92–99. doi:10.1109/MNET.2018.1700284

Hsu, Y.-F., & Matsuoka, M. (2019). A Deep Reinforcement Learning Approach for Anomaly Network Intrusion Detection System Communications and Networking: A Survey. *IEEE Communications Surveys and Tutorials, 21*, 3133–3174. doi:10.1109/COMST.2019.2916583

Huan, G., Liu, G., Liu, J., Zhang, D., & Zhu, X. (2009, December). A hybrid FES rehabilitation system based on CPG and BCI technology for locomotion: A preliminary study. In *International Conference on Intelligent Robotics and Applications* (pp. 1073-1084). Springer.

Huang, S.-C., & Le, T.-H. (2021). Convolutional neural network architectures. In *Principles and Labs for Deep Learning* (pp. 201–217). Academic Press. doi:10.1016/B978-0-323-90198-7.00001-X

Hussain, F., Hassan, S. A., Hussain, R., & Hossain, E. (2020). Machine learning for resource management in cellular and IoT networks: Potentials, current solutions, and open challenges. *IEEE Communications Surveys and Tutorials, 22*(2), 1251–1275. doi:10.1109/COMST.2020.2964534

Hussain, F., Hussain, R., Hassan, S. A., & Hossain, E. (2020). Machine Learning in IoT Security: Current Solutions and Future Challenges. *IEEE Communications Surveys and Tutorials, 22*(3), 1686–1721. doi:10.1109/COMST.2020.2986444

Ibitoye, O., Shafiq, O., & Matrawy, A. (2019, December). Analyzing adversarial attacks against deep learning for intrusion detection in IoT networks. In *2019 IEEE global communications conference (GLOBECOM)* (pp. 1-6). IEEE.

Ilyas, N., Shahzad, A., & Kim, K. (2019). Convolutional-Neural Network-Based Image Crowd Counting: Review, Categorization, Analysis, and Performance Evaluation. *Sensors (Basel)*, *20*(1), 1–33. doi:10.339020010043 PMID:31861734

Irfan, M., Marcenaro, L., & Tokarchuk, L. (2016). Crowd analysis using visual and non-visual sensors, a survey. In *Proceedings of IEEE Global Conference on Signal and Information Processing (GlobalSIP)* (pp. 1249-1254). 10.1109/GlobalSIP.2016.7906041

Irshad, O., Khan, M. U. G., Iqbal, R., Basheer, S., & Bashir, A. K. (2020). Performance optimization of IoT based biological systems using deep learning. *Computer Communications*, *155*, 24–31. doi:10.1016/j.comcom.2020.02.059

Ismagilova, E., Hughes, L., Rana, N. P., & Dwivedi, Y. K. (2022). Security, Privacy and Risks within Smart Cities: Literature Review and Development of a Smart City Interaction Framework. *Information Systems Frontiers*, *24*(2), 393–414. doi:10.100710796-020-10044-1 PMID:32837262

Jaihar, J., Lingayat, N., Vijaybhai, P. S., Venkatesh, G., & Upla, K. P. (2020). Smart Home Automation Using Machine Learning Algorithms. *2020 International Conference for Emerging Technology (INCET)*. 10.1109/INCET49848.2020.9154007

Javaid, M., Haleem, A., Singh, R. P., Rab, S., & Suman, R. (2021). Internet of Behaviours (IoB) and its role in customer services. *Sensors International*, *2*, 100122. doi:10.1016/j.sintl.2021.100122

Javale, D., Mohsin, M., Nandanwar, S. & Shingate, M. (2013). Home automation and security system using Android ADK. *International Journal of Electronics Communication and Computer Technology, 3*(2), 382-385.

Jawhar, I., Mohamed, N., & Al-Jaroodi, J. (2018). Networking architectures and protocols for smart city systems. *Journal of Internet Services and Applications*, *9*(1), 1–16. doi:10.118613174-018-0097-0

Jin, J., & Martin, R. (2019). Exploring the past to navigate the future: Examining histories of higher dance education in China in an internationalized context. *Research in Dance Education*, *20*(2), 225–240. doi:10.1080/14647893.2019.1566304

Juniper Networks. (2022). What is multi-access edge computing? *Juniper*. https://www.juniper.net/us/en/research-topics/what-is-multi-access-edge-computing.html

Kanevski, M., Pozdnukhov, A., Canu, S., & Maignan, M. (2002). Advanced Spatial Data Analysis and Modelling with Support Vector Machines. *International Journal of Fuzzy Systems*, 606–615.

Kang, M.-J., & Kang, J.-W. (2016, June 7). Intrusion detection system using deep neural network for in-vehicle network security. *PLoS One*, *11*(6), e0155781. doi:10.1371/journal.pone.0155781 PMID:27271802

Kannannova. (2022). *Kannannova/deeplearningenablediotdevices*. https://github.com/kannannova/DeepLearningEnabledIoTDevices

Kashyap, R. (2019). Big Data Analytics challenges and solutions. *Big Data Analytics for Intelligent Healthcare Management*, 19–41. doi:10.1016/b978-0-12-818146-1.00002-7

Kashyap, R. (2018). Object boundary detection through robust active contour based method with global information. *International Journal of Image Mining*, *3*(1), 22. doi:10.1504/IJIM.2018.093008

Kashyap, R. (2019). Machine learning for internet of things. *Advances in Wireless Technologies and Telecommunication*, 57–83. doi:10.4018/978-1-5225-7458-3.ch003

Kasongo, S. M., & Sun, Y. (2019). A deep learning method with filter based fea- ture engineering for wireless intrusion detection system. *IEEE Access : Practical Innovations, Open Solutions*, *7*, 38597–38607. doi:10.1109/ACCESS.2019.2905633

Kaur, A., Raj, G., Yadav, S., & Choudhury, T. (2018, December). Performance evaluation of AWS and IBM cloud platforms for security mechanism. In *international conference on computational techniques, electronics and mechanical systems (CTEMS)*, (pp. 516-520). IEEE.

Kaur, C. (2020). The cloud computing and internet of things (IoT). *International Journal of Scientific Research in Science, Engineering and Technology*, 7(1), 19–22. doi:10.32628/IJSRSET196657

Keerthi, S. S., & Gilbert, E. G. (2002). Convergence of a generalized SMO algorithm for SVM classifier design. *Machine Learning*, 46(1), 351–360. doi:10.1023/A:1012431217818

Kegyes, T., Süle, Z., & Abonyi, J. (2021). The Applicability of Reinforcement Learning Methods in the Development of Industry 4.0 Applications. *Complexity*, 2021, 7179374. doi:10.1155/2021/7179374

Khan, A., Shah, J. A., Kadir, K., Albattah, W., & Khan, F. (2020). Crowd Monitoring and Localization Using Deep Convolutional Neural Network: A Review. *Applied Sciences (Basel, Switzerland)*, 10(14), 1–17. doi:10.3390/app10144781

Khan, A., Sohail, A., Zahoora, U., & Qureshi, A. S. (2020). A survey of the recent architectures of deep convolutional Neural Networks. *Artificial Intelligence Review*, 53(8), 5455–5516. doi:10.100710462-020-09825-6

Khan, F. A., Gumaei, A., Derhab, A., & Hussain, A. (2019). A Tsdl: A two stage deep learning model for efficient network intrusion detection. *IEEE Access : Practical Innovations, Open Solutions*, 7, 30373–30385. doi:10.1109/ACCESS.2019.2899721

Khan, K., Albattah, W., Khan, R. U., Qamar, A. M., & Nayab, D. (2020). Advances and Trends in Real Time Visual Crowd Analysis. *Sensors (Basel)*, 20(18), 1–28. doi:10.339020185073 PMID:32906659

Khan, N. A., Nebel, J.-C., Khaddaj, S., & Brujic-Okretic, V. (2020). Scalable System for Smart Urban Transport Management. *Journal of Advanced Transportation*, 2020, 1–13. doi:10.1155/2020/8894705

Khan, Z., Anjum, A., Soomro, K., & Tahir, M. A. (2015). Towards cloud based big data analytics for smart future cities. *Journal of Cloud Computing: Advances. Systems*, 4(2), 1–11.

Kibria, M. G., Nguyen, K., Villardi, G. P., Zhao, O., Ishizu, K., & Kojima, F. (2018). Big Data Analytics, Machine Learning, and Artificial Intelligence in Next-Generation Wireless Networks. *IEEE Access: Practical Innovations, Open Solutions*, 6, 32328–32338. doi:10.1109/ACCESS.2018.2837692

Kimbugwe, N., Pei, T., & Kyebambe, M. N. (2021). Application of Deep Learning for Quality of Service Enhancement in Internet of Things: A Review. *Energies*, 14(19), 6384. doi:10.3390/en14196384

Kim, J.-H., Kim, N., Park, Y. W., & Won, C. S. (2022). Object Detection and Classification Based on YOLO-V5 with Improved Maritime Dataset. *Journal of Marine Science and Engineering*, 10(3), 1–14. doi:10.3390/jmse10030377

Kim, T., Kang, B., Rho, M., Sezer, S., & Im, E. G. (2018). A multimodal deep learning method for android malware detection using various features. *IEEE Transactions on Information Forensics and Security*, 14(3), 773–788. doi:10.1109/TIFS.2018.2866319

Klippel, E., Oliveira, R. A. R., Maslov, D., Bianchi, A. G. C., Delabrida, S. E., & Garrocho, C. T. B. (2022). Embedded Edge Artificial Intelligence for Longitudinal Rip Detection in Conveyor Belt Applied at the Industrial Mining Environment. *SN Computer Science*, 3(4), 1–6. doi:10.100742979-022-01169-y

Kok, İ., Çorak, B. H., Yavanoğlu, U., & Özdemir, S. (2019, December). Deep learning based delay and bandwidth efficient data transmission in IoT. In *2019 IEEE International Conference on Big Data (Big Data)* (pp. 2327-2333). IEEE.

Kouliaridis, V., Barmpatsalou, K., Kambourakis, G., & Chen, S. (2020). A survey on mobile malware detection techniques. *IEICE Transactions on Information and Systems, 103*(2), 204–211. doi:10.1587/transinf.2019INI0003

Krichene, J., & Boudriga, N. (2008, December). Incident response probabilistic cognitive maps. In *international symposium on parallel and distributed processing with applications*, (pp. 689-694). IEEE.

Kruse, C. S. & Beane, A. (2018). Health Information Technology Continues to Show Positive Effect on Medical Outcomes: Systematic Review. *J Med Internet Res 2018, 20*(2).

Kumar, S., Raut, R. D., Priyadarshinee, P., & Narkhede, B. E. (2022). Exploring warehouse management practices for adoption of IoT-blockchain. *Supply Chain Forum: An International Journal*, 1-16. 10.1080/16258312.2022.2082852

Kumar, R., & Goyal, R. (2019). On cloud security requirements, threats, vulnerabilities and countermeasures: A survey. *Computer Science Review, 33*, 1–48. doi:10.1016/j.cosrev.2019.05.002

Kusuma, G. P., Jonathan, J., & Lim, A. P. (2020). Emotion recognition on FER-2013 face images using fine-tuned VGG-16. *Advances in Science. Technology and Engineering Systems Journal, 5*(6), 315–322. doi:10.25046/aj050638

Lee, H.-S., & Kang, B.-Y. (2019). Continuous emotion estimation of facial expressions on Jaffe and CK+ datasets for Human–Robot Interaction. *Intelligent Service Robotics, 13*(1), 15–27. doi:10.100711370-019-00301-x

Liang, S. D. (2018). Smart and fast data processing for deep learning in Internet of Things: Less is more. *IEEE Internet of Things Journal, 6*(4), 5981–5989. doi:10.1109/JIOT.2018.2864579

Liang, Z., Zhang, G., Huang, J. X., & Hu, Q. V. (2014). Deep learning for healthcare decision making with EMRs. *2014 IEEE International Conference on Bioinformatics and Biomedicine (BIBM)*. 10.1109/BIBM.2014.6999219

Liaw, A., & Wiener, M. (2002). Classification and regression by randomForest. *R News, 2*(3), 18–22.

Li, D., Deng, L., Lee, M., & Wang, H. (2019). IoT data feature extraction and intrusion detection system for smart cities based on deep migration learning. *International Journal of Information Management, 49*, 533–545. doi:10.1016/j.ijinfomgt.2019.04.006

Li, E., Zeng, L., Zhou, Z., & Chen, X. (2020). Edge AI: On-Demand Accelerating Deep Neural Network Inference via Edge Computing. *IEEE Transactions on Wireless Communications, 19*(1), 447–457. doi:10.1109/TWC.2019.2946140

Lim, L., & Apple, M. W. (2018). The Politics of Curriculum Reforms in Asia: Inter-referencing discourses of power, culture and knowledge. *Curriculum Inquiry, 48*(2), 139–148. doi:10.1080/03626784.2018.1448532

Lin, T.-Y., Maire, M., Belongie, S., Bourdev, L., & Girshick, R. (2014). Microsoft COCO: common objects in context. In *Proceedings of European Conference on Computer Vision (ECCV)* (pp. 740-755). Academic Press.

Lindsay, G. W. (2021). Convolutional Neural Networks as a model of the visual system: Past, present, and future. *Journal of Cognitive Neuroscience, 33*(10), 2017–2031. doi:10.1162/jocn_a_01544 PMID:32027584

Lin, L., Liao, X., Jin, H., & Li, P. (2019). Computation offloading toward edge computing. *Proceedings of the IEEE, 107*(8), 1584–1607. doi:10.1109/JPROC.2019.2922285

Linthicum, D. S. (2017). Making Sense of AI in Public Clouds. *IEEE Cloud Computing, 4*(6), 70–72. doi:10.1109/MCC.2018.1081067

Liu, N., Li, Z., Xu, J., Xu, Z., Lin, S., Qiu, Q., . . . Wang, Y. (2017). A hierarchical framework of cloud resource allocation and power management using deep reinforcement learning. In *2017 IEEE 37th international conference on distributed computing systems (ICDCS)* (pp. 372-382). IEEE.

Liu, T., Liu, S., Chen, Z., & Ma, W. Y. (2003). An evaluation on feature selection for text clustering. In *Proceedings of the 20th international conference on machine learning (ICML-03)* (pp. 488-495). Academic Press.

Liu, W., Anguelov, D., Erhan, D., Szegedy, C., Reed, S., Fu, C.-Y., & Berg, A. C. (2016). SSD: Single Shot MultiBox Detector. In *Proceedings of European Conference on Computer Vision (ECCV 2016)* (pp. 21–37). 10.1007/978-3-319-46448-0_2

Lonavath, A. K., Virugu, K., Kumar, V. S., & Naik, D. K. (2017). Evolution of Smart City Concept and its Economic Performance: A Study of Cities in Telangana State of India. *International Journal of Research in Geography, 3*(4), 84–99.

Lopez-Martin, M., Carro, B., & Sanchez-Esguevillas, A. (2019). Neural network architecture based on gradient boosting for IoT traffic prediction. *Future Generation Computer Systems, 100*, 656–673. doi:10.1016/j.future.2019.05.060

Lopez-Matrin, M., Carro, B., & Sanchez-Esguevillas, A. (2020). Application of deep reinforcement learning to intrusion detection for supervised problems. *Expert Systems with Applications, 141.*

Louis, M. S., Azad, Z., Delshadtehrani, L., Gupta, S., Warden, P., Reddi, V. J., & Joshi, A. (2019). Towards Deep Learning using TensorFlow Lite on RISC-V. In *Third Workshop on Computer Architecture Research with RISC-V (CARRV)* (pp. 1-6). Academic Press.

Lu & Yan. (2009). Advanced Monitoring and Characterization of combustion flames. *20th annual meeting and meeting of the Advanced Power Generation Division*, 1-25.

Lu, Yan, Cornwell, Whitehouse, & Riley. (2007). *Impact of co-firing coal and biomass on flame characteristics and stability.* Academic Press.

Lu, Lv., Wang, W., Zhang, Z., & Liu, X. (2020). A novel intrusion detection system based on an optimal hybrid kernel extreme learning machine,Knowledge Based Systems, 195, Loukas G, Vuong T, Heartfield R, Sakellari G, Yoon Y, Gan D (2017), Cloud-based cyber-physical intrusion detection for vehicles using deep learning. *IEEE Access : Practical Innovations, Open Solutions, 6*(3), 491–508.

Lundervold, A. S., & Lundervold, A. (2019). An overview of deep learning in medical imaging focusing on MRI. *Zeitschrift fur Medizinische Physik, 29*(2), 102–127. doi:10.1016/j.zemedi.2018.11.002 PMID:30553609

Lv, X. (2021). A quality evaluation scheme for curriculum in ideological and political education based on Data Mining. *2021 13th International Conference on Measuring Technology and Mechatronics Automation (ICMTMA).* doi:10.1109/icmtma52658.2021.00149

Maimo, L. F. (2018). A Self-Adaptive Deep Learning-Based System for Anomaly Detection in 5G Networks. *IEEE Access : Practical Innovations, Open Solutions, 6*, 7700–7712. doi:10.1109/ACCESS.2018.2803446

Ma, J., Nagatsuma, T., Kim, S. J., & Hasegawa, M. (2019, February). A machine-learning-based channel assignment algorithm for IoT. In *2019 International Conference on Artificial Intelligence in Information and Communication (ICAIIC)* (pp. 1-6). IEEE. 10.1109/ICAIIC.2019.8669028

Malik, A. S., Subhani, A. R., & Xia, L. (2019). A physiological signal-based method for early mental-stress detection. In *Cyber-Enabled Intelligence* (pp. 259–289). Taylor & Francis.

Mao, Q.-C., Sun, H.-M., Liu, Y.-B., & Jia, R.-S. (2019). Mini-YOLOv3: Real-Time Object Detector for Embedded Applications. *IEEE Access: Practical Innovations, Open Solutions, 7*, 133529–133538. doi:10.1109/ACCESS.2019.2941547

Martin. (2004). On the Use of Kriging Models to Approximate Deterministic Computer Models. *Proceedings International Design Engineering Technical Conferences and Computers and Information in Engineering Conference.*

McAfee Labs. (2020). *Threat Predictions Report.* McAfee Labs.

McKinsey Global Institute. (2018). *Smart Cities: Digital Solutions for a More Livable Future.* Author.

Memon, A. M., & Anwar, A. (2015). Colluding apps: Tomorrow's mobile malware threat. *IEEE Security and Privacy, 13*(6), 77–81. doi:10.1109/MSP.2015.143

Mijuskovic, A., Chiumento, A., Bemthuis, R., Aldea, A., & Havinga, P. (2021). Resource management techniques for cloud/fog and edge computing: An evaluation framework and classification. *Sensors (Basel), 21*(5), 1832. doi:10.339021051832 PMID:33808037

Mir, M. H., Jamwal, S., Mehbodniya, A., Garg, T., Iqbal, U., & Samori, I. A. (2022). IoT-Enabled Framework for Early Detection and Prediction of COVID-19 Suspects by Leveraging Machine Learning in Cloud. *Journal of Healthcare Engineering, 2022*, 7713939. doi:10.1155/2022/7713939 PMID:35432824

Mondal, K. K., & Guha Roy, D. (2021). *IoT Data Security with Machine Learning Blckchain: Risks and Countermeasures.* Springer Science and Business Media LLC.

Moreno-Vozmediano, R., Montero, R. S., & Llorente, I. M. (2012). Key challenges in cloud computing: Enabling the future internet of services. *IEEE Internet Computing, 17*(4), 18–25. doi:10.1109/MIC.2012.69

Muhammad, G., Alhussein, M., Hossain, M. S., & Amin, S. U. (2018). Cognitive IoT-Cloud Integration for Smart Healthcare: Case Study for Epileptic Seizure Detection and Monitoring. *Mobile Networks and Applications, 23*(6), 1624–1635. doi:10.100711036-018-1113-0

Munavalli, J. R., Merode, F., Rao, S.V., & Srinivas, A. (2014). Healthcare of India: Today and Tomorrow. *International Journal of Innovative Research and Development, 3*(2), 350–356.

Munavalli, J. R., Boersma, H. J., Rao, S. V., & van Merode, G. G. (2021). *Real-Time Capacity Management and Patient Flow Optimization in Hospitals Using AI Methods. Artificial Intelligence and Data Mining in Healthcare.* Springer International Publishing.

Munavalli, J. R., Rao, S. V., Aravind, S., & van Merode, G. G. (2021). Workflow-based Adaptive Layout Design to Improve the Patient Flow in the Outpatient Clinics. *Annals of the Romanian Society for Cell Biology, 25*(3), 8249–8257.

Munavalli, J. R., Rao, S. V., Srinivasan, A., & van Merode, F. (2022). Dynamic Layout Design Optimization to Improve Patient Flow in Outpatient Clinics Using Genetic Algorithms. *Algorithms, 15*(3), 85. doi:10.3390/a15030085

Munavalli, J. R., Rao, S. V., Srinivasan, A., & van Merode, G. G. (2020). An intelligent real-time scheduler for out-patient clinics: A multi-agent system model. *Health Informatics Journal, 26*(4), 2383–2406. doi:10.1177/1460458220905380 PMID:32081068

Nair, R., & Bhagat, A. (2021). An introduction to clustering algorithms in Big Data. Encyclopedia of Information Science and Technology, Fifth Edition, 559–576. doi:10.4018/978-1-7998-3479-3.ch040

Nair, R., Sharma, P., & Sharma, T. (2022). Optimizing the performance of IOT using FPGA as compared to GPU. *International Journal of Grid and High Performance Computing, 14*(1), 1–15. doi:10.4018/IJGHPC.301580

Nair, R., Soni, M., Bajpai, B., Dhiman, G., & Sagayam, K. M. (2022). Predicting the death rate around the world due to COVID-19 using regression analysis. *International Journal of Swarm Intelligence Research, 13*(2), 1–13. doi:10.4018/IJSIR.287545

Nallathambi, A. (2022). *Autonomous Electric Vehicles Auto Monitor and Control.* 202241015720.

Nallathambi,A. B., Kanammai, D. Sandip, S., Gummadi, J. M., Dhanasekaran, S., & Balkeshwar, S. (2022). *Mobile Locking System for Vehicle Using Machine Learning*, Registration Number-1192615. Canadian Copyright.

Natarajan, A., Saideep, A., & Reddy, K. S. (2020). Artificial Intelligence and Augmented Reality driven Home Automation. *2020 International Conference on Electronics and Sustainable Communication Systems (ICESC)*. 10.1109/ICESC48915.2020.9155916

Nawrocki, P., & Osypanka, P. (2021). Cloud resource demand prediction using machine learning in the context of qos parameters. *Journal of Grid Computing*, *19*(2), 1–20. doi:10.100710723-021-09561-3

Nguyen, L., Hu, G., & Spanos, C. J. (2017). Spatio-temporal environmental monitoring for smart buildings. *2017 13th IEEE International Conference on Control & Automation (ICCA)*.

Nguyen, D.-B., Dow, C.-R., & Hwang, S.-F. (2018). An Efficient Traffic Congestion Monitoring System on Internet of Vehicles. *Wireless Communications and Mobile Computing*, *2018*, 1–17. doi:10.1155/2018/9136813

Nguyen, T. T., & Reddi, V. J. (2021). Deep Reinforcement Learning for Cyber Security, IEEE Transactions on Neural Networks and Learning Systems, Ullah, F., Naeem, H., Jabbar, S., Khalid, S., Latif, M.A., Al-Turjman, F., Mostarda, L(2019), Cyber Security Threats Detection in Internet of Things Using Deep Learning Approach. *IEEE Access : Practical Innovations, Open Solutions*, *7*, 124379–124389.

Nirmala., M., Sathya, M., Shukla, A. K. C. S., Ravichandran, P. N. M. H., & Lakshminarayana, M. (2021). An Intellectual Monitoring of Power Sector by Machine Learning Applications, *NVEO – Natural Volatiles & Essential Oils*, *8*(5), 6609–6619.

OECD. (2019). *Enhancing the contribution of digitalisation to the smart cities of the future*. OECD.

Ogiela, L., Ogiela, M. R., & Ogiela, U. (2016, July). Efficiency of strategic data sharing and management protocols. In *10th International conference on innovative mobile and internet services in ubiquitous computing (IMIS)*, (pp. 198-201). IEEE. 10.1109/IMIS.2016.119

Ogiela, L., & Ogiela, M. R. (2020). Cognitive security paradigm for cloud computing applications. *Concurrency and Computation*, *32*(8), e5316. doi:10.1002/cpe.5316

Ogiela, M. R., & Ogiela, U. (2008, December). Linguistic approach to cryptographic data sharing. In *Second International Conference on Future Generation Communication and Networking*, (Vol. 1, pp. 377-380). IEEE. 10.1109/FGCN.2008.89

Oke, A. E., & Arowoiya, V. A. (2021). *Evaluation of internet of things (IoT) application areas for sustainable construction*. Smart and Sustainable Built Environment. doi:10.1108/SASBE-11-2020-0167

Palak, M., Revati, G., & Sheikh, A. (2021). Smart Building Energy Management using Deep Learning Based Predictions. *2021 North American Power Symposium (NAPS)*. 10.1109/NAPS52732.2021.9654262

Pandit, M. K., Mir, R. N., & Chishti, M. A. (2020). Adaptive task scheduling in IoT using reinforcement learning. *Int. J. Intell. Comput. Cybern.*, *13*(3), 261–282. doi:10.1108/IJICC-03-2020-0021

Papagiannakis, A. T., Dessouky, S., Montoya, A., & Roshani, H. (2016). Energy Harvesting from Roadways. *Procedia Computer Science*, *83*, 758–765. doi:10.1016/j.procs.2016.04.164

Papamartzivanos, D., Mármol, F. G., & Kambourakis, G. (2019). Introducing deep learn- ing self-adaptive misuse network intrusion detection systems. *IEEE Access : Practical Innovations, Open Solutions*, *7*(135), 46–60.

Parast, F. K., Sindhav, C., Nikam, S., Yekta, H. I., Kent, K. B., & Hakak, S. (2022). Cloud computing security: A survey of service-based models. *Computers & Security*, *114*, 102580. doi:10.1016/j.cose.2021.102580

Peine, A., Hallawa, A., Schöffski, O., Dartmann, G., Fazlic, L. B., Schmeink, A., Marx, G., & Martin, L. (2019). A Deep Learning Approach for Managing Medical Consumable Materials in Intensive Care Units via Convolutional Neural Networks: Technical Proof-of-Concept Study. *JMIR Medical Informatics*, 7(4), e14806. doi:10.2196/14806 PMID:31603430

Peiravian, N., & Zhu, X. (2013). Machine learning for android malware detection using permission and api calls. In *2013 IEEE 25th international conference on tools with artificial intelligence* (pp. 300-305). IEEE. 10.1109/ICTAI.2013.53

Peng, Z., Li, X., & Yan, F. (2020). An Adaptive Deep Learning Model for Smart Home Autonomous System. *2020 International Conference on Intelligent Transportation, Big Data & Smart City (ICITBS)*. 10.1109/ICITBS49701.2020.00156

Perez, R., Van Doorn, L., & Sailer, R. (2008). Virtualization and hardware-based security. *IEEE Security and Privacy*, 6(5), 24–31. doi:10.1109/MSP.2008.135

Poon, Y.-S., Lin, C.-C., Liu, Y.-H., & Fan, C.-P. (2022). YOLO-Based Deep Learning Design for In-Cabin Monitoring System with Fisheye-Lens Camera. *Proceedings of IEEE International Conference on Consumer Electronics (ICCE)*. 10.1109/ICCE53296.2022.9730235

Poorchangizi, B., Borhani, F., Abbaszadeh, A., Mirzaee, M., & Farokhzadian, J. (2019). The importance of professional values from nursing students' perspective. *BMC Nursing*, 18(1), 26. Advance online publication. doi:10.118612912-019-0351-1 PMID:31312111

Poulopoulos, D. (2021, January 26). Distributed Deep Learning 101: Introduction. *Medium*. https://towardsdatascience.com/distributed-deep-learning-101-introduction-ebfc1bcd59d9

Pradhan, Pal, & Bhattacharyya. (2021). IoT-Based Applications in Healthcare Devices. *Journal of Healthcare Engineering*. doi:10.1155/2021/6632599

Quinlan, R. J. (1992). Learning with Continuous Classes. *5th Australian Joint Conference on Artificial Intelligence*, 343-348.

Rahim, N., Ahmad, J., Muhammad, K., Sangaiah, A. K., & Baik, S. W. (2018). Privacy-preserving image retrieval for mobile devices with deep features on the cloud. *Computer Communications*, 127, 75–85. doi:10.1016/j.comcom.2018.06.001

Rajasoundaran, S., Prabu, A. V., Routray, S., Kumar, S. S., Malla, P. P., Maloji, S., & Ghosh, U. (2021). Machine learning based deep job exploration and secure transactions in virtual private cloud systems. *Computers & Security*, 109, 102379. doi:10.1016/j.cose.2021.102379

Ramachandran, V., Ramalakshmi, R., Kavin, B. P., Hussain, I., Almaliki, A. H., Almaliki, A. A., Elnaggar, A., & Hussein, E. E. (2022). Exploiting IoT and its enabled technologies for irrigation needs in agriculture. *Water (Basel)*, 14(5), 719. doi:10.3390/w14050719

Ramos, J. L., Cano, M. V., Bernabé, J. B., Carrillo, D. G., & Gómez-Skarmeta, A. F. (2015). SAFIR: Secure access framework for IoT-enabled services on smart buildings. *Journal of Computer and System Sciences*, 81(8), 1452–1463. doi:10.1016/j.jcss.2014.12.021

Ranjbar, M., & Ghanbary, A. (Eds.). (2012). *Implications of ICT for Society and Individual. Technologies for Enhancing Pedagogy, Engagement and Empowerment in Education: Creating Learning-Friendly Environments*. IGI Global.

Rathinavel, K., Pipattanasomporn, M., Kuzlu, M., & Rahman, S. (2017). *Security concerns and countermeasures in IoT-integrated smart buildings. In 2017 IEEE Power & Energy Society Innovative Smart Grid Technologies Conference*. ISGT.

Rawat, S., Srinivasan, A., Ravi, V., & Ghosh, U. (2022). Intrusion detection systems using classical machine learning techniques vs integrated unsupervised feature learning and deep neural network. *Internet Technology Letters*, *5*(1), e232. doi:10.1002/itl2.232

Redmon, J., & Farhadi, A. (2018). *YOLOv3: An incremental improvement*. Academic Press.

Redmon, J., Divvala, S., Girshick, R., & Farhadi, A. (2016). You Only Look Once: Unified, Real-Time Object Detection. In *Proceedings of IEEE Conference on Computer Vision and Pattern Recognition (CVPR)* (pp. 779-788). 10.1109/CVPR.2016.91

Redmon, J., & Farhadi, A. (2017). YOLO9000: better, faster, stronger. In *Proceedings of IEEE Conference on Computer Vision and Pattern Recognition (CVPR)* (pp. 7263-7271). IEEE.

Ren, S., He, K., Girshick, R., & Sun, J. (2017). Faster R-CNN: Towards Real-Time Object Detection with Region Proposal Networks. *IEEE Transactions on Pattern Analysis and Machine Intelligence*, *39*(6), 1137–1149. doi:10.1109/TPAMI.2016.2577031 PMID:27295650

Rezvy, S., Luo, Y., Petridis, M., Lasebae, A., & Zebin, T. (2019), An efficient deep learning model for intrusion classification and prediction in 5G and IoT networks, In *53rd Annual Conference on Information Sciences and Systems (CISS)*, IEEE, pp 1–6.

Richert, A., Shehadeh, M. A., Müller, S. L., Schröder, S., & Jeschke, S. (2016). Socializing with robots: Human-robot interactions within a virtual environment. *2016 IEEE Workshop on Advanced Robotics and its Social Impacts (ARSO)*. 10.1109/ARSO.2016.7736255

Rimal, B. P., Choi, E., & Lumb, I. (2009, August). A taxonomy and survey of cloud computing systems. In *Fifth International Joint Conference on INC, IMS and IDC*, (pp. 44-51). IEEE. 10.1109/NCM.2009.218

Ristenpart, T., Tromer, E., Shacham, H., & Savage, S. (2009, November). Hey, you, get off of my cloud: exploring information leakage in third-party compute clouds. In *Proceedings of the 16th ACM conference on Computer and communications security*, (pp. 199-212). 10.1145/1653662.1653687

Robinson, R. P. (2020). Until the Revolution: Analyzing the politics, pedagogy, and curriculum of the Oakland Community School. Espacio. *Tiempo y Educación*, *7*(1), 181–203. doi:10.14516/ete.273

Robnik-Šikonja, M., & Kononenko, I. (2003). Theoretical and empirical analysis of ReliefF and RReliefF. *Machine Learning*, *53*(1), 23–69. doi:10.1023/A:1025667309714

Rocha-Neto, A. F., Delicato, F. C., Batista, T. V., & Pires, P. F. (2020). Distributed machine learning for IOT applications in the fog. *Fog Computing*, 309–345. . doi:10.1002/9781119551713.ch12

Rodriguez-Conde, I., Campos, C., & Fdez-Riverola, F. (2021). Optimized convolutional neural network architectures for efficient on-device vision-based object detection. *Neural Computing & Applications*, *34*(13), 10469–10501. doi:10.100700521-021-06830-w

Rodriguez, E., Otero, B., Gutierrez, N., & Canal, R. (2021). A Survey of Deep Learning Techniques for Cyber security in Mobile Networks IEEE Communication. Survey. *Tutor*, *23*, 1920–1955.

Roopak, M., Tian, G. Y., & Chambers, J. (2019, January). Deep learning models for cyber security in IoT networks. In *2019 IEEE 9th annual computing and communication workshop and conference (CCWC)*, (pp. 452-457). IEEE.

Sabahi, F. (2011, May). Cloud computing security threats and responses. In *IEEE 3rd International Conference on Communication Software and Networks*, (pp. 245-249). IEEE. 10.1109/ICCSN.2011.6014715

Sait, S. (2021, August 19). Distributed deep learning - illustrated. *Medium*. https://towardsdatascience.com/distributed-deep-learning-ill ustrated-6256e07a0468

Sakalle, A., Tomar, P., Bhardwaj, H., & Alim, M. A. (2022). A modified LSTM framework for analyzing COVID-19 effect on emotion and mental health during pandemic using the EEG signals. *Journal of Healthcare Engineering, 2022*, 1–8. doi:10.1155/2022/8412430 PMID:35281542

Sakalle, A., Tomar, P., Bhardwaj, H., Iqbal, A., Sakalle, M., Bhardwaj, A., & Ibrahim, W. (2022). Genetic programming-based feature selection for emotion classification using EEG Signal. *Journal of Healthcare Engineering, 2022*, 1–6. doi:10.1155/2022/8362091 PMID:35299691

Saleem, A. A., Siddiqui, H. U. R., Shafique, R., Haider, A., & Ali, M. (2020). A Review on Smart IOT Based Parking System. In R. Ghazali, N. Nawi, M. Deris, & J. Abawajy (Eds.), *Recent Advances on Soft Computing and Data Mining. SCDM 2020. Advances in Intelligent Systems and Computing* (Vol. 978). Springer. doi:10.1007/978-3-030-36056-6_26

Salih Hasan, B. M., & Abdulazeez, A. M. (2021). A review of principal component analysis algorithm for dimensionality reduction. *Journal of Soft Computing and Data Mining, 2*(1). Advance online publication. doi:10.30880/jscdm.2021.02.01.003

Salih, T. A., & Younis, N. K. (2021). Designing an Intelligent Real-Time Public Transportation Monitoring System Based on IoT. *Open Access Library Journal, 8*(10), 1–14. doi:10.4236/oalib.1107985

Salman, Elhajj, Kayssi, & Chehab. (2015). Edge computing enabling the Internet of Things. *Proc. IEEE 2ndWorld Forum Internet Things (WF-IoT)*, 603-608.

Sanjay & Renuka. (2020). Smart Healthcare using Internet of Things (IoT) for Remote Diagnosis of Covid-19 Patients. *i-Manager's Journal on Software Engineering, 15*(2), 15-24. Doi:10.26634/jse.15.2.18075

Sarraf, Pattnaik, & Vaibhaw. (2020). *Brain-computer interfaces and their applications, An Industrial IoT Approach for Pharmaceutical Industry Growth*. Elsevier. doi:10.1016/B978-0-12-821326-1.00002-4

Sathya, M., Nirmala, S., Shivananda, S., Jeyaseelan. V. D., & Amutha, R. (2022). Smart E-Health Records using IoT. *International Journal of All Research Education and Scientific Methods, 10*(3), 2488–2493. http://www.ijaresm.com/uploaded_files/document_file/Dr.M_.Sa thya_march_2022_l4jL.pdf

Serrano, W. (2018). Digital Systems in Smart City and Infrastructure: Digital as a Service. *Smart Cities, 1*(1), 134–154. doi:10.3390martcities1010008

Sethi, P., & Sarangi, S. R. (2017). Internet of things: Architectures, protocols, and applications. *Journal of Electrical and Computer Engineering, 2017*, 2017. doi:10.1155/2017/9324035

Sha, K., Andrew Yang, T., & Wei, W. (2020). A survey of edge computing-based designs for IoT security. *Digital Communications and Networks, 6*(2), 195-202.

Shadroo, S., Rahmani, A. M., & Rezaee, A. (2022). Survey on the application of deep learning in the Internet of Things. *Telecommunication Systems, 79*(4), 601–627. doi:10.100711235-021-00870-2

Sha, K., Wei, W., Yang, A., & Shi, W. (2016). Security in internet of things: Opportunities and challenges. *Proceedings of International Conference on Identification, Information & Knowledge in the Internet of Things (IIKI 2016)*.

Shakhnarovich, G., Darrell, T., & Indyk, P. (2006). *Nearest-neighbor methods in learning and vision: theory and practice*. Neural Information, Processing. doi:10.7551/mitpress/4908.001.0001

Shalev-Shwartz, S., & Ben-David, S. (2014). *Understanding Machine Learning: From Theory to Algorithms.* Cambridge University Press. doi:10.1017/CBO9781107298019

Shashishankar, A., Dule, C. S., Ananthapadmanabha, K., Rajasekharaiah, K. M., Sathya, M., & Nallathambi, A. (2022). *Cloud based Electric Vehicles Temperature Monitoring system using IoT,* Registration Number- 1191845. Canadian Copyright.

Sheen, S., Anitha, R., & Natarajan, V. (2015). Android based malware detection using a multifeature collaborative decision fusion approach. *Neurocomputing, 151,* 905–912. doi:10.1016/j.neucom.2014.10.004

Sheikh, A., Ambhaikar, A., & Kumar, S. (2019). Quality of services improvement for secure iot networks. *International Journal of Engineering and Advanced Technology.*

Shi, F., Ning, H., Huangfu, W., Zhang, F., Wei, D., Hong, T., & Daneshmand, M. (2020). Recent progress on the convergence of the Internet of Things and artificial intelligence. *IEEE Network, 34*(5), 8–15. doi:10.1109/MNET.011.2000009

Shi, W., Cao, J., Zhang, Q., Li, Y., & Xu, L. (2016). Edge computing: Vision and challenges. *IEEE Internet of Things Journal, 3*(5), 637–646. doi:10.1109/JIOT.2016.2579198

Shon, D., Im, K., Jang, B., Kim, J. M., Lim, D. S., & Park, J. H. (2018). Emotional Stress State Detection Using Genetic Algorithm-Based Feature Selection on EEG Signals. *International Journal of Environmental Research and Public Health, 15*(11), 2461. doi:10.3390/ijerph15112461 PMID:30400575

Shone, N., Ngoc, T. N., Phai, V. D., & Shi, Q. (2018). A deep learning approach to network intrusion detection, IEEE Transactions on Emerging Top Computer. *Intelligence, 2*(1), 41–50.

Shukla, S. N., & Champaneria, T. A. (2017). Survey of various data collection ways for smart transportation domain of smart city. *Proceedings of International Conference on I-SMAC (IoT in Social, Mobile, Analytics and Cloud) (I-SMAC).* 10.1109/I-SMAC.2017.8058265

Silva, J. A. H., & Hernández-Alvarez, M. (2017, October). Large scale ransomware detection by cognitive security. In *IEEE Second Ecuador Technical Chapters Meeting (ETCM),* (pp. 1-4). IEEE.

Singh, M., & Baranwal, G. (2018). Quality of service (qos) in internet of things. In *2018 3rd International Conference on Internet of Things: Smart Innovation and Usages (IoT-SIU),* (pp. 1-6). IEEE.

Singh, U., Determe, J.-F., Horlin, F., & De Doncker, P. (2020). Crowd Monitoring: State-of-the-Art and Future Directions. *IETE Technical Review, 38*(6), 578–594. doi:10.1080/02564602.2020.1803152

Singla, S., Gandotra, E., Bansal, D., & Sofat, S. (2015). Detecting and classifying morphed malwares: A survey. *International Journal of Computers and Applications, 122*(10).

Sivakumar, N. (2018, January 1). *Shodhganga@INFLIBNET: Performance analysis and optimization of microcantilever beam smart structures.* http://hdl.handle.net/10603/257919

Sivakumar, N., & Kanagasabapathy, H. (2018). Optimization of Parameters of Cantilever Beam Using Novel Bio-Inspired Algorithms: A Comparative Approach. *Journal of Computational and Theoretical Nanoscience, 15*(1), 66–77. doi:10.1166/jctn.2018.7057

Sony, S., Laventure, S., & Sadhu, A. (2019). A literature review of next-generation smart sensing technology in structural health monitoring. *Structural Control and Health Monitoring, 26*(3), e2321. doi:10.1002tc.2321

Spring, J. (2011). Monitoring cloud computing by layer, part 1. *IEEE Security and Privacy, 9*(2), 66–68. doi:10.1109/MSP.2011.33

Srivastava, S., Divekar, A. V., Anilkumar, C., Naik, I., Kulkarni, V., & Pattabiraman, V. (2021). Comparative analysis of deep learning image detection algorithms. *Journal of Big Data*, 8(1), 1–27. doi:10.118640537-021-00434-w

Statista: Mobile operating systems market share. (2020). https://www.statista.com/statistics/272698/global-market-share-held-by-mobile-operating-systems-since-2009/

Su, S., Qu, W., Wu, Y., & Yang, Z. (2021). Intelligent evaluation scheme of ideological and Political Education Quality of College English course based on AHP under the background of Big Data. *2021 6th International Conference on Smart Grid and Electrical Automation (ICSGEA)*. doi:10.1109/icsgea53208.2021.00123

Sujatha, K., Bhavani, N. P. G., Cao, S.-Q., & Ram Kumar, K. S. (2018). Soft sensor for flame temperature measurement and IoT based monitoring in power plants. *Materials Today: Proceedings*, 5(4), 10755–10762. doi:10.1016/j.matpr.2017.12.359

Sujatha, K., & Pappa, N. (2011). Combustion Quality Monitoring in PS Boilers Using Discriminant RBF. *ISA Transactions*, 2(7), 2623–263.

Sultana, F., Sufian, A., & Dutta, P. (2019). Review of Object Detection Algorithms using CNN. *Proceedings of 2nd International Conference on Communication, Devices and Computing (ICCDC 2019)*.

Sun, Q., Xu, J., Ma, X., Zhou, A., Hsu, C.-H., & Wang, S. (2021). Edge-enabled distributed deep learning for 5G privacy protection. *IEEE Network*, 35(4), 213–219. doi:10.1109/MNET.021.2000292

Suryawanshi & Vanjale. (2020). Optimum analysis of brain activities by using classification and learning techniques. *International Journal of Advanced Science and Technology, 29(7).*

Taiwo, O., Ezugwu, A. E., Oyelade, O. N. & Almutairi, M.S. (2022). Enhanced Intelligent Smart Home Control and Security System Based on Deep Learning Model. *Wireless Communications and Mobile Computing*. doi:10.1155/2022/9307961

Takabi, H., Joshi, J. B., & Ahn, G. J. (2010, July). Securecloud: Towards a comprehensive security framework for cloud computing environments. In *IEEE 34th Annual Computer Software and Applications Conference Workshops*, (pp. 393-398). IEEE.

Takabi, H., Joshi, J. B., & Ahn, G. J. (2010). Security and privacy challenges in cloud computing environments. *IEEE Security and Privacy*, 8(6), 24–31. doi:10.1109/MSP.2010.186

Talha, K. A., Alper, D. I., & Aydin, C. (2015). APK Auditor: Permission-based Android malware detection system. *Digital Investigation*, 13, 1–14. doi:10.1016/j.diin.2015.01.001

Tan, C. K., Wilcox, S. J., Ward, J., & Lewitt, M. (2003). Monitoring near burner slag deposition with a hybrid neural network system. *Measurement Science & Technology*, 14(7), 232–236. doi:10.1088/0957-0233/14/7/332

Tang, T. A., Mhamdi, L., McLernon, D., Zaidi, S. A. R., & Ghogho, M. (2016). Deep learning ap- proach for network intrusion detection in software defined networking. *International Conference on Wireless Networks and Mobile Communi- cations (WINCOM)*, IEEE, p. 258–63.

Tang, F., Mao, B., Fadlullah, Z. M., & Kato, N. (2018). On a novel deep-learning-based intelligent partially overlapping channel assignment in SDN-IoT. *IEEE Communications Magazine*, 56(9), 80–86. doi:10.1109/MCOM.2018.1701227

Teruela, E., Cortésb, C., Díezb, L. I., & Arauzob, I. (2005). Monitoring and Prediction of fouling in coal-fired utility boilers using Neural Networks. *Chemical Engineering Science*, 60(18), 5035–5048. doi:10.1016/j.ces.2005.04.029

Tewary, S. (2016). A novel approach towards designing a wearable Smart Health Monitoring System measuring the vital parameters and emergency situations in real-time and providing the necessary medical care through telemedicine. *2016 IEEE Students' Conference on Electrical, Electronics and Computer Science (SCEECS)*, 1-8. doi: 10.1109/SCEECS.2016.7509332

Thakur, R. S., Yadav, R. N., & Gupta, L. (2020). Prelu and edge-aware filter-based image denoiser using Convolutional Neural Network. *IET Image Processing*, *14*(15), 3869–3879. doi:10.1049/iet-ipr.2020.0717

Thamilarasu, G., & Chawla, S. (2019). Towards deep-learning-driven intrusion detection for the internet of things. *Sensors (Basel)*, *19*(9), 1977. doi:10.339019091977 PMID:31035611

Thilagam, K. (2022) Secure IoT Healthcare Architecture with Deep Learning-Based Access Control System. *Journal of Nanomaterials*. doi:. doi:10.1155/2022/2638613

Thilakarathne, N. N., Kagita, M. K., & Gadekallu, T. R. (2020). The Role of the Internet of Things in Health Care: A Systematic and Comprehensive Study. *International Journal of Engineering and Management Research*, *10*(4), 2394–6962. doi:10.31033/ijemr.10.4.22

Tien, J.M. (2017). Internet of Things, Real-Time Decision Making, and Artificial Intelligence. *Ann. Data. Sci.*, *4*, 149–178. doi:. doi:10.1007/s40745-017-0112-5

Tiwari, S., Gupta, R. K., & Kashyap, R. (2018). To enhance web response time using agglomerative clustering technique for web navigation recommendation. *Advances in Intelligent Systems and Computing*, 659–672. doi:10.1007/978-981-10-8055-5_59

Toh, C. K., Sanguesa, J. A., Cano, J. C., & Martinez, F. J. (2020). Advances in smart roads for future smart cities. *Proceedings. Mathematical, Physical, and Engineering Sciences*, *476*(2233), 20190439. doi:. doi:10.1098/rspa.2019.0439

Tong, M., Fan, L., Nan, H., & Zhao, Y. (2019). Smart Camera Aware Crowd Counting via Multiple Task Fractional Stride Deep Learning. *Sensors (Basel)*, *19*(6), 1–14. doi:10.339019061346 PMID:30889874

TonyZ1Min. (2022). *YOLO for K210*. Retrieved July 27, 2022, from https://github.com/TonyZ1Min/yolo-for-k210

Torres-Sanchez, E., Alastruey-Benede, J., & Torres-Moreno, E. (2020). Developing an AI IoT application with open software on a RISC-V SoC. In *Proceedings of XXXV Conference on Design of Circuits and Integrated Systems (DCIS)* (pp. 1-6). 10.1109/DCIS51330.2020.9268645

Trojan, W. (2020a, May). Artificial Intelligence for Beginners (1): Object recognition using the Maixduino board. *Elektor Magazine*, 12-17.

Trojan, W. (2020b, July). Artificial Intelligence for Beginners (2): Neural networks with Linux and Python. *Elektor Magazine*, 110-114.

Trojan, W. (2020c, Sept.). Artificial Intelligence for Beginners (3): A stand-alone neural network. *Elektor Magazine*, September & October 2020, 44-49.

Tsai, H. Y., Siebenhaar, M., & Miede, A. (2012). *Threat as a Service? Virtualization's impact on Cloud Security*, IEEE, 32-37.

Tu, Y., Chen, H., Yan, L., & Zhou, X. (2022). Task offloading based on LSTM prediction and deep reinforcement learning for efficient edge computing in IoT. *Future Internet*, *14*(2), 30. doi:10.3390/fi14020030

U.S. National Library of Medicine. (2022). *National Center for Biotechnology Information*. NCBI. https://www.ncbi.nlm.nih.gov/

Udayakumar, K., & Ramamoorthy, S. (2022). Intelligent Resource Allocation in Industrial IoT using Reinforcement Learning with Hybrid Meta-Heuristic Algorithm. *Cybernetics and Systems*. Advance online publication. doi:10.1080/01969722.2022.2080341

Ultralytics. (2020). *YOLO-v5*. Retrieved July 27, 2022, from https://github.com/ultralytics/yolov5

Umar, B., Hejazi, H., Lengyel, L., & Farkas, K. (2018). Evaluation of IoT device management tools. In *Proc. 3rd Int. Conf. Adv. Comput., Commun. Services (ACCSE)*, (pp. 15-21).

Umer, M., Sadiq, S., Karamti, H., Karamti, W., Majeed, R., & Nappi, M. (2022). IoT Based Smart Monitoring of Patients' with Acute Heart Failure. *Sensors (Basel)*, 22(7), 2431. doi:10.339022072431 PMID:35408045

Unal, Z. (2020). Smart Farming Becomes Even Smarter with Deep Learning—A Bibliographical Analysis. *IEEE Access: Practical Innovations, Open Solutions*, 8, 105587–105609. doi:10.1109/ACCESS.2020.3000175

United Nations. (2018). The World's *Cities*. Author.

Usharani, S., Rajmohan, R., Bala, P. M., Saravanan, D., Agalya, P., & Raman, D. R. (2022). Integrated Implementation of Hybrid Deep Learning Models and IoT Sensors for Analyzing Solider Health and Emergency Monitoring. *2022 International Conference on Smart Technologies and Systems for Next Generation Computing (ICSTSN)*, 1-6. 10.1109/ICSTSN53084.2022.9761332

Vathalani, Sathaye, & Peshattiwar. (2017). Anti-Oxidant Potential of Methanolic Extract Of Trigonella Foenum, Trachyspermum Copticum, Nigella Sativa And Their Combination In 1:1:1 Ratio. *International Journal of Pharmaceutical Sciences and Research, 8*(4).

Vermesan, O., Bahr, R., Ottella, M., Serrano, M., Karlsen, T., Wahlstrøm, T., Sand, H. E., Ashwathnarayan, M., & Gamba, M. T. (2020). Internet of robotic things intelligent connectivity and platforms. *Frontiers*. https://www.frontiersin.org/articles/10.3389/frobt.2020.00104/full

Viega, J. (2009). Cloud computing and the common man. *Computer*, 42(08), 106–108. doi:10.1109/MC.2009.206

Vimal, S., Khari, M., Dey, N., Crespo, R. G., & Robinson, Y. H. (2020). Enhanced resource allocation in mobile edge computing using reinforcement learning based MOACO algorithm for IIOT. *Computer Communications*, 151, 355–364. doi:10.1016/j.comcom.2020.01.018

Vinayakumar, R., Alazab, M., Soman, K. P., Poornachandran, P., Al-Nemrat, A., & Venkatraman, S. (2019). Deep learning approach for intelligent intrusion detection system. *IEEE Access : Practical Innovations, Open Solutions*, 7, 41525–41550. doi:10.1109/ACCESS.2019.2895334

Virusshare. (2019). https://virusshare.com/

Voulodimos, A., Doulamis, N., Doulamis, A., & Protopapadakis, E. (2018). Deep Learning for Computer Vision: A Brief Review. *Computational Intelligence and Neuroscience*, 2018, 1–13. doi:10.1155/2018/7068349 PMID:29487619

Walia, R., & Garg, P. (2022). Performance and Security Issues of Integrating Cloud Computing with IoT. In *Emergent Converging Technologies and Biomedical Systems*, (pp. 1 12). Springer. doi:10.1007/978-981-16-8774-7_1

Wang, B., Liu, X., & Zhang, Y. (2022). *internet of things and BDS Application*. Springer. doi:10.1007/978-981-16-9194-2

Wang, Q., Yang, H., Wang, Q., Huang, W., & Deng, B. (2019). A deep learning based data forwarding algorithm in mobile social networks Peer-to-Peer Network. *Application*, 12, 1638–1650.

Wang, R., Wang, Z., Xu, Z., Wang, C., Li, Q., Zhang, Y., & Li, H. (2021). A Real-Time Object Detector for Autonomous Vehicles Based on YOLOv4. *Computational Intelligence and Neuroscience, 2021*, 1–11. doi:10.1155/2021/9218137 PMID:34925498

Wang, S.-H., Muhammad, K., Hong, J., Sangaiah, A. K., & Zhang, Y.-D. (2018). Alcoholism identification via convolutional neural network based on parametric relu, dropout, and batch normalization. *Neural Computing & Applications, 32*(3), 665–680. doi:10.100700521-018-3924-0

Wang, S., Ruan, Y., Tu, Y., Wagle, S., Brinton, C. G., & Joe-Wong, C. (2021). Network-aware optimization of Distributed Learning for Fog Computing. *IEEE/ACM Transactions on Networking, 29*(5), 2019–2032. doi:10.1109/TNET.2021.3075432

Wang, W., Wang, X., Feng, D., Liu, J., Han, Z., & Zhang, X. (2014). Exploring permission-induced risk in android applications for malicious application detection. *IEEE Transactions on Information Forensics and Security, 9*(11), 1869–1882. doi:10.1109/TIFS.2014.2353996

Wang, Y., Cai, W., & Wei, P. (2016). A deep learning approach for detecting malicious JavaScript code. *Security and Communication Networks, 9*(11), 1520–1534. doi:10.1002ec.1441

Wikimedia Foundation. (2021, July 27). Multi-access Edge Computing. *Wikipedia*. https://en.wikipedia.org/wiki/Multi-access_edge_computing

Wikimedia Foundation. (2022, July 9). Artificial Intelligence. *Wikipedia*. https://en.wikipedia.org/wiki/Artificial_intelligence

Wortmann, F., & Flüchter, K. (2015). Internet of things. *Business & Information Systems Engineering, 57*(3), 221–224. doi:10.100712599-015-0383-3

Wu, X., Liu, C., & Wang, L. (2021). *Internet of things-enabled real-time health monitoring system using deep learning. Neural Comput & Applic*. doi:10.100700521-021-06440-6

Wu, Y., Wei, D., & Feng, J. (2020). *Network Attacks Detection Methods Based on Deep Learning Techniques: A Survey*. Security and Communication Networks Volume., doi:10.1155/2020/8872923

Xiang, J., & Liu, N. (2022). Crowd Density Estimation Method Using Deep Learning for Passenger Flow Detection System in Exhibition Center. *Scientific Programming, 2022*, 1–9. doi:10.1155/2022/1990951

Xiao, C., Choi, E., & Sun, J. (2018, October 1). Opportunities and challenges in developing deep learning models using electronic health records data: A systematic review. *Journal of the American Medical Informatics Association, 25*(10), 1419–1428. doi:10.1093/jamia/ocy068 PMID:29893864

Xu, Z., Liu, W., Huang, J., Yang, C., Lu, J., & Tan, H. (2020). Artificial Intelligence for Securing IoT Services in Edge Computing: A Survey. Security and Communication Networks. doi:10.1155/2020/8872586

Xu, R., Zeng, Q., Zhu, L., Chi, H., Du, X., & Guizani, M. (2019). Privacy Leakage in Smart Homes and Its Mitigation: IFTTT as a Case Study. *IEEE Access : Practical Innovations, Open Solutions, 7*, 63457–63471. doi:10.1109/ACCESS.2019.2911202

Yan, L., Wang, P., Yang, J., Hu, Y., Han, Y. & Yao, J. (2021) Refined Path Planning for Emergency Rescue Vehicles on Congested Urban Arterial Roads via Reinforcement Learning Approach. *Journal of Advanced Transportation*. doi:. doi:10.1155/2021/8772688

Yao, Z. J., Bi, J., & Chen, Y. X. (2018). Applying Deep Learning to Individual and Community Health Monitoring Data: A Survey. *Int. J. Autom. Comput., 15*(6), 643–655. doi:10.100711633-018-1136-9

Yerima, S. Y., Sezer, S., & Muttik, I. (2015). High accuracy android malware detection using ensemble learning. *IET Information Security*, *9*(6), 313–320. doi:10.1049/iet-ifs.2014.0099

Yue, Y., Li, S., Legg, P. & Li, F. (2021). Deep Learning-Based Security Behaviour Analysis in IoT Environments: A Survey. *Security and Communication Networks*. doi:. doi:10.1155/2021/8873195

Yu, S., Chen, B., Levesque-Bristol, C., & Vansteenkiste, M. (2016). Chinese education examined via the lens of self-determination. *Educational Psychology Review*, *30*(1), 177–214. doi:10.100710648-016-9395-x

Yusuf, A. A., & Adeshina, S. A. (2021). Deep Learning Methodologies for Genomic Data Prediction: Review. *JAIMS*, *2*(1-2), 1-11. Available from: http://www.oapublishing-jaims.com/jaims/article/view/61

Yu, W., Liang, F., He, X., Hatcher, W. G., Lu, C., Lin, J., & Yang, X. (2018). A Survey on the Edge Computing for the Internet of Things. *IEEE Access: Practical Innovations, Open Solutions*, *6*, 6900–6919. doi:10.1109/ACCESS.2017.2778504

Zafar, S., Jangsher, S., Bouachir, O., Aloqaily, M., & Ben Othman, J. (2019). QoS enhancement with deep learning-based interference prediction in mobile IoT. *Computer Communications*, *148*, 86–97. doi:10.1016/j.comcom.2019.09.010

Zanella, A., Bui, N., Castellani, A., Vangelista, L., & Zorzi, M. (2014). Internet of Things for Smart Cities. *IEEE Internet of Things Journal*, *1*(1), 22–32. doi:10.1109/JIOT.2014.2306328

Zhang, Y., Wang, A. & Hu, W. (2002). Deep Learning-Based Consumer Behavior Analysis and Application Research. *Wireless Communications and Mobile Computing*. doi:. doi:10.1155/2022/4268982

Zhang, C., Li, H., Wang, X., & Yang, X. (2015). Cross-scene Crowd Counting via Deep Convolutional Neural Networks. In *Proceedings of IEEE Conference on Computer Vision and Pattern Recognition (CVPR)* (pp. 833-841). 10.1109/CVPR.2015.7298684

Zhang, J., Chen, S., Tian, S., Gong, W., Cai, G., & Wang, Y. (2021). A Crowd Counting Framework Combining with Crowd Location. *Journal of Advanced Transportation*, *2021*, 1–14. doi:10.1155/2021/6664281

Zhang, J., & Meng, G. (2021). *Evaluation model of practical effect of ideological and political education based on Deep Data Mining. In 2021 Global Reliability and Prognostics and Health Management*. PHM-Nanjing. doi:10.1109/phm-nanjing52125.2021.9612831

Zhang, J., & Tao, D. (2021). Empowering Things with Intelligence: A Survey of the Progress, Challenges, and Opportunities in Artificial Intelligence of Things. *IEEE Internet of Things Journal*, *8*(10), 7789–7817. doi:10.1109/JIOT.2020.3039359

Zhang, Q., Duan, R., Wang, J., & Cui, Y. (2019). Smart building environment monitoring based on Gaussian Process. *2019 International Conference on Control, Automation and Information Sciences (ICCAIS)*, 1-6. 10.1109/ICCAIS46528.2019.9074549

Zhang, S., Li, Y., Zhang, S., Shahabi, F., Xia, S., Deng, Y., & Alshurafa, N. (2022). Alshurafa N. Deep Learning in Human Activity Recognition with Wearable Sensors: A Review on Advances. *Sensors (Basel)*, *22*(4), 1476. doi:10.339022041476 PMID:35214377

Zhang, W., Yang, D., Peng, H., Wu, W., Quan, W., Zhang, H., & Shen, X. (2021). Deep reinforcement learning based resource management for DNN inference in industrial IoT. *IEEE Transactions on Vehicular Technology*, *70*(8), 7605–7618. doi:10.1109/TVT.2021.3068255

Zhang, Y., Li, P., & Wang, X. (2019). Intrusion detection for IoT based on improved genetic algorithm and deep belief network. *IEEE Access : Practical Innovations, Open Solutions*, *7*, 31711–31722. doi:10.1109/ACCESS.2019.2903723

Zhao, C., Min, G., Winkley, J., Yang, L. T., Jiang, P., & Munnoch, R. (2016). An Intelligent Information Forwarder for Healthcare Big Data Systems with Distributed Wearable Sensors. *IEEE Systems Journal*, *10*(3), 1147–1159. doi:10.1109/JSYST.2014.2308324

Zhao, G., Zhang, C., & Zheng, L. (2017), Intrusion detection using deep belief network and probabilistic neural network. In: *IEEE International Conference on Computational Science and Engineering (CSE) and IEEE International Conference on Embedded and Ubiquitous Computing (EUC)*, IEEE, p. 639–642 10.1109/CSE-EUC.2017.119

Zhao, K., Zhang, D., Su, X., & Li, W. (2015). *Fest: A feature extraction and selection tool for Android malware detection. In 2015 IEEE symposium on computers and communication (ISCC)*. IEEE.

Zhao, Z.-Q., Zheng, P., Xu, S.-T., & Wu, X. (2019). Object Detection with Deep Learning: A Review. *IEEE Transactions on Neural Networks and Learning Systems*, *30*(11), 3212–3232. doi:10.1109/TNNLS.2018.2876865 PMID:30703038

Zhen8838. (2022). *K210 Yolo framework*. Retrieved July 27, 2022, from https://github.com/zhen8838/K210_Yolo_framework

Zikria, Y. B., Afzal, M. K., Kim, S. W., Marin, A., & Guizani, M. (2020). Deep learning for intelligent IoT: Opportunities, challenges and solutions. *Computer Communications*, *164*, 50–53. doi:10.1016/j.comcom.2020.08.017

Zou, Q. (2022). Exploring the education reform of architectural drawing and drafting under the background of curriculum ideology and politics. *Journal of Contemporary Educational Research*, *6*(3), 40–48. doi:10.26689/jcer.v6i3.3790

About the Contributors

T. Kavitha is working as a Professor in the Dept. of Computer Engineering, New Horizon College of Engineering (Autonomous), VTU. She completed her Ph.D. in the Faculty of Information and Communication Engineering, Anna University Chennai, India in the year 2014. She received her M.E. degree in Systems Engineering and Operations Research from Anna University, Chennai India in the year 2006. B.E. in Electronics and Communication Engineering from Bharathidasan University, India in the year 2000. She has 21+ years of experience in Teaching and Research from Reputed Engineering Colleges. She is Anna University and VTU recognized supervisor for guiding Ph.D. and M.S. (by Research) Programme. Under her guidance, a scholar completed a Ph.D. at Anna University. She has received Funds from different agencies like ISTE-SRM, VTU-TEQIP, IE, VTU, AICTE-ISTE, and AICTE to organize FDP, workshops, Training, and conferences. She is also a Mentor for the projects who got funds from VTU and KSCKT.

Senbagavalli Ganesan is working as an Associate Professor in the Department of Electronics and Communication Engineering, AMC Engineering College,VTU. She completed her Ph.D in the Faculty of Electronics and Communication Engineering, VTU, Belagavi, India in the year 2021. She received her M.Tech. degree in VLSI system design from JNTU, Andhra Pradesh, India in the year 2008. B.E. in Electronics and Communication Engineering from Madras University, India in the year 2001. She has 18 years of experience in Teaching and Research from Reputed Engineering Colleges. She has published 3 indian patents, 15 research papers in National/International Conferences and various journals.Her field of interests includes Image and video processing, Computer vision and VLSI Design.

Deepika Koundal is currently associated with University of Petroleum and Energy Studies, Dehradun. She received the recognition and honorary membership from Neutrosophic Science Association from University of Mexico, USA. She is also selected as a Young scientist in 6th BRICS Conclave in 2021. She received the Master and Ph.D. degrees in computer science & engineering from the Panjab University, Chandigarh in 2015. She received the B. Tech. degree in computer science & engineering from Kurkushetra University, India. She is the awardee of research excellence award given by Chitkara University in 2019 and UPES in 2022. She has published more than 40 research articles in reputed SCI and Scopus indexed journals, conferences and two books. She is currently a guest editor in Computers & Electrical Engineering, Internet of Things Journals and IEEE Transaction of Industrial Informatics, Computational and Mathematical Methods in Medicine. She is also serving as Associate Editor in IET Image Processing and International Journal of Computer Applications. She also has served on many technical program committees as well as organizing committees and invited to give guest lectures and tutorials in Faculty development programs, international conferences and summer schools. Her Areas of Interest are Artificial Intelligence, Biomedical Imaging and Signals, Image Processing, Soft Computing, Machine Learning/ Deep Learning. She has also served as reviewer in many repudiated journals of IEEE, Springer, Elsevier, IET, Hindawi, Wiley and Sage.

Yanhui Guo received his Ph.D. degree in the Department of Computer Science, Utah State University, USA. He was a research fellow in the Department of Radiology at the University of Michigan and an assistant professor at St. Thomas University. Dr. Guo is currently an associate professor in the Department of Computer Science at the University of Illinois Springfield. Dr. Guo's research area includes computer vision, machine learning, data analytics, neutrosophic set, computer-aided detection/diagnosis, and computer-assisted surgery. He has published 3 books, more than 110 journal papers and 40 conference papers, completed more than 10 grant-funded research projects, has 2 patents, and worked as an associate editor of different international journals, reviewers for top journals and conferences. Dr. Guo successfully applied neutrosophic set into image processing in 2008 and has published many research works in this area. Dr. Guo was a co-founder and chief scientist of MedSights Tech Inc., a high technology company focusing on a computer-assisted surgery system. Dr. Guo was awarded a University Scholar in 2019, the university system's highest faculty honor, recognizing outstanding teaching and scholarship.

Deepak Jain is working as an Associate Professor at Institute of Automation, Chongqing University of Posts and Telecommunications, Chongqing, China. He received the Bachelor of Engineering degree from Rajiv Gandhi Proudyogiki Vishwavidyalaya, India, in 2010, the Master of Technology degree from the Jaypee University of Engineering and Technology, India, in 2012, and the Ph.D. degree from the Institute of Automation, University of Chinese Academy of Sciences, Beijing, China. He was an awardee of CAS-TWAS Presidential fellowship from 2014-2018. He was invited as "Foreign Experts" by Shandong Taian Administration of foreign Expert Affairs. He was an Adjunct Associate Professor in Oriental University, Indore. He has presented several papers in peer-reviewed conferences and has published numerous studies in science cited journals. His research interests include deep learning, machine learning, pattern recognition, and computer vision.

* * *

Latha B. obtained her graduation (2001) and post-graduation (2004) in Physics from Madurai Kamaraj University, Madurai, and M. Phil in 2004 from Manonmanium Sundaranar University. The investigations on "Structure Re-Determination of Nitrobenzene and Growth and Characterisation of Some Amino Acid Crystals" were carried out during the post-graduation. She has been awarded Rank 1 in the academic profile during her post-graduation. In her M. Phil degree, she carried out the project entitled "Computational Investigations on Zinc Telluride." She obtained her doctoral degree from SC-SVMV University, Enathur, Kanchipuram under the guidance of Dr. S. Gunasekaran, Dean (R&D) St. Peter's Institute of Higher Education and Research. She did her investigations on molecular dynamics of some pharmaceutical compounds used to treat hypertension. She has participated in and presented her research paper at more than 15 national and international conferences. She has bagged the Best paper award for her research presentations. She started her teaching carrier in the year 2003 as a Lecturer in Physics Department at Dr. MGR Educational and Research Institute and has been right now promoted as Deputy Dean (Consultancy). She has been awarded the Best Teacher award in the year 2011. She received Sir. C.V. Raman was awarded for her endeavor in interdisciplinary research in the year 2014. She was conferred with Perasiriya Rathna Award in the year 2018 from Namakkal Tamil Sangam. She has coordinated various science projects and activities, wherein a student team coordinated by her won first prize in the Project, in the Science Exhibition conducted by Science City, Chennai. She has coordinated a student team in the 100 Femto Satellites Launch on Feb 7 2021 at Rameswaram, Tamil Nadu. Right now, she is acting as one of the staff coordinators of the 75 Students' Satellites Mission scheduled to launch 75 students satellites to commemorate 75 years of Independence by ISRO.

Sankari B. R. is currently working as an Assistant Professor, in the department of EEE at Dr. MGR Educational & Research Institute. She has also served as a session chair few national and international conferences. 5 Indian patents are published with 1 Australian patent having granted. She has organized and attended many faculty development programs. She has recieved the best teacher award. She is also a member in various professional societies.

Miguel Botto Tobar is Professor at University of Guayaquil. Head of Research Group in Artificial Intelligence and Information Technologies. General Editor of Journals at University de Guayaquil. PhD in Computer Science at the Eindhoven University of Technology in the Netherlands. He is the author/co-author of more than 30 indexed articles; author of "Problem-Based Learning: A Didactic Strategy in the Teaching of System Simulation", editor of "Technology Trends", "Advances in Emerging Trends and Technologies", and "Applied Technologies"; and co-editor of "Information and Communication Technologies of Ecuador (TIC.EC)" and "Technology, Sustainability and Educational Innovation (TSIE)", all published by Springer Verlag, Switzerland. He is editor in chief of Ecuadorian Science Journal, associate editor of Periodicals of Engineering and Natural Sciences, and regional editor of JOIV: International Journal on Informatics Visualization. His current research areas include Software Engineering, Empirical Software Engineering, Model-Based Software Development, and Social Aspects in Software Engineering.

Tamilselvi C. is currently working as Assistant Professor, in the Department of IT at Dr. MGR Educational & Research Institute. She has also served as a session chair few national and international conferences. 5 Indian patents are published with 1 Austrialian patent having granted. She has organized and attended many faculty development programs. She has recieved the best teacher award. She is also a member in various professional societies.

Poorva Devi is currently working as an Assistant Professor at SCSVMV Deemed University, Kanchipuram. Over 12 years of teaching experience and 7 years of research experience in computer science and engineering discipline. More than 70+ research papers published in international journals with a high impact factor on Scopus, UGC care, Web of Science, Thomson Reuters, Indian citation index and so forth. 87+ research papers are published in International conferences like IEEE, Springer conference and so on.

Meghna Dhalaria is currently working in the department of Computer Science and Engineering at National Institute of Technology, Hamirpur, India and has completed her Ph.D in computer Science from Jaypee University of Information and Technology, Waknaghat, India. She received her Bachelor's degree from Baddi University of Emerging Sciences and Technologies. She completed her Master's degree from Thapar Institute of Engineering and Technology, Patiala. Her current research includes the applications of Machine learning and Deep learning.

Angela Diaz Cadena is an Engineer in Business Administration and Master in Creation and Management of Innovative Companies at University of Valencia, Spain. Currently, she is professor and postgraduate manager at University of Guayaquil.

Ekta Gandotra is currently working as an Assistant Professor in the Department of Computer Science & Engineering and Information Technology at Jaypee University of Information Technology, Waknaghat, India. She has around 14 years of teaching and research experience. She has completed her Ph.D. in Computer Science and Engineering from PEC University of Technology, Chandigarh, India. Her research areas include network & cyber security, malware threat profiling, cyber threat intelligence, machine learning, and big data analytics.

Deepak Gupta is working as an Assistant Professor in the Department of Computer Science & Engineering at Jaypee University of Information Technology, Waknaghat (India). He has completed his Ph.D. in Computer Science & Engineering from Thapar Institute of Engineering and Technology (Deemed to be University), Patiala (India). Prior to his foray into academia, he worked in IT industry for a decade performing different roles in software product development and program management. In all, he has more than 20 years of rich experience in IT industry and academics. His research interests include big data analytics, machine/deep learning, cybersecurity, and programming languages.

Nayana Hegde did her bachelor's in Electronics and Communication from Karnataka University, India in the year 2001 and her master's in Digital Communication and Networking from VTU, India in 2014. She did her Ph.D. in Electronics and Communication and Engineering from Reva University Bangalore, India in the year 2022. She is currently an Assistant Professor in the School of Electronics and Communication Engineering, Reva University Bangalore, India. Before that, she worked as Lecturer at Impact College of Engineering Bangalore from 2011-2012. Before that, she worked for Infosys Technologies Bangalore from 2003to 2009. She was Graduate Engineer Trainee at NTTF from 2002-2003.

Udayakumar Kamalakannan was born in Chennai, Tamil Nadu, India. He completed his undergraduate degree in Bachelor of Engineering -Computer Science and Engineering with First Class at Anna University, Chennai, Tamil Nadu, and India in 2005. And he completed his post graduate degree in Master of Engineering in Computer Science and Engineering with First class at Anna University, Chennai, Tamil Nadu, and India in 2009. He presently is doing full time research at SRM Institute of Science and Technology, Chennai, Tamil Nadu, India since 2021. His current research is focusing on optimal resource allocation in Industrial IoT using machine learning. He has published 12 research articles in the reputed Journals and conferences.

Krishnaveni Kesavan did her B.E in Mepco Schlenk Engineering, Sivakasi. M.E in Sathyabama University. She is currently working as an Associate Professor, in the department of EEE at Dr. MGR Educational & Research Institute. She has also served as a session chair few national and international conferences. 5 Indian patents are published with Australian patent having granted. She has organized and attended many faculty development programs. She has recieved the best teacher award. She is also a member in various professional societies.

Sujatha Kesavan is presently working as Professor in EEE, Department at Dr. M.G.R Educational and Research Institute, Chennai, Tamil Nadu, India and heading the Research centre 'Center for Electronics, Automation and Industrial Research (CEAIR). She has 20 years of teaching experience in various Engineering colleges. She completed her BE in the year 1999 from Bharathiyar University, ME in 2004 and Ph. D in 2011 from Anna University. She has presented/published papers in National/International conferences/journals and also published many books with Elsevier and Springer publisher. She is also a reviewer for journals published by Springer and Elsevier publishers. Presently doing her research in the area of Image Processing for Process Control. She is awarded the Best Researcher award for the academic year 2011–2012 and 2014 by IET. Also obtained travel grant from DST in 2014 for attending the conference. She is also awarded the young researcher award at the international conference at China in year 2015. She has also published 4 patents including one international patent with the Chinese University at Huaiyin Institute of Technology, China and also initiated international cooperation research between Huaiyin Institute of Technology, China and Dr.MGR Educational and Research Institute.

Sunilkumar S. Manvi received M.E., and Ph.D., from the University of Visweshwariah College of Engineering (UVCE), and the Indian Institute of Science (IISc.), Bengaluru, India, respectively. He is currently working as a Professor and Director of the School of Computing and IT, REVA University, Bengaluru, India. He has experience of around 29 years in teaching and research. He is involved in research of agent-based applications, multimedia communications, grid/cloud computing, mobile ad-hoc networks, sensor networks, e-commerce, vehicle networks, and mobile computing. He has published 5 books, 10 book chapters, 108 refereed journal papers, and about 150 refereed conference papers. He has presented many invited lectures and has conducted several workshops/seminars/conferences. He is a reviewer for many journals/conferences including IEEE and Elsevier Publications. He is a senior member of IEEE, Member CSI (India), Fellow of IETE (India), and Fellow of IE (India). He received Prof. Satish Dhawan Young Engineers State Award for the year 2015 from KSCST. The award is due for outstanding contribution in research on Engineering Sciences.

Sanjay Mate has combined experience of 8 plus years in IT industries and academics. He authored syllabus based Text book of Machine Learning Application, Mobile Computing, Human Computer Interaction and Big Data Analytics, Introduction to IT System. He has published and invented two Indian patents, and many research articles in reputed journals. He is Editorial board member and reviewer for some international journals. He completed Masters in Information Technology in JNTU Hyderabad, Bachelors in IT in MMCOE, Pune, India. He is working as Lecturer in IT at Government Polytechnic Daman and Research Scholar of Computer Science Engineering, Sangam University, Bhilwara, India. He is a member of ISTE, IAENG.

Jyoti R. Munavalli completed her graduation (B.E. in ECE) in 2001 from Karnataka University Dharwad, Master's (DEC) from Visveswaraya Technological University in 2009 and Doctorate in 2017 from Maastricht University, Netherlands. Currently, she is a working as an Associate Professor in the department of Electronics and Communication, BNM Institute of Technology, Bengaluru, Karnataka, India. She has over 16 years of academic and research experience. She is active in promoting research in academics and has filed two patents. She has published more than 30 papers in National and International Journals and Conferences (Scopus indexed and Web of Science journals), and book chapters. She has guided Postgraduate as well as Undergraduate projects. She is guiding two research scholars for their doctoral degree. She is member of editorial board and reviewer for indexed journals and conferences. She is an IEEE member, Life member of ISTE and Institute of Engineers. Her research interests are Health Informatics, Real-time optimization, hospital operations, biomedical applications and Artificial Intelligence.

Hema N. is an Associate Professor from the School of Computer Science and Engineering at Vellore Institute of Technology, Chennai. Her areas of research interest include Knowledge Engineering, Machine Learning, and Health Care Diagnosis. Has an academic experience of more than 21 years. She is currently involved in research works on Skin Lesions, and Non Invasive health diagnosis methodologies.

Sivakumar N. received his B.E in Mechanical Engineering and M.E in Engineering Design (Mechanical) in the year 2002 and 2004 respectively and PhD from Anna University in the year 2018. He started his career as Lecturer and served as Assistant Professor and Associate professor in various prestigious colleges and universities with a total teaching Experience of more than 17 years as of till date. His research interest is focused on Finite Element Method, Smart Materials, Strength of Materials, Renewable Energy Sources and requiring knowledge of the cloud for the data science. He has contributed as a member in various National and International Committees. He is the active life member of Indian Society of Technical Education, International Association of Computer Science & Information Technology, and International Association of Engineers. He has more than 12 publications in reputed national and international conferences, workshops, and journals. He is associated with a various National and International journals as a reviewer. He has 7 patent publication, One Canadian copyright.

M. Nalini received her B.E in Instrumentation and Control Engineering at Arulmigu Meenakshi Amman College of Engineering, affiliated to University of Madras, Chennai, Tamilnadu, India, during the year 2004 and M.Tech Degree in VLSI Design from Sathyabama University, Tamilnadu, India, in the year 2009. She received her PhD in SCSVMV University, Kancheepuram, Tamilnadu, India, in the Department of Electronics and Communication Engineering in the year 2019. She is currently working as a Professor in the department of Electronics and Instrumentation Engineering, Sri Sairam Engineering College, Chennai. She has a total of 17.1 years of Experience in the teaching field. She had 22 International Journal publications including 18 scopus indexed journals. She also published one book chapter and two patents. Till now she has guided 13 UG projects. She received the best woman faculty award for the year 2019-20 from Novel Research Academy. She is the reviewer for many reputed journals such as IEEE access, Wireless personal communication and Microprocessor and Microsystems. She also delivered many guest lecturers in various fdps. She is a mentor for ATL Tinkerpreneur 2021 Boot camp. She had received 1 lakh DST grant and 3.98 lakh from AICTE for STTP grant.

Amuthan Nallathambi received his B.E in Electrical & Electronics Engineering and M.E in Applied Electronics (EEE) in the year 1997 and 1999 respectively and PhD from Anna University in the year 2014. He started his career as Lecturer and served as Assistant Professor, Associate professor and Professor and Head of the Department in various prestigious colleges and universities with a total teaching Experience of more than two decades as of till date. His research interest is focused on Power Electronics,

Energy Conservation, Auditing, Renewable Energy Sources and requiring knowledge of the cloud for the National Level Integration. He has contributed as a member in various National and International Committees. He is the active life member of Society of EMC Engineers, Solar Energy Society of India, Artificial Intelligence Community (AIC), International Association of Computer Science & Information Technology, and International Association of Engineers. He has more than 31 publications in reputed national and international conferences, workshops, and journals. He is associated with a various National and International journals as a reviewer. He is presently guiding 6 Ph.D students under VTU. He has 7 patent publication, 2 Canadian copyright and 2 textbooks. He has received Alibaba Cloud Most Valuable Professional (MVP) award for the year 2021&2022.

Kannan Nova resides in Miami, United States. He earned a Master of Science (M.S.) in data science from Grand Canyon University in the United States. He holds architect certifications from Microsoft and Amazon, as well as associate certifications from Alibaba cloud, and have 23 years of experience in information technology (IT). Currently, he is a data scientist and cloud architect at Microsoft. He is a goal-oriented IT specialist professional with experience migrating on-premises systems to the cloud (Alibaba, Azure, AWS, and GCP) and assisting clients in embarking on their cloud computing adventures. As a 'Cloud Architect' for Sha Tech Solutions, he has extensive insurance, healthcare, logistics, including transportation, warehouse, customs, and import/export industry experience. He assists businesses and organizations in migrating on-premises workloads to the cloud, from the discovery/assessment phase through the migration phases, which include application, network, storage, database, data, and server migrations. He is an expert in system design utilizing cloud workloads, enterprise architect guidelines (TOGAF), and an ITIL operational framework. In addition to being familiar with all machine learning algorithms and data science projects, he also uses Alibaba Cloud – Platform of artificial intelligence (PAI) for machine learning and data science applications. He is presenting the security considerations for cloud workloads for both at-rest and in-transit data and network. In addition, he endorses data governance, policies, standards, the cloud adoption framework, the landing zone, scalability, security, maintainability, best patterns, and practices. The candidate has demonstrated mastery, proficiency, and knowledge in enabling cloud migration, automation processes, requirements analysis, enterprise resource planning (ERP), and team management. He is always concerned with compliance, laws, rules, and regulations, and he has experience with Python, R, Java &.NET, JSON, website creation, databases, and data analytics. He provides expert mentoring and training across the enterprise. He has worked in Singapore, India, Dubai, Australia, China, and the United States. Received the Most Valuable Professional (MVP) award from Alibaba Cloud for the years 2021 and 2022.

Velrajkumar Pitchandi obtained his B.E in Electrical and Electronics Engineering in 1997 from Noorul Islam College of Engineering, India. He obtained his M.E degree in Applied Electronics in 1999 from Hindustan College of Engineering, India. He has over 22 years of teaching / research experience. Currently he is working as an Associate Professor and Head of Center of Excellence in the Department of Electrical and Electronics Engineering, CMR Institute Technology, Bengaluru, Karnataka, India. His areas of interests are Control systems, Robotics and Automation. He served as Reviewer in International Journals and committee member in various international conferences. His professional memberships are Senior Member IEEE and Member IET.

Sivanand R. is Assistant Professor in EEE Department at Dr. M.G.R Educational and Research Institute, Chennai, Tamil Nadu, India. He has 18 years of teaching experience, Received his Ph.D degree in the year 2021. His area of interests includes Power Electronics, Renewable Energy, Nanomaterials, etc.

Chinnaiyan Ramasubramanian is working as Professor in School of Engineering, Department of Computer Science and Engineering in Presidency University, Bangalore. He is having 22+ Years of Teaching and 16+ years of Research Experiences. He published 80+ papers in referred international Journals and Conferences. He is a life member of ISTE and CSI. His research interest includes Machine Learning, Internet of Things, Software Reliability, Internet of Things, Big Data, Cloud Computing, Deep Learning, Wireless Sensor Networks, and Security.

Balachandar S. is working as a Principal Solution Engineer in Yuga Byte, Bangalore, India. He is having 21+ years of experience in various domains of IT Industry. Currently he is doing his Ph.D Research in the areas of Reliability and Security Issues of IoT, Cloud under VTU Research Centre of CMR Institute of Technology, Bengaluru, India. His research interest includes Internet of Things, Machine Learning and Security Issues.

Bindu S. received her Bachelor's degree in Electrical and Electronics Engineering from Bangalore University and a Master's degree in Power Electronics from University Visvesvaraya College of Engineering, Bangalore University and a Ph.D. degree from Visvesvaraya Technological University, Belagavi. Her Major fields of study are in conducting polymer sensors, Antennas, Image Processing, and Smart & Nanomaterials. She has about 25 years of teaching experience which includes 8 years of research experience. She has published and presented 28 papers in International Conferences and Journals. She is currently a Professor in the Department of Electronics and Communication, B N M Institute of Technology, Bengaluru, India. Dr. Bindu has delivered lectures on Biomedical Nanotechnology, Research methodologies, and Smart Sensors. She is guiding Ph.D., MTech, and BE students for their degree.

Malini S completed her B.Tech in Electronics and Communication in the year 2006, ME in Communication System in year 2009. She completed her Ph.D in 2019 in Image Processing. She has presented more than 10 papers in International Conferences and 5 journals. Her research interests are Image and Signal Processing, Machine Learning. Currently working in AMC Engineering College as Associate Professor and has more than 5 years teaching experience in the field of communication engineering.

Rajarajeswari S. completed her PhD in 2020 from Vellore Institute of Technology. Her research domain includes context aware computing, autonomous computing, knowledge engineering, sematic web and deep learning. She had published many papers in the area ubiquitous computing as a part of her research work.

Ramamoorthy S. is currently working as an associate Professor in the department of computing Technologies, in SRM Institute of Science and Technology, Kattankulathur. Having more than 15 Years of Teaching Experience and 10 Years of Research Experience. The Author also Published more than 100 research articles in the reputed Journals and conferences.

Yasha Jyothi M. Shirur completed graduation in 1997 from Kuvempu University, master's in 2004 from Visveswaraya Technological university and Doctorate in 2017 from VTU, during her education she has received meritorious student awards. Currently is a working as a Professor in the department of Electronics and Communication, BNMIT, Bengaluru, Karnataka, India and has over 22 years of academic and research experience. She is active in promoting VLSI research in academics and has filed Three patents out of which the first one received FER, second one is published and the third one is in publishing stage. She has published more than 51 Technical Papers in National and International conferences and reputed Scopus indexed and Web of Science journals. She has guided more than 20 Postgraduate projects and 30 Undergraduate projects and guiding two research scholars for their doctoral degree. She has presented paper in France and Bangkok and received multiple awards for best papers and best presentation. She is vice chair of IEEE Nano Technology Council, Bangalore Section and is a Life member of ISTE and Institute of Engineers and Fellow member of Institute of Engineers She is awarded as IEEE Senior Member.

Hakki Soy was born in Konya, Turkey in 1978. He received a B.S. degree in Electronics Engineering from Uludag University, Bursa, Turkey in 1999 and a Ph.D. degree in Electrical and Electronics Engineering from Selcuk University, Konya, Turkey in 2013. He joined the Department of Electrical and Electronics Engineering, Necmettin Erbakan University, Konya, Turkey, where he is currently an Assistant Professor. His main research interests include wireless communication systems, vehicular networks, and embedded systems with a focus on edge AI applications.

Renuka Suryawanshi obtained her Bachelor of Computer Engineering degree from Cummins College of Engineering, Pune University, Master in Computer Engineering from Dr. Vishwanath Karad MIT World Peace University, Pune and Pursuing Doctor of Philosophy (PhD) in Brain Computer Interface as Ph.D Research Scholar at College of Engineering, BV (DU) COE, Pune, Maharashtra, India. She is skilled in embedded systems, IOT, BCI and Blockchain. She had around 12 papers published in international journals and conferences. Published two patents and copyright for the application of brain-computer interface. She also attended various national and international workshops on the brain-computer interface. collaborates on several government-funded IOT and blockchain initiatives.

Manjusha Taur is an application support lead. IT professional. Working as software engineer for 14+ years. Author has bachelors in computer science and over 14 years of work experience in Banking sector. She has worked on different OS platforms like DOS, Windows, Unix, Linux, AS 400. She has extensive knowledge of cyber security, software development for waterfall and agile methodology along with code deployments using Jenkins, GIT, PDM pipelines.

Velvizhi V. A. is currently working in Sri Sai Ram Engineering College. She has a total teaching experience of 18 years. She received her bachelor degree from Madurai Kamaraj University in the field of Electronics and communication Engineering during the year 2001. She also received her post graduation degree specialized in Communication System from Anna University in the during the year 2004. She has presented papers in national and international conferences. She has also presented papers in national and International Journals. She has coordinated FDTP and acted as a co-coordinator in organizing a national conference. Her area of interest includes Biomedical signal processing and Image Processing, Artificial Intelligence and Data science, IoT, Wireless Communication.

Kishor Wagh has academic experience of twenty four years (24+ Years). Working as an Associate Professor, Dept. Computer Engineering, AISSMS IOIT, Pune. Completed Ph.D. From Sri Guru Gobind Singhji Institute of Engineering and Technology, Nanded, MH. Masters in Engineering at PICT, Pune and Bachelors at SSVPS COE, Dhule. He has published many research articles in reputed journals, textbooks. Attended several National and International Conferences. Member of IEEE Professional and ISTE.

Index

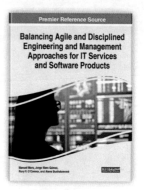

Ensure Quality Research is Introduced to the Academic Community

Become an Evaluator for IGI Global Authored Book Projects

Premier Reference Source

Stabilizing Currency and Preserving Economic Sovereignty Using the Grondona System

Patrick Collins

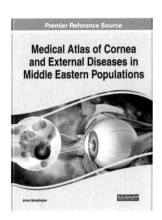

Premier Reference Source

Medical Atlas of Cornea and External Diseases in Middle Eastern Populations

Anna Novakimyan

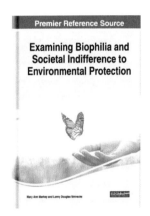

Premier Reference Source

Examining Biophilia and Societal Indifference to Environmental Protection

Mary Ann Markey and Lenny Douglas Meinecke

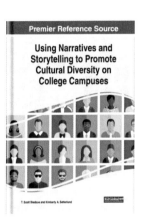

Premier Reference Source

Using Narratives and Storytelling to Promote Cultural Diversity on College Campuses

T. Scott Bledsoe and Kimberly A. Setterlund

The overall success of an authored book project is dependent on quality and timely manuscript evaluations.

Applications and Inquiries may be sent to:
development@igi-global.com

Applicants must have a doctorate (or equivalent degree) as well as publishing, research, and reviewing experience. Authored Book Evaluators are appointed for one-year terms and are expected to complete at least three evaluations per term. Upon successful completion of this term, evaluators can be considered for an additional term.

If you have a colleague that may be interested in this opportunity, we encourage you to share this information with them.

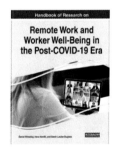

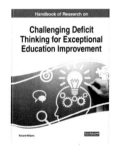

Printed in the United States
by Baker & Taylor Publisher Services